RICHARD STRAUSS

VOLUME ONE

Richard Strauss, 1905

RICHARD STRAUSS

A CRITICAL COMMENTARY
ON HIS LIFE AND WORKS
BY
NORMAN DEL MAR

VOLUME ONE

Cornell University Press

ITHACA, NEW YORK

First published 1986 by Cornell University Press, in cloth and paperback, from the 1978 corrected edition published by Barrie and Jenkins Ltd.

Printed in the United States of America.

The paper in this book is acid-free and meets the guidelines for permanence and durability of the Committee on Production Guidelines for Book Longevity of the Council on Library Resources.

Library of Congress Cataloging-in-Publication Data

Del Mar, Norman, 1919–
  Richard Strauss: a critical commentary on his life and works.

  Bibliography: v. 3, p.
  Includes indexes.
    1. Strauss, Richard, 1864–1949. 2. Composers—Germany—Biography. I. Title.
ML410.S93D4   1986   780'.92'4 [B]   85-19033
ISBN 0-8014-1783-X (set : alk. paper)
ISBN 0-8014-9320-X (set : pbk. : alk. paper)
ISBN 0-8014-1780-5 (vol. 1 : alk. paper)
ISBN 0-8014-9317-X (vol. 1 : pbk. : alk. paper)

TO
THE INSPIRING MEMORY OF
SIR THOMAS BEECHAM
THIS BOOK IS
AFFECTIONATELY DEDICATED

CONTENTS

ILLUSTRATIONS

AUTHOR'S NOTE TO THE 1986 EDITION

THE reappearance of my study on Strauss after an extended period of unavailability, as well as its transformation to paperback, is indeed a glad occasion. All my praise and thanks are accordingly due to the faith and energy of Faber's editor Patrick Carnegy, and also to Walter Lippincott of Cornell University Press whose enthusiastic collaboration has helped make this new edition possible.

It is fortunate that the most vital Straussian documentation was emerging precisely during the time I was writing. New information that subsequently came to light was accommodated in changes to the text which I was able to make for the reprint of 1978. In the seven years since then there has been little scholarship of the kind that would make me want to make major revisions, and so no further changes to the text have been attempted, except to collect all the Appendices together at the end of Volume 3.

A few errors persist, however, and these should be mentioned here. Some are of a minor nature, such as the misspelling of the poet Chamisso on pages 248 and 499 of Volume 3, or the loss of a syllable in Queen Nephretete's name on page 535 of the same volume. More important, though, are momentary aberrations of the kind which led to the attribution to Mendelssohn of Berlioz's Overture *Rob Roy* on page 53 of Volume 1; it was, of course, *Ruy Blas* which had been intended. On page 147 of the same volume, I failed to mention (among the compositions of 1897 which led up to the completion of *Don Quixote*) an elaborate Hymn for composite forces, written for the opening of an art exhibition in Munich; and in the catalogue of Strauss's works (vol. 3, Appendix D) a new entry needs to be inserted together with those for 1888 in the shape of an Andante for horn and piano which, composed for—and dedicated to—Strauss's father on the occasion of his par-

ix

ents' silver wedding, was found and published by Boosey and Hawkes only in 1973. On page 273 of Volume 1, in the chapter dealing with *Salome*, it is of course a *'bird* of prey' to which Herod compared Herodias' hateful screeching, and Strauss must have chuckled when he wrote into the score instructions to the wood-wind to 'screech hatefully' (hässlich krieschend).

Finally come two places where I have to eat my words. In the footnote to page 53 of Volume 3 I wrongly accused Strauss of a faulty knowledge of history. In setting this matter to rights I must quote the admirable letter I received from Dr. David Whitton of Wolfson College, Oxford, to whom I extend my grateful thanks:

> There *was* a Peace of Constance in 1043, under the auspices of Henry III. Unlike Barbarossa's later settlement there it did not simply comprise a peace between the king and his enemies; contemporary sources suggest that the king preached a similar reconciliation to the assembled nobility—all should drop their feuds in Christ's name. As such, it was the first occasion on which the German monarchy associated itself with the Peace of God movement. Properly developed, the theme could have been still more risky to its authors than the eventual collaboration on *Friedenstag*.

Secondly, I have to confess that it was I who was in error when I reprimanded Strauss for misquoting Mozart in his letter to Zweig thanking him for the text of the first act of *Die schweigsame Frau*. Strauss's reference is indeed to the finale of Act 2 of *Così fan tutte* where Don Alfonso is praising the wedding preparations: 'Bravi, Bravi! Ottimamente!' or 'Bravo, Bravo, ganz ausgezeichnet!' as the standard German translation has it.

April 1985   N.R.D.M.

PREFACE

IT was September 1947. Sir Thomas Beecham had conceived the idea of a Strauss Festival to be inaugurated as part of his season of concerts with the Royal Philharmonic Orchestra at the Theatre Royal, Drury Lane. Strauss himself had been invited to visit this country in order to attend the concerts and, incidentally, to collect some of the royalties which had been frozen since the outbreak of war eight years before. Everyone was agog to see this legendary figure from the past, many of whose works—predominantly the earlier ones—are as much part of the classical repertoire as, for example, the Brahms Symphonies. Was he really still alive? Rumours had reached us of the American soldier who, two years earlier, had stumbled on the aged gentleman in the sumptuous villa amongst the Bavarian Alps, and had been roughly told to go anywhere and do what he liked so long as he, Strauss, was left alone to play cards and write a little music. Since then he had migrated to Switzerland and now we were to see him once more.

He came. Sir Thomas gave two concerts at Drury Lane in which three of the Tone Poems were played (*Macbeth*, *Don Quixote* and *Ein Heldenleben*), excerpts from *Feuersnot* and *Ariadne auf Naxos*, and the new Symphonic Fantasia from *Die Frau ohne Schatten*. Strauss attended both concerts with their rehearsals. During my own rehearsal of the *Frau ohne Schatten* Fantasia (Sir Thomas had generously assigned the work to me as part of my London début) he came up to the podium, glumly regarded the score for a few moments, muttered 'All my own fault', and went away. Throughout the entire visit he was very terse and uncommunicative, and only twice do I remember him being roused to any liveliness. The first occasion was when the fireman at Drury Lane Theatre had inadvertently locked the communicating door between house and stage, thus blocking Strauss's way when he wanted to come round to see Sir Thomas. I can still see him stamping and shouting about the 'Gott-verdammte Tür'. The second occasion was after the concert performance of *Elektra* which Sir Thomas gave in conjunction with the B.B.C. At the end the overjoyed Strauss came forward and embraced Beecham. This was an occasion I shall never forget. Nor shall I forget the embrace; I had not realized that Beecham was so small or that Strauss was so large.

Finally Strauss conducted the recently formed Philharmonia Orchestra in a single concert at the Albert Hall, in which he gave *Don Juan*, the *Burleske*, and the *Sinfonia Domestica*. During the rehearsals for this concert he was again monumentally undemonstrative and noncommittal. But he made one very remarkable comment. Something had not quite pleased him and he was heard to say: 'No, I know what I want, and I know what I meant when I wrote this. After all, I may not be a first-rate composer, but I *am* a first-class second-rate composer!'

This was not false modesty, but neither is it by any means the whole truth. *Don Juan, Don Quixote*, and *Elektra* are indeed the products of a first-rate composer, but scarcely *Aegyptische Helena* and *Sinfonia Domestica*. In fact, for two or even possibly three periods in his career Strauss rose to heights of supreme genius, only to fall back in between on merest talent. 'A first-class second-rate composer' is a fair assessment for a certain part of his creative life—but certainly cannot stand as an overall judgement on one of the world's greatest musicians. This paradox is the theme of my book.

The present volume takes Strauss's work up to, and including, *Der Rosenkavalier*, which may legitimately be regarded as the climax of his career, as well as a convenient half-way mark. The mass of songs, however, together with a number of smaller choral and instrumental works of an occasional nature, I have held over from a volume which threatened to become far too long and cumbersome. They will be dealt with as a whole in Volume III.

It will not, I feel sure, go unnoticed that the subtitle is not strictly accurate and that the book so far is considerably more of a critical survey of the works than it is of Strauss's life. There is, of course, a wide discrepancy between the uneventful professional life of this big, conceited man—taciturn to the point of brusqueness, wrapped up solely in his card-playing and his music—and the wide adventurous Romanticism of his artistry.

I have tried to trace the main features of his life in the course of outlining the major works, and I am aiming to give an occasional view of the man himself as seen by some of his contemporaries. But the

overall consideration of his personality and its effect upon his creative
output must wait until the closing pages of the final volume when
the story of his life lies complete before us.

My thanks go out to Mr Klaus Schloessingk-Paul, who has been
endlessly patient and helped me at every stage, both with translations
and with the manuscript itself. Also to Dr Franz and Alice Strauss and
to Dr Roth of Boosey & Hawkes, who have been very kind in putting
scores and documents at my disposal. In addition the research of Mr
Alan Jefferson has been of the utmost value to me, while the Chief
Librarian and Staff of Hendon Public Library have been exceedingly
obliging and painstaking in the pursuit of rare books and other material.

I am further indebted to Dr Franz and Alice Strauss for their
generosity in lending me and allowing me to reproduce the photo-
graphs in this book; and to John and Alix Farrell for preparing the
index.

For their permission to quote from copyright works I am grateful to
the following publishers:

Atlantis Verlag

Bodley Head John Lane Ltd

Boosey & Hawkes, & Fürstner Ltd.

Bote und Bock

Breitkopf & Härtel, Wiesbaden

Doblinger Verlag

Editions Albin Michel

Hinrichsen Edition Ltd, the Copyright Owners of
C. F. Peters

John Murray & Co.

F. E. C. Leuckart Munich-Leipzig

Putnam & Co. Ltd

Steingräber Verlag Offenbach/M.-Wiesbaden

Universal Edition (Alfred A. Kalmus Ltd.)

Wildings, Strathblane

October 1961   N.R.D.M.

LIST OF WORKS DISCUSSED IN VOLUME I

CHAPTER I

BEGINNINGS

BRAHMS used to say with pride that he was 'the last of the classical composers'. He certainly stood in direct line of succession to a series of great masters of symphonic composition which, as the nineteenth century drew to its close, appeared to be in danger of becoming extinct. The advent of Liszt and Wagner together with their hot-headed disciples seemed to proclaim the end of an era. Nevertheless, that day was still, if briefly, deferred and the role of 'last' destined to be reserved for later masters.

In the great German tradition two towering personalities stood at the fatal cross-roads—Gustav Mahler and Richard Strauss—two creative minds which could scarcely have been more different, although they shared a common heritage and spoke a common musical language. Both contributed to the musical revolution which caused the final break in the tradition to which they owed so much; but unlike Strauss, Mahler died in 1911 at the peak of his career.

Despite his small output, consisting of little more than ten symphonies and a handful of songs, Mahler's style had developed steadily until at the time of his death he was in the vanguard of advanced trends in contemporary music. His harmonic innovations, which were more daring with each successive work, had a profound effect on Schönberg and his disciples, and contributed to a large extent, together with his artistic *Weltanschauung*, to the evolution of what is now recognized as one of the most important and far-reaching developments in Western music, the new Viennese school of atonal composers.

Strauss also had an important influence on this movement, and had he died in 1909 immediately after the composition of *Elektra* it might have seemed as if he, too, would have continued on as adventurous a road as his more introspective colleague. Instead, however, he performed an abrupt volte-face and then proceeded to live on for a further forty years, writing prolifically in an increasingly mellifluous vein, opera after opera, work after work, whether the urge was upon him or not, until the very language in which he was writing had ceased to be current musical vernacular and he himself had turned into a legendary figure of a bygone age.

Richard Strauss was born in Munich on the 11th June 1864. He was the son of Franz Strauss, a well-known and highly respected horn player in the Munich Court Orchestra and professor of the Royal School of Music. Richard's mother was Franz Strauss's second wife, the whole of Franz's first family having been wiped out by the cholera epidemic of 1853. Josephine Strauss was the well-to-do daughter of a prominent family of brewers named Pschorr. The marriage relieved Franz of any fear of financial embarrassment for the rest of his life, and enabled him to make several valuable gestures to their son Richard in establishing his career.

That a career was probably in the offing showed itself extremely early, since he eagerly began his musical studies with piano lessons at the age of four and a half, later passing on to the violin. His first attempts in composition began when he was only six. Strauss himself wrote that his actual first effort in this direction consisted of a Christmas Carol, followed by a Polka.[1] Further pieces duly followed one another which we need not take seriously, though the boy Strauss clearly did, since an Introduction, Theme and Variations for horn and piano composed for his father in 1878 is labelled op. 17. This early system of enumeration actually reached op. 30, although it was repeatedly revised as more and more works were gradually considered to be unworthy of inclusion.[2] The compositions completed during these early years are of extraordinary variety, including numerous songs, piano and chamber music. During this period began the first courses in theory under Meyer,

---

[1] According to the composer's sister Johanna, the first composition was the Schneiderpolka, which Papa Strauss notated from the little boy's performance at the piano. The Christmas Carol was, however, the first piece which he wrote down himself.

[2] See Appendix A.

a leading Munich musician. In 1876 the twelve-year-old schoolboy completed his first orchestral score, a *Festmarsch* (Festival March) in E flat which is still the first work of the composer to be known generally to the world at large. It is, of course, little more than a childhood attempt, the remarkable thing being, perhaps, that the boy had the tenacity, let alone the skill, to complete the full orchestral score. It would not even occupy the position at the head of Strauss's acknowledged output had not Uncle George Pschorr taken it into his head five years later in 1881 to subsidize its publication. None but the best-known publishing house was good enough for the little prodigy, and the manuscript was duly sent off to Breitkopf & Härtel, accompanied by the following letter:

> Most honoured Herr Breitkopf!
> I am permitting myself to approach you by letter since I am burdening you on behalf of someone wholly unknown to you. My name is Richard Strauss and I was born on June 11th in the year '64, the son of the chamber music player and professor at the local Conservatoire. I am at present at the Gymnasium in the Lower Sixth form, but have decided to dedicate myself wholly to music and moreover directly to composition. I have had instruction in Counterpoint from Herr Hofkapellmeister Fr. W. Meyer. Accompanying this letter is one of my compositions which I have dedicated to my uncle, Herr George Pschorr, the owner of the beer brewery, and he is most anxious that it should appear in print in the edition of one of the foremost music publishing firms. He would himself defray the printing costs. I am therefore turning to you with the request that you be so good as to take the *Festmarsch* into your edition in order that your famous name which has such influence in the world of music may help the name of a young aspiring musician to become known . . . .

This letter, if precocious, is by no means objectionable, and the piece duly appeared in the famous Breitkopf & Härtel orchestral library. It is clear that even as a boy the little Richard had an extremely fertile and energetic brain. Certainly, being an unusually musical child in the household of a professional musician, he was idolized and, from many accounts, unduly spoilt by his admiring parents and relations. Indeed, it stands much to his credit that he persevered so steadily at composition during this period. The *Festmarsch*, for all its obvious lack of originality and humdrum cadences, is assured in its manner, while the orchestral layout shows an accomplished hand, especially considering that it was the first he completed (a still earlier overture written in 1872–3 was only laid out in short score on two staves). Most commentators have picked on the exploitation of the familiar figure from the finale of Beethoven's Seventh Symphony, but it falls naturally into its new context as an integral part of the principal subject:

Ex. 1

The woodwind melody of the Trio is oddly static in the way it constantly comes back to the same note, but the cello countersubject is nicely invented, recalling many a euphonium solo in the military band. The most interesting features of the work are the return after the Trio section, and more particularly the chromatically extended cadence which leads to the climax of the coda, indicating that the young and self-satisfied composer was beginning to feel the need to experiment beyond accepted formula:

Ex. 2

The March was played shortly after its publication by the amateur orchestra 'Wilde Gungl', which, since it was conducted regularly by Strauss's father, more than once tried out pieces by the boy Richard, apart from giving him the experience of playing the violin in the orchestra and even, it is said, of taking an occasional rehearsal.

2

After the *Festmarsch* of 1876 some further orchestral works began to appear, such as a Serenade, two Overtures, and a second *Festmarsch*. Already Strauss was nothing if not prolific, and the music he wrote during the next three or four years already shows an extraordinarily rapid development both in style and self-assurance.

The next work considered by the Strauss family as worthy of publication was a String Quartet composed three years later. Breitkopf was again approached, but without the bait of a subsidy as the Quartet was considered of sufficient merit no longer to need such cushioning. But under these circumstances the great publishing house showed themselves wholly uninterested. In their defence one might well say that they could not possibly tell that the composer of this conventional essay in traditional formulae would one day be the author of such masterpieces as *Till Eulenspiegel* and *Der Rosenkavalier*. It is indeed ironic that Breitkopf was never to publish a single important work of the composer's, although oddly enough the English branch of that great firm later handled Strauss's works in the United Kingdom. Yet these are the pitfalls of publishing, and it was all the more perspicacious of a certain Spitzweg of the firm of Jos. Aibl that he took the chance of accepting the A major Quartet on promise, and published it as op. 2.

As one might expect, the Quartet shows a considerable advance in making the most of its opportunities, even if the necessary invention did not readily spring to Strauss's mind yet to justify the extra length. After a promising start, the development of the first movement follows exactly the same course of events as the exposition in virtually the same number of bars, a fact which makes one embark with misgivings on the third journey through the same scenery in the recapitulation. Indeed, this was a problem which Strauss always found troublesome, and may have been a strong influence in causing him to turn in later years to forms which by their very nature precluded the necessity of a formal reprise.

R.S.–B

The amiable slow movement never really recovers from the lame symmetry of its themes, and certainly at no time touches even the fringe of one's heart. But then how should it? What did the pampered schoolboy know about life? In the meantime a Mozartian theme will serve well enough for a starting point of the Finale:

Ex. 3

A very similar theme had already proved itself a good opening for a piano trio in the same key.

Except for the occasional bombastic misjudging of the medium, the treatment is Haydnesque and the whole is entertaining, though too long drawn out, three of the four movements being in full worked sonata form. The best movement is undoubtedly the Scherzo, where the limitations of the design keep Strauss from overinflating the slender Mendelssohnian material. And if the main cadence comes again straight from Mozart—well, good luck to him:

Ex. 4

There is perhaps much lost today in the self-conscious reluctance of students to learn to write well-made but stylistically worthless essays in the traditional forms, for without this experience and practice behind him Strauss would hardly have acquired the technique to handle *Don Quixote* and *Elektra* when the time came. The Quartet is dedicated to the Benno Walter Quartet, who gave the first performance on 14th March 1881. Benno Walter was a relative and colleague of Franz Strauss, Richard's father, and had been the boy's violin teacher since Richard was eight. He helped, taught, and encouraged the young composer right up to the early years of his maturity, and the Violin Concerto, op. 8, is also dedicated to him.

The performance of the Quartet was not by any means the only time the boy Strauss heard his works given in public. Apart from amateur performances given by his father, Frau Meysenheim, one of the singers at the Munich Opera, sang three of his songs at a concert two days later.[2a] Moreover, while at the Gymnasium, where he studied between 1874 and 1882, various choruses were performed which had been composed by this unusual pupil. The first of these was a setting of none other than a passage from the *Elektra* of Sophocles. One wonders what thoughts ran through Strauss's mind when twenty-eight years later he was confronted with a new complete libretto on this vividly dramatic subject, out of which he created one of his very finest works.

3

Although still a schoolboy, by 1881 Strauss had become a very acceptable pianist, and in those days it was much more natural than it would be today that he should set down some of his ideas in the form of *salon* pieces for the piano. The set of such miniatures which were published as his op. 3 are this time strongly reminiscent of Schumann (No. 1) and Beethoven (No. 3) as well as Mendelssohn (Nos. 2, 4 and 5). There is little Strauss in them as yet, whereas the *Stimmungsbilder*, op. 9, two of which were written only one year later, in 1882, show many indications of the mature composer's manner of melodizing. The first *Stimmungsbild*—or 'mood picture'—*Auf stillen Waldespfad*, was originally composed as an *Albumblatt*, but the opening bars are strongly suggestive of the 'Hinterweltlern' section from *Zarathustra*.

Ex. 5

Ex. 6

Strauss later tossed off a further four *Klavierstücke*, three of which he added to the two *Albumblatt* movements, revising these to form the complete set of *Stimmungsbilder*. The remaining movement, a Nocturne, has disappeared. The title of the set applies well to four of the five pieces, which are full of Schumannesque romantic atmosphere, especially, of course, the *Träumerei*. The figuration is very much in the style of Strauss's later song accompaniments, so that one is repeatedly surprised not to hear the voice enter. Only the centre-piece, the Intermezzo, is out of place in this respect, but is none the less welcome, since it is an excellent piano piece in its own right. Perhaps the coda shows the immature Strauss finding difficulties in how to round things off, but the bulk shows signs of true Straussian *élan*. The *Heidenbild* which closes the set is in some ways the most freely imaginative, with its two contrasted figurations both set over a persistent drone of a bare fifth. Its extraordinary rapid flourish in the closing bars also suggests some programmatic associations.

The origins of the Piano Sonata in B minor date back to 1880, although it was published as op. 5. This is actually the third of its species, but the hard and fast line drawn by the mere fact of publication has brought the B minor Sonata alone into the range of familiarity. Yet within the limits of Strauss's style of the time, the earlier Sonatas have also points of interest and are by no means to be despised. The first movement of this Sonata, op. 5, has the distinction not only of being built around a somewhat familiar figure:

Ex. 7

but has a dramatic urgency which is quite new and which carries the
composer farther than ever before. It is true that lack of skill in maintaining the argument sooner or later forces Strauss back on empty
repetition, but the movement shows another step taken, and is far ahead
of the remainder of the work. The Adagio Cantabile is for all intents
and purposes one of Mendelssohn's Lieder ohne Worte, and both the
Scherzo and Finale are tremendously influenced by the same master. The
coda of the Scherzo, however, gives one of those horn-call figures which,
while in themselves innocuous and common to all composers, later
become such a predominant feature of Strauss's thematic construction.

Ex. 8

4

When he was eighteen years of age Strauss left school, entering the
University of Munich in August 1882. Here he read philosophy,
aesthetics, history of art, and literature. This is reflected by an abrupt
step forward in the quality of his compositions. So marked is this that
we now reach the first works to survive in the concert repertory of the
present day.

There is considerable divergence of opinion as to exactly when
Strauss wrote the E flat Wind Serenade published as op. 7. Some commentators date it a year earlier, but in style it is far in advance of the
other works of 1881. One first hears of it in connexion with the
première which took place on 27th November 1882 under Franz Wüllner, the conductor who later gave many Strauss first performances,
including *Till Eulenspiegel* and *Don Quixote*. There is talk of many
productions of the piece during the months which followed, but the
most important result came a year later, when it attracted the attention
of the great and influential conductor, Hans von Bülow.

The Serenade is scored for normal double woodwind with four horns plus a contrabassoon for extra support. The score of both this work and the B flat Suite for the same combination gives the option of a bass tuba in place of the contrabassoon, but the alternative instrument is never used and merely indicates the comparative rarity of the contrabassoon in German provincial orchestras of that time. There is also a very curious addition of the string bass to reinforce the tonic in the last two bars. One wonders whether the inexperienced Strauss really expected the extra player to be kept in patient reserve merely to add these notes at the end. At all events the list of players in the early performances makes no mention of a double bass. The single movement work is in sonata form, but without a true development, although there is a brief central episode linking the two main sections of exposition and recapitulation. The development is, of course, the hardest part of a symphonic movement to contrive and so far it had always been the weakest section of Strauss's formal works. Here, having fallen into the trap of rounding off the exposition too completely, it takes him only eight static bars of improvisation on the oboe to work his way into as distant a key from E flat major as he can imagine (B minor); from here he spends a happy period in quicker tempo, gradually building up the spectacular return to the recapitulation in the tonic. The whole ingenuous but undeniably effective sequence of events is immensely typical. Throughout the section the figure,

Ex. 9

derived from the charming second subject, is ever present, thus maintaining the essential unity of the piece even during the independent central episode.

The scoring for the thirteen instruments (not quite the same thirteen as in Mozart's famous Serenade) is by no means without imagination, even though by 1909 the mature Strauss already wrote decrying it as no more than the 'respectable work of a music student'. Of course, to have a wind player for a father must have been a splendid asset in learning how to write for this kind of ensemble, and Strauss clearly already knew just how the sonorities would blend.

Altogether one can well understand Bülow being sufficiently impressed not only to place the piece in his regular repertoire, but to suggest to Strauss during the winter of 1883 that he compose a further and more substantial work for the same combination. Strauss was thrilled, and set to work like mad, only to find that Bülow had his own ideas on the sequence of movements in the proposed Suite including such classical items as a Gavotte and Fugue. He tried hard to oblige his mentor in the last two movements, but the first two were already drafted. The opening Allegretto is in much the same idiom as the Serenade, and like the earlier work is in abbreviated sonata form, though this time without even the semblance of a development.

The second movement however, is a breakaway from Strauss's normal species of Andante, a Romanze made up of motivic themes which are pure Strauss, such as the first subject:

Ex. 10

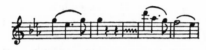

(cf. *Feuersnot*, Ex. 26); and the transition theme:

Ex. 11

(cf. *Macbeth* and *Guntram*. Strauss's personal style was emerging fast.) This movement, like the first, is again in abbreviated Sonata form and in this respect looks forward to the slow movement of the F minor Symphony. Bülow's Gavotte was placed third in the scheme and bore good and original fruit, becoming the most attractive of the four; but the Introduction and Fugue, used by way of Finale, was more than Strauss could handle with interest. The Introduction quotes substantially from the Romanze without adding anything further to what had already been said exhaustively, while, striking as the Fugue subject is, its counterpoint is academic and prevents Strauss from making the most of the medium of the wind ensemble.

Some time after the work was delivered Bülow gave Strauss the opportunity of conducting it himself at an afternoon concert, though entirely without rehearsal. This was Strauss's first experience of conducting professional players and was, for a variety of reasons, a hair-raising occasion. The incident is amusingly described at length by Strauss himself:

In the winter of 1884 Bülow came to Munich and surprised me when I visited him, by informing me that he
would give a matinée performance before an invited audience, after the third official concert, the programme of which
was to contain as the second item my Suite for Woodwind,
which I was to conduct. I thanked him, overjoyed, but
told him that I had never had a baton in my hand before
and asked him when I could rehearse. 'There will be no
rehearsals, the orchestra has no time for such things on
tour.' His order was so categorical that I had no time to
ponder over my discomfiture. The morning of the day
arrived. I went to fetch Bülow at his hotel; he was in a
dreadful mood. As we went up the steps of the Odeon, he
positively raved against Munich, which had driven out
Wagner and himself, and against old Perfall; he called the
Odeon a cross between a church and a stock exchange, in
short, he was as charmingly unbearable as only he could be
when he was furious about something. The matinée took
its course. I conducted my piece in a state of slight coma; I
can only remember today that I made no blunders. What it
was like apart from that I could not say. Bülow did not even
listen to my début; smoking one cigarette after another,
he paced furiously up and down in the music room. When I
went in, my father, profoundly moved, came in through
the opposite door in order to thank Bülow. That was what
Bülow had been waiting for; like a furious lion he pounced
upon my father. 'You have nothing to thank me for', he
shouted, 'I have not forgotten what you have done to me in
this damned city of Munich. What I did today I did because your son has talent and not for you.' Without saying
a word my father left the music room from which all
others had long since fled when they saw Bülow explode.
This scene had, of course thoroughly spoilt my début for
me. Only Bülow was suddenly in the best of spirits.[3]

5

On the whole the Suite is considerably less successful than the Serenade
and through the years it has been rarely performed. This may, however,
be due to some extent to the complicated factors of its publication,
which have led to its being less readily available and thus little known.
Its designation as op. 4 is misleading, since it came into this number
only in 1911, when it first appeared in print. Previously it had been

[3] *Recollections and Reflections*, by Richard Strauss, Boosey & Hawkes, 1953.

intended to be op. 15, but that number was usurped by a group of
songs. Op. 4 was at one time to have been the Concert Overture in C
minor (1883), although this started life as op. 10. In the end the Overture was never published at all; a pity, as it is an exciting piece, strongly
influenced—as Strauss himself acknowledged—by the *Coriolan* Overture of Beethoven.

Ex. 12

The figure ⌐ a ⌐, which replaces Beethoven's infinitely stronger
sustained C's, is interesting in the way it presages Strauss's maturer
manner of forming his themes. The bold opening statement of Ex. 12
calls the Violin Sonata to mind, while the treatment of ⌐ a ⌐ provides a first instance of the famous rushing passage for violins in *Tod
und Verklärung*.

Ex. 13

After a transition making use of a motif anticipating *Don Quixote*,
the second subject, dutifully in the relative major, effects a marriage
between ideas suggestive of *Macbeth* and the Max Bruch G minor
Violin Concerto, a work which was to lend ideas to Strauss on more
than one occasion in later life.

Ex. 14

The Overture marks a notable advance in the young Strauss's emancipation towards a personal style, but it is fascinating to see how this is purely with respect to the thematic ideas and their individual development. The construction of the piece as a whole is still a little stiff, both in the schoolmasterly contrapuntal development and in the triumphal C major coda with its closing plagal cadence, which is disappointingly conventional after so stirring a build-up.

An even earlier orchestral work, a Symphony in D minor written in 1880, was also consigned by Strauss to limbo, after it, too, had occupied the fatal opus number 4. A large-scale work in four movements, this is very much the same vintage as the String Quartet, though on the whole rather less self-assured, especially, naturally enough, in its orchestral setting. It is nevertheless well made and has several interesting ideas, though thematically the slow movement and the Finale are somewhat banal, reflecting, perhaps, the fact that the entire symphony was completed within the space of only three months.

Both Overture and Symphony had the distinction of receiving their first performance at the hands of the Wagnerian conductor Hermann Levi, who was also the dedicatee of the Overture, and who later became instrumental in securing for Strauss his first important post in his home town of Munich. The performance of the Symphony was a great event in the Strauss family. Johanna Strauss has recently written of how she sat with their mother in their subscription seats, pride and apprehension alternating in their excitement. Father Strauss was, of course, in the orchestra, nervous and on edge, while Richard was quite calm, standing in his Sunday suit behind the dress circle.

The occasion seems to have been a considerable success and reflected great credit on the family, much to the father's profound satisfaction. Nevertheless the Symphony is essentially a student work, and Strauss later begged his father not to send it to anyone, as he did not want it performed any more.

6

Strauss's father, old Franz Strauss, was to the end a virulent reactionary
in his musical taste and judgements. He hated Wagner, whom he
regarded as a modernistic upstart, but for whom he had frequently to
play, and violent quarrels were common between the two men. He
desired passionately that his son should compose sound classical music,
well grounded in tradition, and above all, filled with melody which he
insisted was the most enduring quality of music for musician and lay-
man alike. As far as melodic invention was concerned his son Richard
rarely lost sight of this conception, but he was never at ease with the
absolute forms of classical tradition, although he tried them all out
before abandoning them until shortly before the end of his life, over
half a century later.

In this first autumn at University (1882) he completed a Violin
Concerto which had been some months on the stocks, and also followed
it up in rapid succession with a Horn Concerto and a Cello Sonata. In
the latter the influence of Mendelssohn is still strongly marked. The
opening of the Sonata has a fine verve and Strauss wrote proudly home
to his parents that Joachim had congratulated him particularly on the
first lyrical outburst:

Ex. 15

The development is built up of sequential passages which despite
some interesting detail tends to become repetitive. There is an ingenious
four-part fugue which on the collapse of the development whips
up the excitement to an unexpectedly laborious return to the opening
bars for the recapitulation. The effect is of a device employed to extricate matters from an awkward predicament rather than the inevitable
conclusion of a logical argument. I am reminded irresistibly of Professor Tovey's famous dictum: 'How is it that the great masters never
have any difficulty in getting out of pitfalls? Answer: because they
never fall into one.'

The Andante is another Song without Words of which the principal
melody is not very distinctive and which also lacks a well-contrasted
middle section. Strauss had two attempts at the Finale; the first was

almost pure early Beethoven, but was better knit in its opening theme than the revised version, for all the latter's airy and light-hearted play with silent bars. This movement has some surprises in store, however, for after amiably following the pattern of Mendelssohn's Piano Trio, op. 66, with a few ideas drawn from the 'Scotch' Symphony for the sake of variety, it suddenly settles on a cadence straight out of the second act of *Parsifal*!

Ex. 16

And then, as if stirred by the memory, the development builds up a huge quasi-orchestral edifice, full of sequential repetition, but on a scale new to the piece and to Strauss himself in its vehemence and intensity. Soon all the parts soar into the treble clef, the lack of a bass, which in an orchestral score Strauss would surely have supplied, making itself felt when the climax is reached:

Ex. 17

This climax could have swept effectively into the recapitulation, but Strauss had not yet learnt this manœuvre, and he allows the music to subside. As a result he has to contrive a modulatory link, which he does by means of plain unvaried statements of the second subject, giving the misleading effect of having devised a short cut.

However, despite its gaucheries and maladroit handling of the form, the Sonata has some fine moments of panache and occasional indications of Strauss's future mannerisms, such as this cadence which recalls the music of Chrysothemis in *Elektra*:

Ex. 18

A further composition for the Cello, though this time with orchestral accompaniment, also belongs to this period, a most attractive Romanze which has unfortunately remained unpublished.[3a] It is a gentle $\frac{3}{8}$ movement, similar in type to the slow movement of the Violin and Horn Concertos, both of which actually precede it in date of composition. It could easily have formed part of a companion Concerto for Cello, but no doubt Strauss appreciated the unusual difficulties attendant upon such a work, for he never attempted to add to it the outer movements.

The Violin Concerto, though in some ways a less elaborate work than the Cello Sonata, and actually composed slightly earlier, is more satisfactory as a whole and frequently more subtle and original in its melodic lines. It may well have been the presence of the orchestra which put Strauss at his ease, for this is immediately apparent in the orchestral ritornello, with its fanfare-like *Naturthema*:

Ex. 19

[3a] There is, however, some doubt as to whether the orchestration was completed.

The figure ⌐ x ¬ is incorporated continuously into the texture, a
first instance of one of the most characteristic features of Strauss's later
style. The figure itself is of no great consequence; Max Bruch had
already worked it in the Finale of his famous G minor Violin Concerto,[4]
but Strauss's accomplished treatment of it contrasts a little abruptly
with the ingenuous and symmetrical melodies which form the principal
material of the first movement. There are errors of judgement in the
Concerto, especially in the first movement, where the introductory

Ex. 20

[4] A later instance of Strauss's borrowing a theme from this concerto appears in
the *Alpensinfonie* (see Vol. 2).

figuration of the solo violin is repeated both before the short development and again in full before the recapitulation. This seems an elementary mistake of perception which a closer understanding of the great classical concertos might have prevented, but Strauss, who was at that time playing the violin himself a good deal, was probably rather proud of his prowess in devising stylistic passage-work. He seems also to have been in some doubt how to finish the movement, since the long and rather barren orchestral postlude is printed with extensive cuts, albeit different ones, in both the full score and the violin and piano copy. Neither abbreviated version is entirely satisfactory, and moreover it seems surprising that no opportunity is allowed for a cadenza either here or anywhere else in the work.

There is some confusion over the metronome mark of the slow movement. The violin and piano reduction gives $\quarternote=69$, which is wholly inconsistent with the tempo indication 'Lento ma non troppo'. The full score gives $\eighthnote=69$, certainly more in keeping with the sweet and unpretentious character of this miniature, which might have been better described as an 'Andantino'. It begins with a pleasingly asymmetrical ten-bar melody and is altogether on a higher and more original level than the stereotyped Andantes which had so far satisfied Strauss for his slow movements, and points the way to the far more striking parallel movement in the Horn Concerto. There are features also in the Finale which look forward to the later work, notably the dramatic interpolation which brings back one of the principal motifs from the first movement shortly before the end (Ex. 20).

7

It had always been a foregone conclusion that a horn concerto would come sooner or later. One wonders rather that Strauss had not written more for his father by this time. The only horn works he produced before the concerto were a song 'Ein Alphorn hör' ich schallen', with a fiendishly difficult horn obbligato, and the Introduction, Theme and Variations for horn and piano already mentioned above (p. 2). Both works were written at the age of fourteen and dedicated to 'seinem lieben Papa,' whereas the new and important concerto is inscribed to Oscar Franz, a well-known virtuoso on the instrument and author of a tutor still widely used in Conservatoires all over the world. However, old Franz Strauss seems to have been highly gratified with his son's achievement, playing it frequently in the family circle, although it taxed him to the limits of his technique. Johanna Strauss, the composer's sister, recently wrote, on a postcard to the English virtuoso horn player Dennis Brain, that she vividly remembered her father struggling with the solo part, which he found very tiring, even using the high B flat crook. In particular he seems to have considered the recurrent high B flats too daring and dangerous for performance in the concert hall. The first public performance with orchestra was actually given neither by Father Strauss nor by Oscar Franz, but some two years later, when Bülow included the work in one of his Meiningen concerts in March 1885, the soloist being the local first horn, Gustav Leinhos.[5] Strauss wrote to his father that Leinhos was a soloist of 'kolossaler Sicherheit' ('colossal sureness'—a rare quality in horn players) and with a tone very like his father's own.

Formally, the concerto is far in advance of anything Strauss had produced up to the present. The system of holding the work together by means of *Naturmotive*, tentatively tried out in the Violin Concerto, is here exploited to the full. The opening fanfare,

Ex. 21

delivered at the outset by the solo horn and before the orchestral ritornello, not only serves as a framework enclosing the two long and free cantilenas which comprise the first movement, but, transformed into $\frac{6}{8}$ rhythm, constitutes the principal Rondo subject of the Finale,

Ex. 22

an instance of thematic metamorphosis which predates by some three years Strauss's adoption of Lisztian methods under the influence of Alexander Ritter.

[5] A performance had already been given in 1883 (shortly after the completion of the work) by Bruno Hoyer, a pupil of Strauss's father, in the Tonkünstlerverein, Munich, but with piano.

A secondary hunting horn figure of basic simplicity

Ex. 23

also appears in the opening tutti and is repeatedly worked into the texture throughout the concerto, besides being the chief motif in the link
between the slow movement and the Finale, the three short movements all following one another without a break. In the Andante it
forms the principal figure of accompaniment to the gentle $\frac{3}{8}$ melody
which is again based on the notes of the common chord:

Ex. 24

The opening melody for the soloist in the first movement

Ex. 25

is also motivically connected with the second subjects of both the
other two movements.

It will be noticed that, in fact, none of these *Naturmotive* can be
played on the valveless Waldhorn for which this concerto is avowedly
written. Curiously enough, Strauss wrote the orchestral horn parts for
the E flat crook, but the solo part is for the F horn, which was by then
already gradually becoming the standard instrument. Throughout his
life Strauss specialized in the construction of themes which, while based

R.S.–C

on the technique of the natural horn, actually incorporated notes which were not readily obtainable without the use of valves.

Taken as a whole, the unity and conciseness of this concerto is something new in Strauss's more ambitious works. Abandonment of sonata form for the outer movements; the ever-ready flow of melodic ideas; and the ingenious backward glances to the first movement during the Rondo, culminating in the fine declamatory phrase from the last tutti of that movement now blazoned forth by the soloist:

Ex. 26

all these things combine to make this concerto one of the most successful of all the early works.

8

Mention has already been made of an early Symphony in D minor rejected by Strauss shortly after its first performance as unsuitable for further promotion. This anxiety on the part of the now increasingly successful young composer was owing to his desire to create an ever more splendid impression on the important figures in the musical world who had just become aware of him, and because he was now working on a new Symphony in F minor which he considered vastly superior. Since he had now left the university, his father sent him in the winter of 1883 on a trip to Leipzig, Dresden, and finally for a considerable stay in Berlin, a shrewd move, since the precocious youth lost no time in getting himself and his works known in the widest circles. He took with him the first sketches of the new Symphony, on which he worked steadily while putting into order the *Stimmungsbilder* for Piano (see above, p. 7) by way of recreation. He was clearly determined to get this important new symphonic venture finished in time to show to his new professional acquaintances and to sow the seed for future performances. As movements of the Symphony were completed he took them round with him to play to people, until all was ready except the slow movement (Andante Cantabile), which was the last to satisfy him. On 11th January 1884 he wrote to his father that the Adagio (sic) was getting on quite well and that he had thought of a very pretty melody which would serve by way of coda. At last, on 25th January, just over a month after his arrival in Berlin, he sent a brief note exclaiming ecstatically that it was a quarter to eight in the evening and that the Symphony was finished.

Not all Strauss's plans for securing performances matured, but success in an unexpected direction put a tremendous feather in his cap. It so happened that during 1884 the pioneering American conductor, Theodor Thomas, came over to Europe, and in the course of his tour found the opportunity to visit old Franz Strauss. The score of the newly completed Symphony was fortunately at hand, with the result that the same December Thomas introduced the name of Richard Strauss to America by giving the première of the work in New York with the Philharmonic Society Orchestra. The first German performance was given a month later in Cologne under Wüllner, who had already given the first performance of the Wind Serenade. Strauss went to the rehearsal and was moved beyond description by the ravishing qualities of his music. Each movement was more wonderful than the last and the whole 'klingt kolossal'.

It is amusing to find the future composer of *Salome* writing of how monstrously difficult it is and how 'Papa wird Augen machen, wenn er hört, wie moderne die Sinfinie klingt.'[6] However, it clearly impressed other and more experienced musicians, too; Bülow thought so highly of it that when in September 1885 he appointed Strauss his assistant with the Meiningen Orchestra, he encouraged him to conduct the Symphony at his début, while playing the solo part in a Mozart Piano Concerto under Bülow's own direction in the same programme. Strauss may have been full of himself and his own cleverness, but he was certainly 'an unusually accomplished and gifted young man', as Bülow wrote to his noble employer, the Duke of Meiningen, when recommending him for the post. The particular thrill of the Meiningen performance was the presence of Brahms. Not that that venerable figure had any very marked encouragement to offer; his laconic 'Ganz hübsch, junger Mann,'[7] was tempered with advice that Strauss should study the dance music of Schubert and concentrate on the invention of eight-bar melodies. Writing later of the incident, Strauss also recalled the criticism of the great composer, 'Your Symphony is too full of

[6] 'Papa will open his eyes wide when he hears how modern the Symphony sounds.'

[7] 'Quite pretty, young man.'

thematic irrelevancies. There is no point in piling up themes which are only contrasted rhythmically on a single triad.' Justifiable as Strauss may have thought the observation (Father Strauss immediately wrote heartily endorsing all Brahms's remarks), this manner of polyphonic construction remained an important element of his style to the end of his life. Nevertheless the occasion was a great one and was made complete by the arrival of the first copy of the published score of the Symphony, towards the cost of which his father, glowing with pride, had contributed 1,000 marks (£50). The fact that this sum was subsequently paid back by no means minimizes the touching generosity of the gesture.

Unfortunately, viewed from the distance of seventy-five years, the work itself proves to be stolid and even a little unimaginative for this stage of Strauss's development. It was only to be expected that, the Symphony being the arch-representative of sonata form, it should be once again structurally wholly conventional. But the material is less striking than one might have hoped and is presented in thick, almost Schumannesque orchestration. Most of the themes appear in mixed colours doubled at the octave, and since this is true of every one of the principal subjects of the oddly pedestrian first movement, their similarity to each other produces a turgid effect, despite the rhythmic variations dictated by their different functions in the symphonic scheme.

Ex. 27

Ex. 28

Ex. 29

Deliberate as no doubt this thematic homogeneity is, it was misguided in a movement the chief feature of which is its long-winded adherence to every facet and detail of classical sonata form. The result, despite the remarkable technical proficiency, is heavy-handed—a fault emphasized by the slow-moving harmonic progressions.

The Scherzo is possibly the best movement of the four, though it is a little unfortunate in having for its motto-theme the figure employed by one of the most ostentatious contemporary motor-horns:

Ex. 30

It is often delicately treated, however, especially in its combination with the graceful figure:

Ex. 31

A less satisfactory feature of the movement is the similarity between the subsidiary subject and the melody of the Trio, since this is the section which is normally required to provide the strongest element of contrast. However, the sudden premature appearance of Ex. 31 in the latter part of the Trio is amusingly *ben trovato*.

After an uneventful start, the Andante develops some attractive ideas, notably the closing theme of the second subject, possibly the idea referred to by Strauss in his letter of 11th January quoted above:

Ex. 32

Pure Schumann though it is (especially in the continued use of themes stated in octaves) it is nicely handled in a variety of poetic ways, especially as it leads the music gently back to the opening melody. This happens twice, the movement being on a larger scale than Strauss's previous Andantes, which had with few exceptions hitherto been in the simplest ternary (ABA) song form. The material of the second subject actually comes round in full a second time, a final reference to the first subject being used for the coda. A further point of interest is the incorporation of Ex. 29 from the first movement, which makes a fine stirring transition theme in the midst of so much easy-going melodizing in $\frac{3}{8}$ time, and also of a little ascending triplet figure which may not be a deliberate allusion at all, but a natural element in Strauss's manner of composition in similar circumstances.

The Finale tails away into a lame emulation of the symphonic methods of Mendelssohn and Schumann alternately, once the initial fiery impetuosity of the first subject has spent itself. This is at once the most pretentious and the weakest part of the whole composition. Both the themes and their working out are contrived rather than spontaneous, and parts of the development have more than a hint of Bruckner's development sections. Bruckner is, however, a dangerous master to follow unless one can match his nobility of spirit, and this the young Strauss could hardly hope to do. As a result, his mildly interesting Chorales, heavy motifs of descending octaves and long sequential passages of imitative counterpoint lead to an apotheosis scarcely more sophisticated than the closing pages of the *Rienzi* Overture. Nor are matters improved by the unmotivated succession of references to the three previous movements which are strung together and made to form the final dramatic build-up.

I have judged the Symphony not as a student work, although it is but little more than this, but at the highest level of aesthetics, which may on the face of it seem unjust. Yet in its own day it seems to have been praised without condescension and without making any such allowances on grounds of inexperience or immaturity. It is true that the Berlin public were not wholly favourable in their reception, but the critics, with only a single exception, wrote of it in terms of the highest adulation, with remarks to the effect that it would come to be recognized as one of the finest products of the last decade. If this prophecy has not proved well founded, at least the unquestionable promise shown by the Symphony was amply fulfilled and, with the appearance of *Don Juan* only three years ahead, within an exceedingly short space of time.

CHAPTER II

MATURING

THE Symphony behind him, Strauss occupied himself during the remainder of his stay in Berlin, in the spring of 1884, drafting the beginnings of a Piano Quartet and a set of Improvisations and Fugue for piano. The latter was really a kind of diversion combined with exercises in technique, and although originally graced with an opus number (15) and dedicated to Bülow, it cannot rate as a serious artistic accomplishment. It is nevertheless undeniably ingenious, especially in the way the bass of the theme, a fanfare-like motif of ascending thirds, is made to serve both as the theme of the Introduction and as the Fugue subject. The fourteen variations (which is what the 'Improvisations' actually are) contain a good deal of amusing rhythmical contrast, and might well have been published together with the Fugue, which oddly enough appeared by itself six years later, included in a volume of miscellaneous piano pieces.

The Quartet is, however, a very different proposition. Whether it was the experience of symphonic construction which he had been gaining during the past months, or whether his imagination had been fired by hearing the newly composed choral and orchestral music of Brahms, with this fresh chamber work Strauss suddenly took another stride forward. To begin with, the piece is on a very large scale, particularly in the first two movements. The opening Allegro is not only long, but builds up a tremendous dramatic tension which at times oversteps the true province of chamber music:

Ex. 1

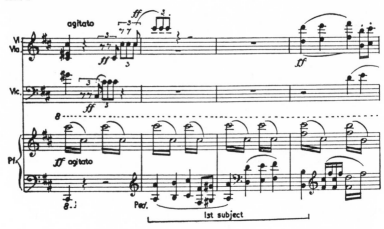

The style is no longer that of Mendelssohn, but is almost pure and unadulterated Brahms, a wholly new influence and exactly what Strauss needed. The handling of symphonic motifs and understanding of the subtleties of sonata form, which were from the first an essential feature of Brahms's style, had been precisely Strauss's greatest weaknesses and in his eagerness he swallowed them whole. Themes from the Symphonies, figures from the Quartets, all were grist to the mill, and as a result, although scarcely an original composition and therefore of only relative ultimate value, the movement solves at a single stroke all the problems that had hitherto baffled Strauss. The development has a logical sense of structure and the lead back to the recapitulation is no longer laborious, but dovetailed in the middle of a paragraph and subtly varied, so that when the tonic cadence arrives the section is in full swing. The coda, too, no longer disappoints expectations as in the Symphony, but on the contrary has a real contribution to make in a passage nearly as long as the exposition itself and containing a fully worked development of a wholly new variant in diminution of the principal subject (Ex. 2). This is not to say that the movement is faultless. The closing melody of the second subject, with its characteristic Straussian retardations, for instance, at first gets stuck harmonically, taking the whole of five bars to get away from its opening tonic chord. Even when it finally takes flight and surges to an ecstatic climax it is suddenly brought back to earth and rounded off too abruptly. But the general gain in technical

Ex. 2

skill, together with the enormous increase in emotional range, far out-
weighs the occasional miscalculation, while the attention to detail is a
constant delight.

None of the other movements quite come up to this remarkable
opening, but the Scherzo has a good many interesting features and is
again on an expansive scale, though the trio is unexpectedly short. The
opening figures ⌐ a ⌐ and ⌐ b ⌐ of the principal subject are obviously full of potentialities and Strauss is now ready to make the most
of them:

Ex. 3

Ex. 4

The picking out of the passing notes in the piano left hand in Ex. 4 is especially ingenious. This movement also boasts an extensive coda in which the Trio subject makes a very necessary reappearance before the piano builds up a splendid frenzy with figure ⌐ b ⌐ hammering away in the strings.

The Andante is another Brahmsian movement with broad melodies in Common Time laid out in abbreviated sonata form. All the thematic ideas are derived from these principal melodies and contrapuntally treated in varying forms of diminution. It is perhaps not Strauss's fault that some of his subjects today bring to mind other and irrelevant associations, but these tunes are undeniably commonplace:

Ex. 5

Ex. 6

It requires taste as well as skill to follow Brahms into the realms of sentiment without trespassing over the border into sentimentality.

In better style is a delicate triplet figure which we shall see again soon in the *Wanderers Sturmlied* (not to mention *Ariadne auf Naxos*):

Ex. 7

(cf.Ex. 10b below)
but which is here nicely contrasted against a series of fragmentary semi-quaver figures.

The Finale turns again to Schumann, though this time in that composer's more impetuous vein. The movement is in full sonata rondo form, with a development for central episode. Both first and second subjects are composite, with a number of pregnant little subsidiary figures, in one of which the features of the later Strauss appear unmistakably:

Ex. 8

The second subject, however, carries with it a melody like a Brahms Lied which, whenever it appears, gives a brief moment of welcome repose from the prevailing busyness:

Ex. 9

This not only introduces the central development episode, but also returns to conclude it (a reversion to Strauss's earlier method) and, as in previous works, robs the exciting working-out passage of its logical climax. Nevertheless Strauss contrives a fine new declamatory ending to the melody, with even greater possibilities for rhetoric in its cleverly delayed return in the recapitulation.

Notwithstanding some weaknesses and plagiarisms, the Quartet is an ambitious scheme bravely carried out, and eighteen months later (when he was already at Meiningen) Strauss heard that the work had been awarded the prize given by the Berlin *Tonkünstler Verein* for the composition of a Piano Quartet. There had been twenty-four entrants and it must be admitted that the judges were by no means unanimous in their opinion. Rheinberger, the famous organ composer, placed the work second, while Heinrich Dorn, a well-known conductor who was a violent opponent of Wagner and who had himself composed an opera *Die Nibelungen*, put Strauss's piece only eighth on the list. The third judge, however, was none other than Franz Wüllner, who had already conducted the Wind Serenade (first performance) and the F minor Symphony, and he swayed the balance in Strauss's favour. Strauss himself played the piano part in a performance of the work in the Meiningen Reunionsaal in early January 1886. The Grand-Duke was present and seems to have taken to the piece, as did also the public—'much to my surprise,' he wrote to Bülow, 'considering that it is by no means a pleasing or ingratiating work'. As a result, when later in the year Strauss decided to leave Meiningen he paid the Grand-Duke the courtesy of dedicating the Quartet to him.

2

On his return from Berlin in the summer of 1884, besides completing the piano variations and the Quartet, Strauss set to work on his first choral composition since his schoolboy days. He chose for the purpose part of an early poem by Goethe entitled *Wanderers Sturmlied*, an admirable vehicle for a single-movement symphonic scheme with its constantly recurring line 'Wen (or Den) du nicht verlässest, Genius', which is reiterated like a motif. It was written in the aftermath of Goethe's early love affair with Frederika Brion, a beautiful fair-haired daughter of a country pastor. Having decided to give her up, and having written to tell her so, Goethe was in a feverish and restless

frame of mind and would go off for long walks in the country by himself. As a result he earned the name of 'The Wanderer' as he roamed
abroad through hills, valleys, fields and woods, singing and composing
'strange hymns and dithyrambs. One of these, the *Wanderers Sturmlied*
still remains' he wrote. 'I remember singing it aloud passionately amid a
terrific storm. The burden of this rhapsody is that a man of genius must
walk resolutely through the storms of life, relying solely on himself.'

Of the 116 lines of the poem, Strauss set the first thirty-eight intact,
since he found these both the most direct in expression and he also felt
with unerring instinct the natural well-spaced climaxes of this section
of the poem, which fall at the words 'Pythius Apollo' and 'Göttergleich'. From here on the text becomes increasingly obscure, with its
references to 'the small, black, fiery peasant' (whom, no doubt, Goethe
encountered as he tramped along); to 'Father Bromius' (an alternative
title of Bacchus); to Jupiter (in his capacity as the god of rain) and so on
with an infinite variety of complex visions which passed through his
mind as he strove vainly to forget his last love. In later years Goethe
vehemently rejected the work as 'half senseless' and Strauss was wise to
stop short of the more incomprehensible passages.

Musically the cantata is cast throughout in a broad Maestoso Sonata
movement, the form of which is divided roughly according to the subdivisions of the poem. The opening stanza, with the three first lines
repeated at the end, corresponds to the first subject—a powerful
orchestral introduction establishing the shorter motivic themes, while
the chorus enters with the more extended melodic strands:

Ex. 10

Ex. 11

Ex. 10b becomes identified with the words '(Nicht der) Regen der
Sturm', a compression of Goethe's line which Strauss allows himself
for the purpose of emphasis. At the climax of the section the chorus
takes part in a restatement of the orchestral opening, using Ex. 10c to
reiterate the 'Genius' line.

A short orchestral modulatory passage introduces the second subject, which consists of two elements: a fine Brahmsian melody:

Ex. 12

wan-deln wird — er wie mit Blu - men - füs - - sen,

and a great declamatory figure which rears itself again and again through the complex polyphonic texture:

Ex. 13

Py - thon, tödtend, leicht, gross,

The interval at | x | between 'leicht' and 'gross' grows wider at each statement, a most exciting development of an impressive idea. This theme in $\frac{3}{4}$ time cuts across the main flow of the music, which is throughout this section in $\frac{4}{4}$ pulse. In the score [1] Strauss emphasizes this cross-phrasing by actually writing each instrument or voice in either three or four time as required, alternating freely and without regard to the other instruments and voices, the bar lines accordingly falling in a number of different places and only coming together at the first great climax of 'Pythius Apollo', in which the whole chorus joins in two mighty and exultant shouts, punctuated by a rising statement of Ex. 12 in the full strings covering two and a half octaves.

A more extended orchestral link now brings the music back to a tranquil mood as the development section begins. This concerns itself principally with Ex. 11 and also with the little rapid figure Ex. 10a, of which great play is made. The return to the recapitulation in the major key is an *a ceppella* passage, as the 'Musen' and the 'Charitinnen' (Graces) are first mentioned. From here to the end, although the sections of recapitulation and coda have each their glowing climax at the common closing word 'Göttergleich', the prevailing mood is elegiac and softly reflective, with harmonic colouring strongly suggestive of Brahms's Requiem. Strauss had heard some of Brahms's choral music during the previous winter and had been particularly interested in the recently

[1] A note informs the conductor that the parts are for obvious practical reasons adjusted and that he should beat the measures according to the notation of the first sopranos.

composed *Gesang der Parzen*, in which Brahms also set a Goethe text for six-part chorus. By pure chance Strauss happened to go one morning to the Gewandhaus in Leipzig when this work was being rehearsed, and there seems little doubt that it gave him the idea of trying his hand at a similar choral piece. Although the result in no way resembles the actual *Parzengesang*, the whole work is full of a thousand and one touches of pure Brahms in the figuration, the orchestral layout and, above all, in the harmonic scheme, which is enormously rich and satisfying. If anything, the fault is now that the whole work is too thick and over-filled with counterpoint, giving an unrelieved heaviness to the piece as a whole. Yet the handling of the six-part chorus is astonishingly resourceful. Only in the development does the sequential imitation become a little mechanical; throughout the bulk of the composition the organization of the many motifs into an intricate polyphonic scheme is no more than a technique used to build up the sonorities of a work conceived in broad outline from the stormy opening to the serene epilogue.

3

Strauss had taken up his appointment in Meiningen as assistant court conductor to Bülow in late September 1885 and stayed there until the following April. Bülow himself resigned in November, so that for the major part of the season Strauss remained in sole charge. He might have remained there for some time, and was in fact invited to renew his contract for three years as Director of Music, but with the offer came the news that the orchestra was to be reduced to thirty-nine players. This was extremely disappointing, since during the five years which Bülow had spent in Meiningen the Court Orchestra had acquired the reputation of being one of the finest in the country, and the decision showed a sad lack of appreciation of the value of what Bülow had achieved, and indicated in addition the Grand-Duke's opinion of the relative standing of his young Director of Music. So, gratifying as it was to be invited to replace his great mentor as First Conductor, on Bülow's advice Strauss relinquished the position and returned to Munich. During his stay in Meiningen he had composed relatively little, even an actual commission for an orchestral Suite not stirring his interest. His unexpected debut, however, as a concert pianist in the Mozart C Minor Concerto drew his creative attention to the piano concerto, and he at once embarked first upon a Scherzo and then a Rhapsody for Piano and Orchestra. Since the former is in D minor and the latter in C sharp it is clear that there was never any intention of combining them into a single major work, and in any case while the composition of the Scherzo went forward magnificently, Strauss lost interest in the Rhapsody, which remained a fragment and has since disappeared. Strauss seems to have become discouraged after the Scherzo, upon which he had built so many hopes, was unsuccessfully tried out with the orchestra. Bülow, for whom it was written, had seen the Lisztian piano part before he left and stated categorically that it was unplayable, and even Strauss felt after the first run through that it was 'pure nonsense'. This was a great pity, as the piece contained much that was highly original, in particular Strauss's splendid idea of beginning with a motif given to four timpani unaccompanied:

Ex. 14

He had been justly proud of this inspiration and quoted it in full in a letter to his father. He had even heard that Spitzweg, of Joseph Aibl, his publishers, was prepared to print the work. But nonetheless he morosely put it on one side. It was not resurrected until four and a half years later, by which time Strauss had come to know the pianist and composer Eugen d'Albert, who pressed him to reconsider his view of the piece. This Strauss did, giving it the title of Burleske and dedicating it to d'Albert, the two friends giving the first performance together on 21st June 1890, in the concert at Eisenach which also included the first performance of *Tod und Verklärung*. The publisher Hainauer was present on this occasion and offered a substantial sum for the work. Strauss still held back, however, although he was tempted by the financial aspect. He had by that time come to feel that he had outgrown the immaturity of its style and could not yet see its qualities in perspective. Four years later again, he finally agreed to its publication, which was undertaken in 1894 by the smaller firm of Steingräber, a fact which has led to the extreme rarity of the orchestral material in recent years. In later life Strauss became reconciled with the Burleske, as was shown by his agreement to its inclusion in his last London concert in October 1947.

It is easy to understand the confusion which must have attended that lamentable first play-through back in Meiningen, especially if, as seems likely, the harassed twenty-one-year old Director tried to combine the roles of conductor and soloist. For the score, despite its debt to Brahms (the continuation of the motto theme Ex. 17 being said to be based on Brahms's D minor Ballade), is full of passages on an entirely new level of quick-witted fantasy and featherweight orchestration of a kind seldom before hazarded by Strauss or any other composer. The sharp, impish, satirical side of Strauss's character is suddenly revealed in a way which does not occur again until we come to *Till Eulenspiegel*; the relationship can easily be seen by the following quotation:

Ex. 15

The whole work is filled with invention of the liveliest character, mostly stemming motivically from the motto theme Ex. 14 and its continuation:

R.S.–D

Ex. 16

together with the theme of the first subject proper, both as presented by
the piano at its first appearance:

Ex. 17

and in its orchestral version:

Ex. 18

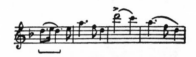

The second subject is a graceful waltz growing out of the figure ⌐ a ⌐
from Ex. 14, while the central episode, which recurs also in the coda, is
another more languid waltz, the theme of which is produced by playing
Ex. 18 in augmentation. There is, moreover, a development section
given to the orchestral tutti which combines all these themes in building
up an exciting climax. As in Strauss's earlier formal works the music
dies down before he can work his way round to the recapitulation, but
the bridge is effected here with so much wit, the piano entering with
curiously obstinate ideas on tonality, that a virtue is made of necessity.
In fact, a most amusing moment occurs when the timpanist refuses to
continue beyond the opening bar of Ex. 14 until the piano agrees to
modify its version of the following bar to enable the piece to continue
in the right key.

    The work is in full sonata form (or it could be regarded as extended
sonata rondo form if Exx. 14 and 16 are considered to be rondo subjects), and it is in the full and uncompromising exploitation of so
extended a form that the main weakness of the work lies. For it is unexpectedly long for its substance, style and content and, enormously attractive though the material is, the inclusion of a recapitulation exact and

complete in every detail was a miscalculation in relative dimensions.
The coda is also too long, partly because of its cadenzas, the more considerable of which spends no less than sixty bars improvising on a single
chord of the dominant minor ninth. Moreover, Strauss had so much to
say that, extended as his scheme already was, he still found room for an
additional subject which he interpolates at the close of both exposition
and recapitulation and which is given its main working out in the coda:

Ex. 19

Once again, so striking is this theme, and so fertile in the development
of its initial rising figure, that it is impossible to regret its inclusion. At
no single moment is the Burleske anything but sparkling and brilliantly
ingenious. Even the 'impossible' piano part can be seen in these days to
be skilfully effective and grateful to play. But in its final impact the
work is never wholly successful, because its seventeen minutes are just
five too many.

                                    4

One of the violinists in the Meiningen orchestra was a man named
Alexander Ritter, who had been a school friend of Bülow's and had
married Wagner's niece. Ritter was not only an excellent musician (he
had once conducted his own orchestra) but a man of wide culture and
encyclopaedic knowledge; having fallen on bad times he had been running a music shop during the last few years before Bülow invited him
to Meiningen, no doubt out of sentiment, as according to Strauss he
seems to have been an indifferent fiddler. He was also a composer with
symphonic poems and operas to his credit, though here again his was no
more than a moderate talent. He was, however, an ardent follower of
Berlioz, Liszt, and Wagner, three names still held by the prevailing
conservative musical opinion in Germany to be mad extremists. Accordingly, his interest roused by the gifted young spark, Ritter lost no
time in inviting him to his house and acquainting him with the programmatic works of the modern school of which, owing to his severely
reactionary musical upbringing, the young Strauss was until that time
entirely ignorant. Strauss was fascinated by Ritter's broadminded

erudition and, in a series of regular evening meetings, absorbed avidly all
the new ideas the older man had to teach him. Opinions differ as to the
extent of Strauss's debt in the development and maturing of his style,
especially since Ritter is said to have been a muddle-headed thinker. It
is difficult to gauge accurately the rights of the matter, as this was the
first time Strauss had come into direct contact with a cultured and
philosophical mind, and was therefore likely to be impressed by a man
who had clearly read widely and spent much time in profound con-
templation. At all events, Strauss himself gave Ritter the complete
credit for having put him on the road in which he almost immediately
found his true stature as a composer, saying that his influence 'was in
the nature of a whirlwind' and that 'he had urged him toward the
poetic, and the expressive in music'. Be all this as it may, the results were
certainly strikingly apparent in the very next work, the Fantasie *Aus
Italien*.

Strauss had always wanted to visit Italy, and with the remark
coming from Brahms that when he finished in Meiningen a journey to
that country would do him more good than frittering away his time in
Berlin, the matter was settled. Within a week of his relinquishing his
post and returning home to Munich he was off on his travels with the
blessing and financial support of his generous father. He clearly had a
marvellous holiday, visiting Verona, Bologna, Rome, Naples, Capri,
and Florence, drinking in the sunshine which always had so strong an
effect upon his creative impulses. While he journeyed he was constantly sketching musical ideas as they came to him. There is a most
amusing letter to his mother in which he outlines some of his experiences, together with marginal remarks as to the keys in which he had
composed at each place. To both Bülow and his mother he confesses that
the beauties of nature stirred him to compose less than the ruins of the
Forum at Rome, where ideas simply flew into his head. The movement
drafted there was of the type of a symphonic opening Allegro, but as a
tentative experiment in the new ideas, so many of which he was now
embracing, he decided to preface it with another slow movement
which had come to him on the Appian Way during an excursion
through the country outside Rome. Two other possible movements
had occurred to him in Capri and Naples respectively, and with regard
to the latter he decided to use a Neapolitan folk song. That the resultant
work would be programmatic music was naturally a foregone conclusion, but although it would clearly be a glorified symphonic poem

Strauss did not yet feel sure of himself, nor had he yet developed the skill to cast the enormous mass of heterogeneous material in a single complex symphonic movement, and the Fantasie has the outward semblance of a traditional four-movement symphony. It is indeed, as Strauss once said, 'the connecting link between the old and the new methods'.

The first movement, 'Auf der Campagna', is easily the most remarkable of the whole work, both in form and content. The broad, spacious Wagnerian chordal structure of the opening, with its little figure of a rising octave, is immensely typical of a side of Strauss familiar to us today, though entirely new at that time, while the Rhapsodic section which follows contains presages of motifs from more than one symphonic poem of the next few years:

Ex. 20

The figure ⌐ a ⌐ built up in the first bar of Ex. 20 emerges at the climax of the movement as part of the great majestic theme for the full wind band which Strauss himself, in an analysis of the work published in 1889, quoted as the principal theme. Before this arrives, however, there is a bridge passage based on the rising octave figure which leads to a melodic section in a warmly distant key which is also referred to briefly before the end of the movement. The most memorable phrase, however, is one which, arriving late on the scene, is extremely short-lived. Nevertheless on reaching it one feels that it was towards this the music has been aiming since the start.

Ex. 21

(An even more remarkable instance of this *modus operandi* will be discussed in due course in *Don Juan*.) The section ends quietly with the atmospheric chordal passage with which it began. The whole most poetic movement, conceived essentially after the manner of a Liszt Symphonic Poem, serves in Strauss's own words as a 'Prelude which evokes the sensations experienced by the composer at the vision of the Roman countryside, bathed in sunshine, seen from the Villa d'Este in Tivoli'.

The second movement, as has been mentioned, was conceived in the Roman Forum. Entitled 'In Rom's Ruinen', it is also headed by the lines, amusingly suggestive of Berlioz, 'Fantastic pictures of vanished splendour, feelings of melancholy and grief amidst the sunniest of surroundings'. After the amazing foretaste of Strauss's mature style in the previous movement, it is with a jolt that one finds him back in his earlier manner contriving a well-behaved symphonic movement based on Schumann's 'Rhenish' Symphony, with a charming second subject strongly reminiscent of Mendelssohn's *Melusina* Overture. Of the vanished splendour, the melancholy and grief there is curiously little in this boisterous Allegro, the most characteristic feature of which is the first subject, recalling still further motifs from future symphonic poems:

Ex. 22

The movement has a fine animal vigour, however, while it is significant in view of what is to come that the greatest interest is now to be found in the lengthy development, not so long ago Strauss's weakest section. The cumulative imitation, working up to a comma which heralds the recapitulation, shows exactly the manner of the parallel passage in *Don Juan*. Occasional but striking features in the orchestration also presage the extreme technical skill the mature Strauss was to expect from his players. The trumpet Top C at the end of the movement anticipates the final bars of *Feuersnot*, but gave the twenty-two-year old composer a certain justifiable apprehension!

Strauss wrote that in the Andantino 'Am Strande von Sorrent' he tried to 'represent in tone painting the soft music of nature, which the inner ear perceives in the rushing of the wind in the leaves, in the songs of birds, in all the fine sounds of Nature, in the distant roar of the sea from which a lonely song resounds on the beach; and to set in contrast against these the experiences of mankind, as expressed by the melodic elements of the movement. The interplay in separation and partial uniting of these contrasts forms the spiritual content of this mood-picture.'

This is a somewhat high-flown description, but one thing clearly emerged; that whatever he may have written, both to his mother and to Bülow, of his insensitivity to Nature, this movement was actually suggested by the natural beauty of the surroundings in which he found himself. It is an exceedingly beautiful and imaginative piece and, bearing in mind that it is still of the same genre of $\frac{3}{8}$ Andantinos of the Violin and Horn Concertos, astonishingly original despite its occasional lapses into pseudo-Mendelssohn. The marvellously colouristic cascades on flutes and violins in the introduction are something quite new in virtuoso orchestral technique and are comparable with his later experiments of the kind, such as the waterfalls in the *Alpensymphonie*. Another feature of the mature Strauss which appears for the first time in the closing bars of this movement is his device of writing a cadence as if it is about to modulate to an enormously distant key, only to slip suddenly into the tonic. Compare the two following examples:

Ex. 23

(*Aus Italien*, 1886)

Ex. 24

(*Le Bourgeois Gentilhomme*, 1910)

The form of this movement is also of considerable interest, since

Strauss takes the plunge of juxtaposing the different sections in the Lisztian manner, following no other rules than those dictated by the poetic idea. The results are magical and Strauss is saved from the routine formula into which his strict adherence to traditional design had led him in the earliest works. Basically the movement is in sonata form, though with an entirely new and independent episode taking the place of the development. This episode, a restless swaying passage with busy string figuration supporting a plaintive oboe solo, corresponds with the 'lonely song resounding on a beach against the distant roar of the sea' of Strauss's analysis quoted above. It is in the recapitulation that the changes occur, since the cadence of the central episode (the rising woodwind figure in Ex. 23). twice interrupts the first subject on its return, until it gives way to the subsidiary theme from the second subject. Conversely, to complete the scheme, the subsidiary theme from the first subject is made to grow naturally out of the second subject proper and thus rounds off both exposition and recapitulation, a role for which it is eminently suitable in its naïve simplicity. The effect, punctuated constantly by the shimmering cascades of the introduction, is of free fantasy, though logically complete, since every theme recurs in due course, and so is entirely satisfying.

If so much of *Aus Italien* is good the question may well be asked why the work is no longer in the repertoire. The answer to that question lies in the Finale, 'Neapolitanisches Volksleben'; for Strauss had the misfortune and lack of taste to mistake the frivolous popular ballad 'Funiculi, Funiculà', composed by one Denza around the newly constructed railway up the side of Vesuvius, for a genuine Neapolitan folk song. The mistake is doubly irksome because not only is the vulgar ditty intolerably faded today and scarcely endurable, but in accepting it for his purpose he missed the golden opportunity of drawing from one of the finest sources of natural and evergreen folk melody in the world.

However, Denza's tune was in high vogue in Naples at the time Strauss was there, and, misguided as he may have been, he certainly had no qualms in the matter, for he launched it with all the gusto he could command, including four extra percussion players who have been silent until this moment. When the 'Volksweise' has been quoted in full, Strauss gets down to the more serious business of working out a Finale. He does this first of all by bringing in themes from the earlier movements, giving the work a cyclic form scarcely in keeping with its programme. The opening chordal passage of the first movement is declaimed briskly, memories of the cascades of Sorrento haunt the transition section, while the second subject combines two further themes from the first movement (figures ⌐ a ⌐ and ⌐ b ⌐ from Ex. 20) with a Tarantella figure actually heard and jotted down by Strauss in Sorrento:

Ex. 25

The movement is in conventional sonata form except for one feature; in the recapitulation the haunting late-comer from the first movement, Ex. 20, is suddenly brought back and is thereafter seldom lost sight of until the bustling coda, a most shrewd and ingenious stroke, which is doubly welcome in view of the relative poverty of the Finale's thematic material.

Strauss took the sketches he had compiled home to Munich and there during the summer and autumn of 1886 he completed the full score, conducting the first performance himself on 2nd March the following year at a subscription concert in the Munich Odeon. It is difficult to understand today why the occasion created such a lively commotion. This was, however, just the time when feelings were strongest over the rival factions of the traditional and reactionary symphonic composers of the classical 'absolute' forms headed by Brahms (though against the wishes of that great figure who had no desire to be the leader of any partisan group), and the *avant-garde* devotees of the *Zukunftsmusik* (Music of the Future), with their joint leaders of Liszt and Wagner, and their passionate interest in the literary associations of programmatic music and the music-drama. Munich was a stronghold of the reactionary clique, and until now it had seemed as if its brightest hope for the future, the young Strauss, was going to remain true to tradition. *Aus Italien* was therefore a considerable shock. The first three movements merely got a poor reception, but after the Finale the uproar was complete, with both lively applause and booing mixed. Strauss could not have been more delighted, and his bewildered father coming round to the artists' room in great distress found his son sitting on the table swinging his legs in high glee. Nor was this mere mischievousness; in the cool light of the following day he wrote to an uncle: 'I now comfort myself with the knowledge that I am on the road I want to

take, fully conscious that there has never been an artist who was not
considered to be crazy by thousands of his fellow men.' More important
to him was the enthusiastic approval he won from Levi and Ritter, not
to mention his family, while the most vital matter of all he tackled
point-blank by writing to Bülow begging permission to dedicate the
Fantasie to him as a small token of his immense gratitude. Bülow replied
with equal enthusiasm warmly accepting the dedication, and one can
readily imagine Strauss's relief and pleasure.

5

From August 1886 to the end of July 1889 Strauss accepted the assignment of third conductor in the Munich Court Opera, a position which
entailed a considerable amount of routine work, although he was able
to use the period to consolidate his position as both composer and conductor by touring Germany, giving performances of his music, and
even returning to Italy, where in December 1887 he conducted two
highly successful concerts in Milan, including the F minor Symphony.
From the standpoint of his creative work these were the most crucial
years of his life, for, having broken away from tradition, he now had
the difficult task of mastering fully his new-chosen technique. He
achieved this aim, incredible as it may seem, in the space of only two
works which he completed during this period—*Macbeth* and *Don Juan*.
But while forging ahead with these new and experimental pieces,
Strauss cast one backward glance at the old forms in which he had first
learnt to compose. This final fling, so to speak, consisted of a Violin
Sonata, his last piece of chamber music before he abandoned the
genre for ever. He occupied himself with it during the summer and
autumn of 1887, the slow movement as in the F Minor Symphony
being the last to reach completion. The work seems to have been
slow in progressing, and one wonders whether he found the task less
absorbing than he had in the past. At all events it was not until a year
later that he wrote home to say that the Andante was finished, the first
performance being given almost immediately afterwards, in early
October 1888.

With the decisions taken which led to the creation of *Aus Italien*, an
unequal work, but nevertheless a successful step in the new direction,
Strauss still felt the need to make his peace with Absolute Music. After
all, there seems no logical necessity to abandon the classical forms of

chamber music and symphony because of a desire to follow the seemingly infinite possibilities of Programme Music. However, although
technically there was no obstacle to the production of dozens of such
perfectly competent works, his imagination was not stimulated by
form as it now was by literary or other extra-musical ideas. Even so,
the Sonata stands as far in advance of the Piano Quartet stylistically, as
does the Quartet relative to the still earlier works. The panache of the
opening statement:

Ex. 26

is no longer merely a reflection of Brahms or Schumann. It is recog-
nizably Strauss in its compact form and directness of expression which
enable it to be incorporated into the texture in a variety of different
ways while suggesting truly symphonic treatment either in Lisztian
unison, declamatory phrases, cumulative imitation, or through
the tension of ostinato. Moreover, Strauss now had a vastly richer
harmonic palette at his fingertips and could construct a well-balanced
paragraph out of a single motif, complete with distant modulation and
characteristically dramatic plunge back into the tonic, before sweeping
into a well-contrasted secondary theme:

Ex. 27

This melody also forms part of the principal second subject, although it
leads into a new and violent figure which supplies a suitable variation
of texture. The transition has a further contrasting element in an
attractively rippling figure of accompaniment. All these features are
exploited in turn in the development which, although by no means
uninteresting is inclined to ramble rather than construct organically,
and, when in doubt, to fall back on recollections of Brahms's handling
of similar circumstances. The recapitulation is carefully approached and
proves as usual to be complete and unvaried, while the coda builds up

a huge climax of such operatic style and proportions as would scarcely
seem out of place in *Elektra* or *Frau ohne Schatten*, which latter it strongly
resembles motivically. Indeed the writing for the two instruments
is generally beyond the realm of chamber music; the piano part resembles nothing so strongly as a Liszt Piano Concerto, while the violin
line, though in no way unviolinistic, rather suggests a full body of
strings, or at times some other orchestral colour of solo wind instruments.

It is difficult to imagine the slow movement of a Beethoven or a
Brahms violin sonata being played, let alone published, apart from its
parent work, and it is perhaps revealing to find the Andante of this
Sonata actually entitled in the complete copy ' "Improvisation" aus
Rich. Strauss op. 18', in which form it has from the start enjoyed an
independent existence. It is, of course, the epitome of Strauss's 'Song
without Words' Andantes, although the sophisticated young man now
travels far beyond the Mendelssohnian simplicity which contented him
as a boy. The opening, Ex. 28, has the melodic charm of a Schubert song,
while the dramatic middle section, Ex. 29, owes something, too, to
'Erlkönig', though touched unmistakably by the emerging hand of
maturity.

Ex. 28

Ex. 29

Richard Strauss, 1888

The surprise in this basically ternery (ABA) movement, and the justification, no doubt, for the title of 'Improvisation', lies in the sudden disintegration of the middle section, after a show of considerable passion, into an infinitely delicate lace-work of rapid Chopinesque figures. These gradually work their way round to the tonic and form the background to the restatement of the principal melody Ex. 28. The coda, surprisingly enough, boldly fulfils the association of ideas which has long been haunting the listener by continuing this opening theme in the manner of the Adagio Cantabile of Beethoven's 'Pathétique' Sonata, as if to forestall and disarm critical comment. The movement is enchanting in its way, and certainly fully within the range of a duo in its exquisite handling of the instruments; Strauss was, of course, an accomplished performer on both. Yet it feels contrived rather than inspired, in contrast with its programmatic opposite number in *Aus Italien,* despite some happy ideas, including further magical examples of the shifting cadences illustrated by Exx. 23 and 24 above.

The last movement is, as so often before, the weakest of the three, though it offers a certain interest in its formal eccentricities. After a slow and sombre Brahmsian Introduction in which the main subject Ex. 30 is gradually formulated, the Allegro bursts in abruptly with considerable sound and fury:

Ex. 30

After successions of orchestral chords and arpeggiando figures (including a startling quotation from *'Tristan'*) have alternated with Ex. 30, two new and broadly melodic themes are announced, the first of which is always closely associated with Ex. 30, while the second breaks easily into a scherzando figure:

Ex. 31a   b

Once Ex. 31 gains the ascendancy the music begins to modulate in earnest, necessarily, since all the themes have so far centred about the tonic key of E flat, thus robbing Ex. 31 of its expected role of second subject.

At this point, despite the unorthodox tonal scheme, some kind of development of the already considerable amount of material seems indicated. Strauss has a surprise in store, however, and an abrupt four-bar shift into C Major introduces a huge melody with a span of nearly two octaves which soars up in both violin and piano alternately, the latter thundering it out while the poor violinist keeps his head above water as best he may by playing rapid arpeggio figures across all four strings. This kind of passage again bears no relationship to true chamber-music style and is a good example of Strauss's lifelong tendency to conceal lack of inspiration by flamboyance. With the full resources of a vast orchestra or an operatic cast of fine voices this grandiloquence could often be turned to good advantage, while the possibilities of colour or a dramatic situation would, in nine cases out of ten, set his imagination on fire once more. With only a piano and a violin to play with, Strauss could not disguise the emptiness of this sprawling melodic line, for all the fervour with which he directs it to be played:

Ex. 32

In due course the violin asserts itself and presents Ex. 30 forcibly. Thereupon the development section passes through all the material and a variety of distant keys before a tremendous downward rush on the piano (a feature for which Strauss soon learnt the right use in *Macbeth*) leads into the recapitulation. But for the first time Strauss cleverly curtails this section by interpolating a brief reference to Ex. 32, after which the first subject, Ex. 30, returns and leads straight to the coda. This final section is, in fact, another surprise, having almost an independent life of its own. It is an extensive movement in $\frac{6}{8}$ time, and in the sudden scherzo-like atmosphere Exx. 30(a) and 31b alternate gaily, until an increase of speed presages the vivacious closing flourishes. The freedom of chromatic modulation in the coda is very striking, and it was perhaps with this in mind that Strauss deliberately invented the harmonically static periods in the earlier portions of the movement. If the experiment was not altogether successful, it gives rise to some interesting moments, and there is not the slightest doubt that Strauss learnt materially from his work on the Sonata. For this piece marks the end of the apprentice period of Strauss's output, apart from some incidental music to *Romeo and Juliet*, for women's voices and small orchestra (written for performances of the play in the Munich National theatre in the later autumn of 1887). Four short surviving numbers, three of which are settings of texts not even by Shakespeare, show the music to have been both inconsiderable and uncharacteristic. This was, however, far from the case with the ever-growing volume of songs with which Strauss punctuated his more ambitious projects from boyhood to old age, and which I shall discuss as a whole in a later chapter in Volume II. Thus nothing now separates us from the great series of Tone Poems which forms the first part of Strauss's important contribution to the contemporary repertoire.

CHAPTER III

THE TONE POEMS (I)

BY 1885 the symphonic poem was at the height of fashion through-out Europe. Unlike most forms, it did not evolve, but came into being at the hands of a single creator, Liszt, who more than thirty-five years before contrived a set of twelve single-movement orchestral works of varying lengths and of diverse origins for which he formula-ted the generic title of *Symphonische Dichtung*. One thing these twelve works had in common, whether they were based on a poem (*Ce qu' on entend sur la Montagne*), a myth (*Orpheus*), a play (*Hamlet*), a picture (*Hunnenschlacht*) or a philosophy of life (*Les Préludes*): they were all inspired by some extra-musical influence; they were the very essence of what had already become known widely as Programme Music. Not that this in itself was anything new. Kuhnau's *Biblical Sonatas* (1689), Telemann's *Don Quixote Suite* and Vivaldi's *Le quattro staggioni* are only a few examples which spring to mind dating back from up to two hundred years.

Yet the validity of this form of music-making had never been widely accepted, purist and conservative opinion having set its face firmly against such experiments as unworthy and a bastard art-form. Even Beethoven felt the need for his famous apologia when composing his 'Pastoral Symphony' ('mehr Ausdruck der Empfindung als Malerei').[1]

But with the coming of the nineteenth-century Romantics, whose enthusiasm for literature led them to combine it with their own art, Programme Music came suddenly and quickly into prominence.

[1] 'More an expression of feeling than painting.'

Berlioz's passion for Shakespeare, Schumann's for Jean Paul Richter—these were the violent symptoms of a far-reaching international movement causing bitterness and opposition.

Even relatively 'classically-minded' composers succumbed to the attractions of the movement. Mendelssohn's 'Concert Overtures' ('Fingal's Cave', 'Calm Sea and Prosperous Voyage', 'Rob Roy' and 'The Legend of the Fair Melusina') are Symphonic Poems in all but name. Liszt not only supplied the title but also strove to create new forms more suitable to the literary conception of such works without sacrificing their essential unity. He failed in the event, because to the end, even in his finest work, the *Faust* Symphony, he never understood that his remarkable technical innovations in the direction of thematic metamorphosis could only implement and not replace organic and logical development. It is the particular failing of his orchestral works that they break up into a succession of disconnected fragments; only rarely does one section grow out of any other.

Nevertheless despite Liszt's limitations as a symphonic composer, the imaginative possibilities of his theories were to stimulate composers far and wide. Yet apart from the early experiments by members of his immediate circle (such as Smetana, whose *Richard III* of 1858, and *Wallensteins Lager* of 1859, based on Shakespeare and Schiller respectively, are obviously directly influenced), the general exploitation of the new form, and indeed the whole Lisztian manner of composition, spread only gradually. For whatever his notoriety as a romantic figure, or in his fabulous pianistic virtuosity, he was largely neglected as a composer, and it was as much as twenty-five or thirty years before some of his orchestral works received their first performances. Thus it was only in 1871 that another Lisztian pupil, the Frenchman Saint-Saëns, began his series of symphonic poems drawing on classical mythology *Le Rouet d'Omphale*, *Phaëton*, etc.), while in Russia, Tchaikovsky was simultaneously embarking on his programmatic Fantasie-Overtures. These are all based on literary subjects (*Romeo and Juliet*, *Hamlet*, *Francesca da Rimini*, etc.) and are essentially symphonic poems, although it was not until late in life that Tchaikovsky actually used the name. He was inspired by Balakirev (who had, in fact, originally proposed both form and subject-matter to Tchaikovsky) and the other members of the Russian circle; Dvořák and César Franck soon followed, and by the 1880s the symphonic poem was being cultivated assiduously by composers in many countries.

R.S.–E

Germany naturally also produced composers of the Lisztian faith who were trying their hand at the form, though few had the genius to produce lasting examples. Bülow, at one time Liszt's son-in-law, had himself composed a similar piece, *Nirwana*, which had impressed the young Strauss enormously, while Ritter had produced not less than six varied examples which in conception, if certainly not in execution, emulated Liszt's breadth of imaginative approach with their programmatic titles of *Seraphische Phantasie*; *Erotische Legende*; *Ritt zum Grabe*; *Olafs Hochzeitsreigen*; etc.

2

When Strauss turned to the symphonic poem[2] he decided to take his subjects from an equally wide range of origins. Beginning with Shakespeare (*Macbeth*), he turned to poetry (Lenau's *Don Juan*), to medieval German Legend (*Till Eulenspiegel*), to philosophy (Nietzsche's *Zarathustra*), to literature (*Don Quixote*), to his own life and experiences (*Heldenleben* and *Sinfonia Domestica*), and finally back to the realization of scenic beauty he had sought to express in *Aus Italien* at the beginning of his experiments with programmatic composition (*Alpensymphonie*).

Such a broad variety of subject-matter naturally calls for an equally varied choice of forms. Alternatively, if no conventional design will answer, complete mastery is essential in the technique of contriving a symphonic structure answerable only to itself and its extra-musical programme. However freely rhapsodic such a work may be of necessity, at no time should the listener be allowed to feel that the sense of logical purpose has been lost and that the work instead of being a-formal, so to speak, has become shapeless. This was where Liszt failed when he abandoned the external trappings of traditional form, as in *Ce qu'on entend sur la Montagne*, which Tovey describes magnificently as 'an introduction to an introduction to a connecting link to another introduction to a rhapsodic interlude, leading to a free development of the third introduction, leading to a series of still more introductory developments of the previous introduction, leading to a solemn slow theme (which, after these twenty minutes, no mortal power will persuade any listener to regard as a real beginning), and so eventually lead-

---

[2] For some reason he changed the title to Tone Poem, although his works were considerably more symphonic than their predecessors.

ing backwards to the original mysterious opening by way of conclusion'. *Les Préludes, Hamlet,* and above all the 'Faust' Symphony, are more successful because they follow a predetermined course based on well-tried formulae: four-part symphony, palindrome, and sonatad first-movement respectively. Each is kept from falling apart by Liszt's ingenious device of overall unification through thematic metamorphosis. In such works the basic design keeps his ideas, always fascinating and imaginatively presented, from dying, as they are apt to do through Liszt's congenital lack of symphonic continuity.

3

It was here that Strauss's training as a composer of traditional forms was of paramount value. As Liszt had done before him with a Shakespearean subject in *Hamlet,* so Strauss in *Macbeth* presented a psychological study of the chief protagonists in a fundamentally formal structure rather than attempting to follow in detail the course of the action.

Yet in writing to his uncle Hörburger he described *Macbeth* as 'a sort of symphonic poem, but not after Liszt'. For his musical language he turned rather to Wagner, and this is strikingly apparent in his quick mastery of what the Germans describe as 'Durchführung' (meaning 'following-through'). *Macbeth* is cast in an elaborate sonata form in which the development far exceeds the recapitulation in length and substance, including, moreover, two self-contained episodes each of which presents a new theme of outstanding importance, the whole unified by a fanfare-like *Naturmotif,* Ex. 1, which is separately presented in a brief introduction.

Ex. 1[3]

This theme should not be taken as referring specifically to the character of Macbeth, but rather, perhaps, to the finer elements of the royal soldier in his personality and so thereby to kingliness as such; at one

---

[3] Notice Strauss's curious manner of accenting the short notes of a figure in the same way as in the Violin Sonata—cf. Exx. 26 and 30 above. No doubt the trick reflected a conviction, possibly developed during conducting, that the short notes are always understressed by performers unless specifically pointed out!

stage of the work it clearly presents Duncan, the king whom Macbeth murdered. Technically, the employment of such a motif was an indication of Strauss's adoption of Wagner's methods, as well as a splendid prop in the sustaining of the free symphonic structure. Macbeth himself is depicted, as is definitely stated in the score, in a section based on two further themes, Exx. 2 and 3, although Ex. 1 is also featured during the section.

Ex. 2

Ex. 3

These composite themes combine to present a character-portrait of Macbeth, martial and ambitious (Ex. 2), passionate yet unstable (Ex.3), and leavened with a definite streak of regal dignity, a vital feature of Shakespeare's conception without which much of the plot would lose its nobility and degenerate to a mere 'penny dreadful'. The section comes to a clear-cut end, and with a single bar of modulation the work passes to the second subject, a parallel character-study of Lady Macbeth. This time Strauss actually quotes Shakespeare in the score, so as to identify the passage with a specific aspect of her personality:

> Hie thee hither,
> That I may pour my spirits in thine ear,
> And chastise with the valour of my tongue
> All that impedes thee from the golden round,
> Which Fate and metaphysical aid doth seem
> To have thee crown'd withal.

From this the emphasis is clearly laid on her influence upon Macbeth in the ruthless pursuit of her ambition rather than on her own personality. Yet the first theme of her section is purely soft and feminine, as if Strauss perceived that the chastisement and valour of her tongue were mixed with conjugal persuasion:

Ex. 4

The subsidiary theme which follows illustrates graphically the appalling contrast between the turbulence within her and the majestic serenity she presents to her husband and the world:

Ex. 5

The exposition complete, the principal protagonists are now presented. Before proceeding with the development, however, Strauss inserts two substantial episodes giving the impression that the drama is proceeding. But there is no attempt to follow the action of the play; in fact, few of the other characters are suggested at all. The tone poem is concerned only with a reflection of the events through the changing character of the two increasingly stark and horrific figures of Macbeth and Lady Macbeth. There is no Banquo even, certainly no witches. The episodes are not explained in the score, though one can more or less guess their significance. The first is clearly a dialogue between Macbeth and his wife, beginning amicably, almost romantically, and gradually becoming more and more heated and frenetic. Macbeth speaks first with a new theme which could be derived from the figure ⌐ b ¬ from Ex. 3.

Ex. 6

This motif constantly rears itself as Macbeth counters his wife's murderous proposals with tender yet apparently inflexible resolution. Macbeth is by no means as wicked at heart as events later force him to become. But gnawing at the roots of his upright morals and arguments of humane loyalty are repeated interruptions by the weak vacillating motif of Ex. 3.

Lady Macbeth argues first with Ex. 4, but before long a new theme is added to her persuasiveness, gracious but insidious in the twisting contours of its melodic line.

Ex. 7

This appears at intervals during the discussion, but it is not as yet brought out as a main subject. Later, however, it becomes one of the most important themes of the work.

A furious *accelerando* leads to a tremendous climax at which Ex. 1 is announced in the form of three mighty fanfares separated by dramatic pauses. Duncan, the king, is at hand. After the third statement the strings burst in with a rushing passage based on Ex. 7 in diminution as the conspirators frenziedly prepare for his arrival at their castle of doom.

Duncan's processional music comprises the second self-contained episode. It is built almost entirely out of Ex. 1, which is transformed into a ceremonial movement worthy of Elgar. At no time has the kindly Scottish king a theme of his own. He represents the epitome of royal dignity and is therefore portrayed by the theme which from the beginning has described those qualities. He is received at the castle by Lady Macbeth (Ex.4), but Macbeth is not present (cf. Act I, scene 6), and it remains for Duncan to ask that he be conducted to him. Ex. 6 surges up in the bass, followed by Ex.7 in a triumphant build up. The procession then dies away to a further series of suave statements of Ex.7 and the work passes directly to the development section proper.

It had already become apparent in *Aus Italien* that the stimulus of a programme showed itself particularly in Strauss's development sections. This was to some extent due to the fact that the necessity for mechanically working through a recapitulation no longer weighed on his shoulders. Naturally the pithy and characteristic motifs which the subjects of a programme awoke in his imagination also lent themselves to symphonic treatment more readily than the discursive themes and melodies he had been in the habit of inventing for his symphonic works. But most important of all was the sense of purpose, of direction, which he had never been able to feel in abstract music in the instinctive way of a Brahms or a Mendelssohn. Faced with the murder scene and the ghastly knocking[4] which disturbed the murderers, Strauss was easily spurred to invent a fine development. Moreover, he had a great deal of eminently workable material to build with, and this he arranged purely symphonically, beginning with Macbeth's themes and passing on to those of Lady Macbeth's much as he used previously to develop his first and second subjects in his sonata movements. The Royal theme, Ex. 1, is, however, ever present, maintaining the continuity of the structure. It is significant that Lady Macbeth, her purpose achieved, is no longer portrayed by Ex.4, but rather by the weird opening figures of Ex.5, indicating her increasing turbulence of spirit despite a calm exterior. In this first character-study Strauss was already showing considerable psychological insight. The orchestral layout of the themes of both characters is now coloured to present an extremely mysterious and sinister picture out of which the figure ⌐ b ⌐ from Ex.5 and the insinuating theme Ex.7 gradually assume pre-eminence as the first main climax is built up. This culminates in the 'knocking' passage, which abruptly collapses into a pathetic colloquy between Macbeth (Ex.2) and the ever more prominent Ex.7

> MACBETH. To know my deed,
>   'Twere best not know myself
>   Wake Duncan with thy knocking;
>   I would thou couldst.[5]

From this point the music works up to a second climax, incorporating Exx.1 and 5 as before, and gradually approaching a repeat statement of Macbeth's music as announced at the opening of the work. The feeling of this moment in the structure is that of a symphonic recapitulation; Macbeth's worst excesses and cruelties when he becomes king are not dwelt upon. We see him only at the extremity of his

---

[4] cf. Strauss's treatment of this with the famous fight music in Tchaikovsky's *Romeo and Juliet*.

[5] This quotation is not given by Strauss, who specifically prints in his score only the passage quoted in connexion with Lady Macbeth's first themes.

downfall, sickened by his degradation as a man of honour, but deter-mined to show himself a soldier of steadfast courage to the last. The recapitulation is extremely brief and in a few bars merely portrays his death and the moral and physical disintegration of Lady Macbeth. There is no sleep-walking scene and she passes away with nothing but a few broken phrases from Ex.4. The coda gives a few distant fanfares suggesting the triumph of Macduff and the coronation of Malcolm in a joyous Scotland freed from tyranny. The lifting of the hitherto un-relievedly oppressive atmosphere is magical. The music then darkens once more, and after some funereal trumpet calls the symphonic poem ends with Ex.6. This, the warmest and happiest of Macbeth's themes, had symbolized that part of his character which, devoted to his wife and so fatally subjected to her will, caused his downfall. The use of just this theme for the final impression is most subtle, especially since it has not been heard since the climax of the Royal episode which preceded the development, a fine piece of thematic organisation.

4

In its first version of 1887-8 the work had closed with a full triumphant march of Macduff in D major, but when Strauss showed the newly completed score to Bülow the latter remarked that this was pure non-sense. 'It is all very well,' he said, 'for an *Egmont* Overture to conclude with a triumphal march of Egmont, but a symphonic poem *Macbeth* can never finish with the triumph of Macduff.' A poetic programme may well suggest new forms, he added, but whenever music is not developed logically from within, it becomes 'literary music'. Strauss saw that this was good advice, and decided to scrap the old ending, putting the whole work away in a drawer, and getting on with the plans for a further symphonic poem to be based on the eternal *Don Juan* legend. In August 1888 he wrote to Bülow drearily: '*Macbeth* rests peacefully in its grave in my desk where, no doubt, *Don Juan* will shortly keep it company.' In his depression it seemed to him for the moment that the pursuit of a new line had spelt ruin for his success as a composer. However, the following January, while in Mannheim, he saw his chance to run through *Macbeth* with the orchestra, which he did exactly as it stood. To his relief it went pretty well and 'sounded far less awful than on the piano'. Even so, 'it was very difficult technically,' he wrote to his parents 'for the fiddles and especially for the trumpets.

The Mannheim orchestra were immensely struck and astounded by the leap from the F minor Symphony to *Macbeth*.' And well they might have been. Nevertheless Strauss felt that the piece could do with improvement, and put it away again until the autumn, when, with *Don Juan* and *Tod und Verklärung* behind him, he set to work not only to alter the ending but to revise the orchestration. The summer of 1889 had been spent as musical assistant in Bayreuth, a very timely opportunity thrown in his way by Bülow, and he brought back with him some fine new orchestral ideas. In particular he inserted into his new score a part for the bass trumpet, an instrument which Wagner had heard in Austrian cavalry bands and brought into the brass ensemble for his *Nibelungen Ring*. The effect of this pleased Strauss enormously, and he wrote enthusiastically after the first rehearsals and performance that 'the bass trumpet has acquitted itself famously; it is the only possible transition and mediator between the trumpets and trombones, and softens the brass *Kolossal*'. Another interesting feature of the instrumentation of the final version is the specification of different beaters for the tam-tam, such as timpani and bass-drum sticks, and more especially the triangle stick with which the tam-tam is to be *rubbed* ('gerieben'). This terrifying effect greatly took Strauss's fancy and he used it several times later in his stage works. Strauss's experiences in the opera house affected his work for the concert platform in a way which assumes significance when we see how his career eventually left the one platform for the other. Already in *Macbeth* there is a wholly three-dimensional theatricality in the Macduff/Malcolm fanfares, with their offstage side-drum roll. It is as if the bodies of Macbeth and Lady Macbeth are still lying dead before us as we look to the background and see the bright vision of the future projected against the grim tragedy which has just reached its bitter catastrophe. Such a visual style was something entirely new to Strauss and looks back to Berlioz for its origin; it is to be increasingly in evidence as the Symphonic Poems unfold.

5

Macbeth was not heard in public until 13th October 1890; the composition had, in the end, been spread over four years, and as a result the chronology of the Tone Poems is disturbed in a way which could be confusing. In discussing the first performance, as it will be convenient to do now, it is necessary for us to bear in mind that although the

first in order of conception, *Macbeth* seemed to its audiences to be the
third Tone Poem to come from Strauss's pen.[6]

Despite the extensive revisions, when Strauss came to the first
performance he found that he was not, after all, entirely happy, though
the idea and shape of the work now pleased him greatly. His doubts
were perhaps strengthened by a pathetic letter from his father, who had
travelled to Weimar specially for the occasion and afterwards wrote:

> I beg you with all my heart, dear boy, to open your mind
> to the views of other knowledgeable people who do not
> happen to share your opinions. I have always been in
> favour of self-confidence, but this should not turn into a
> disease. You have a strong yearning to experiment, but
> no one can combine this with honesty towards art—it
> damages both his art and himself. You will now turn up
> your nose and consider me and my outlook old-fashioned;
> but you are wrong about this. I move with the times even
> if with greater moderation than you; nor do I forget in
> error that youth thinks and feels differently from the aged,
> but in this connexion a certain harmony between the two
> has existed at all times and will always remain; that is pure
> humanity, above which one cannot set oneself unpunished.
> The public that one wants to train and to lead must under-
> stand the guide, or else he cannot lead and clarify but at
> best only confuse and lead astray . . . One can accom-
> plish the highest things without experimenting by setting
> great and noble thoughts in simple clothing, without
> highly coloured instrumentation, and then it will be under-
> stood by all people and in all times. Every great artist has
> in every period and in all forms of art accomplished the
> most artistic things with the simplest means—just think of
> Grecian sculpture and the great Italian painters etc. of the
> middle ages. I counsel you, although heavy-hearted because
> I know it is useless; revise *Macbeth* still once more with the
> greatest care, and throw out the excessive instrumental
> padding; and give the horns more opportunity to stand
> out, as you yourself would say.

From the general to the particular; thus speaks the horn-player!

That Father Strauss could not follow his son's elaborate polyphony
was inevitable, nor would it have been right for Strauss to take his

---

[6] The confusion is further increased by the way in which Strauss allocated the
opus numbers, with *Macbeth* neither before nor after *Don Juan* and *Tod und
Verklärung*, but between them.

father's dictates against experiment too seriously. But there was still much that he needed to learn in the handling in orchestral terms of complex polyphonic structures, and it is clear that when it came to this item of criticism his father's words were by no means in vain. Within two days of receiving the letter Strauss wrote to Ritter that whereas he felt that the work was entirely right in construction and general conception, he was no longer wholly satisfied with the instrumentation. 'With so many inner parts, in many places the principal themes do not emerge as flexibly as I would wish, and I am already very much of a mind to revise the work utterly.' It is clear that he did so, because his remarks after the next performance, which was a full fifteen months later, were unreservedly eulogistic. 'In Berlin all went famously,' he wrote again to Ritter. 'Just think; *Macbeth* has had as good a success in the final rehearsal as in the performance and really seems to have made a profound impression. The orchestra played wonderfully, the piece sounds fabulous and has given me the greatest joy in the clarity of its new version—there is no longer a single theme in it which doesn't come through—and in the mighty surge right through to the end.'

This second performance seems to have been an occasion of high excitement. Bülow wrote to his wife that the atmosphere was electric. It was certainly an important enough setting; a Berlin Philharmonic Subscription concert, in full season, on leap-year-day 29th February 1892. Bülow was to a large extent won over to the work, a considerable triumph, as he had by no means accepted it before on account of its dissonances and lack of immediate appeal. He had even written to Spitzweg, Strauss's publisher back in 1888, when Strauss had shown him the first draft, that 'it would do more to popularize the young composer if the cadenzas he had written for the Mozart C minor Piano Concerto could be published rather than this Macbethian soup from the witches' kitchen.' Even after its success he qualified his enthusiasm by saying that it was mostly mad and bewildering, but a work of genius of the highest order. He also acknowledged with an air of surprise that 'the work also actually sounds well—overwhelming!'

The Berlin reception, even at the *Generalprobe*,[7] was clearly tremendous; Strauss was recalled four times and Bülow said that he had never

---

[7] 'Final rehearsal'. Throughout Germany this has long been by tradition an event to which the public are admitted and in every way comparable with the first performance.

before known a composer get such an acclamation. It is strange to realize that this was for *Macbeth*, and that, owing to the upset chronology discussed above, both *Don Juan* and *Tod und Verklärung* had already appeared, works which are today considered superior beyond comparison. To the contemporary view it is difficult to visualize the first performance of even the final immensely improved version of *Macbeth* as anything but a retrograde step, explainable only by the fact that it was, after all, an earlier—almost experimental work. The assurance, the unmistakable style and fantastic originality of the mature Strauss, although obviously just round the corner, is not completely there. Its neglect today is no matter of unlucky chance, immensely worthy as *Macbeth* is. Far-sighted, introspective, exciting, if a little heavy in its deep-thinking, well shaped (no longer are its eighteen minutes five too many, as in the *Burleske*) and full of good themes—all these qualities it has, even though in later years Strauss cared little for it. When Sir Thomas Beecham announced it for inclusion in his Festival of 1947 Strauss tried to discourage him on the grounds that it was an ungrateful work. This is not quite true; it can certainly make an impressive effect but on the other hand Bülow was overstating the case by using the word 'genius' in his summing up, and here can be found the reason why it has failed to retain its place in the standard repertoire alongside the other tone poems. It is a work of extreme merit; but it was followed immediately by a succession of masterpieces.

6

Strauss's love affairs gave his parents anxiety from the first. Yet it was surely to be expected that an ardent young artist, on his own in the various German townships, would be bound to meet pretty girls to whom he would be attracted and who would surely be attracted to this immensely gifted, incredibly promising and by no means ill-favoured youth. Various letters written both to his parents (by observers who were quick to see what was going on) and by his parents to Strauss, even after he had come of age, indicate that he had quickly become emancipated considerably beyond the point considered respectable by the society of those days. His father wrote to him soon after he went to Meiningen that, nice as it was for him to enjoy himself with good, solid cheerful women (!), where everything was above board, he should be careful not to smear his good name and damage his career now that he had to conduct a women's chorus; to remember the gossip there had been about him and Dora W.——etc., etc. Looking back from these broader-minded times it seems to us that Strauss sowed remarkably few wild oats for so passionate a spirit, and that he found his life-partner remarkably early on.

In late August 1887, Strauss paid a visit to his Uncle George Pschorr, who lived an hour's train journey outside Munich in a village called Feldafing. Prominent in the village was a certain General de Ahna, who lived with his two daughters. He was an amateur baritone of some quality who gave local recitals, chiefly of Wagnerian extracts, and who was therefore gratified to make the acquaintance of the latest star on the musical horizon. The elder daughter, Pauline, was also possessed of a good voice and had actually finished her studies as a soprano in the Munich Conservatoire, without making any headway in the profession. Strauss was entirely captivated by the girl and, like many other musicians, made use of his art to further his courtship by undertaking the instruction of his beloved. This he did to such effect that when two years later he took over the opera in Weimar he was able to introduce her as one of the leading sopranos. In the meantime the effect of this new love affair upon his work was electrifying, for he quickly translated the experience into musical terms, composing his first love music, which proved to be amongst the finest he was ever to write.

As a vehicle for the expression of sexual desire, he chose the greatest erotic subject of all time, the *Don Juan* legend.[8] He found amongst the mid-nineteenth-century German poets a verse play by Nikolaus Lenau which served his purpose particularly well, not so much because of Lenau's dramatic treatment of the legend, as because of his psychological study of the notorious woman-hunter. Published posthumously in 1851 (the poet had died insane a year before), *Don Juan* was Lenau's last work and remained a fragment, a series of short scenes barely forming a coherent plot. It is complete enough, nevertheless, to trace the main outlines of Don Juan's career from the scene where his father vainly sends Don Diego, his brother, to fetch him home from his worthless life of

---

[8] There is some confusion as to when Strauss actually began work on *Don Juan*. Every biographer has accepted the autumn of 1887 as being the approximate time when the first drafts were sketched. Yet Strauss himself wrote that 'during a later Italian journey to Venice (in May 1888) I invented the first themes of *Don Juan* in the courtyard of the monastery of S. Antonio in Padua.' Since the work was undoubtedly completed the same summer, this seems to allow very little time for the composition of so elaborate and complex a score.

sensuality, to the final duel in which he dies not because he is defeated but because he finds victory 'as boring as the whole of life'. During the intermediary stages there is scarcely a form of depravity or dishonour in which he does not indulge or of which he does not show himself capable in what is, in fact, his idealistic search for the perfect woman. But in every successful exploit it subsequently turns out that some great harm has been done, or someone has been desperately hurt. This leaves ineradicable marks on his character, since he is profoundly disturbed to find that his life's philosophy—the glorification of the experience of the single moment above all else—is so utterly unendurable to those on whom he seeks to impose it that they destroy themselves, leaving him completely baffled and demoralized.

All his ever wilder and more assertive exploits are explainable in the light of this deep-rooted discontent which, far from causing him to abandon his mode of life, spurs him on to indulge in further adventures with less and less care for personal safety and honour. As the end approaches he gloomily desires nothing better than the arrival of a mortal enemy who may relieve him of the supreme boredom of living.

Lenau conjures up the images of five of Don Juan's mistresses; Maria who, faced with a stern father and a hateful marriage, abandons all to follow Juan, only to be herself abandoned when the time comes; Clara, whom we only see at the moment of her rejection of Juan, accomplished just in time before his ardour has cooled; Isabella, whom Juan seduces by impersonating her betrothed in total darkness; Anna, who never actually appears, but whom Juan passionately apostrophizes in a Monologue (possibly Lenau would have made more of this episode had he completed the poem); and lastly and most pathetic, an unnamed woman who has just died of a broken heart, the news being brought to Juan at a masked ball, tragedy being dramatically planted into the midst of a carnival in accordance with an age-old and never failing theatrical tradition. Don Juan's attitude in the aftermath of catastrophe is summarized when, after he has desecrated a monastery, the Abbot destroys the entire building in his despair. Don Juan turns to his comrade with the words:

> Das ging zu weit, so hab' ich's nicht gemeint,
> Wer Böses thut, thut mehr stets als er will.[9]

[9] That went too far, that I never meant;
He who does evil ever does more than he intends.

7

Strauss's treatment of the subject is to some extent reflected by the quotations from the poem with which he heads the score. These consist of three passages, all spoken by Don Juan himself; two come from the opening scene and the third from the last, though they are by no means the closing lines, The first two excerpts thus come fairly close together and form the kernel of Don Juan's arguments for rejecting his brother's pleas. Don Diego has come expressly with messages from their father, whose favourite Juan has always been, begging him to return home without delay. Don Juan refuses in a series of replies in which, at considerable length, he expounds his life's philosophy. In the first excerpt, the essence of his worship of the Isolated Moment is immediately manifest:

> Den Zauberkreis, den unermesslich weiten,
> Von vielfach reizend schönen Weiblichkeiten
> Möcht' ich durchziehn im Sturme des Genusses,
> Am Mund der Letzten sterben eines Kusses.
> O Freund, durch alle Räume möcht' ich fliegen,
> Wo eine Schönheit blüht, hinknien vor Jede
> Und, wär's auch nur für Augenblicke, siegen.[10]

Diego finds all this senseless and warns Juan of his inevitable end as a beggar. 'The God of joy is a God of limits as the bonds of the embrace teach you' (a very German form of philosophical analogy). If it were not for his father's commands, Juan could go to the devil. To this remark Juan answers with Strauss's second quotation:

> Ich fliehe Überdruss und Lustermattung,
> Erhalte frisch im Dienste mich des Schönen,
> Die Einzle kränkend schwärm' ich für die Gattung.
> Der Odem einer Frau, heut' Frühlingsduft,
> Drückt morgen mich vielleicht wie Kerkerluft.
> Wenn wechselnd ich mit meiner Liebe wandre
> Im weiten Kreis der schönen Frauen,
> Ist meine Lieb' an jeder eine andre;
> Nicht aus Ruinen will ich Tempel bauen.
> Ja! Leidenschaft ist immer nur die neue;

[10] Fain would I run the magic circle, immeasurably wide, of beautiful women's manifold charms, in full tempest of enjoyment, to die of a kiss at the mouth of the last one. O my friend, would that I could fly through every place where beauty blossoms, fall on my knees before each one, and, were it but for a moment, conquer. . . .

Sie lässt sich nicht von der zu jener bringen,
Sie kann nur sterben hier, dort neu entspringen,
Und kennt sie sich, so weiss sie nichts von Reue.
Wie jede Schönheit einzig in der Welt,
So ist es auch die Lieb', der sie gefällt.
Hinaus und fort nach immer neuen Siegen,
So lang der Jugend Fcuerpulse fliegen![11]

Diego's reply to this outburst deals with the Day of Reckoning in
terms of broken hearts, a consideration which weighs more heavily
with Juan than he is prepared to admit. Its validity becomes increasingly
apparent until the appearance of the third passage, when in the Supper
Scene, unlike Da Ponte's Don Giovanni, he sits gloomily, enveloped in
bitter disillusionment. Surrounded by hangers-on of both sexes, Don
Juan awaits the enemy (Don Pedro as it turns out)who he hopes will
spare him the necessity of continuing the futility of life. Despite Mar-
cello's cheerful assurances that in a few hours he will once more be at
the height of his powers, Juan utterly rejects the idea that he is merely a
victim of depression. He has no regrets and cannot tolerate in man the
weeping and wailing of remorse.

Es war ein schöner Sturm, der mich getrieben,
Er hat vertobt und Stille ist geblieben.
Scheintot ist alles Wünschen, alles Hoffen;
Vielleicht ein Blitz aus Höh'n, die ich verachtet,
Hat tödlich meine Liebeskraft ᵨetroffen,
Und plötzlich ward die Welt mir wüst, umnachtet;
Vielleicht auch nicht;—der Brennstoff ist verzehrt,
Und kalt und dunkel ward es auf dem Herd.[12]

These three quotations carry with them none of the action of the

[11] I shun satiety and the exhaustion of pleasure; I keep myself fresh in the
service of beauty; and in offending the individual I rave for my devotion to her
kind. The breath of a woman that is as the odour of spring today, may perhaps
tomorrow oppress me like the air of a dungeon. When, in my changes, I travel
with my love in the wide circle of beautiful women, my love is a different thing
for each one; I build no temple out of ruins. Indeed, passion is always and only the
new passion; it cannot be carried from this one to that; it must die here and spring
anew there; and, when it knows itself, then it knows nothing of repentance. As
each beauty stands alone in the world, so stands the love which it prefers. Forth
and away, then, to triumphs ever new, so long as youth's fiery pulses race!

[12] It was a beautiful storm that urged me on; it has spent its rage, and silence
now remains. A trance is upon every wish, every hope. Perhaps a thunderbolt
from the heights which I contemned, struck fatally at my power of love, and
suddenly my world became a desert and darkened. And perhaps not; the fuel is
all consumed and the hearth is cold and dark.

play. They are purely psychological and illustrate an attempt on Strauss's part to depict the character of Juan through his own dicta. Yet they are only a partial guide to the music, for the tone poem indulges to some extent in the direct portrayal of dramatic episodes. There are two full-blown love scenes, a carnival, and a clearly defined section in which, at the height of the duel, the victorious Don Juan throws his rapier away and receives the death thrust at the hands of Don Pedro. Nothing of all this is indicated in Strauss's avowed programme. Yet to understand the seeming disparity is to understand Strauss's whole attitude to his task. *Don Juan* is on the one hand a symphonic movement, fully worked out according to the requirements of the thematic material, while on the other hand it portrays the development of a human personality through the impact of events much as Strauss had just done in *Macbeth*.

Even the form of the work is fundamentally the same as that of *Macbeth*: i.e. a sonata first movement with two major independent episodes inserted into the development. The principal subject is a composite theme, all the major features of which are later isolated and extensively developed.

Ex. 8

Ex. 9

This profusion of ideas together presents the figure of Don Juan himself in all his passionate glory and lust for life. Many things strike one simultaneously on being confronted with this astonishing opening of what was still only Strauss's second venture in a new field; the brilliant inventive powers, virtuosity of orchestral technique, and above all the

R.S.–F

stylistic originality. Here suddenly for the first time Strauss has found himself with masterly self-assurance.

The collection of motivic figures which make up Ex. 8 form a natural introduction to the principal theme of the first subject Ex. 9, which is fully worked out in a self-contained section with a clearly defined final cadence. During the course of this section the figures of Ex. 8 are constantly incorporated into the texture, this being a simple matter since they are all easily reducible in terms of the common chord, that is to say, apart from inessential passing notes, they are all *Naturtheme*. A further theme is also gradually introduced which, although scarcely noticeable at its first appearance since it occurs in the bass of an elaborate polyphonic structure, later becomes extremely important:

Ex. 10

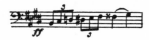

Ex. 10 carries the music impetuously forward after a full cadence supplied by Ex. 8(a), which both opens and closes the exposition of Don Juan's thematic material and leads to the hero's first flirtatious exploit. This episode has little substance and might even be thought too transitory to qualify as a love affair at all if it did not later take its place with all the others in Juan's disillusionment scene. The theme of its heroine is purely capricious and not even the indication *flebile* (plaintive) scattered about the score can suggest that her heart has been touched.

Ex. 11

Yet the chromatically descending figure with which she parts from Juan is said to have been intended by Strauss to represent 'a feeling of satiety in Juan's heart', indicating that an emotional attachment has existed between them. This is represented by Strauss in a single phrase which gives out *fortissimo* the initial bars of the melody which will later dominate Juan's first true love scene:

Ex. 12

With an impatient flourish of Ex. 8(a) Don Juan tears himself from this unsatisfactory mistress, turns round, and is immediately spellbound at the appearance of a new beauty. Her arrival is indicated by a radiant wind chord, and the descending phrases of Ex. 12 in the sweet tones of the solo violin, interspersed by continual soft imitative groups of Ex. 10, show that Don Juan is deeply stirred. Their love scene follows, a tremendous extended section in which Ex. 12 is elaborated in song-like style and with a passion that compares only with such sensual exultation as is experienced in the second act of *Tristan*.

If the earlier flirtation is regarded formally as fulfilling the role of transition passage, this section clearly corresponds with the second subject, even the conventional key of the dominant being used. The music rises to a climax of unbearable intensity, subsiding abruptly as the cellos softly interpose Ex. 8(a) like a question. Don Juan has woken up from the oblivion of love, and although his mistress attempts to make his dreams continue, they have no longer the power to hold him. Once again Ex. 8(a) thrusts upwards in the cellos, the clarinet takes it up, and in a moment Don Juan is out of reach and away in search of further adventure.

The passage which follows is pure development, though only Don Juan's themes are exploited. Ex. 10 is now strongly in evidence and towards the end of the section becomes virtually pre-eminent. The music has reached a pitch of frenzy when there is a halt and a new courtship begins. This time the girl's capitulation is less immediate, though when it comes it is proportionately more complete. Don Juan's wooing is now depicted by a new theme of yearning intensity:

Ex. 13

The girl's resistance is portrayed by a gasping figure on the flute for which Strauss again uses the indication *flebile*, the word clearly being on his brain in the same way as authors tend to overuse certain words when they have first been struck by them. Don Juan's persistence is characterized by the fragments of Ex. 8c which, together with Ex. 13, gradually overcome the girl's pitiable resistance and she finally succumbs altogether.

So complete is her devotion, so touching her love, that the question inevitably arises as to who this crucial figure in the story can be. Yet it is impossible to establish which of Lenau's heroines Strauss had in mind, as there is no comparable episode in the poem. According to at least one version of the legend it is Donna Anna who is the only serious passion of Don Juan's life, but in da Ponte his attempts to seduce her are unsuccessful (as in point of fact are all his subsequent exploits; da Ponte's Don Juan is the most frustrated lover in literature!) and in Lenau she is scarcely mentioned.[13] At all events there is not the slightest doubt that Strauss is now concerned with Juan's deepest love experience, whoever the heroine may be. The section which follows is one of the great love-songs in all music. Nothing in Strauss's previous output could have led one to expect the creation of music so profoundly, so heart-breakingly beautiful as this central episode. Sir Thomas Armstrong expressed its poignance with deep insight when he wrote of its 'strange and ominous beauty . . . the whole passsage (having) that autumnal richness of regret which is so often felt in Strauss's loveliest music and is carried to such a height in *Rosenkavalier*'. Beginning with an oboe solo,

Ex. 14

the melody passes from one wind instrument to another, coming back again and again to the oboe, who brings it to its end in an atmosphere of utter tranquillity. The background of divided strings is generally static, though soft reiterations of Ex. 13 keep us perpetually aware of Don Juan stirring in the arms of his beloved.

The end of the song marks the half-way point of the tone poem and must have caused Strauss some anxiety as to how to continue. That he solved the problem satisfactorily was a feat in itself; the way he solved

[13] It is curious how many commentators give the names of da Ponte's heroines to two of the episodes of Strauss's *Don Juan*. The origin of this may perhaps be traced to the Führer to the work published by Schlesinger about 1905 as one of a set of such analytical essays. As with the guide to *Till Eulenspiegel* (see p. 125), the account of *Don Juan* was written by Willem Mauke, who refers specifically to the three heroines as 'Zerlinchen', 'die blonde Gräfin', and 'Anna'. Even Ernest Newman took it for granted that Mauke's interpretations were substantiated by the composer himself, but, unlike *Till*, there is no evidence for this, and in view of Strauss's avowed derivation solely from Lenau in whose work only the Gräfin appears in person, briefly during the Masked Ball, the identification of these characters seems somewhat fanciful and presumptuous.

it made history. This was through the invention of a new motif for Juan,
a motif so striking that it remains to this day the first theme with which
the whole tone-poem is immediately associated. The stirrings of Ex. 13
turn to impatience, impatience to impetuosity, and after an upward
rush the violins establish a high tremolo pedal-point beneath which the
horns make the grand gesture which is Ex. 15. Don Juan is now not
merely dashing and impetuous; he is heroic.

Ex. 15

It is worth comparing Ex. 15 (a) with Ex. 21 from *Aus Italien* (Chapter
2). Not only are the superficial contours of the two themes markedly
similar, but both are the finest ideas of their respective movements
although appearing only half-way through. As with the earlier heroine,
so this poor girl clings to Juan, her agitation shown in a feverish
version of Ex. 14, but she has even less power over him than her predecessors, and in any case Don Juan is by now in full cry. Repeated
versions of Ex. 15 alternate with Ex. 8(a) which rises higher and higher
until with a dazzling stroke of orchestral colour Don Juan is in the
thick of some wild festivities. This second development section is
generally known as the Carnival Scene, but the nearest parallel to be
found in Lenau is a Masked Ball, and one might justifiably assume that
it was this which Strauss had in mind. There is a new glittering theme
which is developed together with Ex. 15 (a) (on the glockenspiel, of all
unlikely instruments), and then Ex. 8 (a), which becomes increasingly
prominent until it sweeps the music into a powerful series of majestic
statements of Ex. 8 (b) which alternate with the two halves of Ex. 15,
each of which is developed separately. In due course Ex. 8(d) joins in each
downward sweep, gaining in force and momentum until at the climax it
turns into a torrential fall into a terrible pit. This fearful collapse is
psychological although, in the dramatic orchestral language used to
depict it, it is indistinguishable from the actual events described in the
parallel climax towards the end of the work. Don Juan's morale has suddenly reached rock-bottom. The ghosts of his three former mistresses

flit across his consciousness. In his despondency he has taken to wandering through churchyards, and here, as in da Ponte, Lenau makes him come across the statue of a distinguished nobleman whom he has killed, and Juan invites him to dinner.[14] But Lenau is concerned with reality and not with the metaphysical. The Statue does not come; it is the nobleman's son, Don Pedro, who intrudes upon the supper scene. Surrounded by Don Juan's cast-off women (not Maria, Clara, etc., but a new batch with names such as Constanze, Blanka and so on) and their illegitimate children, he challenges the invincible libertine to a death duel. As Ex. 8 (a) tentatively puts out feelers in the different string groups over a dominant pedal, Don Juan gathers strength and confidence for the final stage of the drama or, in symphonic terms, the recapitulation. This build-up to a dramatic comma at the end of the development section is contrived in exactly the same way, although naturally on a far more elaborate scale, as the corresponding passage in the *Rom's Ruinen* movement from *Aus Italien*. Strauss is now a master, but he knows how to use the experience of his apprenticeship.

As in the development sections, the recapitulation deals exclusively with Don Juan's themes and is, to that extent, incomplete. It does, however, incorporate all the new Don Juan material collected on the way including the majestic version of Ex. 8 (b) (which is accordingly omitted from its original position, Ex. 8 (a) leading directly to Ex.9) and culminating in the second and most triumphant declamation of Ex.15 in its entirety, firstly as before on the four horns (being now a third higher it takes them to their high B, a most exciting sound) and then on the upper strings and wind in a tremendous unison. A surging imitative passage based on Ex. 15 (b) leads back to the original matter of the exposition, and the recapitulation closes regularly, only to be carried forward impetuously by Ex. 10 exactly as in the opening section of the work. The logical construction is exemplary, its cumulative power overwhelming. From the opening of the recapitulation the music drives forward without a moment's hesitation from peak to peak until the terrible hiatus in which, at the height of his regained powers, Don Juan, with Pedro entirely at his mercy, realizes that victory is wholly

[14] The invitation by a *roué* of a dead man to supper, and the horror when the invitation is accepted, was one of the earliest aspects of the *Don Juan* legend and dates back at least to the seventeenth century. The first appearance of Don Juan in literature is in a play published in Barcelona in 1630 and attributed to Tirso de Molina; but although he accordingly received a Spanish name, Don Juan is generally regarded as being of widely international origin.

worthless and voluntarily delivers himself to the sword of his adversary. There is a pale minor chord into which the trumpets jab out the dissonant note which with horrible clarity represents the mortal thrust, and with a descending series of shuddering trills Don Juan's life ebbs away. The work ends on a note of bleakness which is the more appalling for the closeness with which it follows on the heels of a scene of unparalleled splendour and exultation.

8

Don Juan was composed during Strauss's first Munich appointment. This, however, came to an end in the summer of 1889, somewhat to his relief, as he had found the conditions at the Munich Theatre disagreeable. This was undoubtedly his own fault to a large extent, as he later acknowledged.

> Although I was handy as a substitute—I tackled an opera by Rheinberger even at this early stage—I was frequently handicapped in the smooth execution of my duties as an operatic conductor by my lack of 'routine' in which many colleagues of far less talent were for a long time superior to me, and by my stubborn insistence on 'my own tempi'. There were, therefore, quite a few upsets, and the usual disagreements between singers and orchestra, especially since the operas I had to conduct at that time did not interest me sufficiently to make me rehearse them carefully, and would really have required far more careful study before the rehearsals—a task which in works like *Nachtlager* and *Martha* bored me far too much.

He had, in fact, felt somewhat low-spirited and neglected in Munich, his home town, but there are not the least signs of this in the creative work of the period. Apart from the usual quota of songs, *Don Juan* occupied his exclusive attention until the late summer of 1888, when, having put it in a drawer 'to keep *Macbeth* company' (see above, p. 60), he immediately set to work on yet a third symphonic poem, to be called *Tod und Verklärung*.[15] The new piece occupied him for a similar period of time and was all but complete when Strauss's fortunes took an abrupt turn for the better. During the winter of 1888–9 Liszt's successor in Weimar, a certain Edward Lassen, an enormously

[15] 'Death and Transfiguration'.

go-ahead music director and himself a composer, secured for Strauss a conductor's appointment by his side in Weimar, his duties to begin on 1st October 1889. Nothing more congenial to a recent convert to the progressive faith could be imagined. The Intendant at Weimar backed Lassen to the hilt in his confidence in the young composer, who was given charge of the entire syllabus of German opera, which included Wagner's *Ring*.

Strauss was not slow in seizing his opportunity, and played, though on the piano, his latest composition *Tod und Verklärung* to his new employers. Their enthusiasm knew no bounds, as also for *Don Juan*, which latter they pressed Strauss to include in the Weimar syllabus for that very season. Although Strauss seems to have had higher aims for the première of *Don Juan*, he allowed himself to be prevailed upon rather than take the risk of waiting for some less certain occasion. This was as it should be, both because the stir it created by its reception even in a relatively small centre was enough to arouse interest in the capital on which Strauss had fixed his hopes, and because his recent experience in taking his own small and less proficient orchestra through the unprecedented difficulties of the piece enabled him to judge the practicability and effectiveness of his latest experiments in orchestration. This time he knew at once he had succeeded and he communicated his satisfaction with both rehearsals and performance in the usual glowing letters to his parents. His experience of the orchestra had served him well and he was able to extend the technique of almost every instrument in the sure knowledge that what he demanded could be accomplished even though it had never been done before. The players seem to have taken it well after the initial shock, though there seem to have been some amusing incidents, such as when one horn player sat breathless and dripping with sweat, sighing: 'Good God, in what way have we sinned that you should have sent us this scourge!' Strauss wrote: 'We laughed till we cried! Certainly the horns blew without fear of death. . . . I was really sorry for the wretched horns and trumpets. They were quite blue in the face, the whole affair was so strenuous.' One is left with an impression that despite the problems which were clearly considerable Strauss conducted the whole enterprise with great good humour. This would naturally be reflected in the attitude of the players and so in the success of the performance. The public response on that exciting day, 11th November 1889, is now an historical byword. The appearance of *Don Juan* established Strauss once and for all as the most important composer to have emerged in Germany since Wagner, while the innovations in orchestral technique, then so startling, have become the recognized basic standards for orchestras of the present day. At twenty-four Strauss had written the first of the masterpieces on which his posthumous position in musical history firmly rests.

9

While Strauss was conducting the first performance of Don Juan the manuscript of his next major work, Tod und Verklärung, was lying on his desk, complete but for three pages of score. Begun just over a year before, this had occupied Strauss during the last months of his Munich appointment, until his temporary assignment as répétiteur at Bayreuth during the summer of 1889 interrupted the work. The well-known biographer, Richard Specht, asserts that the programme of this new descriptive piece originated from personal experience, 'the aftermath of those hours in which the young tone-poet was cast into heaviest suffering on the bed of sickness, in which he felt himself touched by the cool hand of the Angel of Death so that the flame began to burn low and in which his most fervent desires for the completion of his earthly mission mingled with those for joyful release from pain. . . .' This no doubt touching conception, which pursues for some distance the idea that Tod und Verklärung is largely autobiographical (short, that is, of actual death and transfiguration, for Strauss survived a further sixty years), is entirely erroneous, since although the composer was undoubtedly taken seriously ill this was not until May 1891, some eighteen months after the completion of the score.

Strauss himself expressly rejected the idea that the work was inspired by his own experiences; he had neither survived such a severe illness, nor had he been at the bedside of any desperately sick person; he had not even taken the idea from something he had read. In 1894 he wrote a letter explaining the conception on which the tone poem is based:

> It was six years ago that it occurred to me to present in the form of a tone poem the dying hours of a man who had striven towards the highest idealistic aims, maybe indeed those of an artist. The sick man lies in bed, asleep, with heavy irregular breathing; friendly dreams conjure a smile on the features of the deeply suffering man; he wakes up; he is once more racked with horrible agonies; his

limbs shake with fever—as the attack passes and the pains leave off, his thoughts wander through his past life; his childhood passes before him, the time of his youth with its strivings and passions and then, as the pains already begin to return, there appears to him the fruit of his life's path, the conception, the ideal which he has sought to realize, to present artistically, but which he has not been able to complete, since it is not for man to be able to accomplish such things. The hour of death approaches, the soul leaves the body in order to find gloriously achieved in everlasting space those things which could not be fulfilled here below.

Nevertheless, despite the composer's refutation on the subject, the very words 'maybe indeed those of an artist' in the above synopsis, suggest a natural identification of its hero with Strauss himself, an association which he pursued shortly before his death, when he quoted the motif of the 'Ideal' from this work in one of the Four Last Songs. This self-identification with the heroes of his works was a strong part of Strauss's make-up, and one can think of a number of cases where he clearly draws either from his experiences or his dreams of such experiences, as in *Don Juan*, *Heldenleben*, the character of Kunrad in *Feuersnot* and so on.

It has been said that this tone poem stands nearest to the concepts of Liszt than any of the others, but this is scarcely the case, since although it deals with a psychological subject, much as the 'Faust' Symphony, for example, it does so in far more precise detail than Liszt ever attempted. Here for the first time Strauss set himself an actual scenario and followed it deliberately in his composition in a way not to be found in any of Liszt's programmatic works. Moreover, Strauss considered the plot vital to the understanding of the piece and accordingly Ritter undertook to convert it into poetry. The completed poem paraphrased Strauss's sketch of the argument in four stanzas of four lines, each with an introductory couplet, and it was inserted on to the title page of the score and also reproduced in the programmes of the first performance. Ritter subsequently decided, however, to rewrite the poem entirely on a much more elaborate scale, and it was this second sixty-two-line poem which was eventually incorporated into the printed score when the tone poem was published. Although the later version is clearer in intention, neither poem indicates the purpose of the music with anything like the vivid directness of Strauss's own words just given above.

10

The form of the work is even less related to conventional form than
either of the previous tone poems, although it is still possible to analyse
the basic framework in terms of a sonata first movement. Far more
important is the way the various themes undergo development much
as a human personality develops during the different stages of life. The
piece begins with an impression of the scene, the sporadic pulse and
heart-beat of the ill man being suggested by an irregular rhythmic
figure derived from the Prelude to the second act of *Götterdämmerung*
and given alternately to strings and timpani.

Ex. 16

The sighs of the sufferer are also graphically portrayed by the strings,
together with a pathetic little upward twist on the flutes. An already
typically Straussian modulation then changes the colour of the music
and we become aware of the figure on the bed not merely as a body but
as a human personality. Two themes are first presented together:

Ex. 17

after which the 'suffering' music returns. Another modulation of the
same character, though taking a different turning, brings the warmer
colours back once more and another facet of the sufferer is presented.
He is smiling gently as he remembers scenes of his childhood.

Ex. 18

These thoughts are dwelt upon at greater length later, when Ex. 18
comes properly into its own. In the meantime the thematic ideas between them are intended to give a many-sided character study. Since

they all first appear in soft tones to a uniformly cushioned background, it may be thought that they hardly present the contrasts and contradictions normally associated with human personality. Bearing in mind, however, that the primary function of this section is to present the *mise-en-scène*, Strauss was perfectly reasonable in portraying his hero in a subdued and passive state of mind. The motifs are, in fact, extremely skilfully devised with a view to characteristic development during the course of the work.

Suddenly the disease takes a more violent turn and the ill man can be heard writhing in agony. A contrasting section paints with vivid imagination the struggle of the sufferer with the savage onslaught of his affliction. A series of highly suggestive figures punctuated by agitated references to Ex. 16 form an Allegro section of symphonic character, the previous subdued passage falling smoothly into place as a conventional slow introduction. Strauss's solid grounding in traditional form is responsible for the satisfying logic of his architectural sense after he has ceased to obey the rules which were once so sacred to him. A climax is built up at the peak of which the true first subject, a new and important theme, is announced in tones of stern resolution:

Ex. 19

This defiant gesture may be taken as representing the invalid's determination to withstand the threatening approach of death. It is followed by another motif of the will to live, though less staunch in its powers of resistance:

Ex. 20

Exx. 19 and 20 are worked together as in the primary section of an exposition, moving regularly to the dominant for the second subject. During the three bars of transition Ex. 19 is hurled out like a fanfare by the heavy brass against a feverish outburst of Ex. 16 on the remainder of the orchestra. The second subject combines a new panting motif with an important derivative of Ex. 17 (b):

Wedding photograph, Weimar

Ex. 21

It is, however, no part of Strauss's plan to follow the scheme of sonata form even to the partial extent of *Don Juan*. The music returns to the tonic and after a further terse tutti statement of Ex. 19, a long descending passage on a dominant pedal combines Ex. 20 with the panting figure from the second subject. This passage has nearly collapsed when with a superhuman effort the man summons all his remaining strength and we hear the most important motif of the work, the theme of the artist's Ideology:

Ex. 22

The wide range of this figure, with its octave leap approached from without, gives it enormous dramatic power. Every entry becomes an event, even when it appears briefly as in the first isolated reference.

The strain of the attack has been severe, but the sufferer has survived it. As he sinks back, the violins float up to their high D and the central section of the work, the development so to speak, begins in that most innocent of keys, G major. It consists of a series of tableaux representing the different phases of his life; beginning with his childhood, portrayed by Ex. 18 given to the flute and later in imitation on the strings. This alternates with a gentle phrase for oboes and harp which is derived from the opening bar of Ex. 19, and which itself alternates with a lilting version of Ex. 17. The personality of the man is, in fact, already present in embryo in the child. A short burst of pain (Ex. 19 once more fanfarelike, together with fragments of Ex. 16) and the music modulates to the more heroic key of E flat for a picture of the dashing young fellow he has now become, full of hope and vigorous aspirations:

Ex. 23

(Ex. 23 is, of course, none other than a combined metamorphosis of Exx. 17 and 18; here is a purely Lisztian aspect of the piece.)

This tableau culminates in a tremendous sweep on the violins built entirely on repetitions of Ex. 17. (Such virtuoso linking passages for strings had already become a Straussian hall-mark. Parallel places can easily be recalled in *Aus Italien* and particularly in *Macbeth*.) The music then plunges headlong into B major for a love scene, which in its furious passionate intensity outdoes even *Don Juan*. Motivically it is based on Ex. 18, which supports a surging theme, in itself a wild elaboration of Ex. 21.

Ex. 24

Higher and higher it soars, until the sheer memory causes the invalid the most terrible heart palpitations, the trombones and timpani hammering out Ex. 16.[16] There is a brief pause, then gently and with trepidation the dying man tries to evoke the fervent memories once more, but each time he brings on the fearful hammer blows in his chest. Yet, although these are stronger on each return, he courageously ignores them, and passes beyond the scenes of passion towards the magnificent moment when his ideals first present themselves to him (Ex. 22).

Up to this point the tone poem has been exceptionally homogeneous, every passage deriving from one or other of the principal motifs. But here, for the first time, Strauss found himself unable to continue in the same way. His scheme consisted of three widely spaced statements of the Ideology theme (Ex. 22), each one in a more glowing key, and each one slightly more complex, as the artist's vision gradually becomes stronger. It was in the modulatory passages that Strauss found that his imagination, which had carried him forward so far without pausing for an instant, was not really supplying the obvious means of continuation. Although this time he was unable to produce a masterstroke with which to make a virtue of necessity as in *Don Juan*, he did, as before, in-

---

[16] Strauss even put a footnote in his score saying that in order to make the most frightful effect the trombones should point their bells straight at the audience!

vent an entirely new melodic idea, and this he used to begin both bridge passages, though the second time it is soon swamped by increasingly persistent reiterations of Exx. 18 and 20. Before long Ex. 19 joins in, and the whole is consistently accompanied by the gasping figure of the second subject. By now Strauss's imagination was in full swing once more, and he incorporated yet another new figure for which he was later to find excellent use both in *Heldenleben* and the Orestes scene from *Elektra*:

Ex. 25

The glory of the Ideology theme is brought out in these three statements by importing a second harp into the orchestra for the first time in Strauss's work, this together with the triple woodwind making the score of *Tod und Verklärung* the most extravagant in instrumentation so far. In this respect Strauss never looked back in the orchestration of his tone poems, in direct contradiction of his promise to Bülow in a letter just as he was completing *Don Juan*, in which he said categorically: '. . . but to talk seriously now, I definitely promise you double woodwind in my future works.' He also added that he would be exercising the greatest restraint in the employment of severe technical difficulties. Although it was beyond Strauss's power to honour such guarantees once he had tasted the joys of a Wagnerian wind section in *Macbeth*, it is instructive to observe the variations in instrumental demands he made between each new work. In only one respect is *Tod und Verklärung* economical—the percussion, in which department he uses a single extra instrument, the tam-tam. This wonderful effect had had no place at all in the scheme of *Don Juan*, and it was a fine idea to use it exclusively here, saving it, moreover, for the most important moment much as he had done with the second harp.

The third annunciation of the Ideological theme combines it with the surging figure Ex.21, with the result that, for the first time, it summons the power to boil up into an ecstatic afterphrase:

Ex. 26

But the effort has been too great and the whole vision drains away, leaving nothing behind but the scene of the invalid in his bed, exactly as at the opening of the work. A short, almost perfunctory recapitulation follows, in which the dull throbbing of Ex. 16 is followed by another spasm on the lines of the first Allegro section, though drastically curtailed. The ghastly palpitations return, and with an upward slither the music fades away as death brings relief to the sufferer, the moment of expiry being marked by the entry of the tam-tam just mentioned.

Since time immemorial the human race has brooded over what becomes of the spirit after the collapse of the body. New and fascinating lines of thought have been opened up by the recent experiences of individuals who have had their hearts restarted after periods of as much as an hour or two. Tales have subsequently been told of impressions as of moving powerlessly along an extended tunnel at the far end of which a bright light could be seen. It stands to reason that none can testify with confidence as to the validity of such reports, but the idea is one which the human brain can readily grasp and is not far from Strauss's visionary conception. From the utter darkness in which everything is enveloped, only the infinitely deep strokes of the tam-tam are heard, until very little by very little out of the obscurity the opening figure of the Ideology theme Ex. 22 emerges, first on the four horns in turn and then gradually spreading in close stretto to the higher wind instruments. As it builds up it is joined by Ex. 18 on the strings in an ever-increasing weight of glowing sound, indicating that it is the qualities of the child which endure to the Hereafter, outlasting all but the finest ideas of the mature individual.

It is at this point that Strauss's weakness as a mature artist becomes for the first time apparent. For all the skill with which he clothed it in the most gorgeous orchestral texture, Strauss found himself unable to match the exalted level of his conception in profoundness of musical thought.

The strings soar ever higher until the violins finally reach their topmost G. There is a brief pause, and at last Ex.22 is proclaimed in full, as the transfigured soul realizes in the afterlife the aims which it had never been able to accomplish during its earthly existence. But in this C major glorification Strauss's all-important theme now recalls itself as disappointingly commonplace. To portray the transfiguration of the soul in terms of music is, to say the least, no mean task. It had, of course, been Strauss's intention from the first that this *Verklärung* should take place through the consecration of the motifs representing the visionary element in the mind of the dying man. Hence this coda section had perforce to consist of a stately song based from first to last on the Childhood and Ideology themes, complete with the ecstatic continuation Ex.26. However, if inspiration had failed, technique was ready to make good the deficiency. Being a *Naturthema*, Ex. 22 builds easily upon itself and Strauss works it up stage by stage, modulation upon modulation, to a majestic climax from which it descends by way of some magical harmonic effects. Such imaginative manipulation of chord structures came naturally to Strauss, and he used it ever more successfully during the years to come. Eventually the opening notes of Ex. 22, presented in the guise of the famous horn-call figure on which so much of Strauss's technique is based—

Ex. 27

—builds up in a passage which is the precise inversion of Beethoven's treatment of the same figure in the 'Les Adieux' sonata, and the work dies away in what must for practical reasons be a limited suggestion of eternity.

II

The exalted conception is enormously ambitious and the glorious technicolour of Strauss's orchestra unfailingly impressive. Nevertheless this *Verklärung* section lacks ultimately that element of the sublime which was its fundamental *raison d'être*, but which it is given to the very few to achieve. One of the flaws in Strauss's genius was a streak of

R.S.-G

banality which soiled many of his finest works. *Tod und Verklärung* was
for some considerable time the most popular of the tone poems, but it
has largely lost that position today and is considered rather as a retrograde step after Strauss's incredible leap to immortality in *Don Juan*.
Contemporary opinion saw in the new work clear indications that its
composer was, beyond doubt, on the road to the Wagnerian Music
Drama, and they were unquestionably right, as Strauss was already at
work on his own libretto with this intention. What they could scarcely
foresee was his initial failure in that sphere, a failure of which the seeds
were already perceptible in this latest tone poem. For Strauss succeeded
throughout his creative career in inverse proportion to the degree of
sublimity to which he aspired. Thus the high-minded nobility of *Guntram* is a pale shadow compared with the ebullience of *Till Eulenspiegel*;
the inflated wisdom of *Zarathustra* is mere magniloquence against the
sharply outlined exploits of Don Quixote and Sancho Panza; the
abstruse symbolism of *Die Frau ohne Schatten* is pure bombast after the
electrifying portrayal of perversion in *Salome*. Even in the depiction of
character, a field in which Strauss was showing himself to be a master,
the more grotesque or common the personality the more vividly it
comes to life at the touch of his pen. So it is that the spirituality of the
Verklärung is inevitably disappointing after the mundane but undeniably effective *Tod*.

Yet the piece is well composed and holds its own in the repertoire
for all its shortcomings. The thematic material is strongly characteristic
and memorable and there are many passages which are vintage Straussian panache in their orchestral treatment. If there is also a lack of that
jovial bravura which lifted Strauss out of the deep-minded Wagnerianism that threatened every convert to the Lisztian faith, the fault lay in
the choice of subject. The penalty incurred was, however, infinitely
less severe in this tone poem than it was to be in Strauss's first operatic
venture, *Guntram*.

CHAPTER IV

GUNTRAM

S TRAUSS'S experiences as an operatic conductor were of enormous value to him in broadening his outlook. He acquired an even greater practical understanding of the workings of an opera house in Weimar than in Munich, the Weimar authorities being so much more adventurous and also sympathetic to him, with the result that his personal responsibilities were far greater. The repertoire in Weimar was extremely wide, containing the more important pieces of Gluck, Mozart, Beethoven, Weber, Lortzing, Nicolai, Marschner, Meyerbeer (to Strauss's disgust!), Bellini, Flotow, and, most important of all to the young progressive, virtually the entire works of Wagner, even including *Rienzi*. Yet Munich had had its value, though towards the end he incurred the personal animosity of the Intendant, Perfall. This was, however, not before he had served an essential part of his apprenticeship. Moreover, so large and important a musical centre had given him the opportunity of making the acquaintance of interesting rising figures in the German musical scene, such as Gustav Mahler, whose First Symphony he played at the piano in a four-handed version with his immediate superior, the conductor Levi. Mahler's work first came to Strauss's notice with a completion of Weber's *Die Drei Pintos*, which aroused his keen interest, although he poured ridicule on the extravagance and virtuosity of the orchestration.[1]

---

[1] It is fascinating now to remember that the first performance of the three instrumental movements of Mahler's gigantic Second Symphony took place under Strauss's direction.

Ritter's powerful influence led Strauss strongly to champion the Wagnerian Music Drama, with the natural result that he was agog to compose a stage work himself which would follow in the footsteps of the Master. Ritter carefully fed him in this ambition although, ironically enough, it caused the first real rift in their association. Taking his example from Ritter's own operas, *Der faule Hans* and *Wem die Krone*, Strauss determined to draft his own libretto in the Wagnerian manner, basing it upon Teutonic legend or medieval history.

It is scarcely surprising that Ritter played a lively part in bringing this gratifying desire to fruition by drawing Strauss's attention to a newspaper article in the *Wiener Neue Presse* during the summer of 1887, which gave a detailed account of the various secret societies existing in Austria in medieval times. Some of these societies seem to have come into being with partly religious and partly artistic aims, in direct opposition to the concepts of the *Minnesänger*, whom they considered too secular. Strauss was immediately seized wth this idea, inventing the hero on the spot. Thus Guntram came into being, his name a cross between Gunther and Wolfram , his character a combination of Tannhäuser and Parsifal. Freihild and Friedhold soon followed, and Strauss's brain was teeming with Wagnerian ideas. Enthusiastically he wrote to Bülow of his project; Bülow replied guardedly that he relied on Strauss's youthful creative powers 'and wished him success in summoning the necessary degree of artistic somnambulism'.

Before many months had passed Bülow was writing to his young colleague in an attempt to side-track him with one of Ibsen's latest dramas; but it was in vain, and in September 1888 Strauss wrote home that the first draft of the libretto was finished. He seems to have had few qualms over his qualifications for putting his text into shape as a versified libretto, although he could scarcely have had less training for so specialized a task. As he himself put it later in life; 'Unfortunately I lacked poetic talent'. In fact, it took him two years to complete the poem, during which period some most discouraging letters found their way to his parents as to how he was 'kneading the lines round and round until anxiety made his brow wet with perspiration'.

At last it was done, however, and a copy sent home. His father wrote back a carefully considered criticism in which he first discussed the nature of the society to which Guntram is supposed to belong. He had deduced that it could by no means be the Minnesänger, leading one to suppose that he never saw the famous newspaper article. But he went on to say:

> To me the motive for which Guntram kills the Duke is too flimsy; for a servant to refuse him admission into the room might well justify the death of the servant, but not Guntram's killing the Duke. Then, he is allowed to draw his sword and commit this deed without being called to account for it, all of which I don't really understand. Another thing, I find the scene with the mystical tempter superfluous; it is altogether too redolent of Frau Venus.[2] Why drag in the supernatural when it is not necessary? It only holds up the action. You must be very careful not to get too much into the atmosphere of *Parsifal* and *Tannhäuser*. Ritter also suggests that the words are often not significant enough, which comes from the fact that you have read very little in metre. Taken by and large I liked the subject matter, especially the opera's closing scene. But I am sure the whole thing is rather too long, there are too many words in the monologues, and above all, the allusions to the church and the priests must be entirely omitted; they are quite unnecessary and will only make you quantities of enemies.

This was good advice, and Strauss set to work to revise his text, bearing his father's word in mind for once. Many of the points raised in the above letter are so fundamental that nothing remains in the printed score of the passages which gave rise to such vehement criticism. A year later he was still hacking at it, and even as late as the New Year of 1892 he decided to have another attempt at revising Act II, after reading through the whole libretto to Fritz Brandt, his producer at Weimar. Nor was this the end of his revisions, although he now felt he had enough material ready to make a start at composition.

At last in the spring of 1892, nearly five years after the idea of the subject had first been presented to him, Strauss began to sketch the music, beginning with the Prelude to Act I. But by this time the most unexpected thing had happened; his health had failed him and for the last twelve months he had had bouts of extremely serious illness. These had begun during May 1891, when he caught pneumonia and at one stage was on the danger list. Arthur Seidl, the author and critic, visited

[2] He little knew what use a later composer, Hindemith, would make of this idea forty-three years after, with a strikingly similar setting, in his opera *Mathis der Maler*.

him, only to be received with the remark that 'Death wouldn't be so
bad if only it would come quickly', but that he 'would like to have
conducted *Tristan* first'! In fact, of course, he recovered and believed
that he was once more in full health. Nevertheless a weakness remained
which came to a head when in June 1892 he was laid low first with
pleurisy and then with severe bronchitis. It thus became apparent that
he should never have returned so soon to strenuous work and that he
must have a complete break.

In one respect this seemed not altogether a disaster. During the last
season relationships were becoming a trifle strained with even so
accommodating an Intendant as Bronsart. For all his goodwill, Bronsart
frequently found his new young conductor considerably too prone to
sweep aside all other points of view in his determination to press ahead
with his latest progressive ideas. When Bronsart found himself faced
with programmes built of works by Beethoven, Berlioz, and Wagner,
with items by Bülow and Ritter thrown in, he clearly considered it
necessary to apply the brake. Thereupon Strauss, having not yet learnt
the meaning of the word 'compromise', took any such resistance,
however prudent, as the direct opposition of a most hardened
reactionary.

A period of leave from Weimar was thus easily arranged, and in
November 1892 Strauss set off on a tour of convalescence, financed by
his uncle, George Pschorr, the same who eleven years before had paid
for the publication of the *Festmarsch*, op. 1.[2a] In his search for
warmth and sun he travelled as far as Greece and Egypt, spending
over six months alternately sight-seeing and composing. The wonderful
scenery and sunshine were a fine stimulus to his creative powers, and
work on the opera proceeded at a tremendous rate. In addition to the
composition of the music, he drafted a completely altered text of Act III,
which he finished in Athens towards the end of November, writing out a
fair copy which he sent home to Munich. He then moved on to Cairo,
where, working up to six hours a day, he completed the short score on
Christmas Eve, adding the inscription, 'Deo Gratia! Und dem heiligen
Wagner.'

With unhesitating, methodical directness Strauss now proceeded
with the orchestration. All his life, his systematic application of

[2a] In gratitude, while he was in Luxor, Strauss sketched out two movements
for a piano quartet which he completed on his return to Weimar. With some
aplomb, he presented them to Uncle George for Christmas (1893).

routine never altered. He wrote out his time-table in a letter home:

> My day's work is very simple; I get up at 8 o'clock, have a bath and breakfast; 3 eggs, tea, 'Eingemachtes';[3] then I go for a stroll for half an hour by the Nile in the palm grove of the hotel, and work from 10 till 1; the orchestration of the first Act goes forward slowly but surely. At 1 o'clock I have lunch, then read my Schopenhauer or play Bezique with Mrs Conze for a piastre stake. From 3 till 4 I work on; at 4 o'clock tea, and after that I go for a walk until 6 when I do my duty in admiring the usual sunset. [He had read in Schopenhauer that one should never allow oneself to become satiated with nature, but it is clear that, as with his Italian trip, Man and the works of Man interested him far more than scenic beauty. The tombs and monuments of the Pharaohs filled him with wonder and interest.] At 6 o'clock it gets cool and dark; then I write letters or work a bit more until 7. At 7 dinner, after which I chat and smoke (8-12 a day), at half past 9 I go to my room, read for half an hour and put out the light at ten. So it goes on day after day. . . . I shall stay here in Luxor until the middle of March. I hope I shall finish the instrumentation of Act I here. Then the second will follow in Sicily and by next Christmas, I reckon, everything will be done and ready.

Nor was this working plan by any means too sanguine. In Sicily he. stayed for a time in Ramacca as guest of the Count and Countess Gravina. The Countess was one of Bülow's daughters and Strauss was made very welcome with a room overlooking Mount Etna and with much music-making. During this time Act II was finished and the beginning of the third sketched out. By the end of June Strauss had already returned home via Switzerland, where his lungs were given a final exhaustive check-over, and he was pronounced thoroughly fit. He arrived in Munich just in time to accompany his parents on their customary holiday, which was spent regularly at a small and beautiful market town in the mountains called Marquartstein. Here, at the beginning of September, he completed the full score well ahead of schedule, so that he was able to approach the season with the single-minded object of securing the first performance, a very much more difficult and heart-breaking job than with a mere tone poem, as he was to find out only too soon.

[3] Home-made jam.

2

Meanwhile events had been moving fast during his absence in the Middle East, and in a most important direction. In mid-March Strauss's father had a letter from Levi, who was still the principal conductor in Munich, inquiring whether Richard would be well enough and free to accept a position as associate conductor with himself. In the correspondence which followed, a fantastic to-ing and fro-ing of political intrigue is revealed in the different musical centres of Germany, which naturally affected Strauss's decisions and feelings in his choice of rungs in the ladder of his career. Sad to say, he viewed the prospect of leaving Weimar with the same relief with which, so very recently, he had escaped thither from the uncongenial clutches of a hostile Munich. Now he was impatiently considering an exactly reverse process. But in the meantime he knew well enough that he had gained materially in prestige, as the result of which he could count on a very different position from the one he had resigned three years ago. Even so, he also knew that Munich was very far from having turned into a sinecure since he was last there, both from the fact that his old enemy Perfall was still in power, and from the endless difficulties which even so eminent a conductor as Levi had consistently experienced. Bearing also in mind the way he felt Munich had treated him, he was accordingly inclined to keep the offer hanging at arm's length while he put out feelers to Mottl at Karlsruhe and even in Berlin. He only began to think seriously of Levi's proposal when a vehement telegram advising him to do so arrived from Cosima Wagner. This all-important personality had, since Strauss's appearances in Bayreuth, taken an increasingly active interest in the future of so promising a devotee of her late lord and master.

Levi wanted Strauss to take up the position in Munich at the very beginning of the season and Strauss was more than willing, since it would carry great weight if the première of *Guntram* could be given there. Moreover, Mottl had written from Karlsruhe saying that there would be no opening for Strauss, as he intended staying there himself, but that he would be more than interested in taking on the new opera whenever it would be feasible.

In the event, however, Munich made one difficulty after another, and Strauss went back to Weimar for the whole further season 1893–4 while he waited for the contractual arrangements to be concluded with Perfall. Nor when it came to the point was this a bad thing. He had composed little in Weimar except some songs and a bombastic suite of Tableaux for the Golden Wedding Jubilee celebrations of the Grand Duke and Duchess.[4] But he conducted many important concerts and operas, including the first performance of Humperdinck's *Hänsel und Gretel*, which he recognized as the masterpiece it is. Then in 1894 the offer came from Berlin for him to take over from Bülow, who was dying, the concert series of the Philharmonic Orchestra, his most important assignment yet, though a very sad one.

On the other hand, his schemes for *Guntram* were dogged by ill fortune. Mottl had enthusiastically undertaken to give the first performance, but after rehearsals in Karlsruhe had begun, the tenor, Gerhäuser, suddenly turned the part down on the grounds that he could not possibly master it. Gustav Mahler next tried to project it as the opening work for his next season in Hamburg, but this, too, collapsed. So Strauss put it on with his own students in the cast and Pauline de Ahna, to whom he had now become engaged, as the Freihild. Under these circumstances the first performance could hardly help taking place. At this point the story of *Guntram*'s subsequent career is best taken up by Strauss himself:

> My poor and courageous pupil, Heinrich Zeller, suffered torments with the insanely taxing vocal part—people calculated at the time that his role contained so-and-so many more bars than Tristan—became hoarser with each rehearsal and only finished the first performance with difficulty. My fiancée, as she then was, mastered her part completely and gave a performance which was excellently sung as well as acted. After Act II she was enthusiastically applauded in Weimar, as also later in the disastrous Munich performance.
>
> In the course of one of the last rehearsals, when I had to interrupt Zeller time and time again, we at last came to Pauline's scene in Act III which she obviously knew. In spite of this she did not feel sure of herself and apparently envied Zeller because he had been given so many chances of 'repeating'. Suddenly she stopped singing, and asked me, 'Why don't you interrupt me?' I replied; 'Because you know your part'. With the words 'I want to be interrupted', she threw the piano score which she happened to be holding in her hand at my head, but, to the delight of the orchestra,

---

[4] Movements from this were revived in unexpected circumstances. See p. 415 and also Vol. II.

it landed on the desk of the second violinist, Gutheil.[5]

Guntram scored a *succès d'estime*, but after a few futile attempts to revive it in Frankfurt and Prague by making extensive cuts it vanished completely from the stage, and with it disappeared for the next six years my courage in writing for the theatre.

A single unfortunate performance was given in Munich (a year later). The leading singers there, Madame Ternina and Heinrich Vogl, had refused to sing their parts; the orchestra, too, under the leadership of my own cousin and violin teacher, the Konzertmeister Benno Walter, had gone on strike, and a deputation had been sent to the Generalintendant, Perfall, to ask him to spare the orchestra this 'scourge of God'. The tenor Mikorey, whose memory had failed in places even during the first performance, declared afterwards that he would only sing in further performances if his pension was increased. Thus there was no second performance, until on my 70th birthday Berlin Radio broadcast a concert performance with extensive cuts under Rosbaud, which showed that this work—in spite of the many first performances there had been since 1894—contained so much beautiful music that *Guntram* well deserved a revival, if only because of its historic interest as the first work of a dramatist who was later to become successful. Thereupon I published a new edition with cuts, which had a magnificent resurrection in Weimar in 1940 under Sixt; the second half of Act II and the whole of Act III made a strong impression, and even I had to confess that, compared with all the operas which had been written apart from mine in the last forty years, the work was still 'viable'.

Strauss never got over the failure of *Guntram* as long as he lived, and his bitterness against the critics of the work was intense. He wrote to Seidl after the débâcle of the Munich performance: 'It is incredible what enemies *Guntram* has made for me. I shall shortly be tried as a dangerous criminal. Oh yes, one could more easily be forgiven the most serious perjury than that one should write from the heart.' He finally committed the extravaganza of digging a grave in his garden and setting up a tombstone with the inscription reading: 'Here rests the honourable and virtuous young man GUNTRAM—Minnesinger[6]—

[5] Cf. the similar incident described by Lotte Lehmann. See below, p. 121

[6] Strauss's use of the term is presumably generic, since, as we shall see, Guntram belonged, in fact, to a rival society.

who was horribly slain by the symphony orchestra of his own father.
May he rest in peace!'

3

Both Acts I and II start with Preludes which are curious hybrids, being
neither self-contained movements nor brief Introductions setting no
more than the mood of the scenes to come. In a way they are miniature
tone poems, though they lack the symphonic coherence which Strauss
had already mastered so conspicuously in the preceding works. The
Prelude to Act I falls into three clearly defined sections, making a kind
of three-movement suite based on the most vital motifs of the opera.
The first section is calm and static, being an exposition of the 'Love'
themes—that is, love in its aspect of spiritual exaltation (the more carnal
manifestations of love have no place here). A group of themes are presented which are to some extent interrelated. First an extended line,
itself built out of four thematic ideas:

Ex. 1

Presented thus it constitutes essentially a series of formulae strung
together for purposes of development. ⌐ a ⌐ can be taken as broadly
synonymous with 'love' itself, ⌐ b ⌐ with 'pity born of suffering',
⌐ c ⌐ with 'selflessness', and ⌐ d ⌐ with the Cross. ⌐ b ⌐ and
⌐ d ⌐ are reiterated immediately in various keys before ⌐ a ⌐ and
⌐ c ⌐ are redrafted into melodic form;

Ex. 2

This version is likely to be familiar, since it is quoted intact in *Ein
Heldenleben*. It bears considerable significance in the scheme although it

is not fully exploited until the closing scene of the opera when Guntram voluntarily renounces Freihild's love.

The second section of the Prelude states the group of themes which depict the *Bund* (League) and their aims. The solemn tribunal of the Elders:

Ex. 3

is followed by an exposition of their edicts in the pursuit of charity (i.e. the practical application of love) amidst a world of sorrow:

Ex. 4

The phrase ⌐ b ¬ is, of course, identical with Ex.1(b), but its use in this poignant form in consecutive thirds is so consistently introduced as a motif of anguish that it needs to be considered independently. The movement of parts in thirds in this way was quickly becoming a mannerism and later led to a pervading sweetness in much of Strauss's texture (see later, for example, in *Zarathustra*).

A further, more suave theme is used to refer to the activities of the 'Bund' members as minstrels, propagating their creed of peaceful and tolerant co-existence through song:

Ex. 5

(Note the 'horn-call' figure, another increasingly omnipresent hallmark.)

The third section concerns Guntram himself, guileless, innocent and good-natured—another 'pure fool', in fact, though without the dignity of Parsifal:

Ex. 6

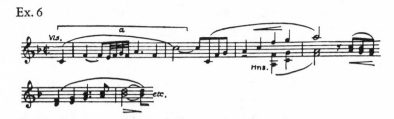

This is the least developed section, possibly because Strauss felt that it would be a mistake to anticipate Guntram's soliloquy from Act I, scene 2, in which the hero's material is worked out at some length. Yet he failed to solve the problem of creating a satisfactory entity out of the Prelude even when supplying an independent concert ending, where he replaced this rather perfunctory third section with a more elaborate structure combining Ex. 6 with other material drawn from later in the opera. Despite the beauty and serenity of this alternative ending, the wholly episodic form of the Prelude has always prevented it from occupying any place in the orchestral repertoire.

In the operatic version, Ex.6 is just beginning to soar when the music suddenly breaks off into fragments suggestive of the Call which Guntram feels he has received from Above.

Ex. 7

These build quickly up into a sudden vivid statement of the motif of Guntram's assignment; Guntram has found where his life's work lies through the League, whose edicts form the final phrase:

Ex. 8

This noble and imperious theme is later associated to a considerable extent with the old Duke, since it is fundamentally with him that Guntram's mission lies. The final chord dies quickly away, the curtain rises and the action begins.

The scene is Germany in the middle of the thirteenth century. Guntram enters leading a group of destitute peasants, refugees from their ravaged homes. Behind them a mysterious figure called Friedhold appears and sits down by himself, entirely apart from the main group. He later turns out to be an emissary of the League into whose charge Guntram has been placed, but the ingenuous novice receives no moral support or guidance from Friedhold's stern and cryptic manner. Guntram ushers the fugitives in and offers them water from a spring—together with bread and fruit—his own simple meal. Simple as it is, it proves enough to divide amongst five of them, and as they eat they put Guntram (and incidentally the audience) into the political picture of the times. They are the victims of an unsuccessful rebellion, for which the Duke has taken revenge..As they describe the oppression and reprisals they are suffering, a gloomy theme is heard:

Ex. 9

while by contrast the reference to Freihild, their one friend at court, is sung to a soft and warm melodic phrase which becomes her principal motif:

Ex. 10

Unfortunately she has been forced by her husband Robert, the young Duke, to abandon their cause. The misery of the peasants is reflected in a wild statement of Ex. 1(b) followed by a new chordal motif:

[6a] 'The only one who heard us, the fair Freihild.'

Ex. 11

Friedhold now comes out of his corner, and approaching Guntram murmurs to him in an undertone that 'life is hard'. He goes on to remind Guntram of the Divine nature of his calling and his oath to the League, a little severely perhaps, since the young minstrel has not yet shown himself lacking in a sense of duty. He then bids Guntram a perfunctory farewell and vanishes, and only reappears at the end of the opera, by which time Guntram, left without the value of Friedhold's moral guidance on his very first mission, is indeed in considerable trouble. As Friedhold disappears Guntram takes a few desperate steps after him calling out: 'When do I see you again?' But it is already too late and the question is left unanswered. Friedhold's exit is accompanied in the orchestra by a figure which only returns when this scene is recalled in Act III.

Ex. 12

This is the same kind of lightning character sketch Strauss later used with other secondary figures in his operas, such as Aegisthus, in *Elektra*.

Poor Guntram turns in alarm at finding himself deserted, even though he realizes that it means he has arrived at the scene of his assignment. Friedhold's last words were 'Streiter der Liebe'[7] and this turns out to be the name by which the League is known. The oldest woman of the party of refugees then delivers a curse upon the Duke worthy of Isolde, and they all move on, thanking Guntram for his ministrations and wishing him a happy lot in the future.

Scene 2 thus finds Guntram left alone for his first big aria in a

[7] 'Champion of Love.'

manner recalling Radames and, of course, Strauss's own *Elektra*. It is a meditative soliloquy taking its point of departure from the last words spoken to him by the peasants—'a happy lot'. This Guntram acknowledges to himself he has never sought, though always secretly longed for. As he considers the pristine innocence of Spring and Youth there is a wistful recollection of the Theme of Childhood from *Tod und Verklärung* (Ex. 18 from the last chapter), suggesting perhaps a self-identification on Strauss's part with his heroes in the light of subsequent experiences. Over a beautiful development of Ex.6, Guntram paints a scene of Nature in full bloom glorifying the Creator. This raises him to a state of ecstasy as a second reference to the *Tod und Verklärung* theme passes once again to Ex.6 and so to sublime peace with the opening bars of Ex.2 at the words 'Schweigen der Liebe' ('Silence of Love'). Then with an abrupt change of mood he turns to the misery with which he finds himself surrounded. Apart from repeated references to the 'oppression' theme Ex.9, a new and important idea is introduced as Guntram speaks of Sinful Mankind:

Ex. 13

He tells with horror of the Peasants' Revolt in which 'father murders son, the prince his own people', and then springing to his feet calls on the Saviour to inspire him in his singing to carry the Word into the hotbed of vice, the court of the Dreaded Tyrant, and stir the heart of the terrible Duke:

Ex. 14

At the climax he shouts aloud: 'Brother! Father! Pray for Guntram! To work, Champion of Love!'

This aria develops in full the material that was only sketched out in the corresponding section of the Prelude, and by way also of Ex. 7 reaches the same climax of the Assignment motif (Ex.8). The music is extremely poetical in conception, and it is unfortunate how present-

---

[8] 'Saviour, my Lord, I recognize thy hand.'

day *Weltanschauung* has so changed as a result of two major upheavals that the highminded sentiments which Strauss ingenuously puts into Guntram's mouth are found not only inacceptable but even amusing by contemporary opinion.

As Guntram concludes and turns to go, the figure of Freihild rushes out of the wood to one side and towards a lake in the rear. She is in the utmost despair, having broken away from the intolerable life of her home and husband, and she sees no course open to her but suicide. She is beside herself and addresses the lake ecstatically as Liberator and Redeemer through Death and Forgetfulness, all of which Guntram finds most odd. The themes which portray her desperation are certainly strange ones and show quite suddenly a strikingly different and original imagination at work:

Ex. 15

The first portion of this wild subject is none other than the B.A.C.H. theme, albeit transposed. There seems no logical reason for this and it is probable that Strauss introduced it for no other purpose than for its chromatically shifting character. Guntram, who has at first hidden, seizes Freihild just as she is about to throw herself into the water and, overcome, she collapses at his feet. After looking round hopelessly for help, Guntram tries to revive Freihild with water from the spring, to a rising figure in the violas for which Strauss was to find a more fruitful place in *Don Quixote*:

Ex. 16

Freihild gradually opens her eyes, only to give way to dismay at finding herself still living. As her delirium mounts once more she tries to break away from Guntram in a renewed effort to drown herself. The sounds of horns offstage, heralding the approach of the Duke and his retinue, add intensity to the feverish atmosphere of the scene as Guntram holds her fast, pleading on the grounds of her youth and beauty. This protestation arouses nothing but bitterness from Freihild and her agony of mind reaches a climax of extreme poignancy as she breaks into hysterical weeping.

A wild climax is built up which subsides as Guntram tries ceaselessly to calm Freihild, who speaks bitterly of her loveless marriage and the joy she has found in good deeds amongst the poor. These sentiments are reflected in two themes, the first an angular theme conjuring up the hated person of the cruel husband to whom she is yoked for life:

Ex. 17

the second a suave melody denoting the maternal joy she feels towards the peasants. The latter phrase of this theme is applied in due course to the paternal love borne for Freihild by her own father, the old Duke:

Ex. 18

Guntram sees his opportunity and presses Freihild to impart the nature of her troubles to him, a brave singer, who has been called to champion her cause. This revelation of his calling arouses scorn from Freihild, who knows nothing of the 'Streiter der Liebe' and accordingly sees in Guntram a mere itinerant minstrel. To a flippant version of what becomes the motif of the Court (Ex.21, below) she contemptuously tells him to be off to the Duke's castle, where his strains may receive their due financial reward. Guntram is cut to the quick that he should be so misunderstood. He clings to her until in her fury she strikes him in the face, so freeing herself and dashing a third time towards the lake as the sound of the horns comes nearer. Suddenly the voice of the old Duke can be heard calling 'Freihild', and as she hesitates Guntram manages to catch her yet again, though he is dumbfounded at the discovery that she is indeed the person he has hoped most of all to meet. To an ecstatic outburst of Ex.10 he throws himself at her feet and begs her vehemently to accept his championship for the sake of the unfortunate peasants. She can make nothing of this strange youth who has balked her intentions, but Guntram persistently urges her to trust him, as the Duke, preceded by his Court Fool, bursts upon the scene.

The whole incident has been too long drawn out and diffuse, but the situations stimulated Strauss's fast-growing powers of thematic and structural organization, so that the interest is well maintained as the symphonic flow passes logically forward to the exciting last pages of the Act. Ex.18(a), now harmonized in a manner suggesting the Trio from the 3rd movement of Beethoven's 7th Symphony:

Ex. 19

is developed together with a rapid figure which for the moment indicates the Duke's joyful agitation at regaining his beloved daughter, although it later forms an integral part of the Court Festival.

Ex. 20

Guntram steps forward and announces himself as Freihild's deliverer, upon which the Duke questions him closely as to his name and mission. Guntram discloses that his goal is the Duke's Court, and the Court motif is declaimed for the first time in its broad and stately form:

Ex. 21

The Duke has just promised to reward Guntram with a boon which he may freely choose, when his son-in-law, the cruel Robert, is heard viciously driving before him the band of peasants to whom Guntram had earlier ministered. His theme Ex. 17 breaks sharply across the texture as Freihild, who has been silent since the appearance of her father, cries out in despair at the sound of her dreaded husband. But Guntram turns to her secretly saying 'I am not what I seem . . . soon you will learn of my mission; till then trust me', and this evokes in Freihild's heart the first glow of love and confidence which Strauss depicts by an important and beautiful theme:

Ex. 22

The plight of the peasants gives Guntram understanding of the purpose for which he has earned his reward. To the theme of his Address to the Saviour (Ex. 14), he begs for their release. His plea is taken up by the assembled company, including the Jester, whose Sancho Panza-like theme is heard for the first time:

Ex. 23

Robert is naturally furious. But the old Duke disdainfully allows Guntram's request, though sternly instructing the minstrel never to impose upon his favour in such a way again. Robert is forced to agree, but instead of showing the least gratitude for the saving of Freihild's life merely warns her that he will need to take greater precautions to clip her wings in future.

Her father is, as always, more gracious, and in a rather touching ariette asks her to come home with them, no more to shun husband and father; but when she agrees it is to the sound of Ex. 22, making it clear that it is only on Guntram's account that she does so. Her recovery calls for celebrations and so the Jester takes the liberty of announcing a Festival of Song, the theme of which begins the coda to the Act as well as dominating the Prelude to Act II:

Ex. 24

From this point the music builds up into a conventional Finale-ensemble with the Court theme (Ex. 21) and Guntram's motifs (Ex. 6) consistently intermingling. The Mission theme (Ex. 8) points one of the main climaxes when the Court Fool turns to the Minnesingers and Vassals who, as the Duke's retinue, have been silent witnesses to the whole last scene, bidding them rejoice at the return of their lady. The final cadence makes further play with the 'horn call' figure:

Ex. 25

in a way almost identical with the use Strauss made of it forty years later in the closing bars of *Arabella*.

4

Strauss subtitled the Prelude to Act II with the words 'The Festival of Song at the Duke's Court' and it is certainly built on Ex. 24 to a considerable extent. But it is also, like the Prelude to Act I, a symphonic movement in which many of the most important themes are developed. If the former presented Love, the League and Guntram, this Prelude introduces the Court, Freihild, the old Duke, the Fool, and the themes of oppression and reprisal (the latter in threatening references to the brass chordal sequence of Ex. 11). These many and varied motifs appear as episodes between constant reappearances of the Festival theme (Ex. 24), which is dramatically interrupted time and time again, though always with undiminished flamboyance, however deep the depression into which the music seems to have descended. Although

⁹ Cf. Ex. 27 from Chapter 3 above (p. 85).

published separately, this Prelude also makes an unsatisfactory concert item, if for a different reason. It is curiously formless and the episodes are incoherent apart from their associations with the body of the opera. Even Ex. 24 has insufficient potentiality for symphonic development—it can only be repeated, and this Strauss does with too little variation of technique to make an effective piece out of context.

The final phrase is cut short as the Fool's theme interrupts the long prepared closing statement of the Court motif, Ex. 20. The curtain quickly rises to show the Fool in the act of entertaining the Duke. He sings a dangerously ironical song (accompanying himself on the lute) in which he tells how some time ago he rejected mercy and rightful deeds in favour of pitiless brutality, as a result of which he now lives well instead of starving. He shrewdly looks at Robert for approbation, knowing well that, although the tale he has told is flagrantly and inexcusably villainous, his master will be pleased. As he expects, Robert is flattered despite his show of sternness at the Fool's audacity.

Some sycophantic Minnesingers then sing a hypocritical chorus of praise to the Duke which the Fool mockingly interrupts from time to time. It is a dull chorus and Strauss treads on delicate ground when he makes the Fool join in the refrain of 'Heil' too soon, since, as he says, 'How can one know when it is going to end?' Guntram is sitting next to three vassals and is astonished to hear them exchange seditious remarks to one another. A new and important figure underlies these comments, symptomatic of the unrest fermenting beneath the surface:

Ex. 26

A tremendous feeling of discouragement envelops Guntram as he sees that, although the Court in all its splendour is doomed, his words can only fall on sterile soil. He actually gets up from his seat and crosses the hall with the intention of leaving. It is hard to imagine what would have become of him had he so faint-heartedly abandoned his post, and it is strange to find Strauss showing his hero, if momentarily, in so pitiful a light.

Fortunately Guntram's eyes fall on Freihild and, as he realizes that he must stay for her sake, another important love-theme sweeps through the orchestra:

Ex. 27

Seeing him standing preoccupied, the old Duke calls on Guntram to demonstrate his art with a song, and the hall hushes to an expectant silence as Guntram prepares to begin. But his thoughts are full of Freihild, knowing that if he sings it is that her heart may be touched— a palpable betrayal of his original mission and intentions. She for her part recalls his words 'soon you will learn of my mission; till then trust me', and a ghost of Ex. 22 is heard.

The aria which follows (beginning much as Wolfram's celebrated "Blick' ich umher" from *Tannhäuser*) contains the passage which was successfully performed separately as the 'Friedenerzählung' shortly before the first performance of the complete work. It is by far the most extended aria in the opera and, together with the soliloquy in Act I, makes Guntram's part extremely exacting. As a result Strauss allowed substantial cuts to be indicated in the vocal score for cases of emergency through too severe demands upon the singer! The complete song falls into two main sections representing Peace and War, the former portion of which is based partly on motifs of the League, partly on those of Freihild (who becomes in Guntram's inflamed mind the personification of the figure of Peace), and partly on a new lyrical idea.

Ex. 28

The War section which follows introduces in its turn two terse and striking motifs which acquire considerable status as the Act precipitates towards what Strauss himself described as the Catastrophe:

Ex. 29

Ex. 30

The former of these intensely dramatic and vivid themes is derived
from Robert's theme, as the second bar shows, while Ex. 30 is a distorted version of Ex. 7.

Guntram's eloquence profoundly stirs his listeners, with the natural
exception of Robert. Even the old Duke, who at first protests and is
inclined to be offended, is won over by Guntram's personal address to
himself in which the minstrel conjures up the concept of a Duke,
generous and just, beloved of his people and behaving towards them as
Prince and Father. An important theme based on Ex. 4b appears here
for the first time; Guntram has accomplished the first requirement of
the League—he has touched the heart of the old Duke.

Ex. 31

Guntram now presents the other side of the picture; a tyrannical
ruler with oppressed people rising in rebellion against a cruel and
hated yoke. Exx. 26 and 30 join in the renewed development of Ex. 9
as Guntram warms to his theme. The song is brought to its end with
a return to the motif of Peace (Ex. 28) in tones of the utmost exaltation,
and the old Duke is wholly won over. But Robert is scornful and angry
beyond measure; to savage ejaculations of Ex. 30 he pours ridicule on
Guntram, bringing into his retort a sneer at Freihild. Robert's evil
derision is too much for Guntram, who, in passionate tones of Ex. 27,
upholds her virtue and purity of spirit. The vassals now take Guntram's

part and events move swiftly to the climax. Robert furiously condemns Guntram to be whipped in the tower, but his commands are intercepted by the arrival of a messenger with news that the rebellion, far from being crushed by the recent victory, has regained strength and is on the point of threatening the castle. The War motif (Ex. 29) is worked up in a feverish movement into which the opening of Guntram's Love theme (Ex. 27) gradually intrudes more and more. In a raging passion Guntram recognizes that peace is an impossibility as long as Robert is alive, and calls upon the vassals to arrest their Duke. Robert immediately thrusts towards Guntram with his sword, but Guntram strikes first and Robert falls dead to the combined cries of Freihild and the old Duke. At the moment of the death blow it is the Love theme which is hurled out in the orchestra, and this is of the utmost significance with respect to Guntram's subsequent behaviour.[10]

Strauss's architectural instinct in the handling of what is, in fact, a very protracted climax is sound, although the almost indefinite extension of the diminished seventh chord sounds banal to our satiated ears. The Duke's grief at the death of his son-in-law is sincere and for that very reason damaging to the situation. With his entry into the world of active violence Guntram has at a single blow destroyed all he had so nearly achieved. A series of wailing statements of Ex.31 (coloured in a way which Strauss rediscovered most effectively in the closing pages of *Ein Heldenleben*) hold the tension of the motionless stage, disturbed only by three rough entries of Ex. 26. The suppressed violence sensed and commented on by the seditious vassals has at last come to the surface.

In the petrified silence the old Duke slowly raises himself and addresses Guntram in a bitter monologue. He invites the murderer to complete his work and slay him, too, as he stands there, a defenceless old man. When Guntram fails to stir a muscle in his horror at what he has done, the Duke's contempt and anger grow bar by bar, together with annoyance at himself for having been so weak as to listen to Guntram in the first place. The repeated statements of Ex. 31 during which he rails at Guntram as a 'Prophet of Pity' gradually come closer together, until from adjacent statements of the opening phrase ⌐ a ⌐ a new theme emerges.

---

[10] It is interesting to compare this definitive version of the action with the original as criticized by Franz Strauss in the letter quoted above (p. 89). The development of Strauss's stage sense is one of the most fascinating studies of the composer's evolution.

Ex. 32

Guntram lets the sword drop, overcome with convulsions of horror. At first the Duke is amazed at such a show of weakness, but gradually realizing that Guntram's immobility has lost him the allegiance of the vassals, he regains control of the situation, asserting in tones of great dignity his God-given power to rule (the 'Cross' theme in military form on the trumpets support this claim). He then calls on his followers to accompany him to the battlefield, where the presumptuous revolutionaries will be suitably punished. A march-theme is declaimed:

Ex. 33

as the Duke strides up to Guntram, ordering him to be removed to a dungeon, there to await torture and death. He then turns to the vassals and with a soft mention of Ex. 1 (d) on the horns (a further reminder of his Divine Right) satisfies himself as to their allegiance. Four monks appear who are directed to carry Robert's body into the chapel, there to await burial after the fearful and glorious battle to come. At last the Duke departs to the sounds of the stirring March, Ex. 33, followed by his vassals and horsemen. The march dies gradually away in the distance, and the stage is deserted except for the numbed and motionless figure of Freihild, with behind her the Fool watching silently and sadly.

After the complexity of the previous action, scene 3 is simple. Freihild slowly realizes that she is free, that her dreams have reached fulfilment. The lifting of the clouds of her life is represented by a series of rising scale figures, while an ingenious extension of the B.A.C.H. theme takes away the madness which was so strong a feature of its treatment. Even the 'fifths' motif of despair (Ex. 15 (b)) is absorbed into the ever more glowing harmonies which also incorporate Exx. 27 and 31 as appreciation sweeps over her that Guntram is the direct cause of her liberation. The excitement grows and a typically Straussian phrase of surging semi-quavers derived from Ex. 22 in diminution becomes increasingly prominent, building the passage to an exhilarating height of jubilant triumph:

Ex. 34

The climax is, naturally enough, built around the motif of Freihild's trust in Guntram (Ex.22) declaimed flamboyantly against a magnificent sunset. Freihild is inspired to declare her love for Guntram in those glorious phrases which, with the fine soprano of Pauline de Ahna in his ears, Strauss came to make a feature of his work. The appearance of Ex. 10 at the end of this outburst indicates that this love is more than mere sympathy and that with it Freihild gives the whole of herself. The orchestral ritornello which caps this aria is cut off abruptly as the sounds of an offstage brass band can be heard accompanying the army on its way to battle.

The sound of the band causes Freihild to turn as she sees the Fool, who says with a voice filled with emotion that he wants to suffer with her, even to die for her. But in such devotion Freihild sees only the means to save Guntram, and she exacts his aid in securing Guntram's escape. To a melody taken from the second part of the 'Friedenserzählung' (Ex. 28) she confirms the Fool's fears that she intends to fly with Guntram into the outer world. Brokenhearted but loyal to the last, the Fool agrees to lead Freihild to the dungeon and, by drugging the guards, enable her to escape with her hero. With little further thought as to what this must cost the Fool, she dismisses him, and the Act ends with a jubilant crescendo culminating in a ritornello virtually identical with the earlier passage which was interrupted by the march. This time, however, the soaring reiterations of Ex. 22 reach their triumphant conclusion and, as Freihild hurries away to join her husband, the curtain falls.

5

At this point Strauss the librettist ran into difficulties. The whole subject of the opera had been suggested to him by Ritter, who had then watched over its development step by step. Ritter, a Catholic and a passionate devotee of the philosophical works of Wagner and Schopenhauer, saw the whole character of Guntram from a strictly religious point of view, with ethics and morality as of primary importance. But ever since he was fifteen years old Strauss had felt intense antipathy for any religion 'which relieved the faithful of responsibility for their actions by means of confession'. This obviously becomes relevant in Act III, since Guntram must either expiate his crime with a penance freely chosen before his own conscience, or report back to the League who sent him in the first place, confess his guilt, and accept whatever punishment is meted out to him, thus remaining within the framework of society and bound by its laws. At first Strauss succumbed to Ritter's influence and in the first draft Guntram reappeared before the League, although Strauss allowed himself the compromise of making Guntram decide of his own free will on a pilgrimage to the Holy Sepulchre. This resolve was reached while Guntram was still in Freihild's arms, the entire Act taking place exclusively between the two principal characters. On his tour of convalescence, however, Strauss found time to make a thorough study of Nietzsche's writings, finding 'his polemic against Christianity particularly to his liking', and this encouraged him to strike out for himself. His self-confidence was also strengthened by reading the works of another German philosopher, Max Stirner, who discourses at some length on the ideal of individualism. As a result Strauss revised the ending of the opera so as to enable Guntram to take the drastic step of ostracizing himself from society altogether, rejecting the League (through the representative figure of Friedhold), and remaining answerable only to himself.

Ritter was shattered. Considering that either way Guntram would be spending the remainder of his existence paying for his crime, Ritter's reaction was unreasonably severe and his language extravagant. He wrote to Strauss:

> As a result of reading your new 3rd Act I have experienced the most profoundly painful emotions of the past ten years of my life. Through this latest form of your 3rd Act you have fundamentally destroyed your work since: (1) the work is now entirely devoid of tragedy, (2) it is robbed of the smallest trace of artistic unity which is so essential, (3) the character of the hero has become psychologically quite impossible and of a patched-together characterlessness [*Charakterlosigkeit*—!], (4) the tendency of the work is now an immoral mockery of every ethical creed. . . . Dear friend! Come to your senses! Do not utterly ruin the first two Acts of so beautiful a work! Take this new 3rd Act—even if you have already set it to

music—and throw it head and tail straight into the fire!
Then go and read with inner enlightenment a chapter
from the gospels or from Schopenhauer's ethical writings,
or Wagner's *Art and Religion*. Then draw up a new 3rd Act
following the earlier draft, reinstating the passage in which
Guntram completes his heroic deed of self-sacrifice by
humbly placing himself under the judgement of the League.

In bewilderment Strauss wrote ruefully to his parents of how Ritter
had begged him for the sake of his salvation to cast out the accursed
tendencies from his poor soul, irrevocably lost to the devil, but that he
really had no idea what Ritter was talking about. He had not changed
Guntram's character in the slightest, but Ritter had obviously always
seen in Guntram something quite different from anything which he,
Strauss, had wanted from the start; anyway, even if Guntram did have
to have tendencies, he could see in them nothing either immoral or
unchristian! However, there it was and he would scarcely get on with
Act II before he came home; perhaps the music would clear up some of
the misunderstandings; but no one could prevent him from now and
then viewing the world through his own eyes, even if they sometimes
saw crooked; after all, it is only what one sees oneself which has any
meaning. An eminently reasonable argument.

That Ritter was being unreasonable and pompously ridiculous was
more than apparent to Strauss. Nevertheless out of loyalty and affection
to his old friend he wrote him a letter of eleven closely filled sheets of
persuasion and self-justification, trying desperately to win Ritter over
at least to toleration of his point of view. All in vain; Ritter never
wholly forgave him Guntram's renunciation of society and for some
time there was a marked coolness in their relations.

6

Unlike its predecessors, the Prelude to Act III is no more than an introduction, and forms an integral part of the scene which follows. It begins
with the stern theme of the League (Ex. 3) in its most menacing form
coupled with the phrase ⌐ a ⌐ from Ex. 4, followed by a brief and
wistful memory of Guntram's theme (Ex. 6) in its first untarnished
innocence. We are to imagine Guntram in his dungeon and can follow
his thoughts as the various images flash through his tortured mind. The
themes of Freihild and their love for each other alternate with the

motifs of his mission, of the Duke, and of Pity. This theme (Ex. 1b) with its various derivatives includes a new chromatic version which in its treatment actually anticipates Schönberg's developments of advanced chromatic harmony in such works as *Verklärte Nacht* and *Pelleas und Melisande*:[11]

Ex. 35

The music flares up momentarily with two cumulative statements of the War motif (Ex. 29), after which it stops short, revealing the dismal chant of the monks who are watching over Robert's body. The curtain has quickly risen, and we can now see, instead of imagining, Guntram like a lion in a cage, alone with his endless self-inquisition. The orchestra broods and explodes in sympathy with his changing moods, while constantly building up a symphonic texture with foregoing material such as Exx. 26, 27, and 30. Guntram's mind is tortured by the riddle of the disaster which has overtaken him; above all, he cannot explain to his own satisfaction his real motives for killing the Duke. The ceaseless chanting of the monks irritates his overheated brain to the point of frenzy and he shrieks a curse at them.

The mournful Requiem dies away, but Guntram's relief is short-lived. He cannot forget what has taken place, and with the appearance of a dark and savage motif (Ex. 36), symbolical of the murder and Robert's corpse, he begins to suffer from hallucinations.

Ex. 36

In an agony of indecision he exorcises Robert's ghost, shouting aloud that Robert had to die that thousands might live; his deed was justified, his hand unstained.

[11] Schönberg was at this time nineteen years old and wholly unknown, as he had not yet begun serious composition. It was not until some eight years later that Strauss came to know Schönberg's work, when he was so impressed by the first part of *Gurrelieder* that he procured for him not only the Liszt Stipendium, but the professorship of Composition at the Stern Conservatoire in Berlin.

At precisely this moment Freihild appears. He immediately takes
her to be the incarnation of his guilty conscience and tries to exorcise
this new vision, too. Freihild is deeply shocked at his condition, and in a
passionate aria tries to restore him to sanity with the offer of herself as
his love and his wife.

Guntram, however, scarcely believing that he is not still experiencing
hallucinations, loses consciousness in Freihild's arms. The love song
with which Freihild revives him is one of the most beautiful passages in
the opera and deserves to be revived. It is a mighty scena of the type in
which Strauss was to become pre-eminent, and it is superbly built up
to a tremendous climax at the peak of which a new theme rings out:

Ex. 37

During Freihild's outpourings of her love and devotion, Guntram has
repeated her name with ever-increasing anguish as the realization
comes to him that his deed of slaughter was inspired primarily for love
of her, and that he has no alternative but to renounce her entirely. Ex.
37 represents his formal act of renunciation long delayed but now
irrevocable, and this moment is accordingly the climax of the entire
opera. The theme itself, it will be noticed, is the starkest of *Naturtheme*,
standing midway between Ex. 1 of *Macbeth* and the 'Nature' motif of
Zarathustra (see below, p. 135, Ex. 13).

Guntram leaps up, repulses Freihild and rushes to the door. As he is
on the point of departure, Friedhold[12] is seen standing in the doorway.
This prefectorial figure, having abandoned Guntram in the first scene,
when his advice and support was most needed by the young minstrel
with his inexperience of life, now makes his re-entry in the final scene in
order to conduct Guntram to trial and to answer for his mistakes. To
his surprise he sees before him no longer the ingenuous youth who will
meekly obey his instructions without question but a mature being who
through suffering has discovered his own mind and is prepared to abide
by his decisions. Stately as Friedhold's pronouncements are, backed up
by the pompous League motifs (Exx. 3 and 4 (a)), they have no longer
their expected effect. At first Guntram seems bewildered and hardly

[12] Apart from the Wagnerianism of the two names, the confusing similarity
between Friedhold and Freihild is an inherent flaw in Strauss's text.

even recognizes Friedhold, who now acknowledges that Guntram's emancipation was premature. Ex. 12 makes its appointed return as Friedhold speaks of the unhappy moment in Act I when he took so abrupt a leave of his young charge. Guntram's reply is that he has not lived until today and that Friedhold has now no right to judge him. Friedhold retorts that if not he, then the League has that right through placing in Guntram's hands a lyre to exalt his power of song. But Guntram impetuously breaks his lyre, swearing that he will never grasp it again. It is the Cross on his breast, which he now clutches, that will in future guide his life; the Cross, the meaning of which he now at last understands. He tries once more to fly from the prison, but Friedhold forces him to remain, as he prepares to deliver a sermon on Guntram's duty and the significance of the League.

This potential aria is introduced by the orchestra enunciating the opening bars of the opera in their original form, and the impression is given that here is the focal point of the work, much as the 'Gralerzählung' in *Lohengrin*. Unexpectedly, however, Strauss never allows Friedhold to bring his homily to a conclusion. Guntram breaks in vehemently, and a philosophical argument ensues which Freihild justifiably finds difficulty in comprehending. The climax comes as Guntram, to repeated declamations of the Murder theme (Ex. 36), insists that the League can only punish the Deed; yet the Deed in itself was good. Light has come to him in the solitude of his imprisonment. The kernel of his reasoning comes at the words:

> Meine Schuld sühnt nur
> Die Busse meiner Wahl
> Mein Leben bestimmt
> Meines Geistes Gesetz
> Mein Gott spricht
> Durch mich selbst nur zu mir[13]

a dictum denounced by no less a person than Siegfried Wagner as a flagrant betrayal of his father's creeds. Friedhold, like Ritter with whom some commentators identify him, is profoundly disturbed and, expressing the strongest forebodings as to what the future may bring, retires from the scene.

Freihild is radiant with joy at what she takes to be her victory and

---

[13] Only the atonement of my choice can expiate my guilt
My life is determined by the decrees of my own spirit
My God speaks to me only through myself.

the beginning of eternal happiness, but her exultation is rudely shattered as Guntram announces his unshakeable resolve to withdraw,
since only by parting from her can he find redemption. The scene bears
considerable resemblance to that of Parsifal and Kundry, with Guntram
alternately dropping on one knee to pray ('Cross' and 'Pity' themes
from Ex. 1) and springing up in a fervent exposition of his innermost
soul ('Love' and 'Murder' themes, Exx. 27 and 36). His reiterated
decision to renounce Freihild brings back Ex. 37, followed by the long-
awaited return of the melodic form of the Love motif (Ex. 2)—now
assuming its true function—that of Wagner's favourite concept
'Redemption through Love'. Finally Guntram speaks of Freihild's sublime future and the last of the melodic themes makes its impressive entry:

Ex. 38

The Fool suddenly bursts in and brings to the lovers the news that
the old Duke has fallen in battle, and the victorious rebels have nominated Freihild as their ruler, calling her 'the angel of the people'. Ex. 18
(the motif of the 'mother-children' relationship she has always had
with her peasants) now finds fulfilment, and a broad climax is reached
with Guntram rejoicing over the splendid mission in life which now
clearly unfolds before her. Exx. 2, 10 and 38 all contribute to the sweeping cantilena in this fine melodic Finale. Freihild finally comes reluctantly
to accept her part in this great renunciation scene as the music takes on
a warmth and nobility of expression quite new in Strauss's work and
which ceases to owe anything stylistically to Wagner. It is an important
new aspect of Strauss's equipment to which he returned in many of his
finest later works. With immense dignity Freihild kisses Guntram's
hand and slowly he takes leave of her as the curtain falls.

7

The importance Strauss attached to *Guntram* has, over the years, proved
to be sadly out of proportion of its intrinsic value as a lasting work of art.
The very great prominence of its many themes in the famous 'Works of
Peace' section of *Ein Heldenleben* is tangible proof of Strauss's devotion

[14] 'I know of a high office for thee, thou pure one.'

to his ill-fated first-born of the stage, but unfortunately the world has shown itself reluctant to share the composer's opinions in this respect. In particular, much of the undiluted Wagnerianism of *Guntram* seems to the modern observer a retrograde step in Strauss's stylistic emancipation after works of such originality as *Don Juan* and *Tod und Verklärung*.

Yet Strauss did not see it at all like that. Although in 1892, when he penned the naïvely reverent inscription to Wagner's memory at the foot of his completed score, the great master had been dead for nearly ten years, his name was still spoken of in musical circles as the most dangerous modernist a young composer could emulate. Thus for the initiated to walk in his footsteps was to tread holy ground, and Strauss, fresh from his visits to Bayreuth, ardently felt himself to be one of the elect. Few of us are able to comprehend which are those qualities in us which the world chooses to respect, and Strauss, being no exception, was totally unable to realize how many of his most valuable characteristics he was sacrificing in embracing the idiom and philosophy of his idol in so uncompromising a manner.

To begin with, Strauss's efforts at formulating his own libretto were, after all his gruelling labour, woefully primitive. They make no attempt whatever at rhyming or metrical stanzas, while the choice of words and turn of phrase are constantly reminiscent of Wagner's worst literary style in every other respect. Moreover, both the language and the behaviour of the characters bear out Strauss's later admission that the opera is a 'witness of my hair-raising *naïveté* at that time'. From the present day point of view he was particularly unlucky in choosing for his subject an aspect of German art which has come to be widely discredited. Ernest Newman put the matter in a nutshell when he wrote already in 1905:

> The world is growing a little weary of all these good but rather tiresome people who are continually renouncing or being redeemed, or insisting on redeeming someone else . . . the occasional slowness of the action and the long stretches of rather nebulous philosophizing are amongst the reasons why the opera has been shelved.

With respect to the music there is a curious conflict, since in the many passages where Strauss is really being himself its value as the progenitor of the tone poems and operas which followed it can scarcely be overestimated. Many themes and sections suggestive of *Don Quixote* and *Heldenleben* have been discussed above, together with the first growth of Strauss's characteristically soaring cantilenas for Soprano, one of the most important features of his later operas and songs. There are even passages which look forward to the experimentalism of *Elektra*, such as the climax of the first scene between Guntram and Freihild, the polyphonic texture of which is in a harmonic idiom of extreme chromatic fluidity such as Strauss contrived for the scene in which Chrysothemis and Elektra hear of the supposed death of Orestes. Yet mingled with these remarkable pages of highly original music are whole sections which are not merely derivative, but frankly plagiaristic. Ex. 11 plainly comes directly from Act III of *Tristan*, the brass passage in the latter part being especially reminiscent. Ex. 27 also comes straight out of the same opera in a way which is so brazen as to be amusing. Similarly Ex. 32 is strongly suggestive of Sieglinde's Fear motif from Act II of *Die Walküre*, and so on.

It thus seems unlikely that *Guntram* will ever find a place in the standard repertoire. The abridged version which Strauss prepared in 1940 served its purpose for the revivals of 1940 and 1942, but the work has since fallen into as deep a neglect as before. The cuts were, in fact, substantial, there being no less than seventeen major excisions, reducing the total length by a full half-hour. Of these the most drastic were:

(1) Two long cuts in the first scene between Guntram and Freihild.
(2) The narrative of the Fool at the beginning of Act II, together with the passage in which Guntram almost abandons his post.
(3) The scene at the end of Act II between Freihild and the Fool.

There were also some revisions in the orchestration, due to Strauss's radical change of attitude over the years with respect to the weight of tone in the pit relative to the clarity of diction on the stage. The young Strauss had very different standards from the mature opera composer, and held no less rigidly to his opinions. A letter from his father in the spring of 1893, criticizing the orchestration of Act I as being too thick, evoked this extraordinarily sharp reply:

> Do you really find it so thickly scored? I had especially pictured to myself that it was so transparent that I had expected less heaving and sighing over the horns in scene 2 than shivers on account of the muted trumpets. To please my dear good papa, the horns must be silent throughout

the opera, or at most blow a few sustained notes in the Finale as in *Don Giovanni* or *Zauberflöte*; I find rather that the bassoons are somewhat too hard-worked, but that wouldn't worry Papchen; he would only be delighted that his dearest neighbours have lots to blow, isn't that right?

Papchen's reply to this attack is not on record.

Of course, it is perfectly true that the original orchestration is frequently thick and heavy, and one looks in vain for the kaleidoscopic use of orchestral colour of the later works. Yet, as might be expected from the composer of *Don Juan*, the score is marvellously euphonous with its triple wind and four bassoons, which latter, as he said, 'appear in almost every French score, and besides I need them, like my daily bread!' The bass clarinet he now used as a basic ingredient, but changed from his use of the Wagnerian notation in the bass clef to what is known as the French notation (i.e. in the treble clef reading a ninth higher than concert pitch.) This notation he retained until *Salome*, when he reverted to his former practice.

In the brass section he experimented further with the bass trumpet, counting on the rehearsals to decide the success or otherwise of his ideas. For the rest he remained content for the time being with the conventional brass with no more than four horns, although he used extra instruments for the offstage band in Act II, including tenor horns. For this group he found himself at a loss as to their practical character and accordingly wrote to his father: 'Would you be so good as to find out how one writes for the tenor horns; what tonality these are in; their range: (1) the absolute limits of possibility; (2) up to how high or low can they blow comfortably?' (!)

The two timpanists and five percussion players are called upon very sparingly and, although Strauss prescribes two pairs of cymbals of different sizes, he scarcely ever indicates which he requires at any given entry. The string parts are written solidly with little use of the solo tone; the conception of a chamber orchestra was still far from Strauss's horizon.

Altogether, despite a great deal of fine music, *Guntram* represents a palpable first attempt. It is an important aspect of Strauss's output that the curve of his operatic productions, a sphere in which he was to be pre-eminent, should begin at its lowest point at a time when his work on the tone poem was at its zenith. As we shall see in due course, the operatic masterpieces begin to appear only when the orchestral works have ceased to be in the front rank of Strauss's achievements.

CHAPTER V

THE TONE POEMS (II)

O N 10th September 1894 Strauss married Pauline de Ahna, dedicating to her as a wedding present his group of songs op. 27. The story of how he became engaged to her is both typical and highly entertaining. I quote it in the form in which Strauss himself told it to Lotte Lehmann—with the radiance with which he always spoke of Pauline:

> She sang Elizabeth in *Tannhäuser* under his baton, and in a rehearsal made some mistake, or dragged or hurried the tempo. In any case, an argument arose between her and the young conductor, which finally reached its climax when she threw the piano score from the stage on to his head, shrieked some frightful insults, and leaving the rehearsal, rushed to her dressing-room.
>
> Strauss, terribly annoyed, laid down his baton, interrupted the rehearsal which had been so violently disturbed, and, without knocking, entered Pauline's artist's room. Those waiting outside heard through the closed door wild shrieks of rage and fragmentary insults—then all was quiet. Turning pale each looked at the other; who had killed whom? A delegation of orchestra members approached the threatening door. A shy knocking. . . . Strauss opened the door and stood in the doorway beaming. The representative of the musicians stammered his speech: 'The orchestra is so horrified by the incredibly shocking behaviour of Fräulein Pauline de Ahna that they feel they owe it to their honoured conductor Strauss to refuse in

the future to play in any opera in which she might have a part. . . .' Strauss regarded the musicians smilingly. Then he said: 'That hurts me very much, for I have just become engaged to Fräulein de Ahna. . . .'

At the beginning of October, Strauss took up his appointment in Munich, having bidden farewell to Weimar the previous summer, where, as he wrote, 'I had recklessly squandered some of the goodwill people bore me, by my youthful energy and love of exaggeration, so that they were not sorry to see Pauline and me leave.' Yet even with this new position in his home town it was not until a further fifteen months had elapsed, in November 1895, with Levi ill and Fischer (the associate conductor who had once been superior to him) away on leave, that he was able to arrange for the Munich production of *Guntram* with the disastrous results we have already seen.

This failure hit Strauss hard, since he was already planning a libretto for a second opera. The first ideas had come to him on the ship when, during June 1893, he was gradually making his way home via Sicily and Italy with the completed score of the second act of *Guntram* in his trunk. The new work was to be a one-act *Volksoper* on the popular legend of *Till Eulenspiegel*. He had already heard an opera on this subject by Kistler, a German composer who has long since fallen into obscurity, and it is probable that the several new editions of the legend with fascinating etchings which had recently appeared in Germany drew Strauss's further attention to the amusing exploits of this national clown.

There seems to be enough evidence to show that there was a real character who went by the name of Tyll Eulenspiegel. The son of a peasant, he was born at Kneitlingen in Brunswick in the early fourteenth century and died at Moellen (a small town south of Lübeck) in 1350, according to some reports, of the Black Death. His life was symptomatic of the growing self-assertiveness of the lower classes at that time against the upper strata of society, whose authority had hitherto rarely been other than taken for granted. Thus Till became the hero of a rapidly expanding legend consisting of a collection of anecdotes based on his practical jokes. To quote Sir Thomas Armstrong: 'Till is essentially a folk-hero; his story has not the distinctive personality of Rabelais or Swift or Cervantes, but is full of broad farce and a rather grim humour. Beneath the farce is a good deal of keen satire upon human nature in general.'[1] The first printed version of Till's adventures had

[1] Strauss Tone Poems, *Musical Pilgrim*, O.U.P.

appeared around 1500, and translations were soon made into many European languages. The earliest edition in English was published in the sixteenth century by Wyllyam Copland under the title of *A Merry Jest of a man called Howleglas*.[2]

All the different accounts of Till Eulenspiegel cover much the same basic group of tales, though most add some extra ones of their own. The stories generally fall into a few distinctive categories; tales in which Till tries his hand as an apprentice at some trade, such as a tailor, shoemaker, etc; tales in which Till plays a deliberate practical joke at someone else's expense in which they suffer either severe loss or even personal injury; tales in which Till triumphs through his lightning wit or repartee, such as his exploits as Court Jester or in outwitting the scholars, doctors or wise men of some city; and tales of adventures by which Till acquires the means of bodily survival either through purest roguery or through some sharp if not illegal practice. All classes of people from a king down to the humblest peasant form the butt of Till's pranks and he is obliged to travel widely as one place after another becomes too hot to hold him. He is more than once sentenced to death, but escapes through his ready tongue, which saves him in the nick of time with some ingenious argument, so that in the end he dies in his bed.

Strauss's first treatment of this legend in his own draft libretto bore only scant relationship to all this, and then only in allusive remarks. The main scheme of the action lay in setting Till against a background of petty narrow-mindedness as shown by a group of city magistrates who are bigoted and misguided to the point of pure imbecility. Till has the brazen effrontery to show them up in all their dishonest simplicity, even at the risk of his personal liberty and well-being. To some extent there are similarities here with the Pied Piper of Hamelin legend, and the conception of a clever individual at variance with pompous local authority was clearly much to Strauss's liking, and we shall meet a similar situation six years later in *Feuersnot*. The opera was tentatively called *Till Eulenspiegel bei den Schildbürgen*. It took place in the symbolical city of German legend, Schilda, and duly incorporated a triangular love interest in which Till emerges bitter and lonely, returning at the end to his original role as the arch-mocker and despiser of humanity and the

[2] The origin of the name Eulenspiegel gives rise to some interesting conjecture. The fact that the French word 'espiègle' denotes 'roguish' seems unquestionably relevant; however, a seventeenth-century tombstone still stands to Till's memory with upon it the engraving of an owl with a mirror.

ways of men. The Schildbürger were themselves part of a folk-legend dating back to the sixteenth century, when they were featured in a satirical book by an anonymous Alsatian. By tradition they epitomized the greatest folly to which man can descend, and it is in keeping with their place in German folk-lore that the members of the town council of Schilda were made by Strauss to be occupied in such unprofitable tasks as capturing daylight with mouse-traps.

Unfortunately the sketch was abandoned before Strauss got near to composing a note of music for it. This was partly owing to a realization of his lack of poetical gifts, and undoubtedly discouragement at the fate of *Guntram* was a strong influence. But there was an additional deterrent in Strauss's difficulty in seeing the character of Till in sufficient detail to present him as a living figure on the stage. He once wrote in a letter: 'I have already put together a very pretty scenario, although the figure of Master Till Eulenspiegel does not quite appear before my eyes; the book of folk-tales only outlines a rogue with too superficial a dramatic personality—the developing of his character on more profound lines after his trait of contempt for humanity also presents considerable difficulties.'

Nevertheless, before giving up the idea altogether he had an entirely new text sketched out by a certain Graf von Sporck. This gave him re-newed interest for a time, but once again the scheme came to nothing. After the disappointment of *Guntram*, the stage had for the time being no attraction for him. In the meantime, however, he had completed a purely instrumental treatment of the subject. Work on this new tone poem already occupied Strauss during the winter of 1894–5; it was finished on 6th May and first performed by Wüllner in Cologne the following November.

2

This time Strauss chose the classical form of the Rondo,[3] giving an indication of the importance traditional form still held for him. He even put the structural aspect of the piece into the heading, the word 'tone poem' not appearing at all. The title is, in fact, unusually long, and thus is rarely printed in full in concert programmes, despite

[3] Best described as 'a b a c a', or in the case of Sonata Rondo 'a b a c a b a' with 'c' marking the main central episode and allowing opportunity for some kind of recapitulation, however brief.

its scholarly unconventionality. It reads: *Till Eulenspiegels lustige Streiche nach alter Schelmenweise in Rondeauform für grosses Orchester gesetzt.*[4] The idea of using the scheme of a Rondo, with some of Till's adventures forming the episodes, was obviously ingenious, even if in the event Strauss's adaptation of it was as free as his adaptations of sonata form had been in the earlier tone poems. The whole work is unified by the employment of two motifs which depict the figure of Till himself:

Ex. 1   Ex. 2

These, as Strauss put it in a letter to Wüllner before the first performance, 'weave in and out of the whole texture in the most varied disguises and moods as the situations press on to the catastrophe in which Till is hanged after the motif has been pronounced over him'.

Ex. 3

To Wüllner, Strauss showed himself unwilling to divulge the exact programmatic significance of the various passages, but when Wilhelm Mauke later wrote a guide to the work, Strauss marked into his score some of the most important references. The opening of the work, for example, a gentle phrase in folk-lore character based on Ex. 1, is naturally enough, 'Once upon a time there was a roguish jester', while the horn phrase which follows (after Siegfried's horn call, the most celebrated solo in the repertoire of the instrument) is inscribed 'whose name was Till Eulenspiegel'.

Ex 4

The figure ⌐ a ⌐ (which is, of course, identical with Ex. 2) is syncopated differently at each repetition, giving a subtle impression of

---

[4] 'Till Eulenspiegel's merry pranks, after the old rogue's tale, set for large orchestra in Rondo-form.'

Till's quick-witted and elusive manner. Yet its subsequent harmoniza-
tion reveals it as little more than the horn figure which has reappeared
again and again ever since the Piano Sonata, op. 5 (see Ex. 8, Chapter 1
and also Ex. 25 from *Guntram*), though brilliantly transformed and
imbued with an unmistakable character of its own. Even its first
slightly tentative entry, followed by a second, identical but fully self-
assured, suggests to the life the figure of Till seeing if the coast is clear
before presenting himself.

Ex. 4 builds to a climax and *fermata*, after which the second 'Till'
theme, Ex. 2, is given in its most vivid and characteristic shape. Here is
indeed the arch-mocker of mankind—thumb to nose and supremely
devil-may-care:

Ex. 5

'Das war ein arger Kobold' wrote Strauss under this phrase, corresponding perhaps with 'That was a rascally scamp!'

The section which follows is a non-programmatic symphonic exposition of the Till themes. Strauss was palpably enjoying himself, and
he filled his score with ingenious devices and thematic references such
as the version of Ex. 1 in double augmentation on the horns when,
with undisguised ebullience, Till shows himself in his true colours. No
specific incident is portrayed here and the next section is even repeated
later in the work in the manner of a formal recapitulation; Strauss's
only comment is ' up to new pranks'. No praise is too high for the taste
and skill with which the material is worked. Gone is all the heavy
second-hand Wagnerianism, gone the turgid texture of *Guntram* and
the more banal moments of *Tod und Verklärung*. As Busoni pointed out,
such lightness and humour had not been handled so masterfully in
German music since Papa Haydn. Here was a side of Strauss which
could not possibly have been foretold in the light of what had gone
before.

A sinister bridge passage of mock innocence prepares the first true
episode ('Just you wait, you lickspittles'); an upward rush of clarinets, a
violent cymbal clash and 'Hop! On horseback straight through the
market women' Till rides, creating pandemonium and havoc as he goes.

He escapes in the confusion, 'Off and away in seven-league boots', as Strauss wrote (Ex. 1 in augmentation on the trombones—he has presumably sold the horse); there is a moment's pause in the music. Till is hidden in a mouse-hole and cautiously puts out his head to see if the coast is clear. A series of jabbing minor seconds suggests his gradual emerging, and soon he is in the midst of his next adventure: 'Dressed as a priest he oozes unction and morality'. This section is the true second subject—the 'b' in formal algebra—of the Rondo design and introduces a suitably ingratiating theme:

Ex. 6

'Yet the rogue peeps out of the big toe' (D clarinet suddenly), while further hints of Ex. 1 penetrate the disguise and show us the figure of Till beneath the mock seriousness of the preacher. In the midst of his sermon however, 'he is seized with a horrid premonition as to the outcome of his mockery of religion', at that time a highly dangerous practice.

Ex. 7

But he banishes his fears, if with difficulty, and a headlong glissando from the very top to the bottom note of the solo violin leads directly into the next adventure.[6]

A gentle new transformation of Ex. 5 presents 'Till the cavalier, exchanging sweet courtesies with beautiful girls':

[5] 'Twice as fast.'

[6] Ever the practical musician, Strauss writes out the bottom octave of this cadenza as the first bar of the new movement, a clear indication that it should be both conducted and played in tempo. Although the run, as Strauss notates it, falls into seven clear groups of sextuplets, many leaders find it convenient to take the passage freely, as a result of which some of the greatest conductors have been known to miss them at the bottom.

Ex. 8

But before long he falls genuinely in love and the music is clothed in richer harmonies. A romantic version of Till's horn theme, Ex. 2, shows that 'he has really got it badly'.

Ex. 9

'He woos her.'

As usual, of course, the girl of his choice will have none of him, and although she is as tactful as possible 'a delicate jilt is still a jilt'. Till is outraged; Ex. 1 strides about the orchestra until with a rearing gesture the four horns shake their fist at the world with a furious declamation of Ex. 2. 'He vows he will take revenge on all mankind.'

The next adventure finds him amongst the pedagogues, whose motif is announced by four bassoons and bass clarinet:

Ex. 10

With a series of jerky statements of Ex. 2, Till poses his questions, after which the learned professors consider their solutions. Strauss explains the episode thus: 'After he has posed a few atrocious theses to the philistines, he leaves them to their fate dumbfounded.' The music of this section is splendidly ingenious, depicting the hopeless complexity of their professorial deliberations which flounder in the mire like so many hippopotami until Till abruptly reveals himself and from a safe

<hr />

[7] 'Glowing with love.'

distance hurls his derision at them with vicious repetitions of Ex. 5, the chord of which is held by the whole orchestra on a mighty sharp-edged trill. Strauss called this savagely powerful gesture Till's 'Grosse Grimasse'.

A climax of this nature might be thought hard to follow up, and Strauss himself had experienced some difficulty at similar moments in his earlier works. Here he was in no quandary; the bitter mockery of the *Grimasse* literally dissolves away into a common ditty, jaunty and vulgar, as, supremely satisfied with his highly successful exploit, Till disappears whistling down the nearest alley:

Ex. 11

This, too, fades away as Till vanishes in the distance and a strange interlude ensues, marked 'fleeting and ghostly'. Though based on Ex. 1, it serves as a link between the great adventure of the Pedagogues which has been the central episode (the 'c' so to speak of the Rondo) and the recapitulation. Till pauses a moment before plunging into further and even wilder exploits.

Strauss's sense of the logical construction is here strong and satisfying. Both the amiable passage which leads from the 'ghostly' section to the reappearance of Ex. 4 (now given in turns to F and D horns, thus giving the tonal variety) and the fanfare-like statement of the same motif to which it leads are interpolations of just the right character and proportions. Although the passage work is filled with contrast and with references to both the Till themes, a light scherzando texture is preserved throughout. An amusing point of style is his employment of the ascending figure which he first invented during the Guntram-Freihild scene in Act I of *Guntram* and which was soon to become such a feature of *Don Quixote*:

Ex. 12

This portion of the work falls into two sections punctuated by their relative climaxes; the first, the fanfare based on Ex. 1 just mentioned; the second, a tremendous reference to the 'sermon' theme, Ex. 6, now hurled out in a similar fanfare by horns and trumpets. The symphonic working out which had emerged from the recapitulation has had no direct programmatic significance. It has, however, suggested a rapidly growing recklessness in Till's behaviour which has inevitably led to his ultimate arrest by exasperated authority, using his blasphemy as the pretext. With a violent side-drum roll he is arraigned before the judges, and although he preserves his debonair nonchalance, 'Still whistling to himself with indifference' (Ex. 5 in its original form on the D clarinet), his accusers are insistent. Finally he realizes with a thrill of horror that he has gone too far. The theme of his earlier premonitions, Ex. 7, returns in agonized tones, but it is too late and he is condemned to the extreme penalty of the law (Ex. 3—the widest interval within the octave, the major seventh). 'Up the ladder with him! There he dangles. the breath leaves his body, the last convulsion and Till's mortal self is finished.' The musical depiction of this grisly scene is graphic in the extreme, with the D clarinet rushing up to its highest A flat, holding it awhile and then slowly descending as the flute gives the final shudder. This is certainly the *non plus ultra* of programmatic music.

Although in actual fact Till is said to have died in his bed, a prey to the terrible epidemic which swept Europe in the fourteenth century, Strauss changed the legend to suit his own dramatic purpose. None of the adventures in the tone poem correspond exactly with those to be found in the various editions of the book. Even the 'Grosse Grimasse' is inverted; in the saga it is the Wise Men of Prague who pose the questions to Till, although they are no doubt as disconcerted at Till's replies as Strauss makes them at his theses. Then, too, when he is arraigned and led to the gallows, as he is in one of the anecdotes, it is merely on account of his theft of some wine. At the last moment he saves himself by his sheer quick-wittedness in exacting the promise of a last dying boon so monstrously undesirable to the judges that they release him rather than cause themselves embarrassment.

However, if in every way as free in its interpretation of the legend as the opera Strauss had in mind, this version makes an excellent plot and the episodes are well within the style of the traditional anecdotes. Even Till's death by hanging is far more poignantly effective than the somewhat unromantic reality. The tone poem ends with an epilogue repeating and extending the 'Once upon a time' version of Ex. 1 with which it opened.[8] The naïve and charming atmosphere suggests strongly the narration of a folk-tale; Strauss seems to be saying that Till was, for all his malicious practical jokes, at heart a good and lovable fellow, and to be recalling with a wistful smile all the *joie de vivre* which, misdirected, led Till to offend society to such an extent as to cause so untimely an end to his career. There is fine insight here and the coda rounds off the tone poem with poetic imagination as well as being profoundly touching with the simplicity of great art. Till is indeed arguably Strauss's masterpiece, and it is to some extent symbolical of his entire career that he should have succeeded so well with a work thrown off in a flash of inspiration, almost casually after the more serious labours on the heavy and uninspired *Guntram*, which at the time seemed by so much the more important undertaking.

3

In *Till* Strauss's ingenuity and resourcefulness of technique reached its first apex. Moreover, it called for the greatest forces of woodwind he had yet used, with four of each group, the extravagance of this particular department being obviously dictated by the subject.[9] The use of the D clarinet is, of course, magnificently apt, with its natural pert, impudent quality. This is its first appearance in Strauss's work, and one of the earliest in orchestral writing. Liszt had already added it to his wind band in *Mazeppa*, though taking good care never to leave it alone for a moment. Precedents in the use of the D clarinet or the still smaller E flat, which replaces it in most countries, are few and far between. An isolated instance is said to occur in an obscure work of Gluck, but in the symphonic field Berlioz led the way with his brief employment of the E-flat clarinet to impersonate the transformation of the 'beloved' into a witch in the Finale of his *Symphonie Fantastique*. In his treatise on Orchestration, Berlioz regrets the neglect of the D clarinet, which he regards as full of possibilities, though he never explored them himself. Mahler used the E-flat clarinet regularly, though mostly in thickly

[8] This is quoted below; see Chapter IX, Ex. 33.
[9] Strauss added brass reinforcements of a further four horns and three trumpets to mark the climax of the work at the point where the 'sermon' theme returns, leading to the trial scene, but these are wholly redundant and have long since been omitted, as they were even by the composer in his own performances.

scored passages for its associations with the military band. Thus Strauss's introduction of a smaller member of the clarinet family as a virtuoso instrument, and in particular his choice of the D clarinet, may be regarded as pioneer.

Apart from the actual instruments employed, Strauss's handling of the orchestra in *Till* is little short of spectacular. It is infinitely more daring than anything in the earlier works, the success of his previous experiments obviously emboldening him to try out more and more infringements of the hitherto accepted limitations of his players, though always (it is important to stress) in the direct line of evolution from the traditional style and character of each instrument. Nevertheless this is virtuoso orchestral treatment the like of which had never been seen before, not in Berlioz, not in Liszt, not even in Wagner. If *Don Juan* and *Guntram* had been the 'scourge of God', *Till* was diabolical. With this new work Strauss became internationally recognized as having inaugurated a new era in orchestral technique.

4

No sooner was *Till* successfully launched than the indefatigable Strauss embarked on another major scheme based yet again on ideas which had taken root in his mind during his tour of convalescence in the Middle East. This proved to be a tone poem based on Nietzsche's finest but most complicated poem *Also Sprach Zarathustra*. No one can say that Strauss lacked courage in his choice of subjects. To compose music about a visionary philosophy, even if much of it is expressed politically, seems little short of foolhardy. One might set part of it, as Mahler did in his 3rd Symphony or Delius in his *Mass of Life*. But to devise a piece of purely orchestral programme music around a series of ideological utterances is to run the risk of becoming dangerously abstruse. Nevertheless Strauss found himself irresistibly drawn towards this undertaking through his preoccupation with Nietzsche as part of his philosophical reading while equipping himself for *Guntram*. Several things about Nietzsche were bound to attract Strauss; his devotion (for much of his life) to Wagner, the poetic beauty of his language, and in particular, as we have seen in connexion with *Guntram*, his antagonism to the established Church, amounting ultimately to an antipathy to all conventional religion. Nietzsche especially opposed those creeds which exalted the weak and humble—'Blessed are the meek, for they shall inherit the Kingdom of God.' *Also Sprach Zarathustra* preaches the very antithesis of such adulation of what was to Nietzsche the most pitiful side of humanity, one which in his view represented that primitive spiritual condition which human beings should ever strive to outgrow.

The figure of Zarathustra, or Zoroaster as the Greeks called him, was an actual person who lived, so far as one can tell, in approximately the sixth century B.C. and was thus a near contemporary of the original Buddha. Zarathustra was a Persian who proclaimed that he was the prophet of Ormazd, the spirit of light and good. In the Zoroastrian religion Man is the focal point of the conflict between Ormazd and Ahriman, the spirit of evil and darkness. Nietzsche used this great prophet of antiquity as a prop on which to clothe his own ideas on the purpose and destiny of mankind. Broadly speaking, Nietzsche's work consists of some eighty discourses, few of them of any great length, purporting to be Zarathustra's pronouncements and views on a variety of different ideas: Of Virtue, Of the Criminal, Of War, Of Chastity, Of Love for One's Neighbour, Of Womankind, Of Priests, Of Science, and so on. At the end of each sermon, as it were, come the words of the title, 'Also Sprach Zarathustra'. But there is also a thread of imagery through the book, showing the figure of the great prophet as he cuts himself off from humanity, returning at intervals from solitude in his cave in the mountains to spread amongst men the wisdom he has gathered during his periods of isolation. This is done first in an extended Prologue, then at the ends and beginnings of the Four Parts into which the work is divided, and finally in a growing crescendo of frequency and fervour as Zarathustra exchanges his faithful disciples of the second Part for an even more devoted group of wild beasts in the third and fourth Parts. In addition to the numerous and complex arguments through which the utterances pass, a single main strand emerges which is the notorious cult of the Superman:

> I teach you the Superman. Man is a thing to be sur-
> mounted . . . what is the ape to man? A jest or a thing of
> shame. So shall man be to the Superman. . . . Man is a rope
> stretched betwixt beast and Superman—a rope over an
> abyss. . . . Man is great in that he is a bridge not a goal. . . .
> The Superman is the meaning of the earth.

Towards this mystical conception Zarathustra constantly strives, shedding the inferior gods, creeds, and customs set up and familiarized amongst less-developed mentalities, as he first preaches and then

R.S.—K

gradually searches within himself for more exalted ideals. The climax of such intense introspection causes him to pass through a kind of mental breakdown, from which he emerges a changed and transfigured being. As Nietzsche deals with this 'convalescence' the element of poetry in the work becomes increasingly prevalent, one particular set of verses recurring as a motif—the tremendous eleven-line poem 'O Mensch! Gib Acht!'[10] the lines of which make their initial appearance at the end of the second Dance Song intoned singly between the strokes of the great Midnight Bell.

Nietzsche himself once said, in his autobiography *Ecce Homo*, that it would even be possible to consider all *Zarathustra* as a musical composition. Strauss could not have known of this remark, since *Ecce Homo* was not published until twelve years later, but it at least indicates that interpretation of the work in terms of music was inherent even in its author's mind, and Strauss had the perception to recognize that such a possibility existed. He reduced the task to three main lines of attack; the chapter headings, of which he selected eight as being particularly suggestive to his musical sensibilities; the conflict between the unyielding figure of 'nature' and the Spirit of Man with its sense of purpose and achievement; and finally the evolution of Man himself from a primitive being towards the Superman through the symbolical figure of Zarathustra. The first of these gave him the sections of the projected composition with their varied characteristics; the second he depicted through a parallel conflict of opposing tonalities, while the third supplied an overall design, a matter of primary concern in so dangerously wide and diffuse a subject. Even so he wisely described the tone poem as 'Frei nach Fr. Nietzsche',[11] realizing that it was simply not possible to convey the contents of Nietzsche's masterpiece in musical terms. At the time of the first Berlin performance December 1896, he wrote specifically: 'I did not intend to write philosophical music or portray Nietzsche's great work musically. I meant rather to convey in music an idea of the evolution of the human race from its origin, through the various phases of development, religious as well as scientific, up to Nietzsche's idea of the *Übermensch*.[12] The whole symphonic poem is intended as my homage to the genius of Nietzsche, which found its greatest exemplification in his book *Also Sprach Zarathustra*.'

[10] 'O Man, Take heed!'
[11] 'Freely after Nietzche.'
[12] 'Superman.'

5

The score is prefaced with a quotation not from any part of the book referring to the Superman, but with the very first opening lines of Zarathustra's Prologue, describing his withdrawal from home and family and giving in full the great apostrophe to the rising sun. Hence the music begins with all the magnificence of a spectacular sunrise. Strauss chose the pure and simple tonality of C to symbolize Nature, and the opening section is entirely built in that key. There is something of the origin of all things in the deep C held over four slow bars which derives from the similarly primeval E flat of Wagner's *Ring*. Out of this deep fundamental C springs the Nature theme, the simplest of all *Naturtheme*, a rising C G C:

Ex. 13

It is declaimed three times by four trumpets in unison and leads to *tutti* enunciations of the major and minor modes in alternation. This vacillation between major and minor is itself symbolical: the Nature theme as it stands (Ex. 13) suggests neither mode, being only a bare fifth. Its modal clothing through the addition of the major or minor third has a human significance and the doubtful ambiguity of the alternation indicates man's perplexity at the sublime but insoluble mysteries of nature.[13] This impressive introduction with its thundering timpani triplets reaches a majestic climax, to which the addition of the organ supplies a solemn liturgical element which Strauss emphasizes by leaving the organ holding on by itself for a full two beats after the orchestra has ceased.

The main scheme of the work now begins. The deep C which has still remained takes on the first semblance of individual shape and after some gloomy meanderings leads to a new motif. Man has stood in awe

[13] These are formidable intentions, and Ernest Newman protested that in this work particularly Strauss tries to imbue musical phraseology with meanings it cannot possibly suggest. Nevertheless it is often necessary to have done one's home-work in order to understand programme music, and once Strauss's purpose has been explained, whether in connexion with the extrovert adventures of Till Eulenspiegel or the mystical ideologies of Nietzsche, its logical aptness becomes apparent and subsidiary to the sheer quality of the music.

before the overwhelming presence of Nature and now the theme of his inquiring spirit rears itself:

Ex. 14[14]

Its key, B (minor at present, though this tonality also alternates major and minor in due course), becomes identified symbolically with the Mind of Man.

Strauss is at first concerned with Man in his most undeveloped state and he labels the section *Von den Hinterweltlern*. This has sometimes been translated by 'Primitive Man' which is not in fact strictly correct, the literal equivalent being 'Of the Backworldsmen'. The analogy is clearly intended with the more usual 'Hinterwäldlern' meaning 'Back-woodsmen,' i.e. beings with the most naïve form of intellect, though in the present instance through the substitution of 'world' for 'wood' Nietzsche intended to suggest beings in a primitive state of spiritual development. So involved a conception is capable of being readily misunderstood and, in fact, Specht actually goes so far as to write:

> That is to say, those who believe and seek behind this world for other better and truer things; a quest which expresses itself in all religion.

On the contrary, the quotation of the traditional plainchant of the Credo, played on the horns immediately after Ex. 14, is palpably cynical, epitomizing the dreaded dogma of the established Church barring the way towards free spiritual evolution. Indeed, Nietzsche's corresponding section depicts this quest for some divine creator of the world as a crude manifestation of purely human imperfection with no origin 'from the beyond'. Hence, since Strauss is now dealing with primitive conceptions, he passes from the dry theme of clerical dogma into a passage of devout fervour depicting the naïve emotional comfort through belief in a benevolent divinity however man-inspired. The section was even originally labelled *Vom Göttlichen*, and the relevant lines from Nietzsche's chapter may be taken to be: 'Thus once upon a time did I also cast my illusions beyond man, like all backworldsmen.

---

[14] Note the enormously wide span of this theme, another Straussian characteristic.

Beyond man, indeed? Ah, brethren, that God whom I created was human work and human madness, like all the Gods!'

A luscious melody for strings divided into sixteen parts with soft organ accompaniment builds up to an ecstatic climax. The individual use as soloists of specific players from the string groups marks the beginning of Strauss's treatment of the orchestra as an overgrown chamber ensemble, a technique which he later exploited to the full in such works as *Ariadne auf Naxos*. The art of melodizing had always been second nature to Strauss and the theme of this section had already been quoted for purposes of comparison with as early a work as the *Stimmungsbilder* for Piano, op.9[15] Apart from the sheer contours of the cantilena, however, the modulations by chromatic descent to a $^6_4$ chord in a distant key are particularly characteristic:

Ex. 15

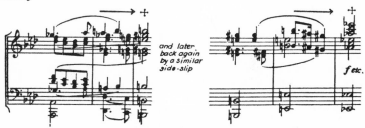

The bitter-sweet tang of the cor anglais breaks into the reflective aftermath of these devotions, and the picture fades away as a solo viola wanders hopelessly upwards, leading to the following section 'Of the Great Longing'.

This in Nietzsche comes towards the end of the third part of *Zarathustra*, between the 'Convalescent' and the second great 'Dance-Song'. Strauss, however, uses the title to suggest the Spirit of Man's first yearning towards self-emancipation from ignorance and narrow-minded superstition. The tonality of B reappears and from it springs Ex. 14, which now grows a new tail in saccharine thirds:

Ex. 16

[15] See Ex. 6 Chapter 1, page 8.

But Man's first bid for spiritual freedom immediately brings him into conflict with Nature on the one hand and his self-imposed religious dogma on the other. The intrusion of the Nature theme immutably in C major upon the prevailing B major tonality is the first instance of a polytonal effect, later of fundamental importance, which has given rise to excited comment ever since the appearance of the work:

Ex. 17

The Church is represented now not only by the Credo theme, but by the opening notes of the traditional Magnificat given out by the organ. Zarathustra's resistance to these influences takes the form first of the opening phrase of the 'devout' music but, soon after, of a new and impetuous motif:

Ex. 18

which gradually overwhelms all other themes in its increasing vehemence, eventually sweeping the music into the wild section 'Of Joys and Passions'. This is an independent and self-contained section with the principal theme a fiercely passionate subject of the kind Strauss had already put into *Tod und Verklärung* (Chapter 3 Ex. 24,).

Ex. 19

This section takes Nietzsche's chapter for the suggestiveness of its title rather than for its philosophy, which concerns itself with self-abnegation and not at all with the passionate sensuality Strauss's music portrays. Nevertheless its setting in C minor is significant, since it indicates the low derivation of Man's emotional life from his nature rather than from his spirit, and this idea leads to the one important instance in which Strauss incorporates the poem's message of renunciation. At the climax the trombones blare out a new theme of fundamental importance,

Ex. 20

a motif usually labelled 'Disgust or Satiety Motif'. It can thus be taken to represent the protest of the spirit against such emotional indulgence, although the parallel passage in Nietzsche is more exalted in its philosophy. Ex. 20 is one of the vital themes of the entire tone poem. It stands mid-way between the two opposing tonalities of B and C through its affiliation to both, although each is distorted—the one into the diminished triad, the other the augmented. This linking harmonic function brings it into increasing prominence during the working-out sections.

Das Grablied[16] follows directly out of the music of 'Joys and Passions' and provides a balancing counter-section to it. The vivid tonality of C has given way to the softer tones of B minor, and the orchestral colour becomes veiled and shadowy as Ex. 19 gradually rises to a second though lesser climax, subsiding once more with the descending chromatic scales of Ex. 19(b) constantly clouding the sinking texture of the score. An important difference exists between this and the previous section in that Ex. 19 is no longer in full and solitary spate; it is now constantly accompanied by entries of Ex. 14 which vainly try again and again to rise above the thick polyphony. At the actual climax the music moves to C major and the *Naturmotif* (Ex. 13) rings out momentarily on the trumpet, as if the sun had briefly pierced the heavy clouds. But immediately a return is made to B minor and its related keys as the Spirit of Man continues the exhausting struggle against the forces which are pressing it ever deeper towards some strange and sinister pit. The prevailing mood is one of nostalgia, matching Nietzsche's chapter, but its purpose here is essentially to serve the musical design by providing a transition to the following passage *Von der Wissenschaft*—'Of Science' or 'Learning'.

[16] 'Song of the Grave.'

Strauss takes the Fugue as epitomizing Learning as such, and writes a dry fugue for the deepest instruments, the subject of which begins with the Nature theme (Ex. 13), passes on from C to B (thus embodying both Nature and Spirit), and employs all twelve degrees of the chromatic scale so arranged as to present five different tonalities in three contrasted rhythms.

Ex. 21

Here is erudition avowedly for its own sake, and opinions differ as to its success on purely musical grounds. It is indeniably dour, but there is an air of strangely mysterious quality about the ingenious counterpoint, which is quite gripping. In particular the passage provides a welcome moment of repose in the hitherto unrelieved tension and excitement.

In the course of the stretto the key shifts firmly to B, and Ex. 14 springs up impetuously as Man's spirit rises above such arid wastes of abstract science. Exulting in its sudden freedom, the theme soars away—into the saccharine thirds of Ex. 16. This time, however, it takes the phrase ⌐ a ⌐ as a point of departure to indulge in hitherto undreamt of flights of fancy:

Ex. 22

Nor is this enough, for the intoxication of the moment sends it into a fantastic dance in upper woodwind accompanied by two harps and high strings rushing and trilling:

Ex. 23

But the Spirit suddenly finds that its dance is premature. The Nature motif interrupts with the same polytonal effect as in the opening bars of Ex. 17. It is now no longer external religion but tormenting doubt from Zarathustra's own soul which alternates with the reiterated statements of Ex. 13. A point is reached at which the constant appearances of the Disgust motif (Ex. 20), now in diminution, burst out feverishly and combine with Ex. 21 in a savage resumption of the fugue. Strauss has now reached the crucial section *Der Genesende* ('The Convalescent'), the significance of which has already been mentioned above (p. 134). It is one of the most vivid chapters in the poem with Zarathustra leaping from his couch in his cave like a madman and crying out with a terrible voice. He then falls like one dead, and fasts for seven days, after which he gradually recovers. But he is a transformed being and now fully understands his mission on earth. This scene inspired Strauss to a series of quite extraordinary feats of invention. The fugue reaches a huge climax in which the whole orchestra thunders out a C major chord, the brass declaiming the Nature motif. There is a terrifying silence, and a sharp B minor chord stabs out, followed by a gloomy passage in which Ex. 20 shuffles about on all the deepest instruments, such as basses, double bassoon, bass clarinet, and second tuba.

The Spirit of Man now makes the most tremendous effort in the form of repeated eruptions of Ex. 14(a) and after two failures in which it slips backwards, suddenly sweeps up into what may best be described as the orchestral stratosphere. 'Up, abysmal thought, from the depths! I am thy cock, thy dawn, thou sleepy worm! Up! Up! My voice shall crow thee awake!'

Ex. 24

The passage which ensues is one of the most remarkable in the orchestral repertoire from the point of view of sheer colouristic virtuosity. Above all, it is handled with that lightness and humour which Strauss had so recently acquired. Ex. 20 on the E-flat clarinet now sounds like

Till Eulenspiegel;[17] Ex. 18 in augmentation makes a well-timed reappearance; the Spirit theme springs up in the solo cello and sets off the
Dance (Ex. 23). The chattering and trilling becomes positively frenzied,
until a climax releases the tension and the fully fledged Superman is
ready for his 'Tanzlied'—the Dance-Song.

Of all the controversies started by this curious tone poem none have
raged more furiously than those around the Dance of the Superman.
For in it Strauss revealed the less discriminating side of his genius as he
had not done since his ill-fated use of 'Funiculi, Funiculà' in *Aus Italien*:
the great Nietzschean *Tanzlied* proves to be a Viennese Waltz. Indeed, as
time went on Strauss was drawn more and more towards the waltz,
using it with far greater relevance than here and at times with a success
which almost rivalled that of his famous namesake. There are few
things more strange than that its first appearance in Strauss's output
should be in *Also Sprach Zarathustra*, and in an odd way this very fact
adds to the significance of the work, even though it scarcely matches its
programmatic intentions.

The sweet chortlings of the solo violin grow out of the Nature
motif and are declaimed against a gentle accompaniment which is a
combination of the motifs of Nature and Man:

Ex. 25

This continues its amiable way, together with occasional hints of Ex. 14
in a wonderfully laid-out passage for strings divided into seventeen
parts accompanied by two harps. It is interrupted by the earlier Dance
figure (Ex. 23) in full tonal equivocation, the statement being harmonized in both B and C with equal validity:

[17] Arthur Hahn in his detailed guide to *Zarathustra* interprets this section in the
light of a passage from the section 'Of Reading and Writing' from the first part of
Nietzsche's work. Although this seems apt with its references to laughing and
flying and coupled with a pair of lines from the Prologue about dancing stars
being created out of chaos, Hahn seems to have chosen passages from the poem
rather too freely in order to fit in with the impressions made upon him by
Strauss's music. This is not the only occasion, as will shortly transpire.

Ex. 26

The dance has hitherto, with its background of the Nature motif, been firmly in C major, but this new dance figure nearly swings the music across into B as peals of chromatically descending laughter shake the earlier harmonic stability. Ex. 13 builds massively up once more, however, from the bottom of the orchestra and re-establishes the key of C, in which it is aided and abetted by suggestions of Ex. 18 and an unusually powerful enunciation of Ex. 14 in cellos, horns, and bassoons. This to-ing and fro-ing between the tonalities becomes more and more an integral feature of the work from here on, especially in respect of the conflict between the motifs of Nature and Spirit (Exx. 13 and 14), although it is important to observe how often the Spirit theme will gladly try out both keys alternately.

This conflict is incorporated into a development section which also includes a mellow variation of the theme of the 'Joys and Passions' section (Ex. 19). The transformation of this motif is certainly justified here on the grounds of purely musical form, but Arthur Hahn has led several subsequent commentators to view it in the light of a programmatic reference to the *Nachtlied* (Night Song) of Nietzsche's poem. Yet I have not been able to find the slightest evidence of this, and it is above all indicative that whereas all the other sections of the tone-poem are carefully labelled, there is no heading whatever at this point in Strauss's score. On the contrary, Strauss is organizing his material in a tremendous last musical build-up towards the most important and final section, the *Nachtwandlerlied*—the Song of the Night Wanderer. As the dance grows wilder, the 'Disgust' theme (Ex. 20) constantly interrupts the flow of the various themes, changing the tonality by its very nature. Its vehemence increases until its savage interjections destroy each motif in turn. Its fury is only momentarily held at bay by a mighty statement of Ex. 14 which sweeps the music up to the climax of the dance, a tremendous C major outburst combining the Nature motif and the Waltz theme (Ex. 25). It then returns exultantly as the *Nachtwandlerlied* follows, hurling its defiance against the strokes of the Midnight Bell.

This great section marks the climax not only of the tone poem but of Nietzsche's book.[18] In it Zarathustra is surrounded by his disciples, and interrupts their joyful dancing and demonstrations of affection by passing through a kind of drunken fit. He recovers just as the Great Bell begins to toll and quietly interprets the solemn strokes by rhapsodizing line by line around the poem 'O Mensch! Gib Acht' before redeclaiming it in full for the last time, its Midnight Message of the Victory of Eternal Joy over Woe now expounded and demonstrated in full. Strauss translates this vision, as he understands it, into musical imagery by gradually taking away the intensity of emphasis from the repetitions of Ex. 20, which spread out in ever widening augmentations as the waves of sound die slowly away, each stroke of the bell being softer than the last. Zarathustra's satiety has reached its height by directing itself even against Nature, even against his own dance-song. But his anger dissolves at the sound of the bell which once inspired his great song of joy, and with a melting side-slip from the garish tonality of C into the velvet harmonies of B major, he gently invokes the radiant melody of his spiritual freedom (Ex. 22), still clothed in its honeyed consecutive thirds.

From this point the music floats upwards into an Epilogue of great beauty, with the Spirit of Man (Ex. 14) appearing as a counter-theme on the bassoon—a magical touch. The motif of satiety (Ex. 20) disturbs the prevailing peace of mind for an instant, but the first motif of freedom (Ex. 16) makes an unexpected return on two clarinets in thirds, and it is clear that the Spirit of Man has found happiness and fulfilment in its B major heaven. This is not to say, however, that Nature is in any way defeated or even superseded. In one of the most notorious endings in musical history Strauss closed this most problematical of all his works with the polytonal passage Ex. 17(a), Nature, rock-like in its immutability on trombones and double basses in the key of C, alternating with the ethereal B major chords of Man's Spirit. At the end, for all Man's achievements and hard-won peace of mind, Nature inevitably has the last word, as Nature always will, whatever beings Earth may conjure up to dispute her sovereignty.

[18] In the definitive version Nietzsche changed the title of this chapter from the *Nachtwandlerlied* to *Das Trunkene Lied* (The Drunken Song).

It will be remembered that Strauss openly avowed the freedom of
his interpretation of Nietzsche's work, and his final view of the problem of Man's spiritual development by no means corresponds with
the conclusion of the poem. Nietzsche ends on a note of climax with
the idea of 'Eternal Recurrence'. Zarathustra emerges from his cave in
the last lines, glowing and strong in the spirit of a new dawn for his
life's work. Such a conception had no place in Strauss's musical scheme
and he closed his tone poem in a mood of utter tranquillity, but showing
the conflict between Man and Nature basically unresolved and as
irreconcilable as the two nearest and yet harmonically so distant keys of
B and C.

6

Zarathustra occupies an odd position in Strauss's output. Built around a
subject which is in itself particularly out of spirit with the times, the
tone poem is more often than not condemned by present-day criticism as representing the least convincing side of Strauss's art. Certainly
when portrayed as the mere bombast of naïve megalomania, there might
seem little to commend it, and since even those who are not antagon-
ized by Nietzsche's ideas are prone to dismiss it as an ingenuous handling of an abstruse philosophy by an artist who was apt to be least
profound when he tried hardest, one might have expected the work to
have faded like *Guntram* into a merciful limbo, only to be resurrected,
as one critic recently put it, 'so that conductors and orchestras may
enjoy themselves with its opportunities for virtuosity'. Yet it obstinately
refuses to die and reappears in frequent recordings and even periodically
in concert programmes, never failing to make a considerable stir.

There is a conflict here which cannot lightly be ignored, for these
adverse criticisms contain an undeniable element of truth. Nevertheless Zarathustra is made up of music much of which is not only extremely well written, but highly interesting and intensely original. It is
not for nothing that a musician like Bartók should have been spurred
into devoting his whole life to composition as the direct inspiration of a
performance of this particular piece. Ultimately it is the sheer quality
of the musical material and its organization which counts, while the
greater or lesser degree to which it succeeds in the misty philosophizing
which conjured it into being is wholly immaterial. In actual fact *Zarathustra*, for all that it speaks the same musical language as all Strauss's

works, is immensely distinctive and possesses a flavour quite unlike the other tone poems, a flavour which somehow suggests the supernatural, even the transcendental, in a way which is hauntingly beautiful and vivid. Only once again did Strauss achieve this extra-musical quality, and write music which is not intimately bound up with purely human characteristics and emotions—in the *Alpensinfonie*, although, despite many fine and impressive sections, he was on the whole less successful in the later work. He attempted a similar vein yet again for the weird supernatural philosophies of *Die Frau ohne Schatten*, but in the more spiritually obscure passages of that uneven opera lapsed into the commonplace which always threatened his more exalted efforts. In *Zarathustra* the lapses of taste may be more readily forgiven, since they are invariably brief, being followed quickly by more sophisticated development sections. Moreover, even the relatively undistinguished invention is clothed in settings of the liveliest imagination for an orchestra substantially larger and more varied than any employed by Strauss so far, with the quadruple wind of *Till Eulenspiegel* reinforced by six horns, four trumpets, two tubas, two harps and organ. It has been said that 'all things may be forgiven an artist but boredom never', and *Zarathustra* is certainly never boring. This in itself is no mean accomplishment, especially with regard to the formal aspect of the work; for the first time in the tone poems Strauss found himself committed by the sheer nature of the subject to working entirely outside conventional form patterns. *Zarathustra* cannot be classified, however remotely, as a Sonata movement, Rondo, or any other such structure, and the fact that its overall design is entirely convincing is a considerable tribute to Strauss's mastery of symphonic thought. The form, although entirely free-fantasia, can be roughly summarized as follows:

I (1) Introduction (including brief linking Exposition)
  (2) 1st Episode (A♭ section)
  (3) 1st Development (largely of themes in (1))

II (4) 2nd Episode (C minor)
  (5) 2nd Development (basically of (4))

III (6) 3rd Episode (Fugue)
  (7) 3rd Development (including working out of Fugue and first climax)

IV (8) 4th Development
   (9) 4th Episode (Waltz)
   (10) 5th Development (incorporating (4) and leading to second climax)
   (11) Coda

7

Also Sprach Zarathustra was completed in August 1896 and first performed under Strauss's own baton on 27th November of the same year. By this time Levi had retired and Strauss had been nominated as first conductor, or Hofkapellmeister, in Munich. He was not, however, to remain long in this much-coveted position in his home town, for in 1898 he accepted an offer from Berlin to become conductor of the Royal Opera House as successor to Weingartner. Nevertheless, though short, it was an important period for Strauss, who was composing prolifically, so that the last years at Munich saw the production of quantities of songs, including the best he ever wrote, the curious melodrama on Tennyson's *Enoch Arden*, some choral pieces—and, by way of climax, a new tone poem, completed in December 1897, taking the form of yet another character study, this time of Cervantes' immortal figure, Don Quixote.

Strauss was by no means the first in the field in depicting the adventures of the grotesque knight and his faithful squire, Sancho Panza. Of classical composers, Purcell and Telemann wrote Suites on the subject, Telemann's in particular being wittily programmatic for its time. Paisiello wrote a full-length opera, while both Mendelssohn and Donizetti built operas out of episodes extracted from the book. Nearer to Strauss's own time, Rubinstein actually wrote a *Symphonische Characterbild*, but there is no reason to believe that Strauss was in the least influenced by, or even knew, Rubinstein's work. Strauss tackled the problem in a way which was entirely novel, though based on a classical form. He cast his piece as a set of variations on a composite theme which delineates the figures of the two protagonists. Each variation follows some adventure or episode, except for one which most ingeniously suggests the arguments which constantly occurred between the down-to-earth and common-sensical Sancho and his fantastically deluded master.

The tone poem begins with an elaborate Introduction, outlining the gradual deterioration of Don Quixote's mental clarity through his preoccupation with books on Knight Errantry, and ends with a most beautiful coda which describes the hero's death in his bed after the enforced abandonment of his misguided career. Obviously in a forty-minute work Strauss was only able to select a few of the episodes recounted in Cervantes' long and rambling narrative. Much of the virtue in his achievement lies in the skill with which the adventures are chosen and rearranged, without regard to their sequence in the original. Indeed, Strauss frequently changed the actual course of events whenever his musical scheme required it.

In a way, a set of Theme and Variations scarcely constitutes a symphonic poem in the normally accepted sense of the term, especially when adhered to so scrupulously from a formal point of view. As in the case of *Till Eulenspiegel* Strauss did not use the word *Tondichtung* at all in the title of *Don Quixote*, which is simply and a little whimsically described as 'Fantastic Variations on a Theme of Knightly Character'. Nevertheless the work is rightly classed amongst Strauss's tone poems on account of both its programmatic intentions and the essentially symphonic nature of its more important sections.

The title heading merely describes *Don Quixote* as being set for *Grosses Orchester*,[19] no mention being made of the soloistic use of individuals. But *Don Quixote* is remarkable in its singling out of the leaders of the different orchestral groups as soloists. The leading cello is particularly favoured in this respect, since during much of the work this instrument takes the actual role of Don Quixote himself. As a glance at the score clearly shows, Strauss actually intended the part for the leader of the orchestral cello section, careful instructions being given to the inside player at the first desk for such occasions as might cause ambiguity when the leader is acting as soloist. Yet Strauss defeated his own object by composing so spectacular and difficult a part that the work is generally given as a Concerto, with a soloist who sits apart from the main group of cellos and remains silent during the many extensive *tutti*

---

[19] A certain anomaly exists between the German use of *Grosses Orchester* and *Kleines Orchester* and the English equivalents of these terms—Large (Full) and Small Orchestra respectively. *Grosses Orchester* originally meant something far more specific than the normal translation would imply. The simple presence of the trombones was at one time sufficient to justify the use of the more dignified appellation, there being thus no way of differentiation in German between a Brahms symphony orchestra and the huge apparatus required by the post-Berliozian schools of orchestrators.

sections. Strauss himself often performed the work in this way, especially in later years; yet such a presentation is misleading, not only because of the elaborate scoring for varying groups of cellos, but also
on account of the way in which the solo part corresponds with the
writing for the first viola, which to some extent plays the role of Sancho
Panza. In the long run it transpires that neither instrument presents an
entire characterization exclusively, the viola sharing with tenor tuba
and bass clarinet, the cello with solo violin. These partnerships are in
some considerable degree obscured when *Don Quixote* is performed as
a celebrity Concerto item.

8

The tone poem begins with an Introduction immediately presenting
Don Quixote himself, 'a gentleman verging on fifty', as Cervantes
describes him, 'of tough constitution, lean-bodied, thin-faced, a great
early riser and a lover of hunting', whose true family name Cervantes
suggests may have been Quexana, the title 'Don Quixote de la Mancha'
being only adopted for professional prestige when he embarked upon
his career. His themes are announced lightly and gayly in the major
key, thus presenting the distinguished gentleman still in his right
mind, albeit obsessed even now with his library of books on Knight
Errantry 'which he loved and enjoyed so much that he entirely forgot
his hunting and even the care of his estates. So odd and foolish, indeed,
did he grow on this subject that he sold many acres of cornland to buy
these books on chivalry to read, and in this way brought home every
one he could get.'

This interesting personage is presented by three distinct and separate
musical ideas. The first, marked 'ritterlich und galant,'[20] suggests his
essentially chivalrous nature, if somewhat volatile of imagination;

Ex. 27

The second theme is the figure which, invented originally for *Guntram*
and incorporated into *Till Eulenspiegel* (see above, Ex. 12), now comes

[20] 'In knightly and gallant manner.'

R.S.–L

into its own in portraying Quixote's courteous and gentlemanly manner:[21]

Ex. 28

Lastly comes a curious theme of an oddly twisted *naïveté*:

Ex. 29

The subtle way in which this cadential motif is altered on each occasion is one of the most interesting features of the entire work.[22] Moreover, Exx. 28 and 29 make admirable capital out of Strauss's penchant, first noticed in *Aus Italien*, for harmonic side-slips. Before and after *Don Quixote* he used the effect for its own sake as a bitter-sweet, delicately stylized mannerism. Here he found its ideal purpose in bringing to life the peculiar distorted reasoning of Quixote's mind.

Having presented the hero's character, Strauss now pursues the course of events leading to his insanity. We see him reading the tortuous phraseology of his books (a placid statement of Ex. 27 degenerating into aimless meanderings) until the oboe enters with a sweet and noble melody. Quixote has determined upon a Lady Patron to whom, after the manner of all true Knights Errant, his valiant exploits will be dedicated:

Ex. 30

There is no passion in this theme, and indeed Don Quixote found himself hard put to it to find a lady with whom he should be in love,

[21] Strauss seems to have been fond of this idea, for he even contemplated using it yet again in the ballet sketch *Kythere* (see below, Chapter 7, p. 201).

[22] Tenschert, in his book on Strauss, lists ten versions which he ingeniously arranges vertically above one another on a single page.

since there was no one of the kind in the whole neighbourhood in which
he lived. At this point Ex. 30 has a certain vague dream-like quality and
stands for the ideal Lady of Knighthood rather than any actual woman.
Thereafter, however, the melody is used to represent the exquisite
Dulcinea del Toboso, as in his emergency Quixote christened Aldonza
Lorenzo, a strapping farm-girl of his acquaintance who happened to
live close by in the little hamlet of El Toboso, and whom he had once
secretly admired.

The idea of the Inamorata leads automatically to the need for springing to her defence, whatever dire peril this may entail. A fanfare of
muted trumpets is sounded and Quixote is visualizing some shining
victory over a monstrous giant or dragon, represented by the tenor and
bass tubas with string double basses also muted. From this point to the
end of the Introduction the strings and brass remain muted, thus giving
a nightmarish unreality to the texture. The lady's astonished delight at
her deliverance knows no bounds, and a brief love duet is played as the
meandering version of Ex. 27 is combined with Ex. 30.

Ex. 31

Her gratitude inspires new protestations of devotion in the breast of the
enraptured knight, now ever increasingly identified by Don Quixote as
himself:

Ex. 32

answered in silken tones by the lady:

Ex. 33

upon which a serenade ensues until the whole vision suddenly collapses like a pricked bubble. But Don Quixote's (and Strauss's) imagination is fired, and as Don Quixote, in reality still alone in his study, reads deeper and deeper into his books, these ideas begin to crowd together in his brain in ever more elaborate profusion, together with new feverish motifs such as the following:

Ex. 34

The complexity of the counterpoint in the pages of score which follow was without precedent even for Strauss, and one can well imagine his father's face when he first saw his wayward son's new extravagancies of orchestration. Yet once again there is no error of calculation, and although this passage is a byword for the number of wholly imperceptible notes it contains, its effect is successful beyond the wildest dreams of Strauss's more careful and reactionary contemporaries. Well might Reger comment, 'It is fabulous what the man writes there!' All the preceding examples appear and reappear in the growing *mêlée* of whirling sound, until at last Don Quixote's overheated brain snaps. Ex. 29 is hurled out in savage discords which work their way round to the dominant of the whole work, the note A. For a time this is jabbed against the most dissonant notes possible, but finally it is heard alone. Quixote has made up his distorted mind; he will himself turn Knight Errant without delay. With the cold quiet logic of insanity he sets out upon his adventures.

9

Strauss now presents the themes for his variations in the form of a character study of 'Don Quixote, the Knight of the Sorrowful Countenance', followed immediately by one of Sancho Panza, the two names being actually indicated in the score. It was, in fact, Sancho who suggested to Quixote the title of the 'Sorrowful Countenance' when, some time after the adventures of the Windmills and the Sheep, Sancho was watching his master by the light of a torch. As he explained when pressed to do so, 'Really Your Worship has lately got the most dismal face I've ever seen. It must be either from weariness after the battle or from Your Worship's losing his teeth' (which were knocked out by the herdsmen in the adventure of the Sheep).

Ex. 35

The subtle way in which this new form of Quixote's principal theme is derived from both Ex. 27 and the meandering version of Ex. 31(a) shows great perception in portraying the misguided knight trying to turn into reality the things he had once been reading so avidly. It is succeeded by Ex. 28, basically unaltered but presented as a trio for cor anglais, solo violin, and solo cello, the two latter instruments appearing already as co-principals in the manner described above. Finally the cadential theme (Ex. 29) appears in its turn, suitably adapted in order to lead into the minor mode appropriate for 'the sorrowful countenance'.

Next comes Sancho Panza, also depicted by three themes. The first shows him as little more than a country bumpkin, although the figure is derived from the theme of the Fool in *Guntram*, who was anything but simple-minded.

Ex. 36

The second of Sancho Panza's motifs describes the rapid and often idiotic wagging of his tongue;

Ex. 37

while the third illustrates Sancho's most amusing habit of talking in strings of proverbs. It consists of a group of splendidly commonplace phrases pronounced by the solo viola with the solemn air of uttering profound truths. One can just see Sancho's face as he earnestly quotes a proverb translated into musical terms thus:

Ex. 38

Yet Sancho's remarks are not all of moronic simplicity; some reflect genuine good humour and others loyalty and affection. The squire may, in his credulous and gullible way, have been as mad as the master, but he has many admirable traits in his character and is a most attractive personality.

Variation I is the adventure of the Windmills, Book I, Chapter VIII[23]. Don Quixote and Sancho Panza are heard setting out on their travels together (solo cello and bass clarinet). Above them like a guiding star in the heavens floats the vision of Dulcinea now firmly identified with Ex. 30. The appearance of the monstrous giants (alias Windmills) is unmistakable, as is also the slight breeze which causes the sails (or giant's arms) to move just as Quixote attacks so valiantly. The knight's fall is sharp and severe, but with great fortitude of spirit and with prayers to his Lady Dulcinea, he allows Sancho Panza to help him re-mount his poor horse Rocinante and prepare for further adventures despite the loss of his spear. All this is described in the music simply, graphically, and with great sense of humour. Gradually Quixote recovers sufficient strength to continue; the brass quietly, but with growing assurance announce Ex. 27(a); a confident version of the ca-dence motif Ex. 29 answers, and Variation II follows without a break.

This is the equally famous adventure of the Sheep from Book I, Chapter XVIII. Strauss shows his two heroes embarking on the adven-ture in full strength and high spirits. Don Quixote has clearly found the power of three men as he is now played by three solo cellos in unison. There is no foundation in Cervantes for this recovery of health and stamina, but it fits in excellently with the musical scheme and balances well with the triumphant end to the variation, another deviation from the book.

[23] The references to Cervantes' text and other relevant explanations are given in full in the piano arrangement, but were for some reason omitted from the orches-tral score.

Strauss's onomatopoeic representation of the bleating of the sheep which Don Quixote took for the mighty armies of Alifanfaron and Pentapolin, King of the Garamantas, is one of the best-known features of the tone poem. It is produced by the woodwind and muted brass playing a succession of minor seconds in fluttertonguing. Its validity was closely questioned at one time, but if descriptive music is once accepted in principle, then this device is undoubtedly more true to the spirit of art-music than, for instance, the introduction of a gramophone recording of a real nightingale which Respighi used in his 'Pini di Roma'.

The piping of the shepherds can be heard behind the bleatings, and also a shimmering haze supplied by the violas, perhaps to represent the dust-cloud raised by the sheep as the two flocks approach each other. The theme of the shepherd's pipes is of importance both for its return at a significant point in this work and for its reappearance in the next of Strauss's tone poems, *Ein Heldenleben*.

Ex. 39

Don Quixote charges and secures a mighty victory. The lamentable sequel in which the shepherds throw stones at the crazy intruder, breaking two of his ribs and knocking his teeth out, is omitted. Strauss was perhaps right to allow at least one of his knight's adventures to have a happy ending.

Strauss called Variation III 'Sancho's conversations, questions, demands and proverbs, Don Quixote's instructing, appeasings and promises'. This describes in detail the course of the variation, which is in two distinct parts. The first section shows knight and squire in conversation. For some time Don Quixote answers Sancho's importunate arguments and protestations calmly and patiently. Eventually, however, Sancho's garrulous prattling does not allow his master to get a word in edgeways. The attempt of the solo violin to intersperse Ex. 29(a) between the phrases of the viola are most amusing, expecially when it only manages to get in the first two notes before the viola is off again on one of its strings of proverbs, including all of the original four and adding five new ones. When at last Sancho has to draw breath Don

Quixote bursts in with vehement fury and, after the turbulent on-slaught of Ex. 27(a) on the brass, the second section of the variation begins in the glowing key of F sharp major.

Now for the first time we see the world of Knight Errantry and its glorious prospects through Don Quixote's own eyes; the giants and dragons he will slay, the maidens he will rescue, the kingdoms he will conquer and the governorships which it will be in his power to bestow (including the famous isle which he promised Sancho Panza early in their acquaintanceship and which the poor squire never forgot or ceased hoping for). Underneath the rich velvety orchestration a long cantilena flows, based on yet another version of Ex. 27:

Ex. 40

(zart, ausdrucksvoll)

Ex. 30 takes up the thread and the melodizing builds to a climax of passionate rhetoric before subsiding gently in terms of such wistful beauty that even Sancho Panza's doubts seem finally allayed (a gentle version of Ex. 36 can be heard at one moment).[24] One last proclamation, on the brass, of Don Quixote's motif (Ex. 27(a)) and, with eyes raised to heaven, the noble knight lets his argument stand.

At this point Strauss's humour shows itself at its keenest. Sancho Panza suddenly thinks of an objection and the bass clarinet gives an impertinent query. Abruptly Don Quixote turns on him like a Fury and we plunge into Variation IV.

Don Quixote is now so angry that he rushes forward as vehemently as poor Rocinante can carry him. Sancho Panza's themes are nowhere in evidence and we must presume him following up woefully in the rear. Suddenly Quixote notices a procession approaching from afar and singing a liturgical chant;

Ex. 41

[24] Strauss's technique of harmonic side-slipping is epitomized in this passage. The music melts out of the tonic key of F sharp into such remote keys as G natural and B flat, and back again with the ease of a Jekyll and Hyde.

This adventure is the last one in Part I of Cervantes' book (Chapter LII). The procession is shown to be, in fact, a group of penitents carrying an image of the Holy Virgin in a petition for rain after a period of severe drought. It comes steadily nearer, accompanied oddly and somewhat mysteriously by constant repetitions of the little figure ⌐ a ⌐ from Ex. 34, made here to sound like muttered 'Ave's'. Don Quixote naturally attacks the group, with the intention of rescuing what he takes to be an abducted maiden, and is instantly knocked senseless to the ground, his prostrate figure remaining motionless in the foreground in the shape of a prolonged note D sustained *fortissimo* in the cellos and basses. The procession then fades away once again into the distance, still accompanied by the mutterings of Ex. 34(a). Sancho Panza believes his master to be truly dead this time and mourns him with groans and lamentations which, however, have the effect of bringing the stricken knight back to consciousness, to Sancho's delight. He gives a whoop of joy on all three of his characteristic instruments— viola, bass clarinet, and tenor tuba[25]—and then, with a touch of poetic licence on Strauss's part, falls asleep with two gargantuan snores, which are, however, not just a touch of unnecessary vulgarity, but can be shown to be a valid variation of Ex. 29 reduced to its barest outlines.

With Sancho Panza safely out of the way for a time, Strauss now returns us to a very early part of the story for Variation V; to a period, in fact, before the squire had even made his appearance. In this most moving section, cleverly re-placed for the sake of the musical scheme, Don Quixote performs the traditional ceremony of keeping vigil over his armour before being formally knighted. The episode is related at length in Chapter III of the book, describing the squalid courtyard of some great castle. In the original, Quixote is disturbed several times by carriers wanting to water their mules from the well in the courtyard, upon whom Quixote inflicts many considerable injuries, leaving them stunned on the ground. He is accordingly recognized as a madman and stoned, all of which tribulations he survives with fortitude. Strauss chose to portray none of this at all; for this episode served as a poetical interlude and he disregarded as musically irrelevant the fact that it

---

[25] Strauss commits an oddity here by writing a phrase which looks like a continuously descending whole tone scale; Since, however, the G flat and F sharp (B.Cl. & Ten. Tuba) are the same note on the two instruments involved, the scale has a hop in it.

should by its very nature precede any of Don Quixote's adventures. Hence instead of depicting still further scenes of violence, he wrote a recitando passage for solo cello in tones of great nobility and pathos. The music centres to a considerable extent around the figure Ex. 34(a), the movement thus growing logically out of the preceding variation. At one impassioned moment Ex. 34 returns in full, thus establishing the identity of the phrase which, derived from it, has acquired so strong a character of its own. Apart from this and isolated references to the second of Quixote's motifs (Ex. 28) the only theme which appears during this interlude is that of Dulcinea, as Don Quixote spends his vigil meditating on the beauties and virtues of his imaginary Lady Patron. There are suggestions of winds springing up as night falls, but otherwise the variation is devoid of action. Here the soloist comes truly into his own in a way that only returns in the coda to the work. He is accompanied for the greater part of the movement only by other cellos from the section behind him, yet the suggestion of the moonlit scene is haunting and vivid. It is in moments such as this that Strauss suddenly found instinctively the profundity of expression for which at other times he sought so strenuously.

10

From the sublime to the ridiculous—for Variation VI portrays the comic episode of Dulcinea's enchantment from Book II, Chapter X. It is perhaps inevitable that Don Quixote should sooner or later decide to visit Dulcinea in person, and so our two heroes visit El Toboso, only to fail utterly in finding her, since neither has the remotest idea where she lives or what she looks like. Don Quixote accordingly puts the entire onus of locating and producing her upon his wretched squire, who, at his wits' end, points out the first three peasant girls who pass mounted on donkeys as the Lady Dulcinea herself accompanied by 'two of her damsels'. Strauss here produced a masterpiece of characterization with an irregular jauntily rustic theme for two oboes in thirds, which conjures up the brash garlic-smelling wench who has appeared in place of the noble aristocratic lady of the knight's expectations. Don Quixote is nonplussed and irritated, but, on being assured by Sancho Panza that she is undoubtedly under an enchantment, pays his respects to her with all dutiful deference with his motif of courtesy (Ex. 28). Sancho is also on his knees before the 'round-faced and flat-nosed country girl', and in order to show his sincerity quotes to her, on the solo viola, not only his own theme (Ex. 36), but a whole phrase from his master's 'vigil' (Variation V), ending with a reference to Dulcinea's own theme (Ex. 30). This is too much for the country girl, who makes off at speed, despite Quixote's frantic protestations, leaving the bewildered knight standing utterly perplexed. His chromatically shifting theme (Ex. 29) is particularly apt here as indicating his confused state of mind as well as playing its customary role of coda, linking the variation with the next.

The outstanding feature of the composition is the extreme variety of the different sections. Mixed in the variations are character sketches, narrative, mood painting, and purely graphic description. Variation VII is an undiluted example of the latter. Its text is one of the incredible leg-pulls played upon Don Quixote and Sancho Panza by the Duke and Duchess (we never learn their names) occupying so substantial a part of Book II; the adventure in question occurs in Chapter XLI. The noble pair play up to Don Quixote, who becomes their guest for a period. During this time they treat him exactly as if he were indeed the Knight Errant he believes himself to be, even to concocting an elaborate hoax concerning a Bearded Woman in Affliction whose Wrongs Quixote is to Right; this involves the knight and his squire in a journey of some 9,681 leagues, which they are to travel through the air on a flying horse controlled by a peg in his forehead as in the Arabian Nights. Don Quixote readily accepts this farrago of nonsense, and even Sancho Panza is, if with some difficulty, persuaded to join his master in being placed blindfold upon the toy animal. They are then led to believe that they are travelling high above the world by means of an orchestra of bellows wielded by the whole retinue of the Duke and Duchess.

Strauss realized well enough that the intricate plot could have no possible place in his scheme, but enjoyed himself hugely in building a colourful orchestral picture based on the different fragments of Don Quixote's and Sancho Panza's themes, Exx. 35 and 36. The whistling of the wind is given by harp glissandi and flutes fluttertonguing with the addition of a Wind Machine, suggesting the flight of the horse with its two passengers through the air. At the same time Strauss slyly reveals the true state of affairs by keeping the feet of the horse firmly on the ground with a continuously sounding pedal D. This is not the most subtle of variations, but it is an entertaining piece of virtuoso orchestration.

Variation VIII is on an altogether higher level and describes the adventures of the Enchanted Boat from Chapter XXIX of Book II. The two travellers come upon a boat tied up by a river-bank. Don Quixote is immediately seized with the idea that it has been deliberately planted there with the intention of carrying him to the scene of some important assignment, and insists upon Sancho Panza joining him in embarking downstream whithersoever the boat shall take them. The gentle undulation of the water is beautifully suggested by some most poetic contrapuntal writing, ingeniously incorporating Don Quixote's two principal themes (Exx. 27(a) and 28). In point of fact, the river takes them to a weir amidst some water-mills and they are in some danger of being dashed to pieces by the great mill-wheels. The boat actually suffers this fate and the two occupants are only saved by being turned overboard into the water. They are rescued by some millers whose efforts to avert the disaster had been mistaken by Don Quixote for diabolical interference with the Hand of Knightly Rescue to the Oppressed. The plunge of the couple into the water is clearly portrayed in the music, together with their arrival on dry land, drenched and miserable; it is extraordinary just how wet the succession of pizzicato notes and chords sounds. The variation ends with a brief prayer marked 'religioso' built on Quixote's motif (Ex. 27a), although Cervantes states that it is Sancho Panza who 'went down on his knees and, with hands joined and eyes fixed to heaven, implored God in a long and devout prayer to deliver him from all his master's rash plans and enterprises in future'.

By contrast with the last elaborate movement, Variation IX is short and straightforward. The exploit it describes comes from the same chapter as the adventure of the Windmills. Don Quixote sees a group of horsemen accompanying a coach containing a Basque Lady travelling to Seville to join her husband. Preceding this group, but not, in fact, part of it, are two Benedictine monks mounted on large mules and wearing riding masks against the dust. Convinced that they are enchanters bearing off a princess, Quixote attacks them, despite their courteous explanations, and easily puts them to flight, although Sancho Panza comes off exceedingly badly at the hands of their servants.

Strauss depicts this episode with supreme simplicity, omitting all reference to Sancho Panza. The movement consists of a rumbustious statement of Don Quixote's principal subject (Ex. 27), leading to a long and exceedingly amusing mock-religious dialogue for the two Benedictines represented by two bassoons entirely unaccompanied. After their discourse has continued for some time Don Quixote can be heard creeping stealthily towards them (lower strings pizzicato), and then, with a short reprise of the earlier ebullience, sending them packing, 'crossing themselves more often than if they had had the devil himself at their backs'.

The tenth and last variation follows without a break. A gentleman from Don Quixote's own village, profoundly concerned over Don Quixote's well-being, decides to take a hand at influencing the knight to stay at home peacefully, instead of risking his health and that of his long-suffering squire in these hair-brained escapades. The Bachelor Sampson Carrasco, as he is named, actually encourages Quixote to embark on a third expedition, and then, no sooner has he set forth, than Carrasco follows dressed as the Knight of the Mirrors. In this disguise he challenges Quixote to a joust with the intention of using the inevitable victory to sentence his misguided friend to give up all idea of Knight Errantry for a whole year. Unfortunately it is Don Quixote who wins the contest and Carrasco hobbles home very much the worse for wear and unable to renew his purpose until a further fifty chapters have elapsed. He then reappears, now redisguised as the Knight of the White Moon, and at last fulfils his design, exacting the necessary promise from the defeated knight.

It is this latter incident which Strauss depicts, much as it occurs in Chapter LXIV, together with Don Quixote's dignified retreat homewards and resolve to spend the prescribed twelve months in sheep farming and other pastoral occupations. Strauss's version of the battle is stirring, even though he portrays the contestants as too unevenly matched, the solo cello of Don Quixote fighting the whole wind and brass of Strauss's large orchestra. But the journey home must be rated amongst Strauss's most moving conceptions. It takes the form of a powerful pedal-point reinforced by regular strokes on the timpani, and has been cited as one of the most elaborate and technically advanced examples of that long-established device. It has both dignity and pathos, while Sancho Panza's themes scuttle around, barely audible in the midst of the funereal majesty of the resolute gait of the stricken knight. At the climax the great discord is reached which in the introduction marked the beginning of Quixote's insanity, and now at last that discord is resolved as, with his knightly defeat, his reason slowly begins to return.

First, however, he toys with the conception of becoming a shepherd, and the theme of the shepherds' piping from the relevant variation

returns aptly (Ex. 39) accompanied by a new version of Sancho's motif
as the squire sees himself as the shepherd Panzino:

Ex. 42

The agony of his affliction returns briefly to Don Quixote, the fatal
discord this time incorporating the third of the motifs (Ex. 29), with
which it was originally associated; but the worst is over and the clouds
lift from his confused mind once and for all, as the harmonies clear and
settle into a series of high and simple chords of the dominant in
preparation for the Finale.

II

As so often happens, the passing of madness has left the sufferer very
feeble and with his return home Quixote takes to his bed for the last
time. The closing chapter of Cervantes's great novel is perhaps more
sad than tragic and Strauss concludes his version in a similar vein. The
leading cellist is again treated as an out-and-out soloist and begins with a
preamble based on a new and tender version of Don Quixote's principal motif:

Ex. 43

This eventually leads to an onset of death pangs strongly reminiscent of those suffered by the invalid in *Tod und Verklärung*. The cello
then, after recalling a moment from the 'vigil' (Variation V), passes in
review the original form of Quixote's three principal subjects as they
were heard at the beginning of the work. The theme of the famous
harmonic side-slips (Ex. 29) is now heard for the one and only time as
an absolutely straight cadence. The poignant closing phrase of Don
Quixote, the player dying by tradition over his cello, is familiar to all
who have been present in the concert hall during an actual perfor-

mance. One further augmented statement of Ex. 29, with the side-slip not only restored but extended, and the work is over.

Don Quixote stands with *Till Eulenspiegel* as twin peaks in the achievement of its creator in purely orchestral composition. Only its extreme difficulty of execution, particularly with respect to the cello part, and perhaps one or two features of the instrumentation such as the tenor tuba and two extra horns, have prevented it from being as regular an item as its sister work in the concert repertory. It is never turgid or bombastic, and its occasional banalities are deliberate and fitting to the subject. On the side of humour and incredible fertility of invention Strauss at no time surpassed what he accomplished throughout *Don Quixote*, though he equalled it perhaps during some of the stage works which lay ahead. Whatever may survive the passing of the years in Strauss's output, *Don Quixote* is sure to remain a firm landmark in the Post-Romantic School of orchestral music.

CHAPTER VI

THE DECLINE OF THE TONE POEMS

FOR the last three years Strauss had produced an annual tone poem
in addition to the still rapidly increasing volume of songs, and
with the world of opera still a bitterly closed door for him he automatically cast around for a subject which would be suitable for the next
work in the series. For the first time since *Tod und Verklärung*, however,
the world of literature momentarily failed him and he fell back upon his
own imagination. His sketch-books seem to indicate that while he was
still at work on *Don Quixote* the idea of a companion work had already
occurred to him, and so during the summer holidays of 1898 he
decided to go ahead with the plans for this new work which was to
follow the life-span of some imaginary hero-figure. Strauss's account
of the *raison d'être* for the work is characteristically boisterous; 'Beethoven's "Eroica" is so little beloved of our conductors, and is on this
account now only rarely performed', he wrote from Marquartstein in
the summer of 1898, 'that to fulfil a pressing need I am composing a
largeish tone poem entitled *Heldenleben*, admittedly without a funeral
march, but yet in E flat, with lots of horns, which are always a yard-
stick of heroism.'[1]

In a sense, then, it might be said that *Don Quixote* and *Heldenleben*
were to some extent conceived simultaneously, and many commentators firmly regard them as complementary. Strauss himself when

[1] It is amusing to be able to record that an obscure Danish composer by the
name of Horneman anticipated Strauss by composing a concert overture entitled
Ein Heldenleben!

writing from Berlin to Gustav Kogel shortly before the completion of the full score even said, 'I think so strongly of *Don Quixote* and *Ein Heldenleben* as being directly linked together that in particular *Don Quixote* is only fully and completely comprehensible when put side by side with *Heldenleben*.' The connexion between the new tone poem and its predecessor was, it seems, to be based on a co-relationship of ideologies. If *Don Quixote* portrayed the 'crazy striving after false ideals,' the new composition was to show by contrast 'a more general and free ideal of great and manly heroism'. This constitutes a preoccupation with the hero and heroism as such in a disembodied philosophical form which is generally regarded as a particularly Teutonic phenomenon. Yet although its prominence in Germany is undeniable, and can to a large extent be ascribed to Wagner's researches into the heroic aspect of Nordic legend, it was the British author Carlyle who in 1841 wrote the first important treatise on heroism and hero-worship.

However, it seems dubious how far Strauss delved into the cult of the hero whether in its Carlylian or Wagnerian origin, since when he came to plan the details of his scheme he finally drew to a large extent upon autobiographical subject-matter. The reason for such derivation of his programmatic outline from personal experience must remain to some extent conjectural, especially since of all composers Strauss's life was supremely unromantic, even uneventful, and equally Strauss's personality was one of the last which might be labelled heroic. Yet this was the first time that Strauss was planning a tone poem on an abstract subject. Even in *Tod und Verklärung* he began with at least a sequence of events or mental images, albeit imaginary. Now he had to superimpose a scheme upon an idea and he may very well have found the need for something more definite to build upon. In that case what could be more convenient than his own life, if this could be incorporated without his having to identify himself immodestly as his own hero? Before long he did indeed take the further step of founding a work, the *Sinfonia Domestica*, entirely upon himself and his family circle, and it is arguable that under these precarious circumstances he aimed at a perceptibly more intimate melodic style despite the brilliant orchestral gestures which abound equally in both works.

But while at least three of the main sections of *Ein Heldenleben* are indisputably taken from Strauss's own life, it is wrong to proceed from this to the all-too-frequent denunciation of the tone poem as a flagrant instance of personal aggrandisement. The closing sections of the work in which the hero retires from the world are purely imaginary, while even the portrayal of the hero's character in the opening section bears no resemblance to Strauss's opinion of himself as shown in his avowed self-portrait at the beginning of the *Sinfonia Domestica*. Strauss had too much sense of humour pompously to proclaim himself a hero to all the world, even though he had sufficient idea of his own importance to find no embarrassment in repeatedly introducing personal affairs by way of analogy.[2]

The scheme of the work and the first sketches were already in existence before Strauss finally left Munich, and the score was completed according to plan shortly before the end of 1898, during the composer's first season as Generalmusikdirektor with the Berlin Philharmonic Orchestra. Always a methodical worker, Strauss had a particularly clear idea of his plan in this new tone poem, which goes back to the earlier scheme of *Macbeth* and *Don Juan* in turning the programmatic outline into a musical design based on symphonic form. The six main sections correspond broadly with the subdivisions of a sonata first movement as follows:

I   The Hero   1st Subject
II The Hero's adversaries (or critics)   Transition
III The Hero's companion (or wife)   2nd Subject
IV The Hero's deeds of war   Development
V   The Hero's works of peace (and   Recapitulation
        struggles in the face of continued   (with added episode)
        criticism)
VI The Hero's retirement from the world Coda
        and the fulfilment of his life.

These sections are all continuous (except for the dramatic pause at the end of I) and there are no indications of form or content in the printed score. Once again, Strauss made a careful point of refraining from positive identification of his programmatic intentions in the published editions of the work, even though he betrayed them at various times to his numerous friends and biographers. Thus Friedrich Rösch,

[2] Romain Rolland quotes Strauss as saying, 'I do not see why I should not compose a symphony about myself; I find myself quite as interesting as Napoleon or Alexander.'

Wilhelm Klatte, and Richard Specht all wrote guides to the music claiming the author's approval for these section headings which they quote identically and upon which the above synopsis is based. An elaborate poem was even written around the scheme by one Eberhard König following Ritter's example with *Tod und Verklärung*. The meaning of the tone poem is, however, perfectly simple and clear without any such misguided elaboration.

2

The opening section, devoted to a character-study of the hero, is a self-contained exposition of his various motifs. The first of these is an unaccompanied statement of a long and elaborate theme containing in itself a number of motivic ideas:

Ex. 1

A climax is reached with a further related figure:

Ex. 2

This enormous sentence is then firmly rounded off and the first four bars repeated, this time against a harmonic background supplied by five trumpets which are added to the prevailing string colouring. There are some important features about this unusual theme. To begin with, ⌐ a ⌐ is once again a *Naturthema* apart from the added sixth supplied by the C in the second bar. Indeed, with this exception, and the rapid descending figure of ⌐ b ⌐ the whole of the opening four bars are built entirely around the notes of the common chord of E flat. Thereafter, the remainder of the theme consists of nothing but a descending scale, barely disguised by the changes of octave supplied by the hugely characteristic rising sevenths and the curious colouring of the flattened notes in bar 7 which momentarily suggest the whole tone scale. Yet the effect is extremely arresting, partly on account of the great variety of the motivic content including surging, plunging or striding figures all finely suggestive of a great heroic personality in the prime of life; its effect is also partly due to the enormous span of the theme (three octaves, all but a semitone), a feature of Strauss's melodic ideas which has been traced from as far back as the Violin Sonata. In the hands of a Reger a rambling theme of this kind might have become weak and indeterminate, but although it is patently less concise and direct than its sister-theme, the *Don Juan* motif (Exx. 8 and 9 from Chapter 3), it has great dignity and Strauss always manages to keep the interest powerfully alive through his masterly sense of thematic construction.

A second composite theme grows naturally out of the restatement of Ex. 1 as follows:

Ex. 3 and 4

These two themes acquire importance independently of each other, while the figure Ex. 3 (a) before long becomes one of the salient themes of the hero. It is even incorporated immediately into the next motif which follows upon the heels of Exx. 3 and 4:

Ex. 5

Out of all this material Strauss builds a symphonic structure by juxtaposing the ideas, modulating, beginning Ex. 1 again in various new
keys, and gradually working up a series of ever more imposing
climaxes, at one of which Ex. 5 is hurled out by six horns[3] with
splendid panache. A four-bar dominant pedal leads to a grand cadence
in the tonic, heralding a splendiferous return of Ex. 1. The end is not yet
reached, however, and as Ex. 1 rears itself, a new and defiant theme is
declared as if by way of challenge:

Ex. 6

Six times the hero proclaims his ultimatum, which is followed each
time by a dramatic silence. The section then closes with a final statement of Ex. 1(a) on the heavy brass and, with a mighty chord of the
dominant seventh, the hero awaits the answer of the world.

3

The second section comes with something of a shock. If the hero
expected his nobility of spirit to be matched with a parallel loftiness on
the part of his adversaries, he is rudely disappointed. His critics are
shown to be without exception a mean and petty collection of narrow-
minded or smugly reactionary nobodies.

Exx. 7 to 13 give the numerous voices of the opponents, from which
it can readily be deduced that they vary from the thin and spiteful to the
fat and complacent. The whole passage is a caricature which is the
equivalent in music to some of the most grotesque drawings of Mervyn
Peake. There is, of course, not the slightest doubt that Strauss meant
this section personally. He wrote to his father after the performance,
'Of the critics so far, *Lokalanzeiger* (Klatte) and *Vossische Zeitung* (Urban)
were very good; the others spit poison and gall, principally because on
reading the analytical note they believed that they could see themselves identified with the really hatefully portrayed "grumblers and
antagonists" and that I myself am meant for the hero, which last is only

[3] Not eight horns as given in the condensed form of the score published by
Eulenburg.

Ex. 7

partially so.' It is strange that Strauss, who of all artists had so consistently had the lion's share of success, should feel so venomously about the critics, however vituperous some may have been. Only with respect to *Guntram* had he experienced anything which could in any way be described as a flop, though this, as we know, he never forgave the world. Yet he felt so strongly such criticism as he had met that, like other great artists and authors before and since, the bitterness came out in his work and, in the present instance, soiled a potentially great achievement, as the intrusion of personal spite always will. A truly great hero needs equally great and honest opponents or his victory will be a worthless bubble, and the adversaries with which Strauss's hero finds himself confronted are certainly unworthy of him. He is utterly downcast. Ex. 1(a) is heard in the minor, dolefully delivered by the cellos and basses. It is followed by an extended section built upon a new and sorrowful melody.

Ex. 14

As this grows in intensity it makes increasing use of the figure Ex. 1(d). A climax is reached and as the song dies away the critics renew their attacks. But now the hero is irked and he retaliates with Ex. 1(a). The more they rail at him, the stronger his replies become, until with a violent gesture (Ex. 5(a)) he shakes himself free of them altogether.

It is at this point that the hero's companion makes her appearance. She is represented by the solo violin and the passage that follows is one of the most taxing for the orchestral leader in the entire repertoire. In a long series of cadenzas her character is presented from every conceivable angle, and by no means in a flattering way. Many comments have been made on the extraordinary personality Strauss chose to give the hero's wife, and the distinguished French writer Romain Rolland, who came to know the composer first at about this time, took the step of asking him about the matter. Rolland wrote in his journal:

> I asked Strauss about the hero's wife, who had intrigued the audience so greatly—some found her a perverse woman, others a coquette, etc. He said: 'Neither one nor the other. A little of all that. It's my wife I wanted to show. She is very complex, very feminine, a little perverse, a little coquettish, never like herself, at every minute different from how she had been the moment before. At the beginning the hero follows her, and gets into the mood in which she has just been singing; she keeps going further away. At last he says 'No, I am staying here.' He remains wrapped in his own thoughts, back in his own mood. Then she comes to him. For the rest, this long and very fully developed section serves as an interlude, as contrast between the two noisy outbursts of the opening and of the Battle. It would be impossible to go on in the same vein.

In the course of her many tirades, which range from the seductive to the frankly shrewish, her principal themes are introduced, though separated by numbers of a-thematic violinistic cadenzas, including two-part inventions, arpeggios, broken chords, rapid scale passages, and treble-stoppings. The themes themselves all portray her gentler feelings for the hero:

Ex. 15

Ex. 16

Ex. 17

The hero replies in subdued tones with fragments of Ex. 1 and partly with a new theme which emerges more and more as the lash of the woman's tongue stings him to protest;

Ex. 18

Ex. 19

Note the rising fourth common to all these examples, symbolizing the hero's awakening interest. At last with Ex. 19 he speaks to her of love, and it is upon this fervent theme that the ensuing episode is built, together with the themes of her affection (Exx. 15 and 16). This third section, the second subject of the symphonic scheme, is truly operatic in character, and one feels acutely Strauss's need for voices to complete the picture of this *Liebesszene*. Into it he threw all his most colourful orchestral devices; soaring strings and horns, tremolos, wind trills, harp glissandos—everything to evoke the most erotic and passionate scene possible. The themes are good and the music beautiful, yet somehow it fails to sweep the listener off his feet as does the equivalent passage in *Don Juan* so irresistibly.

The passion subsides into tenderness as another last love theme makes its appearance:

Ex. 20

This leads by way of a rhetorical passage of unexpected vigour to an equally important closing phrase:

Ex. 21

These last two melodies reflect the deep and very real affection between the hero and his wife and become of extreme significance at the end of the tone poem.

The manner in which the call to action once raised Don Juan from his bed of love is here re-enacted, though on a larger scale. First it is the critics whose irritating bickering can be heard in the distance, but it requires no more than a reminder of Ex. 21 with its languidly falling phrases to banish them wholly from the hero's mind, the soft warm tonic chord of G flat major never having been disturbed for an instant. It is, however, a different matter when an elaborate trumpet call is sounded by three off-stage trumpets:

Ex. 22

This time the hero rises vehemently, and although the companion draws him back to her (Ex. 15 *molto espressivo*), an abbreviated repeat of the trumpet call spurs him to leave her side and arm for war. Fragments of the trumpet call mix with motifs from Ex. 1, figures 1(a) and 5(a) being especially prominent. Before long his companion, now reconciled to the necessity of the hero's return to action, takes a busy hand in the preparations with repeated statements of Ex. 15, and in a very brief space of time the hero is fully armed and ready for conflict.

4

The ensuing Battle Scene was for many years the most notorious part of the tone poem and one of the most widely discussed passages in all 'modern music'. The aggressive ugliness of the opening has not become softened over the years, even though the technical means by which it was effected have been vastly exceeded by countless composers including Strauss himself. But whereas the far more revolutionary excesses of *Elektra* are as fresh and interesting today as when they were first written, much of this once so shocking section now sounds merely crude. It is built primarily on augmentations of figures ⌐ a ⌐ and ⌐ b ⌐ of the adversaries' first theme, Ex. 7, set against an all-pervading drum figure ♫♫ ♫♫♫ and various explosive pizzicati and woodwind flips suggestive of the clashing of swords and spears. The hero is represented initially by the first four bars of Ex. 1 together with quotations from the trumpet call, Ex. 22. As the battle proceeds his companion's theme joins in, suggesting perhaps that the inspiration of her image spurs him to greater deeds than ever before. With her appearance the hero's theme is joined by Ex. 4 and the figure ⌐ x ⌐ from Ex. 5 becomes increasingly prominent. The battles waxes more and more furious and Ex. 1 is gradually given in larger sections together with Ex. 4(a) in diminution which builds up from the bass instruments in rapidly rising sequences.

The texture broadens and simplifies, showing that the hero is in the ascendency, although the adversaries still keep up their attacks to the last. Finally with a tremendous effort he deals the decisive blow (Ex. 5(a)) and exultantly he sings the love themes (Exx. 15 and 19) as his enemies flee before him in terror (rapidly descending figures derived from the hero's belligerent motif, Ex. 5(a)). There is no doubt that the love of his companion is a major factor in the hero's strength. There is a broad cadence and Ex. 1 is proclaimed as a mighty song of victory. The phrase Ex. 1(c) is picked up by the eight horns, while the strings and

oboes chant a hymn-like version of another of the love motifs Ex. 16,
and the tone poem builds up majestically to its great central climax.

One has become conscious during the battle that Strauss's inventive
powers have warmed perceptibly to the task, so that by the time the
hero is on the way to victory we are in the midst of a highly satisfactory
and well-planned symphonic development. The feeling at the point
now reached is in every way that of a regular recapitulation, and
Strauss appropriately sets off to do the required thing (although Ex. 1 is
now combined with Ex. 15, as the hero is no longer alone but strides
through life arm-in-arm with his companion). But at the seventh bar
Strauss suddenly takes a new turning and an entirely fresh theme is
announced, surging and impetuous:

Ex. 23

There is clearly no question of the hero resting on his laurels, and
Strauss's mind, warmed to fever heat by the excitement of creating the
last few stirring pages, was bursting with new ideas. The way in which
the work now gathers new life at just this most dangerous formal junc-
ture is one of its strongest and most inspired features. This new melody
epitomizes the hero's unfailing dedication to his work and his bound-
less ambition, and it is therefore of particular importance that it is this
theme which later dominates the section devoted to the hero's old age,
shortly before the end of the work. It swamps completely the earlier
themes of the hero (Exx. 3 and 4)[4] and surges forward, statement after
statement, reaching ever higher until when the climax finally comes it
proves to be a surprise fully worthy of such tremendous preparation.
The horns suddenly peal out the great theme from *Don Juan* (Ex. 15
Chapter III) upon which the strings and wind follow up with two more
themes from the earlier tone poems, the love theme—again from *Don*

---

[4] The figure ⌐ a ⌐ is, in fact, an inversion of the ubiquitous figure ⌐ x ⌐
from Ex. 5, which latter made a brief and scarcely noticeable appearance in the
basses at the moment Ex. 23 was born, as if to point out its all-important relationship to its new cousin.

Juan (Ex. 12, Chapter III) and the 'Spirit of Man' motif from *Zarathustra* (Ex. 14, Chapter V). In his exultance the hero presents to the whole world excerpts from his mightiest conceptions. Here is the crowning moment of his ambitions and Strauss interprets it personally by quoting from two of his own finest creations. The *Zarathustra* motif merges into a chromatic form of the figure ⌐ d ⌐ from the hero's theme and Ex. 1(a) rears itself vehemently before the music fades away in an anticipation not unmixed with anxiety.

5

There is a silence into which the two tubas interpose Ex. 10, the intolerable voice of the smug critic who has been entirely silent throughout the battle and has therefore never been fought or defeated. Nothing could be more unexpected or deflating. The hero reacts as if stung in the back by a hornet:

Ex. 24

His pique subsides quickly, however, and he settles down in a calmer and less domineering frame of mind to an account of his Works of Peace. The section now takes the form of a reverie, and Strauss, continuing the analogy with his own career, embarks on a potpourri of his principal earlier compositions. Introduced by a barcarolle-like version of Ex. 1(a) against which Ex. 5 is played in canon on the bassoon and cor anglais, the numerous quotations soon pour out in profusion, beautifully worked into a flowing symphonic texture. Naturally enough this amusing device has since aroused unceasing interest amongst succeeding generations of musicians and the passage is a *locus classicus* of the musical quiz. Here then is a list of answers in order of appearance. The page references are from the original Leuckart edition of the full (and miniature) score:

Richard Strauss and his father

p. 105, bar 3 *Don Juan*	(Ex. 15, Ch. III)
5 *Don Juan*	(Ex. 12, Ch. III)
Zarathustra	(Ex. 14, Ch. V)

p. 110, bar 1 *Tod und Verklärung*	(Ex. 22, Ch. III)
Tod und Verklärung	(Ex. 18, Ch. III)
3 *Don Quixote*	(Ex. 27, Ch. V)
4 *Don Quixote*	(an extra phrase adapted from the coda on the cor anglais, not quoted)
5 *Don Quixote*	(Ex. 28, Ch. V, with original accompaniment on horns and bassoons)

p. 111, bar 1 *Don Juan*	(Ex. 14, Ch. III)
Don Juan	(Ex. 13, Ch. III)
Don Quixote	(Ex. 42, Ch. V)
3 *Till Eulenspiegel*	(Ex. 5, Ch. V)
6 *Guntram*	(Ex. 22, Ch. IV)

| p. 112, bar 3 *Guntram* | (Ex. 10, Ch. IV) |
| 5 *Guntram* | (Ex. 38, Ch. IV, with original triplet accompaniment) |

p. 113, bar 1 *Guntram*	(Ex. 6, Ch. IV)
2 *Tod und Verklärung*	(Ex. 22, Ch. III)
Zarathustra	(Ex. 13, Ch. V) combined with:
Guntram	(Ex. 37, Ch. IV)
4 *Macbeth*	(Ex. 4, Ch. III)
'Befreit'	(Bars 20–22)
5 *Macbeth*	(Ex. 3, Ch. III)
6 *Macbeth*	(Ex. 1, Ch. III)

p. 114, bar 2 *'Traum durch die Dämmerung'*	(Bars 15–18)
3 *Guntram*	(Ex. 31, Ch. IV)
5 *Guntram*	(Ex. 2, Ch. IV)
Don Quixote	(Ex. 40, Ch. IV)

| p. 115, bar 4 *Guntram* | (Ex. 6, Ch. IV) |

| p. 116, bar 3 *Tod und Verklärung* | (Ex. 24, Ch. III) |
| 5 *Zarathustra* | (Ex. 14, Ch. V) |

| p. 117, bar 1 *Guntram* | (Ex. 1(d), Ch. IV) |

Worked in with these references are the various themes of the hero and his companion, Exx. 5, 20, 4, 18, 19 and 15 (in that order), and the section tails away into the same question mark which followed the initial outburst of quotations. This time the hero repeats the querying phrase as if making a desperate plea of self-justification. A poignant version of Ex. 6 is twice screamed out by the upper woodwind before this third question floats away into a long silence.

The answer comes as before; an unmoved, unaltered, implacable restatement of Ex. 10 by the two tubas. Again maddened beyond endurance by the narrow and uncomprehending criticism, the hero breaks into a repeat of Ex. 24 which leads into a feverish, tormented passage of turbulent figures based on Ex. 2 and the chromatic version of Ex. 1(d). The opening phrases of the hero's theme are added at one moment, but disappear again, overwhelmed by the wild frenzy of the hero's agony of doubt as to the value and purpose of all he has been striving for. This inner battle is in its way the counterpart to the earlier actual battle.

There is a savage collapse and some tearingly dissonant cadences ensue which recall in augmentation some of the ugly trumpet calls from the Battle Scene. Against these the chromatic Ex. 1(d) first struggles and then sinks exhausted. The ugly cadence softens and melts into a chord of C major as, against a throbbing drum-tap, the cor anglais begins a pastorale based on Ex. 1(a).

Ex. 25

Like Don Quixote, his heart beating painfully, the hero considers becoming a shepherd. The parallel between this passage and the corresponding section of Variation X of the earlier tone poem is apparent and intentional. However, so absolute a retirement from the world would be too drastic for a hero with so great a character and sense of mission, and like Don Quixote he never actually takes to the fields. Yet his recent inner conflict has won him the power of renunciation and in retirement he finds the peace of mind he needs for his old age. Perhaps Strauss, in drafting these closing pages, had a vision of himself as the country squire in his future retreat in Garmisch, at that time not the overgrown suburban town it is today, but still a sparsely built and peaceful resort among the Bavarian Alps.

6

Strauss once said that in the coda to *Heldenleben* he aimed at producing the effect of a free and fanciful improvisation. Yet the invention is always cogent and relevant. Repeated statements of Ex. 25(b) on high violins gradually modulate back to the tonic of E flat, in which key the final melody is sung in tones of the utmost warmth and nobility by the mellow combination of strings and eight horns. Arising out of Ex. 25(b), the first notes of which are identical, the melody proves to be synonymous with the impatient passage Ex. 24, which was itself a caricature of one of the love themes, Ex. 17. Thus the hero's retirement is built both on the love of his youth and on that part of his nature which has been refined by internal struggle. There is still one element missing, however, and his desire for this—the sublimation of his ambitions—brings back nightmare memories of his combat with the critics. A grotesque section is suddenly interpolated, giving the impression of a bad dream experienced by an old man dozing in his armchair. An augmented version of the first antagonist's motif, Ex. 7, alternates with one of the hero's protesting themes, Ex. 18, against a background of weird trills, tremolos and strangely rushing figures in the basses and muted horns.

The hero's wife, once again taken by the solo violin, dispels these horrific apparitions and restores him to the world of reality. The strings and horns resume their melodizing, but that last vision of his adversaries has restored to the hero his faith in the completion of his work. The theme of his ambitions, Ex. 23, now returns on the horn in conjunction and in alternation with the two tenderest of the love themes, Ex. 20 (the contours of which it now resembles to a marked degree) and Ex. 21.

The last voices are those of the first horn and the solo violin, the one falling while the other ascends. Each reaches its respective E flat, high and low, as the full brass presents the final apotheosis of the hero's theme by building up the chord of E-flat major in terms of the opening notes of Ex. 1. At the end the hero's life has known the happiness of complete fulfilment.

7

Ein Heldenleben is from many points of view the high-spot in the series of Strauss's tone poems. Quite apart from its intrinsic quality, the sheer size of the orchestra employed, with its eight horns, five trumpets, two tubas, two harps and quadruple woodwind, labels it a *tour de force*. Then the frankly extrovert style of the greater part of the work with its cumulative climaxes makes it an irresistibly thrilling experience, while the glowing richness of the coda leaves the listener with a feeling of deep satisfaction after the last majestic wind chord has died away. Nor is this satisfaction an illusion; much of the work is built out of really fine material by a composer whose symphonic powers were at their height. The performance of *Ein Heldenleben* in a concert programme more than sixty years after its first appearance is still an exciting event.

Yet despite all this, from an artistic angle there are a number of features about the work which point to a deterioration from the pre-ceding tone poems. To begin with, it fails in precisely the field in which Strauss had recently shown his strength to lie—character port-rayal. The unnamed hero never comes to life as a human being in the way that *Don Juan*, *Till Eulenspiegel*, and *Don Quixote* did so signally. This failure reveals Strauss's limitations as a creative artist. He could illustrate in music an already existing character brilliantly and with profound insight, but he was never able to create an entirely new figure himself and breathe life into it. Here again we encounter the factor which contributed so largely to the failure of *Guntram*. As with *Guntram*, we are made infinitely aware of the hero's aggressive self-confidence, of his lofty aspirations, also, of course, of his tenderness and passion in matters of love, but little of any breadth or depth of person-ality—even in the section specifically devoted to the exposition of his character. Only the portrait of the hero's companion (drawn, it will be remembered, from life) is wholly vivid, and the best sections of the tone poem are those devoted to her or the hero's relationship with her. The remainder, for lack of any positive and already existing characters or situations to be transformed into music, is apt to fall back on bom-bast in a way which was particularly characteristic of Bismarck's Germany at about the turn of the century. This aspect of the work is therefore the most vulnerable to the passing of time, in the same way as Elgar's musical expression of Imperialist Britain during the Edwardian era is becoming increasingly discredited. Moreover, the very size of the orchestra, which at the time seemed to be a special venture, subsequently turned out to be an unhealthy sign; a symptom of Strauss's growing tendency towards over-protestation in the face of insecurity. It will have been noticed that with the passing of the years Strauss's orchestra was growing steadily larger, and the symphonic poems which followed *Ein Heldenleben* showed that this was no mere coincidence arising out of the requirements of each new subject-matter, but a continuous trend, which was only justified when Strauss once more found his natural means of expression in the symphonic drama.

8

Although Strauss's next important work proved at last to be his second opera, it will be more convenient to discuss immediately the symphonic poem which followed *Ein Heldenleben*, reserving Strauss's return to the stage for a later chapter. No less than five years separate *Ein Heldenleben* from its successor, *Symphonia Domestica*. The reason for this sudden gap was nothing short of a turning-point in Strauss's career. A chance meeting in Munich with the writer Ernst von Wolzogen ripened quickly into collaboration over a comic opera to be directed maliciously against both the stage in general and Munich in particular. Anything more providential could not be imagined, since it required some such spur of artistic revenge to break down the psychological barrier Strauss had built up within himself since the *Guntram* episode, and so open the way for the masterpieces which this born master of the theatre had it in him to produce.

But what was to be gain in the theatre was loss in the concert hall. The creation and production of *Feuersnot* occupied Strauss until the end of 1901 and it was mid-April 1902 before he felt ready to embark on a new symphonic poem. The opera had in no way disturbed the autobiographical line of thought started in *Ein Heldenleben*, as there was a strong personal allegory connected with the action of *Feuersnot*. Hence the line of least resistance was to crystallize these hints of personal reference and compose a work openly around himself and his family.

After a difficult birth, Pauline Strauss was delivered of a son on 12th April 1897. Richard was away on a short concert tour at the actual time, and matters were not improved by the doctor's false diagnosis that he was about to become the father of twins. His pride over the boy was in the finest traditions of fatherhood, writing to his parents detailed dimensions of the baby (width of head 39 cm., breadth of chest 37 cm., etc.), eyes like his own, nose a cross between Pschorr and de Ahna, and so on. Then, after a sentimental account of the way he slept so peacefully, the letter closes with the familiar words, 'The boy is screaming like hell.'

The child's progress is recounted duly in Strauss's letters home—at two-and-a-half he is reciting the list of portraits on the wall. 'Wagner, Backhoffen, Liszt, Bülow', a year later he is learning daily 'a Christmas carol a yard long' and is 'full of humour, getting up to every kind of prank'. At five years old he is having some not too strenuous piano lessons with Papa, 'which he finds the greatest fun; he already knows the white notes'.

By this time (April 1902) the new symphonic poem[5] was under way. The new operatic venture had occupied him exclusively for the past three years and, apart from the steady flow of songs, he had composed nothing since the completion of Heldenleben at the end of 1898. A potential symphonic poem on an alpine subject (!) had come to nothing, as also some sketches for a full-length ballet. Now he was trying to stimulate his imagination with a large choral work, Taillefer, which was to be a setting of a Ballade by Uhland accompanied by an enormous orchestra. Together with this, he was also making some progress with the autobiographical symphonic poem (the subject of which he carefully refrained from revealing), but at first he found it heavy going. He persevered, however, and by September had got back into the swing of symphonic composition. Work proceeded steadily, often late into the night, but even so it was not until the following June that the sketch was virtually complete, the last bars being drafted during a holiday in the Isle of Wight after the famous London Strauss Festival. He seems to have struck lucky with the English climate, speaking of 'Bubi running about all day in the hot sand and going in and out of the sea'. More favourable circumstances for the completion of a Sinfonia Domestica he could hardly have wished for, and he was the more high-spirited as the result of having just heard from Heidelberg that the Faculty had decided to confer upon him the honorary Doctorate of the University. This eminently satisfactory news he quickly passed on to his parents, while simultaneously letting the cat out of the bag over the

---

[5] It is amusing to notice that in describing the progress of the work he uses the title 'Symphonische Dichtung', which he assiduously avoided throughout his life for the published works.

title of his new symphonic poem. Despite all his diplomacy, his father's reaction was much as he had feared, though for an unexpected reason:

> The title of your newly projected symphonic poem [he wrote], which is intended to depict German family life, has not struck me as very pleasing on account of the word 'Domestica', which so far as I know means 'domestic', i.e. servitude, and so would place the whole centre of gravity on the matter of inferiority, which in my opinion will do the work great harm in the eyes of the public. One must give no cause for malicious sallies on the part of one's opponents. Try to find a title which will point towards the gaiety of the piece.

Nevertheless Strauss paid no more attention to his father's words than he had ever done. Seldom can parental advice have been more regularly or more uselessly given.

The sketch was revised during the next few weeks and the orchestration put in hand during the autumn. By dint of hard labour, often when he was overwhelmed with business affairs, correspondence, and his extremely heavy duties as conductor of the Berlin opera, the score was at last finished on 31st December 1903. The instrumentation was on an even more flamboyant scale than in *Heldenleben*, with five clarinets and bassoons and a quartet of saxophones added as a daring innovation.[6] There are, however, it must be admitted, only four trumpets this time and one tuba. Nevertheless his father was eminently reasonable when he expressed surprise: 'Is the *Symphonia Domestica* so long, that you need nearly 200 pages for it?—are you orchestrating it as heavily as *Taillefer*? —in the home one can't make so much noise!'

9

As far as the length is concerned, *Domestica* takes approximately the same time to play as *Heldenleben*, although it bears the title of Symphony. Some comment has even arisen over Strauss's return to the symphony as if in deference to his father's views after an interval of nearly twenty years. The title is, however, the merest lip-service and the work is as much a continuous symphonic poem as its predecessors,

[6] Even Strauss must have had pangs over the judiciousness of these thickening instruments, for he never gave them any solo work, marked them *ad lib*, and (like the extra brass in *Till Eulenspiegel*) omitted them in his own performances.

even though it follows the superficial outline of a four-movement symphony with its 'Scherzo', 'Adagio' and 'Finale' with which Strauss carefully headed the more striking subdivisions of the work. There is, on the other hand, no proper first movement, other than the introduction, which consists of a straightforward presentation of the three principal thematic groups on which the whole work is built, again all carefully labelled in the score. First comes Papa:

Ex. 26

Ex. 27

Ex. 28

Ex. 29

Ex. 30

This array of motifs should be compared with the far more homogeneous themes allocated to the hero in *Ein Heldenleben*. Here Strauss is openly painting his self-portrait. The first thing which strikes one is the wide variety of his own moods and impressions which he lays before us, all yet again specifically marked into the music. We are to perceive without fail that he is a 'gemächlich' (comfortable—easy-going) fellow, inclined to be 'träumerisch' (dreamy) or 'mürrisch' (morose) at times, but with a decidedly 'feurig' (fiery) and 'lustig' (gay) side to his nature. Strauss is disarmingly honest here—perhaps even more than he intended. We never learnt so much about the hero, although his themes were infinitely more distinguished than any of these. The groups end with a dazzling upward-rushing scale in triplets.

As for Mama, we already know her through and through from her previous appearances on the solo violin in *Ein Heldenleben*, but Strauss bravely tries to depict her again; nor was this the last time in his career, as we shall see in connexion with the opera *Intermezzo*. He suffered much at her hands, but there seems to have been an element in his character which needed that quality of suppression. As he said to the Mahlers on one particularly provoking occasion after the première of *Feuersnot*, 'My wife is a bit rough at times, but it's what I need, you know.'

Ex. 31

Ex. 32

Ex. 33

Ex. 34[10]

[7] It is significant that the figure Ex. 31 (a) is the direct inversion of Ex. 26 (a); husband and wife are demonstrably one. Moreover, a case could be made for the likeness of Bubi to his father, the last five bars of Ex. 35 being an elaborated augmentation of Exx. 26 (a) and 27 (b).

[8] 'angry—in a temper.'

[9] 'tender—sentimental.'

[10] The extremely strong resemblance of this theme to Tchaikovsky's Waltz in A flat, op. 40, No. 8, may well have been intentional, especially in view of a second such plagiarism later in the work. Possibly a private joke lies behind the allusion; Pauline Strauss was always chiding her husband for his lack of originality.

She works herself up into a perfect paddy before Papa cheerfully turns aside her wrath with a gay, four-square version of Ex. 26 in folk-song style. Strauss's penchant for folk-like airs, implicit in some of his songs, had come to the surface in *Feuersnot*, where the subject naturally called for them, and remained prominent in *Domestica*, written so soon after, while the style was still strongly in his mind. The remainder of Mama's section is devoted to a conversation between her and her husband, their themes alternating and combining in the course of the discussion. A clear-cut end is reached, after which Bubi's theme is given out quietly against a soft string background.

Ex. 35

This innocent little theme is given to none other than the oboe d'amore, an instrument which had fallen into total disuse since the time of Bach. It had, however, featured prominently in such repertoire works as the *St Matthew Passion*, and Strauss accordingly felt safe in calling upon it with the reasonable likelihood of finding players in any major centre of music throughout the world.[12] Its choice was a clever piece of casting; certainly no other instrument would have served nearly so well.

10

With a start the child is awake and shouting lustily. Wind trills and muted trumpets reflect Strauss's heartfelt remark to his parents concerning the vocal powers of his offspring. Papa and Mama leap into action and quickly get Bubi ready for presentation to the assembled relations. The upward-rushing scale is followed by a more sedate descending one and we hear a somewhat arch suggestion of the voices of uncles and aunts, whose inevitable remarks are indicated in the brass parts in the printed score (Die Tanten: 'Ganz der Papa!'—die Onkels: 'Ganz die Mama!')[13] as the appropriate instruments play the relevant

[11] 'dolcissimo.'

[12] This was by no means his only instrumental resurrection; from *Elektra* onwards he incorporated the basset horn into his normal orchestra, while in many of the later works he used the C clarinet in preference to the little E flat or D.

[13] The Aunts: 'Just like Papa!'—the Uncles: 'Just like Mama!'

versions of Exx. 26(a) and 31(a) respectively. These are all that remain of countless such identifications of Strauss's inspirational sources for the work which he originally noted into the score but later removed. A brief cadence now leads directly into the Scherzo which the composer described sentimentally as 'The child at play; his parents' happiness'.

Naturally enough this section is built primarily on variants on Bubi's melody (Ex. 35), which is first presented as a kind of Ländler in a manner somewhat recalling that of Mahler:

Ex. 36

It is in this work that the styles of the two masters, Strauss and Mahler, approach each other most nearly in their simplicity, the folk-like quality of these quieter themes and their 'Innigkeit'.[15] That this should be so was perhaps the natural outcome of their closer association during these years, this being the only time in their careers that the two important figures had the occasion to work on and hear each other's music, while at the same time meeting regularly in the course of their professional activity. Even so, in the case of characters so utterly opposed, it stands to reason that while each absorbed something from the technique or manner of the other, both remained utterly true to their own already fully formed personalities. Mahler, the introvert battling with increasingly advanced technical problems arising out of a tormenting desire to express the innermost struggles of the human soul; Strauss, the professional musician *par excellence* stretching the instrumental and vocal resources of the time to unheard of lengths in ever more enterprising schemes of imaginative pictorialism.

The Scherzando episode pursues its happy way, to the apparent satisfaction of the admiring parents, whose themes are heard from time to time. An accompanying figuration is derived almost entirely

[14] 'merry—gay.'

[15] This is an essential word for which there is no adequate translation; 'intimacy' of a particularly moving and introvert kind is perhaps the nearest approximation.

from the figure ⌐ a ⌐ from Ex. 36, although an extended flute solo in triplets takes flight in a manner strongly anticipating the parallel passage in the first act of *Der Rosenkavalier*. An important climax in the section is reached when a broader version of Bubi's theme is combined with its scherzando variant, the two derivatives proceeding simultaneously for some time.

Ex. 37

The music gradually subsides and a restatement of Ex. 35, in its original form but ending in an upward sigh, suggests that Bubi is becoming somewhat sleepy. Papa approaches the child with a new and whimsically affectionate idea which is to become important not only for its function in the present work but for what becomes of it at a much later date in *Capriccio*.

Ex. 38

The enormous range of the melody and its wide leaps are most characteristic and the melody can be taken to represent Strauss's personal pride in his son and his desire to share in the details of his upbringing. As preparations are put in hand for Bubi's bed-time, this new melody is combined with Ex. 26 (Papa's theme) and with yet another variant of Bubi's theme which is to become the principal subject of the Finale and will be quoted later (Ex. 44). Papa plays merrily with Bubi, but as this does not get him any nearer to bed, Mama firmly interposes Ex. 31 in augmentation, only to be greeted with a frenzied return of the woodwind trills with muted trumpets to show that as before Bubi himself has a strong opinion to express on the subject. It is of this passage that Hans Richter is reputed to have invented the famous *bon mot* that all the cataclysms of the downfall of the gods in burning Walhalla do not make a quarter of the noise of one Bavarian baby in his bath.

The turbulence dies away and the work passes gently into a Lullaby which for some personal reason, perhaps, is lifted verbatim from one of Mendelssohn's 'Lieder ohne Worte',—the Venetian Gondolier's Song. I quote at length from the passage, not merely on account of the melody, the likeness of which to Mendelssohn is obvious (see bars 7 et seq. from Ex. 39), but also because of the treatment ,which is of great interest, since it embodies in an extreme form Strauss's favourite method of cadencing through shifting tonality (as in bar 4 of the quotation). Much of this smoothly flowing section, the subtle and deceptive simplicity of which is very typical of many passages in the later works, could almost be a study for the great music of the Marschallin in the closing scene of Act I of *Der Rosenkavalier*:

Ex. 39

Even the 'goodnight' kisses form a cadence in which the tonic is approached obliquely:

Ex. 40

(Mama: Gute Nacht! Papa: Gute Nacht!)

The clock strikes seven (Strauss uses the glockenspiel here for the purpose as also for the Marschallin's time-pieces), thus fixing Bubi's bedtime exactly, and a gentle quartet for flute, oboe, clarinet and bass clarinet based on Papa's dreamy theme, Ex. 27, and its inversion suggest Strauss himself standing contemplatively over his sleeping child. The violins take up the melody before this interlude leads to an infinitely soft and moving statement of a new folk-like fragment which stands for the profound tenderness and affection which lies at the heart of his stormy relationship with his wife:

Ex. 41

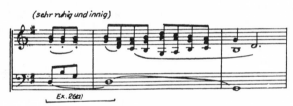

(sehr ruhig und innig)

Ex. 26(a)

Papa's reverie is roughly interrupted by Mama, who vehemently sends him away from the nursery and, grumbling (Ex. 28(a)), he complies, going to his study for his evening's work as the third movement, the Adagio, begins.

The first section of this part of the symphony was called by Strauss 'Schaffen und Schauen'[16] and represents the paterfamilias in his capacity as creative artist. Here, one might have thought, would be the ideal opportunity of further quotations from earlier works, but Strauss, having exploited this device to the full in Heldenleben, wisely refrains from repeating himself. There is a passing hint of the Don Juan motif on

[16] Meaning roughly, 'Doing and thinking'.

the horn, but otherwise the material is entirely derived from Papa's themes (Exx. 26—29) which are combined and worked together with those of his wife (Exx. 31—34). This is essentially the development section of the symphony rather than an independent movement and even the appellation 'Adagio' in the score has no significance beyond the first nine bars. Bubi's themes, however, have naturally no place here and remain dormant like the character they represent. Mama's material might indeed seem somewhat intrusive upon her husband's creative mood, and there is more than a hint of impatience in the handling of his themes. There might well have been historical substance here slyly mimicked in the music; we know from the countless anecdotes told by artists who had occasion to visit Strauss's household, with what contempt Pauline Strauss regarded her husband's work; she would be unlikely to leave him to compose undisturbed during a whole evening without at least a struggle. At last, however, with an augmentation of Ex. 31 followed brusquely by Ex. 32 in the basses, she sails out of the room and the composer turns to his work, his mood rising quickly to elation as in a majestic passage he picks up the thread of some grand conception which is occupying him. Most of his themes are present, but it is Ex. 27 which dominates the picture and remains in sole possession after the first flush of inspiration has passed.

The passage which follows is the most laboured and uninteresting part of the work. Intended as an idealistic vision of the composer projecting and envisaging new artistic conceptions, it emerges as a dry working out of Ex. 27 and its inversion in the manner, perhaps, of Bruckner though without that controversial composer's dedicated loftiness of spirit which shines through his most pedantic developments. Strauss had come once more to one of those *impasses* in his work which we have often seen before in the earlier tone poems. Inspiration had flagged and a period of marking time was necessary before the ideas would flow again. One important phrase, nevertheless, occurs at the top of the curve, a phrase which Strauss calls upon to a considerable extent in later parts of the work:

Ex. 42

At last an augmentation of Ex. 31, softly given in the basses, indicates that the wife has returned, this time discreetly, and she is rewarded by a double statement of the motif of tenderness, Ex. 41. This leads directly into the second part of the 'Adagio', the '*Liebesszene*', to give Strauss's own description. To build up a surging flow of erotic orchestral music with such fertile themes offered no problems for a composer like Strauss, and here he was determined to overreach even his own previous achievements in this direction. Yet although the music is almost hysterically exciting in its graphic detail, the final impression left upon the listener is curiously disappointing, as if Strauss's heart was not really in the task, congenial as it must have been. Ultimately, as at other times in the tone poem, the passage is remarkable not for what it says but for how it says it. The abandon of its expression points directly to the next work *Salome*, where it found its true place, while a device exploited to the full in that same masterpiece also owes its origin to this same section, that of pouring out a salient theme, such as Ex. 31, in a streaming diminution:

Ex. 43

Moreover at the climax, the simultaneous outbursts of the themes of husband and wife are given polytonally, another technical innovation which foreshadows *Salome*.

This culminating corner-stone of the symphony represents in extraordinary detail the composer's own sexual relations with his wife, and it is difficult to avoid the feeling that in an autobiographical work it becomes somehow disagreeable even if it is skilfully carried out. Romain Rolland was by no means alone when he wrote in his Journal: 'Strauss's *Sinfonia Domestica* begins, after hearing it a few times, to fill me with a certain repugnance. . . . In the Night Scene, there is gravity, dreaminess, something rather unexpected and moving—all in extremely bad taste.'

The passion subsides and melts into affection with a last statement of the relevant theme Ex. 41, and a few gentle phrases of their two initial themes show husband and wife asleep. The section which follows, the third and last of the so-called Adagio, is by far the most remarkable of the entire work. It suggests the dreams of the sleeping couple and is impressionistic in a way hardly exploited by Strauss at all up to this time, except in a few isolated moments in *Don Quixote*. In view of the works he was so soon to undertake, the experience and imaginative stimulus he gained in this passage were to prove invaluable. Strauss called it '*Dreams and worries*', and it suggests with uncanny success the troubled visions of the two sleepers whose themes are twisted and turned, whole or in fragments, used as ostinati or introduced in weird combination, the whole orchestrated with superlative instinct to create the unreal atmosphere of a Dali dream-sequence. One important motivic entry must be chronicled; that of Ex. 38, which has not been heard since the Scherzo, when Papa observed that Bubi was tired and tried playfully to prepare him for bed. The extremely sparing use of this beautiful melodic idea is significant, for its reappearance here is one of the very few in the whole work. It is interpolated between phrases of Bubi's theme, Ex. 35, and is followed immediately by ghost-like memories of the splashing and trills of the bath incident. The dreams fade away into total stillness as the Glockenspiel strikes once more— 7 a.m.—time to get up.

II

The entire remainder of the work, amounting to nearly half of the printed score (though not, of course, quite as much in terms of timing) is devoted to the finale—'Double Fugue—merry arguments—reconciliation—happy ending'. Here the descriptive aspect of the work is definitely relegated to the background; only the opening, with the trills and muted trumpets, indicates the awakening of the child, and with him the whole family. (There is something analogous to the ringing of an alarm clock in the trill at this point.) Papa's and Mama's themes are heard in violent alternation with Bubi's theme, which is now given again in the form in which, during the Scherzo, it was heard in conjunction with Ex. 38, and it is in this lively version that it is used as the first subject of the double fugue:

Ex. 44

The second subject is entirely built on Mama's themes, beginning with Ex. 34 (though without the opening figure) and carrying Ex. 31 in its

train. Papa's themes are introduced to a considerable extent during the
exposition of the first subject, whilst during that of the second subject
Bubi's theme appears in the background in its original form, Ex. 35.
The two fugue subjects are then combined and further material from
the themes of the parents are worked into the texture. The rising
triplet run and the trumpet figure Ex. 30 mark off a phrase point in the
music after which Ex. 44 is worked in close canon. Figure ⌐ a ⌐
from Ex. 34 then emerges as an ostinato figure and a tremendous
climax forms around it. The trills and muted trumpets now reach
their apotheosis, with the fanfare-like Ex. 30 thrusting upwards regularly at four-bar intervals through thick clouds of the seething orchestral texture. A penetrating statement of Ex. 44 can also be heard on the
trombones driving across the mass of sound and degenerating into a
pounding rhythm before dying away, together with the general fading
of the music.

Exhausted by the argument, Papa duly gives in to his wife. A soft
statement of his Ex. 29, no longer 'fiery', combines with her still loud
and vehement Ex. 31; this is followed by Bubi's theme serenely sung by
the violins and imperceptibly merging into the melody of Papa's concern over his say in the boy's upbringing (Ex. 38). But he has lost the
battle of wits with his wife and the theme is now marked 'geschmeidig'
(pliant, yielding). The quarrel was quite certainly less merry ('lustig')
than Strauss's subtitle would try to have us believe and is said to have
concerned little Franz Strauss's future. No doubt his father dearly wished
him to become a musician, but since Mama only grudgingly accepted
what she considered to be the socially degrading position of a musician's
wife, she certainly had no intention of becoming the mother of another
musician. Considering that she herself pursued a career as a singer for
so long, this attitude was curiously illogical. The good humour with
which Strauss portrays himself as finally accepting the situation is a
true mark of the philosopher, and in all probability a genuine self-
portrait, from all we know of his behaviour in the home.

The ostinato figure of Ex. 34 (a) which has persisted throughout this
capitulation now gradually falters as Exx. 26 and 28 show a slight protest at the continual underlying ill temper of the wife's motifs, and the
music finally melts into a most remarkable and beautiful little vignette.
This consists of a quasi-folk-song given entirely to wind band, based on
and around Bubi's theme, though never actually quoting it. It is now
transformed into a touchingly simple tune which would make a fine

Christmas carol. Its appearance here after the hurly-burly which both precedes and follows it has precisely the freshness of inspiration which has been lacking during much of the work and is perhaps all the more moving on that account.

From this point of extreme tranquillity, the 'reconciliation' of the title, the music gathers itself for the long final peroration. The mood is at first wholly cordial and light-hearted. After a succession of running figures derived from Papa's themes, the descending melodic phrase Ex. 42 making an amiable counterpoint, a development is built out of the folk-song-like variant of Papa's first theme (Ex. 26), a derivative which has not been heard since near the opening of the work. Mama having won her point, she, too, is in high spirits, and fragments of her themes can be heard here and there amidst the polyphony. Bubi's theme Ex. 35 is then added and there is a long and steady crescendo of speed and volume. The texture becomes exceedingly elaborate with Ex. 35 combining with a reprise of the '*Schaffen*' section of the Adagio. In this, it will be remembered, the composer-father's idealistic theme Ex. 27 and its inversion were built up to a climax out of which sprang the descending phrase Ex. 42. Now the process is repeated on a grand scale, but with Ex. 42 strongly in evidence from the first. This is, in its way, a glorification of the father's products, both paternal and artistic, and it culminates in a fine declamatory passage in which two versions of the child's theme are combined as in the corresponding section of the Scherzo quoted above as Ex. 37. This time, however, the majestic version is played with the fugal form of the theme Ex. 44. Moreover, the mother's principal theme is added as a powerful extra counterpoint fortissimo on all the violins in unison. As the music continues to rise, however, all the themes other than those of the child drop away, the section thus forming the Apotheosis of Bubi. Suddenly, at the climax, Papa's first theme re-enters in a proud augmentation. There is a pause and it might seem that the end is at hand. But Mama is not to be left out and her theme bursts in to start what is, in fact, the closing section of the work.

This whole finale has been justly criticized for being much too long and digressive, many commentators observing that Strauss seems to have experienced some difficulty in stopping. There is no doubt that, left with so intangible a subject, Strauss failed to make this elaborate movement formally convincing. All that he says in the last twelve pages of score he has said before, not once, but often; yet he says it this last time with irresistible brilliance and a virtuosity of orchestration which leaves one open-mouthed. Still one further variant of the child's theme sends the horns squeaking up into altitudes which had been considered unfit for human habitation since Haydn last experimented with them in some of his earlier symphonies:

Ex..45

The ending, with its heroic gestures, the two great tutti fermatas (at least five bars long, says Strauss in a footnote), and the fantastic *élan*, is tremendously exhilarating, while Papa seems to come out of the whole affair most satisfactorily after all, even having the last say.

12

But when it is all over and the sheer elation of the orchestral sound is a thing of the past, one is filled with appalling doubts. For there is, as Romain Rolland said, so very great a disproportion between the subject-matter and the means of expression. The utter lack of sensitivity as to how such bombastic immodesty would strike the world is reflected in Strauss's typical letter to his parents after the première, which took place in New York during his American tour at the beginning of 1904:

> I have succeeded with *Domestica*; it sounds splendid, but is very difficult (especially for the horns, who squealed out their high A famously) on account of the large amount of detailed work, which must be played exceedingly well and accurately, which these miserable bread-and-butter musicians are by no means accustomed to. But it went all right and the reception was overwhelming; perhaps eight recalls; two laurel wreaths; even the critics, who here in New York were to some extent very antagonistic, had gradually to turn round and shut their traps. *Domestica* is splendid, brilliant, too, although it lasts about forty-one minutes, yet it holds the public in breathless suspense. The double

fugue comes off magnificently, the virtuoso coda with its colossal build-up is most grateful to play, the Adagio sounds wonderful; in short, I am content.

Behind this charming self-satisfaction, the passing reference to the critics hides a severe heartache. For the Americans were as merciless as only the American critics can be, beginning immediately in typical style with a headline reading 'Home Sweet Home as written by Richard Strauss—Papa and Momma and Baby Celebrated in Huge Conglomeration of Orchestral Music'. Elsewhere even so great an admirer as Ernest Newman wrote that it 'contrasted badly with the earlier symphonic poems; the instrumental colour is grossly overdone; the polyphony is often coarse and sprawling; the realistic effects on the score are so pitiably foolish that one listens to them with regret that a composer of genius should ever have fallen so low'. In fact, the view began to be widely expressed that this major talent which had held the scene for over a decade in German music was now fading fast and that little more could be hoped for in his direction. Strauss began to perceive that, despite his apparently continued success with the public, he had offended his admirers and detractors alike. It took a true friend such as Rolland to mix advice and understanding with his censure:

> . . . but if you give the work in Paris, believe me, don't publish the programme. What good is this programme which belittles the work—makes it appear puerile. It is enough to put *Symphonia Domestica* without any other indication. Here is an ordinary symphony, you are free to interpret the programme in any way you like. But why publish it? There is nothing to see in the programme but pretty mediocre events. What is interesting in the work is not the recounting of these events, but the powerful interior forces which stirred them up. The programme can only mislead one's attention and falsify the character of the work.

At first Strauss protested that he had never given any such programme to the piece at all, and that in any case Rolland had misinterpreted the purpose of such a programme, which must be general rather than detailed. Nevertheless he wisely complied with Rolland's suggestion, though he was not particularly pleased to discover that he was now hailed as a true symphonist gathered back to the fold:

> Isn't it wonderful [he wrote in a letter to the author Oscar Bie], how if today one has added a literary programme to the title of an orchestral work one is reckoned as

one of those composers of Programme Music (do you
happen to know the difference between Programme Music
and real music? I don't!)—and if instead tomorrow it
so happens that one keeps quiet about the poetic idea, or
only suggests it, one is welcomed as a penitent back into
the bosom of the one and only holy Absolute Music, (Do
you happen to know what Absolute music is? I don't!) like
a Prodigal Son.

This was, of course, the over-protestation of an embittered artist,
but his pique was perhaps understandable even if he was being absurd
in suggesting that in his view there was no such thing as Absolute
Music, as if he could forget not only the days when he had written no
other, but the whole commotion on this very subject in which he had
taken a leading part.

In the end Strauss tried to exculpate himself on the major indictment
of exploiting and inflating his private life in an inartistic and immodest
way. He published a manifesto on his intentions, stating that he had
from the first meant the work sincerely as an exposition of its subject
in the most general and universal way possible:

The symphony is meant to give a musical picture of
married life. I know that some people believe that the work
is a jocular exposé of happiness in the home, but I own that
I did not mean to make fun when I composed it. What can
be more serious a matter than married life? Marriage is the
most serious happening in life, and the holy joy over such
a union is intensified through the arrival of a child. Yet life
has naturally got its funny side, and this I have also introduced into the work in order to enliven it. But I want the
symphony to be taken seriously and it has been played in
this spirit in Germany.

This rather shamefaced apologia reads sadly. Despite his unreliable
taste, Strauss was too great an artist to have put himself so much in the
wrong. Nor was the world hoodwinked for one moment; his intentions were explicit in the music and as always it is this which counts for
the most, and on this the work is judged. If it has been found wanting,
it is for less than was at first thought. Strauss's affection for it, which
caused him to include it in his last Albert Hall concert in 1947, was not
mere sentimentality. True enough the programme is intolerable.
Equally true and on that very account, the music is markedly less great
than in any of the previous major works since his maturity. There is,

nevertheless, much fine writing in it, and in particular a vast amount which prepared the way for the truly great works which lay so very near over the horizon. The symphonic poems of the concert platform had traced their curve in Strauss's output and were now descending fast. For if *Heldenleben* had shown the beginning of the decline after the last peak of *Don Quixote*, *Domestica* was well on the way down. Only one work remains, near the bottom, the *Alpensinfonie*, which will be discussed in a later chapter in Volume 2. Another curve, equally great, was rising which would amply replace the old; the curve of the stage works, on the summit of which Strauss's reputation stands as securely as on the masterpieces which crowned that earlier spate of genius, now all but spent.

CHAPTER VII

THE RETURN TO THE STAGE

ALTHOUGH Strauss lost the courage to write for the stage after the failure of *Guntram*, this is not to say that theatrical projects were no longer of interest to him. On the contrary, few years passed without his being tempted by some new project, as libretti or scenarios presented themselves to him in various degrees of completion. Some were outlined for the composer by a number of different authors, others emanated from Strauss's own mind. We have already seen how Strauss drafted part of a libretto on the subject of *Till Eulenspiegel bei den Schildbürgern*, and how two years later Graf von Sporck prepared a revised text for him. In this version the figure of Eulenspiegel himself is gradually supplanted and in a still later sketch of 1897 he disappeared entirely; the last draft is even renamed *Die verlassenen Weiber von Schilda*.

The next scheme was the result of a brief association with Frank Wedekind, the author of the notorious plays *Erdgeist* and *Büchse der Pandora*, upon which Alban Berg later based his opera *Lulu*. Wedekind had a number of ideas in hand which he outlined to Strauss. The only one which took the composer's fancy for a short time was a ballet panto-mime on the subject of a flea which thrived under the hoop skirt of a noble lady. An opera text by the poet Otto Bierbaum entitled *Lobetanz*, which was naïve in character like a children's game, had no appeal for him and was soon abandoned. A scheme for setting Goethe's *Lila* was also considered at one point. Nor was this the first time, for as a child Strauss had already set some excerpts from *Lila*. Once again, however, he did not progress far with the subject.

In February 1899 Strauss himself began a sketch for an opera libretto in one act, a *Diebeskomödie* which occupied him on and off during the course of the next few months. It was said to have been called *Ekke und Schnittlein* and to have taken place in Spain. Papa Strauss thought the idea frivolous and said as much, but he need not have worried. Richard's heart was not in the scheme and although he returned once more to the sketches later in the year he never proceeded with the plan. The same fate overtook another ballet proposed to him by the poet Paul Scheerbart, although at first Strauss was enthusiastic about the idea of a *Dance of the Comets*. It would have been a 'very pretty astronomical ballet' in which he could at least 'have stormed about in the orchestra without worrying over any singers'. Yet a further ballet scheme based on Watteau's picture *Embarquement pour Cythère*[1] held Strauss's attention during much of the year 1900 and reached quite advanced stages, including a fair copy of as much as he had done, before even this was laid aside[2]. It was to have been a large-scale undertaking in three acts, the scenario by Strauss himself, under the title of *Die Insel Kythere*. The action was to have been extremely elaborate, with a vast list of characters ranging from pilgrims, a group of noblemen and women, representatives of the *Commedia dell'Arte*, Moors, Chinamen, and Apes, to a complete cast of peasants, supplemented by a further complete array of classical figures such as Venus, Adonis, Diana, Hermes, Amor, Nymphs, Cyclopes *et alia* for the second act, which was in itself to have been a vast transformation scene.[3] No less than ten numbers were projected for the six scenes of Act I and four for the four scenes of Act II. Of Act III less was planned, only two pieces reaching any degree of continuity, though sketches exist for some nine further movements. The particular interest in the surviving draft lies in the enormous number of ideas it contains which Strauss used in later works. Act I has two major themes from *Feuersnot*, the Ländler which appears as a Peasant Waltz from the opening scene, and the Nocturne from the later part of the same act which Strauss took

[1] This same picture gave Debussy the inspiration for his well-known 'L'isle Joyeuse'.

[2] It might be thought strange that Strauss considered it worth his while to make a fair copy of a mere sketch, but throughout his life this was a characteristic of his method of work. All his surviving manuscripts are impeccably neat.

[3] It is only fair to admit that many of the characters doubled with the classical gods for the second act, but even so the number of performers on the stage would have run into several hundreds.

for the closing love scene. In between, one is astonished to find none other than the Minuet and Gavotte which are two of the most familiar movements from the incidental music to *Le Bourgeois Gentilhomme* composed twelve years later. One of the other pieces is unexpectedly based on the second Don Quixote theme (Ex. 28, Chapter 5 above), though this must have been a deliberate reworking of a fertile idea.

The second act contains ideas later used for *Josephslegende* and *Ariadne auf Naxos*, the latter being the familiar B flat *Naturthema* 'Bald aber naht ein Bote', which seems to have begun life as a solemn entrance hymn for the arrival of Venus and Adonis. Altogether, as Strauss later said, there was enough material to fill three ballet evenings, and there is no doubt that the fascinating scheme would have come to fruition had it not been submerged by another project the affinity of which to Strauss's frame of mind was so striking that it carried all before it.

2

It was in Munich towards the end of 1898 that Strauss first met Ernst von Wolzogen, a popular satirical author who had already written a novel around the life of Liszt and who was the father of the *Überbrettl* movement.[4] Strauss seems to have opened his heart very quickly to his new friend, confiding to him his qualms over his future in the theatre due to the failure of *Guntram*. Opportunist as Wolzogen was, he immediately encouraged Strauss in his idea of an operatic revenge, and the two men rapidly cast about for a vehicle for the scheme. It was Strauss himself who discovered the central idea in a collection of Dutch legends which included one entitled *The Extinguished Fires of Audenaarde*. In this story a young lover who has been spurned by the girl he adores seeks the assistance of a wise old magician, who draws out from the youth the details of his humiliation. It seems that he has allowed himself to be drawn in a basket half-way up the

---

[4] This was a semi-artistic development of the German cabaret song which began in Munich and later spread to other German cities. The songs often had a political flavour and were largely satirical in character. Another poet who contributed to the movement was Otto Julius Bierbaum, who was mentioned above in connexion with the projected *Lobetanz*, and three of whose poems Strauss had already set to music as his op. 29, including the evergreen *Traum durch die Dämmerung*. The *Überbrettl* became very lively during the early part of the new century and had a strong influence on such important post-war writers as Bertholt Brecht. Wolzogen's first ideas leading to the formation of this movement date from as far back as 1900, the year in which he completed the libretto of *Feuersnot*.

side of his beloved's house in the promise of fulfilment of all his desires. At this frustrating point, however, he has been left to cool his ardour the whole night long and only lowered to the ground in the morning amidst the jeers of the assembled townspeople. The magician listens sympathetically to the sad tale and resolves to give the unfortunate youth his revenge. To effect this he puts out all fires in the town and makes it known that they can only be rekindled one at a time from the flame which will spring from the girl's back when her naked body is publicly exhibited in the market square. Thus the wretched girl has to suffer a humiliation comparable with that which she inflicted upon her poor lover.

Naturally enough the story as it stands could scarcely be enacted on the stage. Yet as a jumping-off point it had decided possibilities which Wolzogen was not slow to exploit. Already the following March (1899), after a visit to Munich in which he attended a performance of *Zarathustra*, he wrote to Strauss:

> This has given me the urge to get on with our opera at once. I have now got the following idea; *Feuersnot*—one Act —scene of action Munich in legendary Renaissance times. The young hero lover is himself a magician, the Grand Old Man, his master, who was once thrown out by the worthy people of Munich, never appears in person at all. The malicious young girl must in the end sacrifice her maiden-hood in order to redeem the town from their 'Feuersnot' (fire famine—fire need) upon the pressing demands of the High Council and the Bourgeoisie. When love unites with the magic of genius then even the greatest spiritual philistine must see daylight!
>
> And the motto, which will be written behind the ears of the dear narrow-minded townsfolk and mixed in with some ideal pan-pipe strains will go something like this;

> Hold him right fast, that curious man
> Who'll magic you all a bit if he can!
> You think of virtue he will tell
> And banish need and spite as well.
> Just swill away and fill your paunches
> And quarrel for the fattest haunches
> To heaven he will never go,
> There must be magic there, you know—
> If bad from good you'll only learn
> Then will your light for ever burn.

That's just improvised, but you will already be able to get the idea from it. I have in mind a linguistic style of rough joviality if somewhat archaic and with a decided tinge of dialect.

Wolzogen also cleverly wooed Strauss by pressing the analogy of his role as Wagner's successor (Richard III; there is no Richard II, as Bülow once said), and so contriving the libretto that the young magician Kunrad was plainly identifiable with Strauss himself, the very names of Wagner, Strauss, and Wolzogen appearing in the text through a series of double and even triple meanings, as will be shown in detail later. This fitted in splendidly with Strauss's preoccupations over autobiographical references in his other works of the period and was palpably irresistible. By October 1900 he was in possession of the completed poem and was already sketching out the music. At first his letters home sound a little half-hearted, 'the opera, which will be very simple, quite amuses me', but very quickly he warmed to his work, composing day and night, until before the end of November he had already set thirty-four out of the fifty pages of libretto. He now wrote enthusiastically that the score would be pure Lortzing ('supremely popular and melodious'), and that his use of well-known local folk-tunes would make the good people of Munich sit up! The sketches were finished by the end of the year, and the orchestration began on 1st January 1901. The whole work was finished on Wagner's birthday and the last page of the score is inscribed: 'Completed on the birthday and to the greater glory of the "Almighty"! Charlottenburg, 22 May, 1901'.

3

As we have seen, Wolzogen transferred the action to Munich and made much of the 'Fire' element in the old Netherlandic legend. In so doing he drew freely from the various customs and beliefs which actually existed in former times both in Germany and elsewhere. His very title Feuersnot has a basis of fact in the old 'Need-fires' which were lit in some parts of Central Europe during the Middle Ages. There was no fixed day of the year, as there was with the many fire festivals, but it is known that in some parts of Germany Need-fires were lit annually as a superstitious precaution against cattle-plague. All the fires in the neighbourhood would be extinguished, the Need-fire lit—often by children working in the dark, rubbing sticks together—and a great bonfire

would arise from the resultant flames. The household fires throughout
the village were then rekindled individually from the bonfire, thus providing the origin of the legend of Audenaarde. Wolzogen, however,
times his action for Midsummer's Eve (the Johannesnacht of *Die Meistersinger* fame) and so links the story with the fire festivals of the
Solstices, the Winter Solstice falling on 21st December and the Summer
Solstice accordingly on 21st June[5] which latter was known in Germany
as Sonnwend or Subend. He then described the period as 'fabelhafte
Unzeit',[6] but it is plainly the Middle Ages which are depicted and the
twelfth century is specifically mentioned in the stage directions. The
scene is old Munich, a description of which is given in some detail, even
down to the historical names of the old streets. Unlike *Guntram*, there is
no Prelude and a brief introduction serves to announce the motif,
which throughout the *Singgedicht* (as Wolzogen calls the work) refers
to the Solstice fire itself:

Ex. 1

[5] It is important to differentiate between the Solsticial fires and the Celtic
ritual Beltane fires which were lit on 1st May. The English translation of the
score, made by no less a person than the author and composer William Wallace,
translated 'Subend' and 'Feuersnot' throughout as 'Beltane fire'. Though obviously
practical, this is, in fact, technically wrong, despite Wallace's elaborate self-
justification, printed in the English textbook of the opera.

[6] 'Fabulous no-time.'

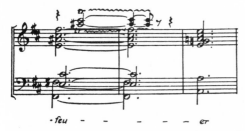

- *feu* - - - - - - *er*

A gay theme then bursts in, setting the mood for the action, and almost immediately the curtain rises. A horde of children are crowding through the streets, followed by a group of amused townsfolk. The children, heralded by fife and drum, are pushing a large hand-cart which is filled with wood. They are collecting this wood, solicited from door to door, for the great evening bonfire which is shortly to be lit according to ancient annual tradition. The very custom of the children begging for fuel in this way is not only true to history, but survives to the present day in some parts, notably in Provence.

The style of the music describing the children and their activities marks an important development in Strauss's idiom, which had remained basically unchanged for the past dozen years, ever since the enormous step which produced *Don Juan*. The sparkling simplicity of this material could have been foreseen in parts of *Till Eulenspiegel*, perhaps, but it is only now that Strauss exploits it to so great an extent that it becomes integral to the lighter element of his operatic manner. We shall see in many places that *Feuersnot* is a preparatory exercise for, in particular, *Der Rosenkavalier*.

Ex. 2

The children sing stanzas of quasi-folk-song, in broad dialect, punctuated by fragments of Ex. 2. The words are such as the following,

> Wer ma a Scheit giebt, is a braver mö
> wer ma koans giebt, is a rechter Gockelhô![7]

set to music much of which sounds like a parody of the Dance Song from *Hänsel und Gretel*. The children are rowdy and often rude, but they are encouraged with sweets by the townsfolk, few of whom grudge the wood for which they are asked in so impolite a manner. From time to time the singing breaks into a refrain of the 'Eeny, meeny, miny, mo' variety:

Ex. 3

This links up easily with Ex. 1 and forms part of the enthusiastic song in praise of the great solstice fires. Soon the Burgomaster comes forward benignly and promises the children enough wood to baptize even the Evil One with fire, and this reference to diabolism is accompanied by a motif suggestive of licking flames:

Ex. 4

The burgomaster is followed by his daughter Diemut, the local beauty, who enters with her three playmates. Her melody, again a simple folk-song strain, is with its refrain one of the most prominent melodies in the opera.

---

[7] Wallace, faced with an impossible task, translates this as:
'Those who give wood are surely proper men,
Those who give none are not worth a silly hen!' (!)

Ex. 5a

b

The typical use of the old horn-call figure,  so often commented on before, is especially prevalent in the accompaniment to this melody and reappears again in a further motif which follows directly. One of the older girls in the gang of children sings a little couplet in praise of Diemut, foretelling that since firewood has been satisfactorily forthcoming, undoubtedly she will be betrothed that very day:

Ex. 6

[8] 'Sweet cherries, candy by the ton . . . Emma, Ursula, Elizabeth, all girls like mead.'

[9] 'Miss Diemut looks like an angel: Miss Diemut will be a bride today.'

Richard Strauss with his wife and son

A remarkable feature of the whole of this opening section is the trans-
parency of the orchestral writing. Instead of the thick Wagnerian texture of *Guntram* there is a most imaginative use of solo groups of both
wind and strings. This is particularly suitable for the succession of folk-
like tunes such as occur in this scene.

The children's verses become increasingly ribald until they verge on
the blasphemous. The townsfolk turn on them angrily. In no way
abashed, the procession moves on to the next house, where the children
create a tremendous hullabaloo, hammering on the door and crowing
like cocks. This brings the innkeeper to the door of his tavern, pompously announcing to the children that they had better leave that house
alone. The man who lives there is apparently a very strange and fearful
individual who never mixes with any of his neighbours even when he
goes to eat at the inn. At the reference to the inmate of the weird house
the orchestra introduces a motif which tells us who is meant, as this
theme later grows into a surging melody characterizing the passionate
leveller,[10] Kunrad (and hence, by analogy, Strauss himself). Here, however, we see him only through the superstitious eyes of the ignorant
innkeeper:

Ex. 7

As Pöschel elaborates on the uncanny character of the house, the motif
of Evil (Ex. 4) is heard from time to time on the flute or solo viola.
Abruptly Kunz Gilgenstock, the baker and brewer, bursts in with hot
dispute. He is characterized by a jaunty theme which is very typical of
the popular idiom Strauss was intent on cultivating for this work:

[10] There is some confusion over Kunrad's trade or occupation. In the German
text he is an 'Ebner', the dictionary translation of which is 'Leveller'. It is probable,
however, that the word was used in medieval times for some kind of wood-
worker. The translations mostly avoid the issue by diverting him to the far more
mysterious and romantic calling of alchemist.

Ex. 8

Before long this is combined with a genuine old Munich drinking-song
Der Alte Peter:

Ex. 9

Gilgenstock protests that the 'strange neighbour' is, in fact, fully
accredited and that Pöschel has no grounds on which to revile him.
His defence is supported by Hämmerlin, the haberdasher, who paints a
very different portrait of a well-spoken young man of proud bearing, a
description which is substantiated by a new and important form of
Kunrad's motif (cf. Ex. 7):

Ex. 10

But Gilgenstock and Hämmerlin are not allowed to complete their
eulogies. The old cooper Tulbeck (taken by a high tenor of the kind
who usually sings the part of Mime in Wagner's *Ring*) screeches out a
fanatical attack to a further and frenetic transformation of Ex. 7:

Ex. 11

Tulbeck hints of dark secrets which only he knows and the crowd is
naturally curious. Ex. 11 envelops the texture and sinks to silence as the
malicious old gossiper prepares to tell his awful story. It is a foolish
tirade and largely irrelevant, but it makes a good contrasting episode
and gives Strauss the opportunity of introducing another old Munich
drinking-song, *Mir san net von Pasing*. This is done in a way which also
gives a deliberate reminiscence of the Giant's motif from *Das Rheingold*:

Ex. 12

The gist of Tulbeck's tale is that the original inhabitant of the gruesome house was descended from an ogre, a slander on the memory of the old magician which is vehemently refuted by another old man, Kofel, the smith. While Tulbeck sings, Ex. 12 is given in deeper orchestral colours and is interspersed with the fire-like motif of Evil (Ex. 4) and the more horrific version of Kunrad's theme, Ex. 11. By contrast Kofel's rebuke is given a very mellow setting, the folk-song Ex. 12 appearing in the major against a gentle triplet figuration. Kofel affirms that the old man was a 'würd'ger Hexanmeister, hat an der Stadt nur Gut's gethan'.[11] It is of course clear that this further controversy is a caricature of the battle which was waged over the head of Strauss's master, Richard Wagner, though the direct allusion is reserved for a more striking position in the opera.

The children sing a new and equally ribald song, later to acquire some importance

Ex. 13

Is a frem der Herr im Haus [12]

as they renew their attacks on the door of the strange house, beating and hammering on it. Ex. 11 is repeated emphatically on the full woodwind, behind which Kunrad's voice can just be heard calling from inside. The orchestra suddenly plunges into the depths and he at last appears on the threshold. He is described as 'about twenty-five years old, dressed in a dark, becoming costume, bare-headed, long-haired and pale'.

Musically he is announced by a new motif which, although later to

[11] 'A worthy necromancer who only did good for the city.'
[12] 'Is there some stranger in the house?'

develop melodic interest, is first given as a Wagnerian chordal sequence:

Ex. 14

Such harmonic themes are a great feature of Strauss's later works such as the *Alpensinfonie* and *Die Frau ohne Schatten*; the first entry of Orestes in *Elektra* springs particularly to mind (cf. Ex. 33, Chapter 8(b)). To a sinister form of Ex. 7 Kunrad asks the children whether they are trying to arouse some monster, not dreaming that it is he himself who is universally regarded as an ogre. At first fearfully (Ex. 13 in hesitant phrases), but with rapidly growing courage, the children make their demand for faggots, the request being clothed as usual in a threat. Their reference to the impending burning of Kunrad's immortal soul, should he have the temerity to refuse, sparks off a wild burst of fire from Ex. 4 leading into the gay Ex. 2 as the children, now wholly at their ease once more, chatter away their impertinent verses, ending with mocking cock-crows. Unperturbed, Kunrad comments on their festive appearance, his themes taking on the friendlier guise of Ex. 10 as he does so. He is answered this time by Diemut's three companions, who tell him that it is the Solstice today and tease him for having slept through it. Their taunts have a most gratifying reaction and to the 'Sonnwend' themes (Exx. 1 and 3) Kunrad exclaims with distress at having missed this all-important occasion. His ecstasies over this 'boldest and happiest of festivities' evoke a new and luscious theme in Strauss's favourite thirds:

Ex. 15

Such a gorgeous melody, in itself the quintessence of Strauss, inevitably conjures up the magic of love, and it is in that aspect of 'Subend' that Ex. 15 specializes. Immediately on its heels yet another vital motif enters which epitomizes Kunrad himself as the Solstice Lover:

Ex. 16

It is, of course, immediately apparent not only that the figure ⌐ b ⌐ is a variant of the phrase ⌐ a ⌐, but that both are directly related to Ex. 14.

Kunrad warms to his theme of self-reproach and turning to the children invites them to take what wood they need from the very structure of his house. He then sets the example by wrenching off one of the shutters and smashing it under his feet. This demonstration is greeted with enthusiasm by the children but, naturally enough, extreme scepticism by their elders; even Hämmerlin, who had previously spoken in his defence, now decides that poor Kunrad is clearly no more than a simpleton, and Gilgenstock is also inclined to believe in the young man's powers over the spirits if he can indulge in such extravagant pranks. (Gilgenstock's theme, Ex. 8, in the minor.) An ensemble is building up amongst the townsfolk, based generally on Kunrad's motifs (Exx. 10, 11 and 16), when the three companions interrupt with a new taunt. They have not failed to notice that this weird sorcerer, as everyone had imagined him to be, has turned out to be an exceedingly presentable young man. 'Who', they ask, 'will dare to leap over the flames with him?' in which they refer to the universal custom, where-soever Midsummer fires are lit, of lovers jumping together over the burning pyres. Belief had it that should the girl emerge entirely un-harmed she would fail to conceive for the whole of the current year. This vision of Kunrad as a dashing young lover of Solstice-time naturally conjures up Ex. 16 now suitably transformed:

Ex. 16a.

The companions now turn on Diemut and to seductive music built around Exx. 15 and 16 suggest that she may be already smitten by the charms of the mysterious young man. Diemut breaks away from them in fury, but her angry retort is given together with Ex. 10, suggesting that the figure of Kunrad is by no means repellent to her. The com-panions accordingly renew their thrusts in a scherzetto based on Ex.

16a, but containing a sly reference to the theme Ex. 8, in which one of the townsfolk defended Kunrad in the earlier ensemble.

Ex. 17

Diemut, however, shows nothing but contempt for either her provocative companions (whom she suspects of having designs on their own account) or Kunrad, who so far as she can see is likely to have no roof over his head, seeing how the children are setting upon his house, and whose worldly goods are likely to be entirely consumed by the 'Subend' fires. Even the worthy Burgomaster, her father, interrupts at this point, blaming Kunrad for permitting what has become destruction on quite a serious scale. But Kunrad is not to be shaken. His determination to sacrifice his melancholy cell has been strengthened by his growing admiration for the spirited Diemut. Ex. 16a builds up to a climax and breaks off abruptly as he plunges into a passionate outburst in which he publicly abnegates book-learning and gloomy study in favour of Nature and Life. These will teach him the magic towards which his old master had led him.

In much of this arietta there is an unmistakable sound of the orchestral texture of *Tannhäuser* which, deliberate as it may have been under the circumstances, sounds oddly conventional. The arrival of a set piece of this kind was well timed, but although Strauss had plenty of material at hand he failed to derive from it an entirely convincing opening subject; moreover, in his preoccupation with following an existing text[13] he could not so easily depend on his hitherto reliable instinct in organizing the formal scheme with that elusive but all-important quality of inevitability. As a result the section is less successful as an exposition of its hero than, for example, the parallel exposition in *Don Juan*, which it initially resembles to some extent. Nevertheless all Kunrad's many motifs are introduced and developed in their many guises, including even the sinister Ex. 7, suggesting that Kunrad has caught a glimpse of himself as the outside world has seen him. More-

[13] One is conscious here and there that in this first opera written to another man's libretto Strauss was not yet sure enough of his ground to make the criticisms, alterations, and demands with which he was soon to plague Hofmannsthal.

over, a further theme appears here for the first time which will before long come into its own in Kunrad's great love song. I quote it already in full, although so far only the two opening phrases are stated:

Ex. 18

This fine melody represents the inner Kunrad, no longer the sorcerer's apprentice, but himself a master of fire, and with it love, knowing that both will ultimately consume him. In due course Ex. 18 has an exposition to itself which forms part of the main lyrical centre of the opera. By comparison the present outburst is far less significant as an entity in its own right and serves rather to heighten the tension in the hitherto somewhat easy-going drama.

As Kunrad speaks of burning all he has accomplished, he directly addresses Diemut, at whom he has been gazing throughout his aria. Then asking her vehemently whether she will spring through the flames with him, he leaps towards her and kisses her full on the lips.

So brazen an action naturally causes a furore. The Burgomaster quickly comes forward and denounces Kunrad, in which he is supported by the townsfolk, all of whom are suitably shocked, except for the three playmates, who dance round the shattered Diemut in huge delight. Ex. 16a here undergoes a transformation which reminds one strongly of the double fugue from *Sinfonia Domestica* (cf. Ex. 44, Chapter 6)

Ex. 19

while Diemut's utter shame and humiliation are portrayed in a new and most expressive melody:

Ex. 20

The playmates' good-humoured raillery takes the form of a folk-like melody of the kind which Strauss was soon to cultivate more and more, though it had never been far from his natural idiom:

Ex. 21

The relationship of this pretty tune to the religious section of *Zarathustra* and so back to the *Stimmungsbilder*, op. 9 can easily be seen by comparing its contours with those of Exx. 5 and 6 from Chapter 1. The feeling behind the three themes is widely varied, but their formation is almost identical. Within the present work Ex. 21 is most closely related to such similar songs as that of the children (Ex. 13) and that in which the people acknowledge Kunrad's integrity and persuade Diemut to yield to him, later in the opera (see below, Ex. 34).

Diemut reacts with bitterness and ill humour to the taunts of her companions, while the gaiety of the children (Exx. 2 and 3) only adds to her misery. The mood of banter grows steadily, with Diemut vowing passionately that she will make Kunrad pay for his insult and that they will all be the witnesses of her revenge, until suddenly the music bursts into a stylish Viennese Waltz. The children now all dance round Kunrad, shouting their conviction that Diemut will be married before winter:

Ex. 22

[14] 'Diemut, are you going to drink the love potion? Did the fire fly at you even before you left?' The reference is to the custom of leaping over the flames (see above and p. 213).

leading to:

This reappearance of the Waltz in Strauss's work is, of course, of salient importance. As we have seen, the first example was in the most unlikely setting, that of the Dance of Nietzsche's Superman. Here was a more suitable opportunity, and Strauss threw himself into it with the utmost abandon as if born to it by his very name. Actually its relevance to the time and scene of the action is only questionable on grounds of sheer tempo. The Waltz evolved during the eighteenth century from the Ländler, an extremely popular traditional dance which had flourished in Bavaria as well as Austria for at least two hundred years. The only difference between the two dance forms was that of speed, the Ländler being generally danced at a rather deliberate pace. The present-day view of the Waltz as being predominantly Viennese is due to its outstanding exploitation and development by composers, especially as a very quick dance, for Viennese ballrooms, from the mid-nineteenth century up to the present day. Yet there is no doubt that especially in Bavaria it was, from early times, a highly characteristic feature of popular life and that here at least Strauss was fully justified in introducing it.

Strauss treats it much like his famous namesake though in a more concentrated and, at the same time, more elaborate way. Theme follows theme in an extended panoply of waltz-tunes. Even the motif of Diemut's humiliation, Ex. 20, is incorporated with effective major-minor contrast, as the poor girl tries to escape the mockery of the children. A further strain follows, calmer in mood, and this in turn passes to another genuine and rollicking Munich folk-song, *Guten Morgen, Herr Fischer*, which bears the strangest resemblance to the waltz from Tchaikovsky's *Eugen Onegin*.

Ex. 23

Exx. 2 and 3 convert easily into waltzes and the whole section constitutes a splendid development of the material in $\frac{3}{4}$ time, marking both the climax and the conclusion of the first main scene of the opera.

The Burgomaster now tells the children to be off and start the fire before the Bailiff locks them in his tower for breaking up Kunrad's house, and they go away with their cart, screaming and laughing. The playmates also depart, though not before there has been much whispering with Diemut, as they concoct some secret plot. The stage clears gradually and the Bailiff, Herr Schweiker von Gundelfingen,[15] enters with some stupid-looking constables, a trifle disturbed at the breach of the peace. The Burgomaster assures him that it is best to leave things alone; only one or two hearts have been set on fire (references to Ex. 17); then, taking Diemut's hand, he tries to cheer her up and take her indoors. Her distress arouses the Bailiff's curiosity and he is even more astonished when he hears that Kunrad is to blame, as he personally has never heard anything to the young man's discredit.

The children can be heard in the distance singing their refrain of 'Maja, maja, mia, mô!' while Diemut disengages herself from her father and, with a tearful disclaimer to the perplexed old Bailiff, goes alone into the house. Kunrad's theme, Ex. 10, gradually breaks up, passes back into its initial form, Ex. 7, and disappears into the bass. The fragments ⌈ x ⌉ from the waltz theme, Ex. 22, now form the basis of a transitional passage together with a jerky version of Diemut's humiliation theme, Ex. 20. The Burgomaster and Bailiff exchange a few words over the incipient lovers and then, the Burgomaster going off to the Fire, the Bailiff approaches Kunrad. The chordal motif Ex. 14 supplies the background harmonies as the old man suggests that Kunrad's method of courtship may have been too abrupt. He gets no reaction from the young lover, however, who is gazing dreamily at the sky as darkness falls completely. People can be discerned leaving their homes, the distant horizon glows red with the now raging fire and the singing of the children is again clearly audible as they shout with joy and beat their drums. There is a surging in the orchestra and a great build-up of the 'Subend' love theme (Ex. 15) launches Kunrad upon his fine song of passion and philosophy:

[15] I confess to finding the Dickensian names irresistible.

Ex. 24

This rearing form of Ex. 15 from the bottom to the top of the orchestra anticipates to a remarkable degree the mighty octave motif from *Elektra* (see Ex. 11, Chapter VIII(b)). At this point the emotional level of the music deepens as the characterization of Kunrad takes on a warmer and richer colour. His whole being has been transformed by his awareness of Diemut, and he expresses his new emotions in metaphysical terms full of allusions to the magical conquest of fire and the burning pain of glorious longings. The poetic philosophy is worthy of *Tristan* at its most abstruse and one feels with the Bailiff when he bursts out with the remark 'Ye Gods! He's mad! I'd better be off', and departs at speed through the city gates.

Musically this passage consists of an extended melodizing based on and around Ex. 18 and, together with the duet which follows, is one of the chief lyrical passages of the opera. It is, however, better known in the orchestral version in which, during the closing scene, it appears complete for a second time. In fact, the music gives the impression of having been composed first in the purely orchestral form, and the voice part, which is musically superfluous, added later. This is demonstrably true of much Wagnerian vocal music, but at its most successful the technique is disguised better than Strauss manages to achieve here. Yet the fervour and beauty of the music matches so well the spirit of what Kunrad is trying to express that one readily ignores the fact of the melodic line lying wholly in the orchestra, the voice contributing a disjointed series of subsidiary phrases. One

portion of the violins' cantilena demands quotation both for its subsequent metamorphosis and for its splendid example of Strauss's surprise cadences:

Ex. 25

Kunrad's last imploring question 'wer mag den Zauber zwingen?'[16]
melts into the soft poetic theme of Diemut's Song to the Midsummer
Night:

Ex. 26

(cf. Chapter 1, Ex. 10)

Diemut has lit the lamp in her room and has moved out on to the
balcony, combing her long hair as she sings. Kunrad hides in the
shadow of the house.[17] The derivation of Ex. 26 from Diemut's second
motif Ex. 6 is apparent and later becomes important when the two
themes are used in close conjunction. References to Kunrad's themes
(Exx. 10 and 16 (b)), as she sings of her aching heart, lead to a new and
pathetic figure of a kind which reappears all through Strauss's works:

Ex. 27

As Diemut sings of 'him who wished to choose her' and the foolish
way in which he went about it, Kunrad quickly moves under the

[16] 'Who can conquer the magic'?
[17] There is a most extraordinary mistranslation in the English vocal score which
gives 'laughing to himself' for 'Lauschend' ('listening').
[18] 'find her weeping.'

balcony and addresses her. He is full of excited eagerness: 'Will she not teach him better? Has he not paid penance enough? Let her open the door that he may make atonement to her in all her beauty.' Kunrad's passionate wooing is made to the melodies of his great song Exx. 18, 24 and 25, though with the addition of a syrupy little figure which we shall meet again in both *Elektra* and *Rosenkavalier*:

Ex. 28

Diemut replies sharply in a series of passages based on repetitions of a pert motif derived from Ex. 20, the theme of humiliation:

Ex. 29a.

Kunrad then changes this into what ultimately becomes the very theme of her capitulation:

Ex. 29b.

Her threats that Kunrad has still to know the meaning of penance do not affect him; he will not stir from the spot until she surrenders to him with her golden crown of hair. Even her taunt at the word 'crown'— that the idea of coronation is inapposite now that his palace is reduced to firewood—merely spurs him to greater enthusiasm as he elaborates on his kingdom of the wide world in which their royal wedding will be celebrated under the flaming sky of the midsummer night.

This whole section is in many ways the most imaginative and accomplished in the opera, and shows in an advanced stage most of the elements of Strauss's future operatic style: the instinctive power of thematic synthesis; the freedom and beauty of the writing for soprano voice, including leaps of as much as two octaves;[19] the use of soft brass

[19] Such apparently wild treatment of the voice originates from Wagner's writing for Kundry in Act II of *Parsifal* and leads forward through Strauss in direct line of succession to Schönberg's second Quartet and *Erwartung*. Gawky as it looks on paper, this form of tessitura has proved itself not merely practical but dramatically effective in the highest degree.

to point a motivic reference, such as the appearance of Ex. 17 in augmentation set for three trumpets in a manner employed repeatedly in
Salome; and in particular the mysterious, shadowy orchestration which
becomes such a feature of *Elektra* and *Die Frau ohne Schatten*. Exx. 10
and 15 sweep against a series of shining tremolo pedal-points in rows
of consecutive thirds and the instrumental colouring takes on a trans-
parent lucidity which lasts until the love duet. Diemut pretends to be
won over by the poetic image painted for her by Kunrad. All the last
themes (including Ex. 29 in both forms, the pathetic figure Ex. 27 and
Kunrad's Ex. 24, complete with his fervent declamation of the title
word 'Feuersnot') are hurried along in a rapid swirling movement
which fades away as a fine glowing statement of the midsummer-night
melody (Ex. 26) begins, sung together by the two lovers. This now
extends into a passage in sixths derived from Kunrad's Ex. 10, which
melting phrase henceforth forms a part of the love music, whether
Diemut is merely pretending, as here, or whether she is sincere, as
during her true capitulation towards the end of the opera.

Ex. 30

Throughout the duet the orchestra supplies rapid figuration suggestive
of the fiery background now raging fiercely in the distance. The
graphic instrumentation grows stronger as the lovers sing of the flames
which 'fliessen in Fluten, leuchtende Gluten'.[20] They then co-relate this
to their *Herzeleide*[21] with the lamenting theme Ex. 27. The language is
again pure Wagnerianism, and with the identification of this theme
with the word 'Herzeleide' it suddenly becomes apparent that Strauss
took it straight out of the *Herzeleide* section from Act II of *Parsifal*,
an instance of plagiarism justified after the event through ingenious
cross-reference.

Strauss directs that both singers should greatly exaggerate the
pathos in this duet, a surprising instruction, since although Diemut may
well be making sport of Kunrad, he for his part is undoubtedly in

[20] 'flow in floods, gleaming flames.'
[21] Heart's sorrow.

earnest. Perhaps beneath her hypocrisy Diemut, too, is profoundly moved, although her pride will not allow her to admit it, even to herself.

A glowing cadence is reached in which the theme of Diemut's capitulation (Ex. 29b) is hurled out triumphantly by the horns against a flickering version of Ex. 1, the 'Subend' fire theme, which is reminiscent of the Fire Music from *Die Walküre*. The children are then heard yet again, chanting their 'Maja, maja, mia, mô' and the vision fades. With soft but importunate phrases from his many motifs, Kunrad begs Diemut for admission to her room, and she, shyly pleading that onlookers will see if she admits him openly, points out to him the basket which lies at the foot of the wall of her house, all roped up with pulleys for hoisting wood and other commodities to the top floor. After only the most formal of objections, Kunrad accedes to this extraordinary suggestion and seats himself in the basket, contenting himself with her promise that he will soon be hidden on the balcony with her. His theme Ex. 16 performs the upward journey (through the orchestra from horn to piccolo) in optimistic expectation that his body will shortly do the same.

At this point Diemut's three playmates return through the gateway and sing an extended trio as they hide, in order to watch the fun they know is to ensue. Their music, though not motivic, is of the simple folky species which Strauss had already used, and will soon use again in connexion with the people of Munich.

Ex. 31

The light, gaily staccato style is to become a striking feature of *Der Rosenkavalier*, while the vocal writing with its close harmony for female voices anticipates the parallel sections for Najade, Dryade, and Echo in *Ariadne auf Naxos*. The three girls are accompanied partly by appropriate giggling in the woodwind, partly by the motifs of Diemut's

[22] 'Softly, softly, let's see if the bird has already been caught.'

revenge (Ex. 27 in diminution, transformed into a figure startlingly like the oboe figure of Salome's *Dance of the Seven Veils*, together with Ex. 29a,) and Kunrad's themes, also in diminution, suggesting his discomfiture. As they sing, the pulleys are set in motion and the basket with Kunrad straddled across it moves slowly upwards. It rises to a point somewhat short of the balcony and then stops. Kunrad hears the girls' tittering and answers them with commendable good humour before calling up anxiously to Diemut, who complains of his weight. She disappears, ostensibly to find new means of helping him up to her balcony, though the constant repetitions of Exx. 19 and 29a hint at her true purpose. The companions renew their whispering mockery with the resumption of the staccato theme Ex. 31. Kunrad, still un-suspicious, attributes their lack of courtesy to envy of his future happiness and sings ecstatically of Diemut's beauty as the strings pour out the love theme Ex. 15 in its sensuous thirds.

At last she returns and stretches down in turn her sleeve, her arm, and her hair. The first two prove too short and Kunrad's attempts to grasp some strands of Diemut's hair naturally cause her pain. She cries out in distress and then, with mounting mockery, invites Kunrad to use his magic to fly through the air into her arms. This section is a splendid development of the love theme (Ex. 18) and the motif of Diemut's revenge (Ex. 29a), which naturally comes fully into its own as the manner in which she has planned to humiliate his bold love be-comes apparent. A particularly ingenious use of his material is the way Strauss exploits one of the later figures from the love music which began with Ex. 18,

Ex. 32

The leap of the seventh which, just failing to reach the octave, always drops back, makes a splendid parallel with the form of Kunrad con-stantly stretching in vain to reach the balcony of his desires.

At last Kunrad realizes that the predicament in which he finds him-self has all along been part of a preconceived plan. He first threatens and then cajoles Diemut, but her triumph is complete. Exultantly she tells Kunrad that he is about to pay in full for his insult (Exx. 20—the original form of the Shame motif—and 19—the vigorous version of

Kunrad's theme showing him as a brazen wooer—both reintroduced in firm tones) and then calls out to her companions to come and see the strange bird she has caught. This section of mockery is set to a scherzando development section strongly reminiscent of *Till Eulenspiegel*, both thematically and in the orchestral treatment. The love duet (Ex. 26) and Kunrad's love theme (Ex. 16) are reduced to a lively ⁶⁄₈ movement, the leading subject of which is the companions' scherzetto Ex. 17. The three mischief-makers have crept out and spread the news of the great practical joke amongst the townsfolk, who all come flooding back on to the stage to join in the fun. The children, too, add their 'Maja, maja, mia, mô' to the general derision, and only the old Burgomaster, Diemut's father, puts in a word of censure at her ill-treatment of Love.

Ex. 33

Das tat noch   nie___ kei·ne Sentlinger-in 23

The figure ⌐ a ⌐ , though derived from the love music Ex. 18, and later referred to in connexion with it, acquires independent motivic significance in the closing scene.

Though undoubtedly meant in good faith, this chiding remark of the Burgomaster provokes a general outburst of laughter which is instantly silenced as Kunrad cries out in a mighty voice to his dead master for help in his extremity. He calls for the Spirit of Magic (repeated statements of Ex. 4 on the piccolo) to quench the fires of a people who have poured disdain on the demands of Love. Need-fire now shall become Need of Fire, Solstice-Fire shall die the Red-Death, and all that has flickered shall be quenched in deepest night in retribution for laughter at Love's power. The 'Feuersnot' theme (Ex. 24) is declaimed in augmentation punctuated by dramatically contrasted chordal sequences. This kind of despairing cadence has been part of Strauss's natural expression ever since he discovered the formula for the closing bars of *Don Juan*. Kunrad raises both his arms high in the air in

---

23 'No girl of the Sentlinger family has ever done such a thing!' Sentlinger was a prominent old Munich name and to this day the Sentlinger Strasse and the Sentlinger Thor ('street' and 'gate' respectively) stand in the busiest part of the city.

invocation and abruptly every fire in the city from the merest candle
end to the great glow, which had hitherto been strongly visible beyond
the city gates, is extinguished. There is a shriek from the crowd and a
ghastly silence.

4

Until now the action and thereby the shape of the musical scene has
been complicated. From this point to the end, however, the dénouement is effected by means of four clearly defined set-pieces: a chorus;
Kunrad's big scena-cum-aria; a second chorus; and the closing scene
(often described as the *Liebesszene*), which is the only section to have
survived away from the stage performances of the complete work.
The first chorus is essentially an extended *crescendo* as the bewilderment
of the dumbfounded townsfolk turns to menacing anger. The children
whine to a pitiful transformation of their once so cocky Ex. 2, the fear
of the people is portrayed by a snarling return of the folk-song *Der
Alte Peter* (Ex. 9) on muted horns, and old Tulbeck says to everyone,
'I told you so', against a continuous reiteration of Ex. 27 in its 'Seven
Veils' figuration. As the music builds more and more, the frenetic
version of Kunrad's theme (Ex. 11) becomes increasingly prominent
and forms the basis of the latter part of the chorus as the people shake
their fists at the young man. The climax comes with a development of
Ex. 24 (a) (the 'Feuersnot' theme itself, which was derived from Ex. 1)
repeated with frantic insistence against rising statements of Ex. 16 (the
motif of Kunrad as Solstice Lover) in the heavy brass.

Kunrad's monologue follows, this being the symbolical kernel of
the whole opera. In the darkness he has at last succeeded in climbing
up on to the balcony[24] and is clearly silhouetted in the moonlight as he
leans against a corner pillar, smiling down at the enraged townsfolk.
The gist of his address is that the people of Munich who once turned
out the great 'Ruler of the Spirits' out of small-minded fear, nevertheless failed to banish a new enemy who had arisen. However, many
people to whom the new magic was a joyful thing removed themselves
to a beautiful country over the hills and there flourished. But at last the
spirit of the old master addressed itself to him, Kunrad, bidding him to
return to continue the good work in his old house of sorcery; he must
not be turned aside by discouragement, nor become complacent

---

[24] It is never made clear how, after all the fuss, he manages to achieve this.

through praise; when his heart might fail he would find a spark of flame in the loyalty and passion of woman. Alas, the everlasting fire has failed him, without which how is he to show that he is indeed the true apprentice of his master? His chosen one has mocked his love with high-minded virtue. To show that he is above such virtue which prized fire and passion so little, he has extinguished all their fire and light.

Lastly comes Wolzogen's motto which the poet explained in his reminiscences twenty-two years later:

> All creative power springs from sensuousness. Creative spirit possesses the magic power to fashion a living entity out of nothing. Now, if this magic can only become effective through the fire of the senses, then I claim full right to clutch this fire to myself wherever I may find it. I have given poetic expression to this artistic bravado in the *Singgedicht, Feuersnot,* which I thought out together with Richard Strauss in Munich and wrote down in a few days on the island of Rügen in the splendid elation of a delightful love affair.
>
> Not a soul has understood the hidden sense of this allegory. The Philistines naturally were morally upset as usual, but even the professional art *cognoscenti* remained without any idea. Only art invests life, at least for men of culture, with light, colour, warmth and depth of meaning. Each true artist is a Prometheus who creates mankind in the likeness of God. But he has no need to steal the distant light of heaven for his creation; he can take fire from the earth, since,
>
> > 'All warmth springs from woman,
> > All light stems from love. . . .'
>
> Here, namely, is the moral of this little poem.

Kunrad proclaims these last lines as the climax of his sermon, adding that only from the body of a hot-blooded young maiden will fire once again spring for the people.

To set an extended symbolical and philosophical tirade of this kind stretched Strauss's powers to the limit. However, he did his best, matching Wolzogen's puns and allusions to his own Wagnerian heritage with appropriate quotations. Wolzogen imbued the name of 'Wagner' with a triple meaning: (1) the key figure of the composer, whom he calls Reichart der Meister, (2) that of a waggoner: 'Er wollt' euer Wesen auf Räder setzen' (he wanted to put your being on

wheels), and (3) deriving Wagner from the word 'Wagen' meaning
'dare'—hence 'one who dares' as in:

> 'Sein Wagen kam all zu gewagt Euch vor;
> da triebt Ihr den Wagner aus dem Thor.'
> (His daring was all too much for you;
> So you drove the darer [i.e. the waggoner—
> i.e. Wagner] from the door.)

Strauss makes no attempt to parallel this far-fetched punning, and
confines himself to two straight quotations; the 'Walhalla' theme at
the words 'Herrscher der Geister' and the 'Flying Dutchman' theme at
the 'daring' allusion just discussed.

Next comes Strauss's name, which Wolzogen introduces in connexion with the new 'enemy' with which the people of Munich find
themselves confronted;

> den bösen Feind, den triebt Ihr nit aus—
> der stellt sich Euch immer auf's Neue zum Strauss
> (the foul enemy, him you did not drive out—
> he presents himself to you ever again in combat.)

'Strife' or 'Warfare' being one of the meanings of the word 'Strauss'
in the German language, the composer Strauss depicts himself through
the 'war' motif from *Guntram* (Ex. 29 from Chapter IV).

Finally Wolzogen, finding the temptation too strong for him, uses
his own name in the very next lines which change the picture to 'the
more valiant people who rejoice in more daring (Wagnerian) activity:'

> Wohl zogen mannige wackere Leut
> die ein wagendes Wirken freut.

Here poor Strauss was placed in an impossible position and he
solved the problem as best he could in what was at least an ingenious
way. Two things guided him; first, the meaning of the text, and
secondly Wolzogen's position in German literature. The passage
describes the activity of the more venturesome spirits in German art.
These built a retreat for themselves (so Kunrad says) in the Isargau,
the mountainous district of the River Isar, in South Bavaria, where
they were enjoying a carefree and elevated spiritual existence amidst the
beauties of nature. To Strauss such a conception smacked strongly of

the Bavarian people enjoying themselves, and so in turn of folk-song and the Ländler. Add to this Wolzogen's position as a well-known author of ballads, popular ditties and cabaret songs, and the treatment of this section as light music seemed eminently appropriate. The somewhat ridiculous appearance of Kunrad standing solemnly in the moonlight, on the balcony of Diemut's house, lecturing at considerable length a stunned populace while the orchestra play a potpourri of folk-songs and waltzes, seems to have escaped Strauss in his equally ingenious discovery that here was a fine opportunity to bring back in formal recapitulation the Ländlers and folk-tunes which ended the first scene of the opera. One new theme in folk-song idiom must be quoted, as it forms the basis of the opening section of the succeeding chorus. Although by no means identical, its relationship to earlier themes of the kind, such as Ex. 21, is self-evident:

Ex. 34

If, of the three folk-like themes in this vein, Ex. 13 represents the children and Ex. 21 the three companions, this new melody stands for all the people of Munich, though from the position of its first appearance in the score at the words 'Wohl zogen mannige wackere Leut', it would seem to indicate Strauss's hope of their becoming the people of whom Kunrad speaks, the courageous people who are prepared to abandon the reactionary territories in order to experience the spiritual elevation provided by both his own new artistic trends and those of Wagner before him.

The waltz section which follows embraces most of the earlier themes, including an important section of the love music Ex. 25, which is now transformed into a waltz with a cadence figure worthy of, and indeed strongly reminiscent of, Baron Ochs's great waltz in Act II of *Der Rosenkavalier*:

R.S.–Q

Ex. 35

Gradually the music becomes more serious in character, with increasing references to the various motifs connected with Kunrad and his love as the section is reached which deals with the artist's need for earthly fire drawn from the passion of a woman. Finally the motto lines are reached, declaimed against the glowing, surging sounds of Ex. 15, culminating in the all-important phrase 'from the body of a hot-blooded young maiden'.

Ex. 36

5

The townsfolk are won over, albeit unwillingly, and in their second chorus, like the last an extended crescendo, they address themselves to Diemut, pressing her to yield to Kunrad's advances. They knew all along he was of noble blood! The first section is based entirely on Ex. 34, after which a soft short link of Kunrad's theme Ex. 10 hands the lead to the three companions, who sing their passionate persuasions to their own folk-like tune, Ex. 21.[25] Meanwhile, unseen in the obscurity (the moon having gone conveniently behind a cloud) Diemut has quickly taken Kunrad by the hand and pulled him into her room.

A second link follows, based on the theme of Diemut's triumph over Kunrad (Ex. 29a), as the companions, together with the old townsmen who had once sided against Kunrad, now upbraid Diemut for her treatment of him. This leads to the next main section, an exceedingly bawdy song which is combined with the previous material in a very aggressive and rowdy way. When Strauss, during the rehearsals for the première, insisted that nothing should be cut or soft-pedalled he was undoubtedly thinking especially of this passage:

Ex. 37

With the suggestiveness of many a present-day comedian, Strauss delays the first statement of what exactly it is that the maiden is going to have to lose, so that when it comes two beats later one has been led to expect something quite different from 'Lirum-larum-lei'.[26]

Oddly enough, whether because of the crudity of the text or because its cabaret style at this point was foreign to Strauss, this section is in fact musically vulgar and leads badly to the next passage, itself of no great distinction, but well motivated with the gradual reintroduction of Ex. 29b, showing that Diemut's capitulation is approaching. The music then dissolves into the love theme, as the complete cast unite in

[25] Trenner rightly shows, by a side-by-side comparison, that the crowds *volte-face* appraisals of Kunrad are set to words which are a deliberate skit by Wolzogen on Goethe's *Gretchen am Spinnrad*. The last line however, in which the three companions add the poignant 'Und ach, sein Kuss!' was maliciously added by Strauss.

[26] It is of course, wholly typical of our British sense of the proprieties that these lines should have been rendered in the English version as follows:

'Now don't you shilly-shally
You know the only way
So honi soit qui mal y pense!
Fol-de-rol-de-ray.'

singing Wolzogen's motto about 'Warmth springing from woman', followed by Kunrad's last lines (Ex. 36), which, with the exception of the children—a nice show of sensitivity on Strauss's part—they all quote verbatim. They then call out as with one great voice to Diemut to listen to Love's commands and so help them in their 'Feuersnot'. The tremendous diminished seventh chord which marks the climax of this second chorus sinks to a series of ever softer and more widely spaced chords and then to total silence in preparation for the closing scene.

The final section of the opera is the formal synthesis of all that is best in the music, and fully justifies its status as an independent concert item, apart from the purely practical consideration that the very few vocal lines it contains can easily be omitted or cued into the orchestra. It is in three main parts; the wooing in its affectionate and in its passionate stages, and the aftermath with its universal jubilation. The first section consists of a short slow introduction based on the first chordal version of Kunrad's theme Ex. 14.[27] This is followed by two complete statements of Diemut's melody (Ex. 5a), separated by the love theme (Ex. 15), given in its pristine consecutive thirds on the violins. Diemut's music is most delicately coloured with harps, glockenspiel and harmonium. It dissolves into an extended recapitulation of Kunrad's love-song (Exx. 18 and 25), but given entirely free without voices and with Ex. 29a, the theme of Diemut's capitulation as it is now becoming once more, interspersed between the phrases.

Ex. 16 (a) given dramatically on the horns heralds the passionate section of the love scene. It is answered in sweeping tones by Ex. 10, which, contrasted with the previous motif in this way, has a feminine touch about it. Both themes are, however, motifs belonging to different aspects of Kunrad, and it was not until the Introduction to Act I of Der Rosenkavalier that Strauss repeated the formula in almost identical tones, but following the natural suggestions of the music, that is to say, the man identified by the horns' motif and the surging string melody of the answer characterizing the woman (see Chapter IX, Ex. 1).

In this passage Strauss really found himself and wrote music of the freshness and convincing passion of Don Juan and the best part of Tod und Verklärung, which latter it strongly resembles in the orchestral texture. As the music surges upwards towards the climax, the upper

[27] Although this derivation is demonstrably true, the section is one of those which, as we have seen, was lifted in toto from the sketches for Kythere.

woodwind emphasizes the outline of Kunrad's motto Ex. 36 against the insistent thrusting of Ex. 16 (a) of the horns.

There is a petrified silence and all the lights and fires of the city blaze forth in a sudden flash as the orchestra bursts into a tumultuous version of Diemut's and Kunrad's themes in combination. The assembled people, who have been waiting silently in breathless anticipation since the beginning of the scene, burst into a shout of jubilation. This time Diemut's melody has its afterphrase, Ex. 5b, which lets the music gently down to Ex. 26, the theme of the Midsummer Night. The lovers can be heard singing together as they did earlier in the opera, and as at that time the duet moves through Ex. 30 to the same glowing cadence, with Ex. 29 on horns and violins. Now, however, Diemut's capitulation has been real, and the whole crowd sings her one-time refrain 'Imma, Ursel, Lisaweth' (Ex. 5b), the orchestra passing triumphantly on to the motif of the loving tribute of Diemut's companions to her beauty and goodness (Ex. 6), which has been skilfully reserved for this final moment of happiness. One last fanfare of trumpets declaims Ex. 16 (b), thus pointing to Kunrad as the key figure, there is a harp glissando and, amidst general embracings, dancing, rejoicing, and congratulations to the old Burgomaster, the opera is over.

6

Feuersnot has never been considered the equal of the operas which immediately succeeded it, although there are stirring passages and it is full of splendid ideas. But it contains few grateful opportunities for the principal characters, except for Kunrad, whose three arias fail, the first two because they are too fragmentary, and the third, by contrast, because it is too diffuse. Moreover, there are numerous exceedingly difficult small parts and a children's chorus, all of which, as Strauss realized only too well, mitigate against its being retained in the standard repertory. Yet even these deterrents would be immaterial if the general level of cheerful invention rose to sufficient peaks of true inspiration during the work. Only, however, during the closing scene can this really be said to happen.

Feuersnot is thus, above all, a transitional piece, as Strauss himself partly recognized when, just before he died, he wrote:

In nearly all the biographical articles which I now find myself reading in profusion, I miss the correct attitude,

particularly towards the text book of *Feuersnot*. One forgets
that this certainly by no means perfect work (especially in
the all too unequal handling of the orchestra) still introduces into the nature of the old opera a new subjective
style at just the very beginning of the century. It is in its
way a sort of upbeat.

There is much truth here not only in the broader historical sense but
in its relation to Strauss's own operatic output. Strauss continued
however:

> Why do people not see what is new in my work, how
> in them Man is visibly linked with the work, as only in
> Beethoven [!]—this begins already in the third Act of
> *Guntram* (the renunciation of collectivism), *Heldenleben*, *Don
> Quixote*, *Domestica* and in *Feuersnot*. There is a conscious
> tone of mockery, of irony, of protest against the conven-
> tional opera text, the individual newness. Hence the
> cheerful satire of Wagnerian language; for it is precisely
> because of Kunrad's address, which must not be omitted,
> that the whole little non-opera ['*Nicht-Operchen*'] came
> into existence!

At this point, in his desire to be coupled with Beethoven's artistic
expression of the Importance of Man, Strauss failed to appreciate the
approach to his work of critical opinion. Although Kunrad's address
may indeed have been the starting-point of the entire scheme, by the
time Strauss penned these grievances such philosophizing was already
out of date, the Wagnerian battles a thing of the past. The lengthy
sermonizing had ceased to be interesting, and the laborious references
and double meanings had become merely whimsical. Thus, the address
is not only the least satisfactory section on purely musical grounds, but
has become, directly contrary to its *raison d'être*, the chief stumbling-
block to the general acceptance of the entire piece.

In its day, however, the opera's greatest hurdle was its provocative
bawdiness. In particular, the 'Lirum-larum-lei' chorus caused considerable offence in many quarters. In striking contrast to his lamentable experiences with *Guntram*, the now famous Strauss found himself
in the gratifying position of having two of the most influential opera
houses of Europe, Dresden and Vienna, clamouring for the privilege
of producing his new work. Yet he nearly lost this powerful bargaining
position through the objections of the Viennese to the histrionic
implications of the closing scene. There were even troubles over the

publication of Wolzogen's text, culminating in an attempt to replace the more offensive lines with some milder but utterly commonplace doggerel to which Strauss objected vehemently, preferring to cut some of the lines altogether rather than agree to so banal a substitution. Nevertheless he ignored these difficulties while negotiating with Dresden, to whom he had decided to offer the first performance, and even wrote to Ernst von Schuch, the conductor, stressing the importance of not softening the work in any way at all:

> To take away from the opera its biting sharpness is to achieve a success of misunderstanding. This I would gladly forfeit; better a gigantic flop, in which case you have at least thrown in the faces of that pack of Philistines a few thorough coarsenesses and beneficial impertinences, which should cleanse both their brains and their gall.

A new but henceforth extremely significant aspect of Strauss's personality comes out in a letter to Schuch during these negotiations;

> In haste. . . so 1,500 marks is still too much! O this theatre! To hell with all opera composing! Well now, what would you have? Perhaps I should send you something more for nothing? Say a fire-engine? So as to put out the Need-of-money-fire? I must set aside the first performance for you and you want to do absolutely nothing in return? I find 1,500 marks really not too much. Anyway let Fürstner[28] do as he likes. If it doesn't come off then I can wander off to Vienna where Mahler will do anything if I will only give him the first performance. I am going to change my name to Riccardo Straussino and have my works published by Sonzogno, then you would agree to everything.

This shows Strauss in a new light. In the first place he was by no means sure of being able to substantiate the threat of Vienna, and his use of it notwithstanding is a piece of shrewd bluffing more common to the world of business than of art. Moreover, this preoccupation with pure finance was already a strong part of his personality and was to become even more so as time went by. Alma Mahler gives a revealing account of Strauss's behaviour during the first performance of

[28] Adolph Fürstner had recently begun the publication of Strauss's more important works, an arrangement which continued for some forty years, though with the advent of the Nazis the firm was taken over by the purely 'Aryan' Johannes Oertel, previously only a junior member.

Feuersnot, for which the Mahlers shared a box with the composer and his wife—'Strauss thought of nothing but money . . . the whole time he had a pencil in his hand and was calculating his profits to the last penny.'

The Dresden first production of *Feuersnot* is historically important, being the first of a long series of such Straussian events, for in gratitude for Schuch's courage and belief in his operatic future, Strauss reserved for the fine Dresden opera house the first performance of most of the later stage works. Despite repeated objections on grounds of morality, *Feuersnot* secured a considerable success (Wolzogen himself causing a furore by coming on to the stage after the opening performance with an aster the size of a cartwheel in his buttonhole) and was immediately taken up by Vienna and then Berlin. In this latter city, however, after only a few performances it received an unexpected setback. At the instigation of the Empress, Kaiser Wilhelm II suddenly forbade all further representations of the work, upon which Count Hochberg, the General Intendant of the Berlin Opera, immediately handed in his resignation. Hochberg told the composer that he would fight like a lion for the free presentation of the work, and indeed his self-sacrificing gesture was effective, for the ban was lifted soon after.

Though Strauss wrote home rather bitterly to his parents over the affair, such a storm was just what he had been trying to stir up, ever since he had greeted with amused satisfaction the scandalized impact of his *Aus Italien* on that first audience of 1887. He was, in fact, working up to his greatest period of deliberate provocation, by comparison with which the schoolboy crudities of *Feuersnot* were to pale into insignificance. It was here that his heart lay and consequently he never pursued the next, less controversial text which, at his own request, Wolzogen prepared for him (with far less relish and endless pains) on a subject by Cervantes. This scheme seems to have arisen out of the *Diebeskomödie* to which reference was made above and for which Wolzogen triumphantly found a fantastic new name: *Coabbradibosimpur*. Possibly realizing that he was losing his hold on Strauss, and being in increasingly serious financial straits, he persevered stubbornly with the piece, which gradually turned into a major project and was further subtitled *Die bösen Buben von Sevilla*. Unfortunately even poor Wolzogen had to agree that it had become 'fearfully long', and it is clear that it never aroused Strauss's interest sufficiently for him even to begin sketching musical ideas for it.

There is a rather pathetic sequel to this episode. In 1942 Strauss wrote in his reminiscences;

> Ernst von Wolzogen later arranged a short story by Cervantes which I had already planned as a one-act opera. I have mislaid the libretto I know not where.

The libretto has since come to light among Strauss's effects—a manuscript of no less than eighty-four closely written sheets with a title-page bearing the words 'Coabbradibosimpur, oder Die bösen Buben von Sevilla. Ein Gaunerstückchen in einem Akt nach Cervantes von Ernst von Wolzogen. Musik von Richard Strauss.'

Manuscript of the opening of *Salome*

(By courtesy of Boosey & Hawkes)

THE STAGE TONE POEMS (I)

OSCAR WILDE wrote his *Salome* during the winter of 1891-2, although the subject had been brewing in his mind ever since he had visited an exhibition of pictures in Paris on this theme by Gustave Moreau. Moreau, who was to be the teacher of such artists as Matisse and Rouault, had achieved a considerable success with his *Salome* pictures, and in 1876 his representation of the climax of the legend in a canvas entitled *L'Apparition* was voted the picture of the year by the *Salon*. Wilde was much struck by the possibilities of the idea for dramatic representation, and the recent publication of Flaubert's short story *Hérodias*, followed by Massenet's opera *Hérodiade*, had brought the subject to the foreground of artistic consciousness of the Paris of those days. The appearance of Salome and especially the idea of her dance made an extraordinary impression upon Wilde, who confessed to dreaming endlessly about her. He even went to enormous pains to find and compare the widely different conceptions of the Oriental princess and her dance by such painters as Titian, Leonardo da Vinci, and Dürer. But Moreau's pictures came closest to his ideals, and in imagination Wilde sensuously clothed her 'unchaste body' with endless varieties of precious stones whenever he passed a jeweller's window.

It was no doubt as the direct result of having been inspired by what was essentially a Parisian movement that Wilde wrote his play in French, even though at the time he actually set pen to paper he was

living in Torquay. He was virtually bilingual[1], of course, and the
French language must have appealed to him as more suitable for the
setting of 'quelque chose de curieux et de sensuel', as he later described
it to Sarah Bernhardt. There was probably also a stylistic reason, however, in Wilde's adoption of the enigmatic, cryptic, yet often flowery
style of Maeterlinck, an idiom particularly and uniquely French.

It is unlikely that the true story of the events which culminated
in the death of John the Baptist will ever be fully known and compre-
hended in all its psychological undercurrents. The versions given in the
two gospels correspond very closely, although, as so often, Mark is
more detailed than Matthew. John lived and stirred up his religious
revival about A.D. 30 in Galilee during the reign of Herod Antipas,[2]
the son of Herod the Great by his fourth wife, Malthace. John (or Jochanaan in the Hebrew form of the name), the son of a priest called
Zacharias, believed that he had been chosen by God to announce the
imminence of His appearance upon Earth and to call mankind to
repentance. John's practice of bathing his converts in the waters of the
Jordan earned him the popular nickname of 'The Dipper', from which
sprang the more respectful title by which he is known today. He
acquired a considerable following, though he at no time constituted a
danger to the security of Antipas's throne. There were nevertheless two
reasons why the Tetrarch felt happier with him safely incarcerated in
a fortress at Machaerus, a place east of the Dead Sea some eighty miles
from Herod's Northern Palace at Tiberius. In the first instance Antipas
was unsure of his hold over the Jewish people, and there was really no
telling where apparently vague and harmless phrases such as 'Kingdom
of God' might not lead when fed to large bodies of religious fanatics.
But more dangerous to the Tetrarch personally were John's frequent
attacks on his marriage. For Antipas had recently returned from
a visit to his half-brother Herod (not Philip as stated in the gospels,
possibly to avoid ambiguity), during which he had fallen in love
with Herod's wife, Herodias, who was incidentally the half-niece
of the two brothers. There is not the slightest doubt that Antipas had

---

[1] Nevertheless Romain Rolland in his correspondence with Strauss over the
French translation of the opera wrote: 'But when there is a "mistake of French"
do not hesitate to correct Wilde's original. However remarkable Wilde's knowledge of French may have been, it is nevertheless impossible to consider him as a
French poet.'

[2] Unlike his father and elder half-brother, Antipas had no birthright to the
name Herod, but adopted it for official purposes in his capacity as Tetrarch.

every intention of getting rid of his first wife, though shrewdly she anticipated the turn of events, which might have proved disagreeable, by fleeing the country. Thus honourable divorce was made impracticable, a fact Herodias never forgot and for which she never forgave the middle-aged Antipas, whom she married for his superior political prestige and position as Tetrarch. Herodias thus never felt wholly secure in her new position and suffered keenly from the scurrilous attacks which John the Baptist showered upon her name in public wherever he went, on account of what he regarded as her incestuous remarriage. There was also a rumour that Antipas had had to do away with his brother Herod in order to win Herodias for himself, and this, if true, materially adds to Herodias's motives for wishing John safely out of the way. It is fascinating to follow Christian legend through countless elaborations, amongst which the vile figure of Herodias emerges from time to time as a kind of female Wandering Jew, seeking salvation after her appalling sins, which include laughing at Christ as he carried the cross. Wagner made use of this version of the myth, linking it with the figure of Kundry in his opera *Parsifal*.

It is thus generally accepted that Herodias was directly responsible for John's death, taking as her opportunity Antipas's infatuation with Salome, the daughter whom she had by her first husband Herod. Apart from an odd suggestion, in Heine's long and diffuse poem *Atta Troll*, that Herodias herself had conceived a violent and hopeless passion for the Jewish prophet, there seem to be no theories put forward to explain in any other way Salome's reasons for her gruesome choice of reward in the shape of John's head on a silver charger. Wilde's attribution of her motives to frustrated passion appears to be entirely original, plausible though the reconstruction certainly is. It is considerably more satisfying dramatically to find Salome holding her stepfather to his oath, against his strongest superstitious disinclination, on grounds of her own personal vendetta rather than merely as a characterless dupe of her vindictive mother. Passions run high in the East and Salome was no innocent child at the time of these events.

2

Wilde himself wrote of his *Salome* (in *De Profundis*) that it contained 'refrains whose recurring motifs make it like a piece of music and bind it together as a ballad'. Such an analysis of a literary work by its author in terms of musical form is reminiscent of an earlier source of inspiration for Strauss, Nietszche's *Also Sprach Zarathustra*.[3] The exploitation of motivic words, phrases or ideas is in itself a primarily musical technique and is characteristic of the late nineteenth-century interrelationship between literature and music. Wilde's handling of the device lent itself especially well to musical treatment and was ideal for a composer with a predominantly symphonic style such as Strauss. In addition it enabled Strauss to tackle the problem of writing for the theatre in a manner which he had already fully mastered in his orchestral works, that of Lisztian organization and metamorphosis of motivic germs as in the symphonic poems. The result gives the opera a tremendous unity unusual in stage compositions outside Wagner's music dramas. *Salome* immediately impressed its early listeners as having been composed 'in a single breath', the long and complex structure forming one vast span.

Strauss's greatest gift was his power of realizing in vivid thematic material the musical potentiality implicit within a literary conception. When the author himself pointed out the link with music already existent in his work, Strauss had his opportunity to hand. However, Wilde's *Salome* was not immediately a ready-made success. For it was only after various vicissitudes, including a flop in Paris and the total refusal on the part of the British censor to grant a licence for its production, that the play was at last acclaimed as the masterpiece it is. This was not, however, until over a year after Wilde's death, when, in 1901, it was given in Breslau in a translation by Dr. Kisper. The following year it was produced with enormous success at Max Reinhardt's *Kleines Theater* in Berlin, where it played for the unheard-of run of two hundred performances.

Meanwhile a certain Anton Lindner, a young Viennese writer, had already had the perception to send the play to Strauss with the offer of turning it into a libretto. Lindner was no stranger to Strauss, who had, in fact, set a poem of his, *Hochzeitlich Lied,* as one of the songs op. 37. Nevertheless, his ingenious rewriting of the opening scene pleased the composer more in its choice of subject than its handling. Strauss's letter to his parents telling them of this new project of a Pendant to *Feuersnot* (!) reflects his qualms as to the successful outcome of Lindner's aspirations. Fortunately Strauss was able at once to perceive the vast possibilities in Wilde's text as it stood without alteration

[3] See p. 132.

other than extensive cuts. With this in mind he began making a few preliminary sketches, and then early in 1903 took the opportunity of the Berlin production to go and see the play for himself, drawn additionally by the appearance of the prominent actress Gertrud Eysoldt in the title role. At the theatre he encountered a close friend, one Heinrich Grünfeld, who immediately commented that here would be some real material for an opera for him. Strauss at once replied that indeed he was already at work on it, for the visit had confirmed him in his determination to set Wilde's original text. Hedwig Lachmann's translation, which was the one used in Reinhardt's Berlin production, was accordingly cut to his specifications and the composition of the music went forward like lightning. The whole conception and Wilde's poetic language fired Strauss's imagination, while the Orientalism of the subject touched strongly upon his belief that 'operas hitherto based on Oriental and Jewish subjects lacked true Oriental colour and scorching sun'. Accordingly he exercised his penchant for passionate melodizing and his experience in the virtuoso handling of large orchestras to produce the most gorgeous and kaleidoscopic score possible. He himself felt that he had been inspired to produce 'truly exotic harmonies which sparkle like taffeta, particularly in the stirring cadences'. As we have seen, he had been experimenting with unusual cadences for some considerable time, but there is much truth in his conviction that the subject had stimulated him to give of his best. Shortly before his father's death Strauss played him part of the nearly completed score of *Salome*, and the poor old man remarked, 'Oh God, what nervous music. It is exactly as if one had one's trousers full of maybugs', a pretty fair comment, even allowing for his notorious conservatism.

Franz Strauss died on 31st May 1905 at the age of eighty-three. For much of the latter part of his life he had failed to follow the trends of the more advanced school of composition and the music of his famous son meant little or nothing to him. But Richard was always extremely affectionate and grateful to his father for his strict musical upbringing, which reaped its due harvest, both in his performances of classical masters and in the secure technique on which even his most daring innovations are built. In later years he wrote a short article on his father, painting him oddly unsentimentally as a bigoted and irascible old man. Yet he seems to have been genuinely fond of him and respected his artistic integrity, though, as we have seen, rarely took his advice.

The score of *Salome* took Strauss two years to complete, no very great period of time, especially allowing for the disturbances of his American tour in the spring of 1904 and the fairly heavy toll imposed upon him by his conducting duties in Berlin. There has been some controversy as to the order in which the various sections were written. Ernest Newman was strongly of the opinion that Strauss completed both the *Dance of the Seven Veils* and Salome's closing solo scene before he composed a note of the remainder of the opera.[4] In the case of the closing scene there may well be truth in this surmise, since although no evidence has survived to establish it definitely, a number of artistic factors point in that direction. For the dance, however, we have Alma Mahler's account, which points to the precise opposite. Her description of a most entertaining incident not only fixes the matter but brings the scene to life splendidly:

> Strauss. . . was cheerful and communicative. He had finished *Salome*, and asked Mahler whether he might play it through to him from the manuscript score. There is a story behind this. When he told Mahler he was going to make an opera of Wilde's *Salome*, Mahler was violently opposed. He had a thousand reasons; there was first of all the moral objection, but also, neither last nor least, that the production might be barred in Catholic countries. Strauss was unconvinced, but somewhat irritated all the same, though not for long. I told Mahler afterwards I was surprised he should have tried to dissuade him. It was as if he had advised a man against marrying a woman he loves.
>
> And now the composition of the opera was finished, and there was a note of triumph in his proposal. He had discovered a piano-shop and the three of us made our way to the showroom, where there were pianos by the dozen. It had huge plate-glass windows on every side and passers-by loitered and stood still to peer in at what was going on.
>
> Strauss played and sang to perfection.[5] Mahler was charmed. We came to the dance—it was missing. 'Dös hab i no net g'macht' (haven't got that done yet), Strauss said, and played on to the end, leaving this yawning gap. 'Isn't it rather risky,' Mahler remarked, 'simply leaving out the

---

[4] Newman points out that the orchestral rehearsal figures do not follow through the Dance, which on the contrary has its own system of letters.

[5] Rolland gives a somewhat different account of Strauss' prowess in this capacity: 'Le soir, il vient dîner. X. l'a retenu 3 heures, à lui jouer son nouvel opéra. Il joue et chante très mauvaise [sic].'

Dance, and then writing it in later when you're not in the same mood?' Strauss laughed his light-hearted laugh: 'Dös krieg i schon.' ('I'll soon put that right'). But he didn't, for the Dance is the one weakness in the score—only a hotchpotch of all the rest. Mahler was completely won over. A man may dare all if he has the genius to make the incredible credible.

When in May 1905 Strauss saw that the end of his task was in sight he quickly contacted Schuch, for whom he had once more ear-marked the first performance. There were, he hastened to reassure the conductor, no chorus problems such as there had been on the last occasion, but on the other hand there would be large numbers of small parts, while the orchestra and principal roles would be about twice as difficult as in *Feuersnot*! A month later, on 20th June, the score was completed by the addition of the famous dance, the delay in the composition of which held up the printing of the work all along the line. Nevertheless this did not prevent the parts going out to the prospective principal singers, upon which the troubles began. Strauss wrote:

> At the very first piano read-through the singers assembled in order to *give back their parts* to the conductor— all except the Herod, a Czech singer called Burian, who when asked last of all, answered 'I already know it off by heart.' Bravo!—At this the others felt rather ashamed and the work of the rehearsal actually started. During the casting rehearsals the dramatic soprano Frau Wittich went on strike (she had been entrusted with the part of the sixteen-year-old princess with the voice of an Isolde) on account of the strenuousness of the part and the thickness of the orchestration—'one just doesn't write like that, Herr Strauss; either one thing or the other'. With much to-ing and fro-ing she protested angrily like any Saxon Burgomaster's wife 'I won't do it, I'm a decent woman'.

Writing of the incident in later years, Strauss conceded that she had a certain right on her side in view of her unsuitable figure (!) and the exaggerated perversity demanded by the producer, but at the time he did not exactly see it in that light. He held her misbehaviour, and her sluggishness in learning the role, over the head of the miserable Schuch with threats of competition for the first performance from rival opera houses which strongly remind one of his parallel tactics over the première of *Feuersnot*:

R.S.–R

In haste!

Dear esteemed friend,

So now everything has come out blissfully just as I had feared. Editor, printer and myself, we have all fallen over ourselves to get you the piano score by 1st September and the high and mighty Frau Wittich has left the rotten thing lying around for five weeks and can't even do it in the end; but you mustn't be cross with me if under the circumstances I can't any more guarantee you the first performance.

In Leipzig Nikisch is already hard at work at it. Mahler tells me today that (in Vienna) the piece has at last been pushed past the censor[6] and that work is now forging ahead. He has got four singers covering the part of Salome; should he get in before you I can't do a thing about it. As I already wired you, I will reserve the first performance for you until 9th December at the latest, and if you can't bring it off by then, whoever is ready first can do it.

Ruthless as one might consider this letter to an 'esteemed' colleague towards whom an undertaking had been given, it certainly had the required effect. Schuch managed to give the wildly successful première on the actual date of the deadline Strauss had given him, 9th December 1905.

3

If *Guntram* had an incomplete Prelude, and *Feuersnot* no more than a brief introduction, *Salome* has nothing at all. Indeed, the opera is unusual in that the curtain should rise before a single note of music has been played. The strange scene thus makes its impact upon an unprepared audience, like a frozen tableau into which the music then breathes life. The great terrace in front of Herod's palace is shown bathed in the light of an enormous moon. The moon is one of the chief motifs in Wilde's drama and constantly recurs in various guises right up to the very last page. It was fitting therefore that Beardsley should have chosen this theme as the subject for the Frontispiece for his famous illustrations. Strauss, however, made no attempt to parallel this use of textural motif by a recurring musical theme depicting the moon, although he endorsed Wilde's stage direction 'Clair de Lune' by insisting that 'The moon shines very brightly' and matching this with the veiled yet curiously luminous colouring of the orchestration.

[6] This turned out to be quite untrue. More will be said about these censorship troubles in due course. (See p. 280 et. seq.)

Thematically it is Salome's motif that is heard in the very first bar, stated sinuously, with rapid runs before and after, by the clarinet.

Ex. 1

It is answered by a theme which springs up in the cellos, and depicts the hopeless longing for Salome which burns in the breast of the Young Syrian. Strauss describes this touchingly pathetic character throughout by his name, Narraboth, although in Wilde's text the name only appears on one particular occasion in the mouth of Salome herself.

Ex. 2

Narraboth is rhapsodizing on Salome's beauty, while the young Page of Herodias, who is utterly devoted to Narraboth and never appears except in relationship to him, is fascinated by the appearance of the moon, which he likens to a dead woman looking for dead things. Narraboth takes him up, but in a way which shows clearly that his thoughts have never left Salome. As he says 'She is like a princess who has little white doves for feet. You would fancy she was dancing', Strauss introduces a derivative of Ex. 2 which comes into prominence when Salome herself dances.

Ex. 2a

An uproar emanates from the banqueting hall below, in which Herod is entertaining important emissaries from Rome. A number of violent and strongly contrasted themes are hurled out against one another to depict the religious disputes of the Jews. The motifs (a) and

(b) from Ex. 3 acquire primary importance later in the opera, although it must be conceded that (b) is virtually inaudible in its present context on the double bassoon. The indication 'heulend' (howling) is worth attention,[7] the whole passage is full of fantastic instrumental effects.

Ex. 3

The uproar dies down and Narraboth resumes his rhapsody on the subject of Salome. This time the Page's anxiety disturbs the mood of the music, finding expression in a dual theme which arises out of the setting of the words.

Ex. 4

The shadowy form of Salome's theme in diminution on the violas should on no account be missed, although it flows past so swiftly. It is the first instance in the opera of a device which recurs constantly and which had only previously appeared in the Dream episode of the *Sinfonia Domestica* (see above Chapter 6, p. 192).

[7] Wilde goes into some detail by means of a conversation between two soldiers to describe the point of doctrinal controversy which has given rise to the hubbub. Strauss omits much of this as irrelevant, although he retains the soldiers for their value in essential explanation.

[8] 'You are always looking at her . . . something terrible may happen.'

As Narraboth comments on Salome's pallid appearance, a startling motif like a knife-thrust screams out in the orchestra:

Ex. 5

This intensely dramatic idea represents a vital aspect of Salome's character, her impetuous impatience sharpened to the point of perversity. Its initial appearance here shows that her pale expression as she sits at the feast is due to wellnigh uncontrollable anger at the unwelcome admiration of her unsavoury stepfather.

At this point Strauss cuts Wilde's dialogue between the soldiers and various hangers-on, a Cappadocian and a Nubian (the latter, indeed, never appears in the opera at all), and the Page's anguished cry (Ex. 4 (b)) is interrupted directly by the new and all-important episode of Jochanaan's voice.

For purposes of his drama, Wilde put John's prison into the actual palace in the form of an old subterranean cistern. From here he can be heard by all as he proclaims his prophecies and recriminations. The Cappadocian discusses with the two soldiers the merits of the cistern as a prison. They tell him that, unhealthy as it may seem, the Tetrarch's brother (the first husband of Herodias) was left to rot there for twelve years, and even then did not die, so that it proved necessary in the end to have him strangled. This whole course of events seems to have no substance in history (though it is ominously mysterious that nothing is known of what became of Herod after Antipas had stolen Herodias from him) and Strauss omits the discussion of it entirely.

Jochanaan's proclamations are set to music which is solemn and majestic, but Strauss failed to give it the necessary quality of sublimity which he desperately needed in order to contrast with the otherwise prevailing moral decadence, the morbid colour of which he captured with singular success. This failure was, of course, integral to the whole nature of Strauss's genius, as we have already seen, and it was inevitable from the first that the lofty passages in Wilde's text, many of which are direct biblical quotations, would prove the weakest sections of Strauss's musical realization of the work.⁹

Although broadly improvisational, Jochanaan's first utterance contains two vital motifs:

Ex. 6

Ex. 7

Both themes represent the prophet, though Ex. 6 tends to depict the figure of the man himself and Ex. 7 his stern warning of the imminence of the Day of Judgement as heralded by the coming of Christ. The two motifs are bandied about (Ex. 7 in aggressive diminution) as the two soldiers and the Cappadocian discuss Jochanaan, his coming and his strange incomprehensible sayings. A brief link concerned only with Salome's theme (Ex. 1), as, with agitation, Narraboth watches the princess's irritable withdrawal from the banquet, now ushers in scene 2 and the appearance on the stage of Salome herself.

4

Salome's entrance is greeted by the orchestra with a huge arch of melody containing Ex. 1 as its keystone and with new motifs intimately associated with her on either side:

⁹ Romain Rolland, in a letter to Strauss, expressed his view of this in terms of exceptional sympathy and perception: 'I have a clear impression that you have not experienced the faith of the savage Precursor in the slightest degree. You have nevertheless represented it in a manner which is both strong and true—but some-what detached and without a really personal emphasis.' Strauss tried to excuse himself when they were together and with a friend of Rolland's who also found the prophet's themes decidedly commonplace. First of all he protested: 'Oh, no! no! I don't think so at all.' But after a while he conceded rather lamely:'Besides, I didn't want to treat him too seriously. You know, Jochanaan is an imbecile. I've got no sympathy at all for that kind of man. I would have preferred above all that he would appear a bit grotesque.'

¹⁰ 'When he cometh.'

Ex. 8

The motif of irritability breaks in as she cries out that she neither can nor will stay at the feast, after which Ex. 8 is repeated and leads into a new theme:

Ex. 9

The figure has been variously labelled 'Herod's weakness' and 'Herod's desire'. Certainly the lack of character in its presentation and the shifting harmonies which form the background to its repetitions well suggest the shifty Tetrarch, indeterminate of purpose, untrustworthy and sensuous, of Wilde's imagining. But it later becomes associated more specifically with Herod's passion for his beautiful stepdaughter. At this first entry it accompanies Salome's fretful complaint over the way she finds herself ogled by the 'mole's eyes' of her mother's husband.

A swaying dance-like version of one of Salome's new themes (Ex. 8 (b)) follows, one of two variants which become of particular importance in the delineation of her character. In this form it depicts the graceful, apparently naïve, sixteen-year-old princess:

Ex. 10

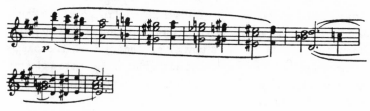

It will be seen that the familiar seductive thirds are strongly in evidence, while the Viennese waltz lurks no great distance behind.

Fragments of Ex. 3 return as Salome describes the horror of the feast with the odious guests who are present at it. An interjection of Ex. 4 (b) from the Page then leads back into the waltz-like Ex. 10 as Salome in her own way comments on the moon. Unlike the Page, who sees it as a dead woman, and Narraboth, who sees a dancing princess, Salome sees in it the coldness of chastity, the beauty of virginity. The prevalence of her own motifs behind the shimmering harmonies seems to suggest that her words imply a reference to herself.

She is interrupted by Jochanaan announcing briefly the coming of the Son of Man (Ex. 7 softly on the trumpets). The sound arouses her strong curiosity over this strange prophet of whom the Tetrarch has evinced a superstitious dread, and her various themes are reiterated in different ways as she questions the soldiers about him. Ex. 1 in particular is spelt out note by note in flute and harp as Salome waits with ill-disguised impatience for Narraboth to finish uttering foolish courtesies to her (Ex. 2 in cellos and basses). When she is crossed, as by a wretched slave who has been sent by Herod to summon her to return to the banquet, Ex. 8 (b) is hurled out viciously in the second of the two variants mentioned above, revealing behind her grace and sweetness a savage character:

Ex. 11

Narraboth tries to press Salome to return, but only receives in his turn a thrust of Ex. 11 as she presses the soldiers for more details of the mysterious prophet in the cistern. Jochanaan's voice is heard prophesying once more, to a new theme so strong and pregnant that it is with surprise that one discovers that it never recurs throughout the work. Salome is fascinated and her determination to see and speak with Jochanaan is emphasized by constant upward surgings of Ex. 8. The soldiers excuse themselves and Salome peers down into the cistern to a gloomy theme on tuba and deep horns, the bass clarinet meandering aimlessly about in its lower register.

Ex. 12

Finding the soldiers inflexible, Salome turns to Narraboth, of whose infatuation she is fully aware. The Page at once perceives the danger of the impending situation (Ex. 3 (a) threateningly on bassoons and horn), but is powerless to intervene. To seductive music of a kind which presented no problem to Strauss she sets out to achieve her desire through him. Her themes, delivered in melting tones, mingle tantalizingly with his as she promises to drop him a little green flower[11] as she passes by in her litter, perhaps even to smile at him. This is the moment, indeed a highly significant moment, when as Salome seduces the young Syrian, Wilde makes her utter his name, which at no other time is given in the text, not even in the Dramatis Personae. There is a subtlety here which Strauss has missed, and in so doing he has also failed to do full justice to a horribly important section of the work. For, strangely enough, Strauss seems ill at ease in the voice parts, the last thing one would expect in the setting of such suggestive phrases, especially when he has already caught their mood and meaning so precisely in the orchestra. But, as Salome gabbles Wilde's text ('Sehr hastig', so Strauss directs), the words still seem too verbose, even after considerable pruning, to fit the carefully constructed symphonic structure. Much of *Salome* is in conception far more tone poem than opera, and here, as in other vital passages to come, the voice part detracts instead of adding to the meaning of the music, as Wagner in similar circumstance always succeeds in doing.

Narraboth, in agony of mind, tries to do his duty and resist Salome's persuasive tactics, but his desire for her overcomes his qualms, and before long he issues the command that the prophet be fetched for the Princess. There is a last surge of Exx. 2 and 8, for poor deluded Narraboth feels that at this moment he stands higher than ever before in Salome's regard. At the climax, however, Jochanaan's stern 'Wenn er kommt' theme Ex. 7 is blazoned out on horns and cellos and we

[11] This was a passage which Wilde was fond of quoting on account of its deliberate absurdity, though it must have been disconcerting when he was told by a friend that some flowers really are green.

know that he, and only he, is in Salome's mind. The intensity fades momentarily and the orchestra embarks on the first of the opera's main dividing interludes, beginning with the development of an important variant of the cistern theme (Ex. 12a) while the soldiers go down to fetch Jochanaan:

Ex. 12a.

mf espr.

5

Wilde covers the pause in the action at this dramatic cornerstone by reintroducing his motif of the Young Syrian and the Page, with their discussions on the appearance of the moon. Ernest Newman elaborates this point with great perception in his article on the work in *Opera Nights*:

> The moon is almost a character in the work, certainly a symbol. . . . The aspect of the moon changes with the psychological changes in the drama. As we have seen, it figures at the opening as the symbol of super-terrestrial whiteness and purity, an aspect of it which both Narraboth and the Page instinctively associate with the young Salome they have so far known. But now, when the action takes on a definitely darker tinge, the face of the moon changes, and the Page and Narraboth are nervously sensitive to it.

Perhaps Strauss made a sacrifice in omitting the motivic interchange between these two important if minor characters. Yet to have reverted to the weird mood of the opening for the sake of a few lines would have seriously slackened the tension. Strauss realized that in a musical work the dramatic problem was entirely different, and that the inexorable progress of the tragedy was better maintained by a symphonic passage which would develop and build to a climax the musical motifs impinging on the situation with its deadly implications.

Salome's motifs Ex. 8 (a)[12] and Ex. 1, the latter in diminution and

[12] With sublime disregard for practical considerations, the opening figure is given to the violins even when it goes below their compass, viz.: When tackled on the subject Strauss remarked impatiently, 'Well then, what would you expect me to have written—a G?'

turning into a rising chromatic scale, are worked up to suggest her feverish anticipation at the prospect of seeing Jochanaan. The prophet's theme, Ex. 6, however, never loses its calm dignity, whether played alternately with Salome's turbulent music or combined with it. New motifs are now introduced on behalf of both characters. Salome's is an impassioned lyrical theme which portrays the growth of her physical passion for the Prophet,

Ex. 13

while Jochanaan's is another dignified pronouncement suggestive of the divine nature of his visionary utterances:

Ex. 14[13]

Beneath the elaborate polyphony the gloomy music of the cistern, Ex. 12, meanders oppressively, the bass clarinet figure rumbling below on tremolo double basses.

As Jochanaan appears, the washes of orchestral sound die away and Ex. 14 is nobly proclaimed by the oboe band, complete with cor anglais and heckelphon[14]. This leads to a statement of Jochanaan's first theme, Ex. 6, now elaborated at length by the six horns. Against this impressive background Jochanaan embarks on the first of a series of prophesies and accusations.

The long scene which follows resolves itself formally into three clear sections:

(1) Jochanaan's pronouncements and their growing effect upon Salome's emotions until she forces herself into his awareness.

(2) Salome's three-verse love song with Jochanaan's rejections.

[13] In its full version this theme is extended by an undulating figure and ends with a true Straussian modulation to a chromatically distant key.

[14] The heckelphon, a continental type of bass oboe, appears here for the first time in the symphonic orchestra.

(3) The first climax of the action; Salome's abandonment, Narraboth's suicide, Jochanaan's sermon and curse.

The first section contains a number of new and important motifs. As Salome asks Narraboth whom it is that the Prophet is denouncing, Ex. 8(a) appears coyly on the clarinet with a new twist to its tail, a twist which is shortly to grow into the principal theme of Salome's love song.

Ex. 15

Jochanaan warms to his subject and two new themes enter into the structure of the symphonic design. Though first heard together, they later acquire independent importance:

Ex. 16 and 17

If Ex. 16 represents the intense fervour of Jochanaan's personality, Ex. 17 is associated more specifically with his anger and reproachful attacks against Herodias. In this respect they form a pair much as Exx. 6 and 7 belong together.

Despite Narraboth's urgent pleas (accompanied always by his Ex. 2), Salome is transfixed. Jochanaan is terrible; his eyes above all are terrible. At the mention of his eyes—'black caverns where dragons dwell'—a strange eerie theme is heard on the clarinets:

Ex. 18

This theme, the relationship of which to Ex. 14 is obvious but vital, recurs only once in the work, but at a particularly sinister and significant moment in Salome's closing solo scene. Little by little Salome's motifs mingle with those of Jochanaan as she becomes increasingly fascinated by him. Exx. 1 and 16 in particular are repeated like ostinati against the wailing chromatic tail which grows on the end of Ex. 14. Salome insists on making herself known to him and out of his horror-struck and vehement rejection of her, Strauss builds the electrifying passage which leads into Salome's love song. A particularly ingenious transformation of Ex. 17 with the upper and lower parts reversed in double counterpoint makes the venom in the motif turn into lust as Salome begs Jochanaan to go on talking. His voice, she urges, for all its denunciations, sounds like music in her ears. The growing hysterical excitement is horrible and is greatly intensified not only by the feverish repetitions of motifs often telescoped into rapid diminution, but by the elaborate detail of scurrying scales and arpeggios with which Strauss fills the score. There is one moment of calm as Jochanaan refers to the Son of Man. Salome naïvely asks who that may be: 'Is he as beautiful as thou art, Jochanaan?'—scarcely the reply he had looked for. In his fury, Jochanaan cries out that he can hear 'the beating of the wings of the angel of death'. There is a brief rushing and flapping, a premonition of the wind and beating of wings which Herod, too, is to hear at certain crucial moments in the drama. There is a last upward plunge of Ex. 16 and as the music resolves triumphantly into the rich and highly coloured key of B major, Salome bursts into her ecstatic paean in praise of Jochanaan's beauty, the second main section of the scene.

6

Salome's eulogy dwells in turn on three aspects of Jochanaan's physiognomy; his body, his hair, and his mouth, while in between each stanza come the episodes of Jochanaan's rejection and Salome's deliberate distortions of all she has just said, as a child may wilfully destroy the toy it has just built with such patient care. Wilde's language here is extravagantly poetic, erotic, and voluptuous. Once again, therefore, music is redundant for its true appreciation, while in its turn it is too elaborate to fall simply into place in Strauss's symphonic scheme, which, for formal reasons, still needed to be kept fairly concise. The first verse is by far the most inspired—a natural outpouring of sheer melody based on Ex. 15 and the passionate phrase Ex. 13. The second verse, based on Jochanaan's hair, consists of little more than note spinning around Salome's light-hearted dance theme (Ex. 10, punctuated periodically by Ex. 8(a)) until the words are duly exhausted; but in the third verse Strauss clearly strove to overreach all his own achievements in the expression of the erotic in music. Phrases in thirds press upwards ever higher:

Ex. 19

the descending figure Ex. 15(a) is emphasized in augmentation and linked to passage work reminiscent of all Strauss's most ardent love music from *Don Juan* onwards. Yet the final effect is somewhat forced and seems to lack the spontaneity of the earlier stanza. Possibly Strauss recognized this, for it is only that first section which finds a place in the great reprise of the solo scene; there is, however, perhaps another explanation in Newman's conjecture as to the order of the composition of the opera which will be discussed in due course.

Each section ends with the little refrain 'Let me touch (kiss) thy body (hair, mouth)', which Strauss sets in the most ingenious way with three different cadences based primarily on Ex. 15 (though Ex. 1 enters slyly to round off the first two), modulating each time abruptly and unexpectedly into a different yet always totally unrelated key. The first verse (in B) slips down into A, the second (in D flat) crosses the whole spectrum of keys into the most distant tonality of G, while the third (in E) raises itself winningly up to F. Here is an extension of the mastery of harmonic technique which was already so apparent in *Don Quixote*.

Jochanaan's reactions to the first two stanzas are in turn proud and vehemently angry. Salome's retaliations are on both occasions full of the ugliest caricatures of Strauss's own orchestration which he could conjure up. Violas are marked to smear the phrasing in passages which contain the craziest double octaves, violins play the love music with only the wood of the bow; the brass are constantly muted, in which condition the horns indulge in chromatic scales and trills; the harps clatter away *fff* at the very highest octave in an attempt to depict in sound the idea of the hair now having become a crown of thorns; muted violas give an inversion of Ex. 16 as a symbol of negation of all that Salome had previously seen as fine in Jochanaan. The reactions to the third verse, however, are entirely different. Jochanaan is utterly disturbed, though he is filled with shuddering at Salome's demand that he let her kiss him. She for her part is now beside herself, and her raging thirst inspired Strauss to the creation of one of the most glowing themes in the opera:

Ex. 20

Ich will dei·nen Mund küs·sen, Jo - cha - na - an

At this point Narraboth's theme (Ex. 2) returns into the texture of the complex polyphony. The wretched Young Syrian can bear no longer what he sees going on before his eyes and after a brief and ineffectual protest kills himself, his body falling between Salome (Ex. 1 in viciously descending sequences) and Jochanaan (Ex. 15 rearing itself in ferocious indignation).

But Salome, being now launched into Ex. 20, is, as it were, on a different plane. The death of Narraboth is less than nothing to her, and she merely repeats her ecstatic desire to embrace the prophet, who is not merely disgusted but shocked to the depth of his soul. (He even mentions Herodias directly by name, for the only time in the work, thus identifying the meaning of Ex. 17 beyond question.) Jochanaan earnestly exhorts Salome to seek out Jesus, who is on the Sea of Galilee with his disciples. A new collection of motifs accompanies this sermon, which is set in the simplest harmonies and sweet, plain orchestration, on an undulating pedal, suggestive of a boat at rest on calm waters;

Ex. 21

As Jochanaan conjures up a picture of a penitent Salome begging for-
giveness of Jesus, a soft version of Ex. 20 follows and leads both into and
out of a fanfare motif which marks the climax of the words 'Call unto
Him by Name.'

Ex. 22[15]

The function of Ex. 20 in this context is of the greatest interest. When
the whole section recurs later in the work the opening figure of this
melody is retained, but with a different continuation. In each case the
marked repetition of the tonic rising to the mediant is the focal point of
the entries and this connects up with Jochanaan's 'Wenn er kommt',
Ex. 7. Since it is this very looked-for coming of Jesus that we are now
dealing with, the allusion is plain and can be pursued to include the
opening of Ex. 22, the interval now justifiably being major, since we
are in the presence of the Divine. What is less plain is why Ex. 20, the
theme of Salome's passion for Jochanaan, should from the first have
been connected in the same way. Specht in his analysis of the opera,
discusses the point at great length and offers a number of alternative
explanations, including Jochanaan's hope for the expiation of Salome's
sin through Jesus. It is possible that Strauss may indeed have intended to
give point to Jochanaan's line 'ask of Him the remission of thy sins', not
only by sublimating in Jesus's music the theme of her terrible lust, but
by linking it motivically with that of His coming.

The sermon ends with a full statement of Ex. 14 which dissolves into
a soft swaying repetition of her erotic request from the now despairing
Salome. Jochanaan, at his wits' end, curses her and, leaving the wretched
girl beside herself with desire and frustration, descends into the cistern
once again.

7

As before, Strauss replaces Wilde's linking passages with an orchestral
interlude, this time one of the focal points of the score, not only on

[15] It is interesting to note here again Strauss's penchant for alluding to the
supreme Divinity in terms of basic triads (cf. *Guntram* Ex. 1 (d)).

account of its intrinsic quality, but by virtue of its position as the main turning-point of the entire drama. In it Strauss pursues Salome's thoughts and yearnings as she watches Jochanaan descending into his prison (Ex. 12). Her love song is poured out wildly in canon, even the timpani contributing the whole opening figure of Ex. 15, with Jochanaan's themes worked into the texture as the music surges higher and higher. The tempo quickens and Ex. 6 is given out by increasing bodies of brass instruments in alternation with the other motifs, the alternation itself gradually quickening until only rapid sweeps separate the entries. The climax is reached with frenzied chromatic scales simultaneously rising and falling in a figuration which owes its origin to the climax of the Introduction to Act III of *Siegfried*. The full cadence is reached after powerful reiterations of Jochanaan's themes of recrimination (Exx. 16 and 17). A simple cadence after so great a build-up seemed to Strauss, however, too abrupt, so he extended it with a passage of terrifying impact. The violins sustain a tearing fortissimo tremolo, while the brass savagely force through it a series of spaced-out cadences in which the tonic C sharp is repeatedly approached from a dramatically new direction:

Ex. 23

On one occasion Salome recalls the gentle subtle modulatory cadence of her refrain 'Let me kiss . . .,' but the phrase, timidly ventured on woodwind and lower strings, is never completed, being brusquely dismissed by Ex. 23 cuttingly delivered three more times as it descends through the depths of the orchestra.

Salome's sanity, never very stable, now gives way altogether. She cowers brooding over the lip of the cistern while her Ex. 1 is played by a solo contra-bassoon against the tearing tremolo which in its turn has now descended to the violas *sul ponticello*. The effect is indescribably sinister, and grows steadily more threatening as, out of the contra's phrase, there springs a new figure, symbolic of some insane resolution.

R.S.–S

Ex. 24

Suddenly the E-flat clarinet pipes out a grotesque caricature of Jochanaan's prophetic motif Ex. 14, and with a new theme solemnly declaimed in the brass we not only know that Salome has determined to have her revenge on the man who has spurned her advances, but are given a premonition as to what form that revenge is to take:

Ex. 25

[Salome (later): *Ich will den Kopf _____ des Jo - cha - na - an.*]

The relationship of this theme to Ex. 13 and so in turn back to Ex. 7 is important. The rise and fall of the characteristic minor third later becomes a familiar form of this motif as an isolated figure, viz.

Ex. 25a

In this form the fragment ⌐ x ⌐ which is later repeated so often becomes first cousin to the opening figure of Ex. 15. This homogeneity of Salome's motifs is remarkable and of great importance.

The uproar theme (Ex. 3) breaks into the ghastly tension accompanied by hectic streams of descending whole tone scales. Herod, with Herodias at his heel and his whole entourage in train, bursts unceremoniously upon the scene in search of Salome.[16] The music has never been diverted from the changing character of Salome, and all other matters have now become irrelevant distractions. As a result the rapid entry of the Court has the startling effect of an explosion.

[16] Wilde brings Herod's entry immediately after a contradictory remark of one of the soldiers, viz. 'The Tetrarch will not come to this place. He never comes on the terrace. He is too much afraid of the prophet.' (Enter Herod) . . . This delightful piece of irony has no place in Strauss's scheme any more than the heartbreaking mourning speech of the Page over his dead friend.

Apart from the reckless descending whole-tone scales, which Strauss uses with sure insight to suggest Herod's petulant weakness (the whole-tone scale is entirely characterless, though it can create atmosphere), the Tetrarch is portrayed by a series of animated motifs. Only when at last seeing the figure of Salome once more before him and momentarily regaining his calm, is he shown in some semblance of dignity.

Ex. 26

Motifs descriptive of principal characters built in this way out of chromatically shifting block chords have appeared before in Strauss's operas (cf. *Feuersnot*, Ex. 14) and will appear again, for example, at the entry of Orestes in *Elektra*. Unlike Kunrad and Orestes, however, Herod is a neurotic tyrant who scarcely deserves so solid a theme, and Strauss finds few occasions in which to introduce it. Here it manages to persist against the whole-tone scales while Herod gives his view of the extraordinary moon, which he sees as a mad, naked woman looking for lovers. Herodias spitefully replies that the moon is the moon and nothing else. Her deliberate lack of imagination brings with it momentary calm, but it is short-lived, for her own motif is as insanely restless as most of Herod's:

Ex. 27   or later

A dreadful feature of the drama is the prevailing air of insanity which is spread like a cloak over the scene and which Strauss has brought out with horrible vividness in the score. Herodias announces that they will go back into the palace. Even setting his obsession over Salome on one side, this is enough to make Herod decide to stay. He has no sooner called to his slaves for torches, carpets, wine, and so forth (repetitions of Herodias's Ex. 27 in mounting fury) than he slips in the blood of Narraboth, whose corpse is still lying where it fell. Ex. 27 immediately inverts and turns into a new motif which henceforward portrays the frenzy of Herod's superstitious fears:

Ex. 28

Herod cannot understand the reason for this death (Ex. 1 on the oboe slyly explains it, could Herod but hear and understand)—he gave no order for the Young Syrian to be killed. Strauss even has a motif for the word of command which Herod denies having given:

Ex. 29

Herod is recalling the love-sick glances the Young Syrian cast at Salome (Ex. 2) when an icy wind springs up. Each gust begins with Ex. 28, implying that they exist solely in Herod's overwrought imagination. Herodias hears and feels no wind, just as she saw the moon purely and simply as the moon, and her retorts bring absolute and abrupt calm in the orchestra.

Nevertheless Herod continues to experience the rushing of the ghostly wind and as it grows he seems, like Jochanaan before him, to hear the beating of mighty wings. Exx. 14 and 15(a) rise up in the furore, indicating a wilder purpose in the visit of the Angel of Death than just poor Narraboth. For a moment the wind sinks again, then rises a third time. Herodias decides that Herod is clearly a sick man, but he retorts that it is Salome who is deathly ill, and certainly she gives that impression in her appearance and behaviour. Herodias's sharp attack on Herod for looking at Salome, clearly an attack already made with maddening regularity, is enough to rouse Herod's perversity, and he immediately proceeds systematically to make advances to the girl. In turn he presses wine and fruit upon her in snatches of rather commonplace song based partially upon her motifs,[17] though the second verse begins like the

[17] It is apparent again and again in the full score that Strauss was amusing himself while working on the orchestration. At this point there is a young concerto for bass clarinet hidden in the texture, and quite superfluous to its meaning. It is at best scarcely audible, though extremely difficult. Even Strauss seems to have realized that this was an instance of detail for its own sake, for he adds a footnote to the effect that if the bass clarinettist is not absolutely excellent the whole passage is best omitted altogether!

passage from *Samson and Delilah* and continues with a vulgar tune which is later brought back in the most unpleasant circumstances in the last scene:

Ex. 30

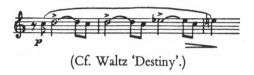

(Cf. Waltz 'Destiny'.)

Let Salome only put the imprint of her little white teeth on the fruit, says Herod, and he will eat what remains. So it had also been with the wine and her little red lips, but each time Salome in a dull expressionless voice refuses (Ex. 1 on the heckelphon, a very odd effect) to the undisguised satisfaction of Herodias. Herod turns upon his Queen, saying, 'See how you have brought up this daughter of yours', to which she retorts 'My daughter and I come from a royal race. As for you, your father was a camel driver! He was also a robber!'[18]

In bitter exasperation Herod embarks on a third verse in which he meaningly offers Salome her mother's throne, but quite unmoved she merely replies as before that she is not tired, while the contra-bassoon recalls the closing bars of the interlude, showing that Salome's mind is still focussed on her revenge, so that she is quite incapable of taking any part in the scene that is being played for her benefit. Herod, somewhat put out of countenance, dithers and is only saved by the voice of Jochanaan, who begins to prophesy once more. The prophet's brief announcement is a virtual repetition of the one which first attracted Salome's attention near the beginning of the opera. In Wilde's text there is no very great similarity between the two speeches, but Strauss needed a formal symphonic reprise of earlier material, and so by careful cutting and slight adjustment of the translation a co-relationship of the two sections was made not only possible but natural.

Herodias reacts violently. Ex. 27(a) makes its first piercing entry, indicating the state of Herodias's nervous system, which is frayed almost to the verge of hysteria. Herod coldly asserts that Jochanaan is a

[18] Wilde also adds the exchange which Strauss unfortunately did not set:
'Herod: Thou liest!
Herodias: Thou knowest well it is true.'
Upon which Herod hastily changes the subject. The whole makes a splendid interplay between the terrible Tetrarch and his appalling spouse.

very great prophet, upon which Herodias accuses him of being afraid of him (the descending whole-tone scales reveal the truth of this). Although Herod replies that he is not afraid of anyone, Salome's theme Ex. 8(a) in the violins shows that there is certainly one person he fears. This is no invention of Strauss; the English translation of Wilde's text gives the phrase as 'I am afraid of no man', a subtlety which, while in neither the original French, nor the German version, may have emanated from Oscar Wilde, who played a considerable part in the revision of the text published under the name of Lord Alfred Douglas.

Herodias makes the further taunt that if he were not afraid of the Prophet he would hand him over to the Jews, who have been clamouring for him these past six months, and one of the Jews who have followed the Court out on to the terrace eagerly presses this proposal. Taken unawares, for one might have thought that Herodias would be the last person to make such a suggestion, Herod angrily refuses on the grounds that Jochanaan is a man who has seen God. (The implication that he is in a form of protective custody is a delightful one.)

The idea of any man actually seeing God touches directly upon religious doctrine, and in a flash the Jews are in heated theological argument. Strauss sets this as an extended Scherzo-development of the motifs which make up the 'hubbub' theme Ex. 3. At its climax Herodias screams out to Herod to stop them, but, although they are momentarily halted, Herod himself is interested in the subject of whether Jochanaan may indeed be a reincarnation of the prophet Elias, and the discussion breaks out again, to the despair of Herodias. It is interrupted this time by Jochanaan's voice heralding the Saviour of the World. With the appearance of this phrase the subject is put on a different level. Two Nazarenes enter the argument, claiming that the Messiah has indeed come (one Jew refutes this so frantically that he is pushed right out of key, the first of a series of instances of dramatic polytonality in this section), and they go on to an account of Jesus' activity in Galilee, giving Strauss the opportunity for a development of Exx. 21 and 22, the latter with great magnificence and nobility of utterance. This is also the place, referred to earlier, in which the opening phrase of Ex. 20 is featured with a series of different continuations. All goes well until one of the Nazarenes reports that Jesus has raised people from the dead. Abruptly Herod is shocked right out of key like the first Jew before him, a device which caused excited comment when the work first appeared. That the dead should return is as terrible a prospect as Herod can imagine, bearing in mind his brother and what he did to him.[19]

The voice of Jochanaan is now heard attacking Salome and prophesying her death by various extreme forms of violence, including the actual fate which overcomes her in the drama—i.e. that the soldiers shall crush her beneath their shields.[20] Herodias, however, continues to take the attacks as directed personally against herself, and her cries of rage (Ex. 27(a)) become frantic in their insistence. They combine with Exx. 16 and 17, as well as with distortions of the Prophecy motif (Ex. 14), fuel being added to the fire by repetitions of Ex. 27 in its original form. At the very moment of extreme exasperation there is an abrupt silent pause, followed by a complete change of subject.

8

In Wilde's original text the episode of Salome's dance is brilliantly prepared, but in a way which it was impossible for Strauss to incorporate. From the very entrance of the Court on to the stage remarks have been passed by Herod to show his profound consciousness of the presence of important envoys from Rome. Like the distinguished ruler he is, he never wholly forgets his position as host,[21] though at times the provocation of his Queen and his burning desire for her daughter force undignified retorts from his lips. Yet when he slips in the blood of the Young Syrian, one of his first thoughts is of his guests, and he says: 'What does this body here? Think you I am like the King of Egypt, who gives no feast to his guests but that he shows them a corpse?' Now he makes a brave effort at conversing with them, but it is his misfortune that even as he does so he cannot take his eyes off Salome, with the result that he talks hopeless rubbish. He forgets his first question before he has completed the sentence, while in the second he commits the crass indiscretion of asking about the rumoured disappearance of the sanctuary veil in the Temple. Herodias spitefully answers: 'It was thyself who didst steal it. Thou speakest at random. I will not stay here. Let us go within', at which unendurable provocation Herod, whose eyes have never left Salome, can contain himself no longer and calls her to dance for him.

[19] Since Strauss, as we have seen, has omitted the reference to the brother's fate (see above, p. 241), an important point is lost here in the opera.

[20] This was an invention of Oscar Wilde. In real life Salome lived on to marry Antipas's younger brother Philip.

[21] Strauss himself used to make a great point of this to performers of the role.

Strauss had from the first omitted the characters of the Roman guests altogether, so that it became necessary for him to cut this splendid scene also. He solved the problem by a *coup de théâtre*, hoping that the sudden silence and switch to Herod's 'Dance for me, Salome' would bridge the gap effectively. Nevertheless the final impression remains as of a cut in the score.

Until now Jochanaan's declamations have remained isolated and set against a background of his relevant motifs, all the other characters of the drama listening to him or waiting for him to finish before continuing their roles in the main drama. Here for the first time Strauss makes his solemn prophecy of Herod's own downfall go for nothing against the greater urgency of the situation which is developing in the foreground. Even in the music there is no reference to Jochanaan's themes, but only to Salome's Exx. 8 and 11, with Herod's descending whole-tone scale cutting across. The Tetrarch presses Salome to dance, against her own icy refusals and her mother's violent objections. He now promises her complete freedom of choice up to half of his kingdom for her reward. His supplications carry with them a new composite theme which, although seemingly unimportant at present, builds to great dramatic intensity in due course, when Herod finds himself exhorting Salome in a very different way.

Ex. 31

Suddenly Salome sees the possibilities latent within such a promise, and forces Herod to make it upon oath. All unsuspecting, Herod agrees readily and in an infinitely banal C major phrase (which the complexity of the orchestration does nothing to hide) chortles away at the thought of the beautiful Salome as queen. As Ex. 31(a) takes the strains away into the deep bass the eerie wind makes an unexpected return. Herod's oath has brought about the reappearance of the Angel of Death in the palace. Strauss makes the music prophetic by repeating Jochanaan's Ex. 6 in a disagreeably beheaded form during the subsiding of the stormy wind passage. The next section is one of the most adventurous in the opera, and, with some passages in *Elektra*, represents the farthest Strauss travelled into the regions of progressive stylistic experiment in company with composers such as Bartók, Stravinsky, and above all, Schönberg. There will be more to say on this subject later. The extreme imaginative juxtaposing of countless motifs, of Salome, of Jochanaan, of Herod himself as he alternately shivers with cold and perspires with fever, takes Strauss to the brink of atonality.

At last the storm subsides and, with a sighing reference to the whole-tone scale on the clarinet and Ex. 31(b) on the oboe, Herod breathes again. Herodias's protests are now in vain; Jochanaan makes the last prophecy of his life as Salome tells Herod that she will dance for him. Her Ex. 8 and Herod's Ex. 26 rise through the orchestra; there is a silence, two sharp chords on harps and celeste and Salome is ready to dance the Dance of the Seven Veils.

9

Alma Mahler was not entirely wrong when she wrote that the Dance is no more than a hotchpotch of all the rest, though this need not necessarily be taken quite so devastatingly as she meant it. Strauss undoubtedly took a risk in leaving it till last, when he had to rely on technique rather than the inspiration which had carried him through the main body of the opera. Yet despite its banalities, and they are many, it remains an extremely brilliant symphonic piece, well balanced and skilfully constructed, whilst histrionically and in its use of the motifs of the opera it takes its place effectively in the total scheme. In performances it always comes off, but discerning opinion frowns upon it as the weakest section of one of Strauss's best works, and laments over its offensive lapses of taste. Strauss's taste, as we have seen, was fallible when he aimed high, which explains the banalities of the music composed for the divine elements of the score as compared with the vivid inspiration of the sections describing the deeds and emotions of the more grotesque characters. It does not explain the Dance, however, which might have been expected to stimulate his imagination immediately. The reason why it did not do so lies surely in his wish, expressed from the first, to succeed where others had failed in the musical representation of 'true Oriental colour and scorching sun'. This Orientalism was a tremendously important facet of the period in the widely prevalent desire on the part of Western intellectuals to experience ever more exotic emotions, believing that the sensations to be found in forms of existence nearer home had been thoroughly exhausted and were now *vieux jeu*. Wilde's play itself was a typical product of the *fin de siècle* atmosphere of the late nineteenth century in its bogus gestures and extravagant exploitation of Oriental sensuality and erotic searchings. To match its atmosphere in music was to conjure up new sonorities and a style of orchestral colouring which came more easily to the French and Russian composers than to the Germans. So it was that Strauss, for all his virtuosity of orchestral technique a German through and through, found it harder than he had expected to evoke the delicate but morbid air of perfumed decadence which oozes out of Wilde's text. When he set out on the composition Strauss firmly believed that he had succeeded in finding the appropriate style, but by the time he reached the dance (where the need for local colour was by far the strongest) it had become apparent that all he had succeeded in producing was mere embellishment and that his thought and invention had remained obstinately Teutonic. Despite the quasi-Orientalism of the opening bars of Salome's dance, its flavour is unmistakably—even disconcertingly—Viennese.

Basically, then, the Dance of the Seven Veils is a super-potpourri of the main themes of the opera. It is in three main sections, in turn slow, lyrical and virtuoso, flanked by the introduction and coda. The introduction presents a brief attempt at barbaric local colour, containing the first ideas which are exclusively indigenous to the Dance:

Ex. 32

This leads to a furious announcement of the theme of Salome's revenge (Ex. 25) which naturally enough forms the motivating impulse of the piece. In various diminutions similar to Ex. 25a it forms the ostinato accompaniment to most of the different sections from the first slow dance movement. This is a seductive passage for solo woodwind instruments which, beginning with the oboe turns from Ex. 32, gradually incorporates most of Salome's motifs, including the irritable Ex. 5 which has long been neglected. Narraboth's Ex. 2 finds an important place in the course of the working out, though Strauss's purpose here can only be purely musical. If anything is sure, it is that Salome has not one thought in her head for the unfortunate Syrian who has died in anguish for her. Gradually the halting steps of the first section weld into a flowing movement for which Strauss composed a nice warm, juicy tune:

Ex. 33

A graceful waltz soon follows, and further themes of the dancing Princess are happily and ingeniously transformed for this second lyrical section. A brief return to the slower opening ushers in the waltz-like Ex. 10, which now finds its rightful milieu. The rhythm stumbles and then passes into a very quick tempo for the third virtuoso section of the Dance. The link is effected by means of the derivative of Narraboth's theme (Ex. 2a), which has never been repeated since its first important appearance near the beginning of the opera.

The brilliant Presto section combines Ex. 33 with the savage viola figure Ex. 32(a), to the accompaniment of a complex ostinato formed out of the oboe turns (Ex. 32) and constant repetitions of Salome's Ex. 1. Against this, moreover, the violent fanfare-like motif of Herod's word of command (Ex. 29) constantly thrusts upwards in the trumpets. There is a breathless pause and Salome hurls herself into the coda, a prestissimo of the utmost impetuosity based on the theme of Salome's lust for Jochanaan, Ex. 13. This reaches its climax on an isolated trill sustained high up in violins, clarinets, and piccolo, against which flutes and oboes give out twice the opening phrase of Ex. 15 in a way which is charged with terrible purpose. The tonal ambiguity of the trill is in itself the motif of Salome's kiss on Jochanaan's dead lips, as will transpire when the time comes, though it is anticipated here and each time later when she insists on her gruesome reward. The stage directions at this point show Salome pausing for a moment by the cistern in a visionary manner. The last phrase of the same theme (Ex. 15) then hurtles down in the combined strings and woodwind as Salome flings herself at Herod's feet.

10

Herod's jubilant enthusiasm sends his theme Ex. 26 cavorting all over
the orchestra, accompanied in dance-like fashion by the two harps and
pizzicato strings. The clarinets then resume the eerie trill as Salome
prepares to name her trophy. Such is Herod's excitement that she gets
no further at first than stipulating the silver charger before he breaks in
with transports of delight while the woodwind and celeste enjoy themselves with cheerful arabesques. By establishing a mood of light-hearted
fervour, Strauss thus intensifies the shock when Salome completes her
request. As she does this, the trills which have duly appeared again for
the purpose, creep upwards with a horrid expectancy.

Herod leaps up flabbergasted. The whole-tone scale crashes down on
the brass, Ex. 31(a) plunges about on the bass instruments (including
tuba), and the strings rush hither and thither. Herod's immediate
thought is that the idea of such a request was put in Salome's mind by
her mother, but in a sullen voice (the trill now being in the lower
register) Salome repudiates the suggestion and reminds Herod that he
has sworn on oath. Herod argues with her, but she is firm, and Herodias
soon adds her approval of what her daughter is doing. The character of
Herodias comes alive at the touch of Strauss's pen even more vividly
than that of Salome herself. In her vitriolic hate she is first cousin to
Elektra and Klytemnestra. As she shrieks her triumph a new form of
Ex. 27(a) bellows out in the horns:

Ex. 34

But even while she rants, the theme of Salome's vengeance, Ex. 25,
rearing up through the orchestra, gives the lie to her fond idea that
Salome has indeed made her choice for love of her mother and in vindication of her honour against Jochanaan's attacks.

Herod now changes his tactics. To the theme of his own passion,
Ex. 9, he acknowledges that he has been too much attracted by Salome
and begs her not to bear him a grudge on that account. He gives her in
turn a series of reasons why she cannot want such a ghastly reward: the
object itself is dreadful; the prophet is a holy man, possibly sent by God;
she cannot want him to commit sacrilege. In exchange he offers her

various alternatives, consisting of endless jewels and his prize white peacocks. But in view of the fact that he has already offered half of his kingdom these are small fry, and one sympathizes with Herodias when she turns on him with the comment 'As for you, you are ridiculous with your peacocks', as one does also with him when he retaliates with 'You cry out always; you cry out like a beast of prey'.

Herod's agitation is accompanied by a new theme which we shall meet again in *Der Rosenkavalier*:

Ex. 35

During his description of the jewels there is a surprising return of the ecstatic Ex. 19. Ex. 31(a) also is ever more strongly in evidence until, as Herod's offers to Salome become increasingly wild—firstly the mantle of the High Priest and finally the veil of the sanctuary itself (The Jews: 'Oh, Oh')—it thunders out in the full brass. All is in vain, however, and the trill returns, now fortissimo on the complete range of flutes and clarinets,[22] against which Salome wildly screams out yet again her horrific demand.

From this point onwards Strauss lets his imagination run riot. The results made history in the same way as did *Till Eulenspiegel* and *Don Quixote* some ten years previously. The whole-tone scale thunders in brass and timpani[23] with Ex. 26 cutting across it. A vast chromatic scale then leads to a ferocious augmentation of Herod's superstition theme Ex. 28. Ex. 26 then rears itself in desperation as Herod dully says: 'Let her be given what she asks! Of a truth she is her mother's child!' and sinks back hopelessly in his seat.

The B-flat clarinets trill away down below, while the A clarinets rush uphill in scales a tone apart. Trumpets proclaim the motif of Herod's command Ex. 29, while Salome's Ex. 15 combines with her mother's Ex. 34 in a horrible display of hysterical triumph. Herodias has drawn the ring of death from the Tetrarch's hand and given it to a

[22] In addition to the usual extras in the clarinet department, the little E-flat at one end of the compass and the bass clarinet at the other, Strauss uses two B-flats as well as two A instruments, a most interesting method worthy of close study.

[23] Strauss gives a diagram of how the drums should be laid out.

soldier, who has passed it to the executioner. The latter, though visibly scared, goes down into the cistern and as he does so Herod becomes conscious of the loss of his ring (Ex. 29 softly on woodwind and pizzicato strings). He also has the impression that someone has drunk his wine. He is, in fact, on the verge of delirium in his superstitious terror. A distortion of Jochanaan's theme Ex. 6 sighs in the strings and muted horns. Herodias shrilly calls out that her daughter has done rightly (Ex. 27(a) in piercing tones) and the low trill which has continued right through the section doubles over upon itself and disappears into the depths.

Salome leans over the cistern and listens. There is not a sound but a bass drum roll and infinitely soft tremolo basses on their lowest note. A succession of fantastic jabs break the petrified silence from time to time. This is obtained by four double basses, who are instructed to clutch the string high up between the thumb and forefinger and give it a short sharp stroke with the bow. The result has been rightly described as grisly, despite Strauss's assurances that these notes 'do not represent cries of pain uttered by the victim, but sighs of anguish from the heart of an impatiently expectant Salome'. The composer went on to say: 'The ominous passage proved so shocking during the dress rehearsal that Graf Seebach (the Dresden Generalintendant) for fear of causing merriment, persuaded me to tone the double basses down by a sustained B-flat on the cor anglais.' Strauss also took the precaution of adding a footnote in the score to the effect that 'the sound should imitate the stifled sighs and groans of a woman'.[24]

In her fever of anticipation, Salome tries to picture the scene that is being enacted in the cistern. During the dreadful silence she cannot understand how it is that Jochanaan does not cry out, as she would if

[24] Strauss took this whole idea *en bloc* from Berlioz, who, in his famous treatise on Instrumentation, wrote as follows:

A Piedmontese artist, M. Langlois, who played in Paris about fifteen years ago, obtained with the bow, by pinching the high string of the double bass between the thumb and forefinger of the left hand instead of pressing it on the fingerboard, and by rising thus nearly to the bridge, high sounds of singular acuteness, and incredible power. If there were need to introduce in the orchestra a loud female cry, no instrument could better utter it than double basses employed in this way. I doubt whether our artists are acquainted with M. Langlois's method of producing acute sounds; but they would soon be able to make themselves familiar with it.

Only a few years previously Strauss had made his own translated edition of Berlioz's work and clearly noted this effect for future use.

someone sought to kill her. The need for self-expression which this thought stirs up within her causes her to cry out to the executioner to strike. The vengeance motif begins to stir, first as in Ex. 25a, but quickly building up to the complete phrase, upon which Ex. 24 also rears itself, culminating in its jarring dissonance. Here at last is to be the fulfilment of Salome's obsession which first crystallized within her at the end of the central orchestral interlude. A short reprise is thus apt and the contra-bassoon also adds its sinister solo. This, too, dies away and the tension becomes unbearable.

Suddenly there is a nasty thud, supplied by cellos and basses on a deep trill. There is no doubt at all what this represents, but Salome's diseased brain forces her to think that it was the sword of the executioner which fell and that he has shirked his task. Strauss depicts her demented ravings with fiendish zest. The cistern theme in its varied form Ex. 12a is used as a restless ostinato, and the strings and woodwind hurl out the theme of Salome's savage temper (Ex. 11) again and again, while the mad Princess turns to the Page and with supreme contempt for his feelings, tells him as a friend of the dead Syrian that 'there have not been dead men enough' and that he should go to the soldiers and order them to bring her 'the thing the Tetrarch has promised me, the thing that is mine'. The Page recoils and she turns herself to the soldiers. They, too, turn from her in horror and ultimately she shrieks straight at the Tetrarch to order his soldiers to give her the head of Jochanaan. The music is again entirely built on Exx. 24 and 25, hammered out with hysterical insistence. Her voice and the music die away, and a huge black arm appears bearing the long-sought object on its silver charger. Only the bass drum roll accompanies this terrible apparition. Herod hides his face with his cloak. Herodias smiles and fans herself. The Nazarenes fall on their knees and begin to pray.[25] Salome seizes the head and the great final Scena bursts out in the full orchestra.

II

At various times during the opera it has seemed as if the setting of Wilde's words has been to Strauss a difficulty, a problem to be overcome. Certainly the opening lines suggested their own musical formulae, as he discovered when he turned away from Lindner's adaptation

[25] These essential stage directions are inexplicably missing from the score.

and back to the original text. But this was not always the case and much of the vocal line is forced and unnatural in places where one would expect it to be lyrical, such as Salome's seduction scenes with Narraboth and Jochanaan.

No such charge can be levelled at the present soliloquy which ends the opera. On the contrary, so well do the words fall into the melodic shapes that they seem to have motivated all the chief themes of the opera as one by one they recur. Many of them indeed, which seemed unspontaneous and awkwardly worked in earlier places, appear perfectly right and natural in their positions and development here. This could, of course, be the case if the closing scene had been written at a very early stage, perhaps even first of all, and I feel strongly with Ernest Newman that this may very well have been what happened. 'The later allocations of the motifs', he wrote, 'to this or that passage in the earlier part of the opera were seemingly a matter with him of the suggestion of the moment. Strauss, I imagine, would already have in his mind most of the main motifs of the work, but as yet principally as constituents of this superb piece of writing which is, in essence, a closely and organically symphonic poem with a vocal solo.' The whole long section sounds as if it was conceived in a single outpouring of inspired melodic thinking, and, in contrast with so much of what has gone before, it is all gloriously singable.

Newman further described the Scena as a tremendous emotional release to Salome. It is this opening of the spirit after so long and severe a tension which is so moving. What tears at the heart is the pitiful cry 'What shall I do now, Jochanaan? Ah, wherefore didst thou not look at me?'—the searing nostalgia of which was something which Strauss was able to catch better than almost any other in the entire gamut of human emotion. This burning misery is established at the very first flood of orchestral sound and dominates the music except only for the outbursts in which Salome exults in the victory she has won over him. As a result of this victory she can throw Jochanaan's head to the dogs and the vultures in revenge for his insults. This taint of brutality is incorporated into the polyphony not only by a series of violent new figures such as:

Ex. 36a   b

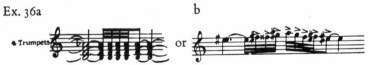

but by a new theme for which Strauss seems to have found no use in the main corpus of the opera:

Ex. 37

Gradually the fervour subsides and an air of mystery takes its place. The theme which now enters is musically exactly right for the context. But we have heard it once before earlier in the opera, when Salome first noticed the terrible eyes of Jochanaan (Ex. 18). The words here are also about Jochanaan's eyes—which are now shut. The textually motivic reason for the borrowing of the theme speaks for itself, but it is significant that the use of it in the Scena arises naturally from musical reasons. Again, when Salome described a little earlier how she can now not only kiss his mouth but bite it like a ripe fruit, Ex. 30 enters, not in the vulgar style in which it occurred during Herod's invitation to Salome to bite a real fruit,[26] but with an intense morbidity which may be nasty but is not artistically commonplace. Moreover, it is soon developed at length during the passage in which Salome compares Jochanaan's tongue to a viper spitting its venom upon her, a context which bears not the least relationship to the previous ideas which it was used to accompany. 'Herod's Graciousness' or 'Teeth of Salome' are thus equally misleading labels, though both have been used by reputable, even distinguished, authors. Newman cites Strauss's use of this theme to prove his point that when Strauss came to an apt place in the earlier portions of the opera his mind would 'revert to the parallel passage in the final monologue' instead of the other way round.

So also the recapitulation of Salome's great love song to Jochanaan falls upon the ear as an original conception, the words now fitting the musical cantilena in a way which was not the case when the identical passage was used for the first stanza of the song sung to the living Jochanaan. As for the third stanza of that song, its theme, Ex. 19, which seemed so forced when spun out to full length, falls perfectly into place at the tragic words, 'but me, me thou didst never see. If thou hadst seen me thou wouldst have loved me', and leads into the most disturbing passage

[26] See above, p. 265.

R.S.–T

of all, in which Salome describes her terrible thirst for Jochanaan's beauty, a thirst which 'neither floods nor the great waters can quench' and which can now never be quenched. Well might she say 'What shall I do now, Jochanaan?' The emotions here described by Oscar Wilde might be vile, but they are real. Strauss evokes the utmost erotic yearning as Ex. 20 builds upon itself ever higher, horns and other wind straining up to their top notes and falling away chromatically. Ex. 15, the love-song motif, shrills on flutes and piccolo and hammers on tuba and drums as the Vengeance motif Ex. 25 thunders in on the trombones.

And when the burning passion subsides all is still nostalgia. Even Ex. 14 is turned into a love song, this theme of prophecy which Salome has already evoked in full when she spoke of the strange music she heard when she looked upon him. Only when she compares the mysteries of Love and Death does the glow fade from the music and a shuddering cold envelop the atmosphere.

Herod turns to Herodias and mutters in an awed voice: 'She is monstrous, your daughter, she is altogether monstrous,' to the dull thudding repetitions of Salome's love theme on the timpani, and a shadowy reference to his own Ex. 26. Herodias is quite unshaken and says loudly that she approves of her daughter's behaviour, against screams of Ex. 27(a) on strings and wind. 'Now,' she says perversely, 'I will stay here.' Herod, however, is adamant. He calls to his slaves to extinguish the lights and the moon and stars, too, if they could but manage it. His words are obeyed by the elements and a huge black cloud covers the moon as he begins to climb the stairs. The music rushes desperately to the very upper regions and settles on a tremolo minor second. This fades to the trill which we have learnt to recognize and to fear. That trill from A to B flat plays a crucial part in the final stage of the drama. Against it piccolo and oboe declaim Ex. 15 as before, but are now answered by a deep awesome, dissonant chord which is sustained as Salome in a dead voice speaks of the kiss she has just given to Jochanaan's mouth, and of the bitter taste on his lips. The phrase to which she sings has a sigh in it which is echoed by the muted violins as by a ghost. The whole effect is unspeakably eerie and nauseous. 'Was it the taste of blood,' she asks, 'or rather, perhaps, that of love.' At the word 'love' the first violins take the lower note, the A, of the trill as the essential harmony note and sing Ex. 20 in the key of F:

Ex. 38

The enigmatic deep dissonance returns and the harmonic glow fades from the music as Salome says that love is reputed to taste bitter. Then the thought comes to her that even though it was not a pleasurable experience she has nevertheless had the kiss which the living Jochanaan had tried to deny her. At this idea Ex. 15, which has been restated at intervals, sinks on to a C sharp. Taking now the upper note of the trill, the B flat, as an A sharp the violins play Ex. 38 in the far warmer key of F sharp major. No sooner have they done this than the cellos again take the lower note of the trill as the harmony note and play Ex. 38 in A major against the persistent F sharp major of the upper voice. The dual tonality is extremely striking and for its day enormously daring. Psychologically it is a masterstroke, since in Salome's mind the nostalgia of love, and exultancy at having achieved her desire, are equally present while she forces her triumph to gain the upper hand. Thus even when she has sung her final song of victory in the even more glowing colouring of C sharp major, the chord of the alternative tonality is jammed against it in a shattering dissonance over which the musical world continues to dispute and comment more than half a century after it was written:

Ex. 39

The moon breaks out from behind the clouds and lights up the enraptured figure of Salome. Herod turns from the stairway and in an outbreak of revulsion calls out for his soldiers to kill her. The Command theme (Ex. 29) springs up on the four trumpets. The soldiers, who ask nothing better, rush forward and batter Salome to death with their shields, thus fulfilling Jochanaan's prophecy (see p. 267). There is a brief ironical reference to Ex. 27(a) depicting Herodias, who at her moment of triumph finds herself watching the life being crushed out of her daughter's body, but the rest of this brief coda, which is in the brutally cold key of C minor, is devoted to Salome's themes, which reiterate wildly and then break up into fragments. The last savage enunciations of the figure ⌐ x ⌐ from Ex. 25a sound like nothing so much as the final pounding of the soldier's shields upon the broken remains of Salome, Daughter of Herodias, Princess of Judea.

12

Mahler had foreseen, and had warned Strauss, of the difficulties he would inevitably encounter when he tried to get his new opera staged. Yet for his part Strauss was not wrong to persevere. True that the *succès fou de scandale* which *Salome* achieved in Dresden led to an outcry in which naturally the churches were strongly to the fore. In Vienna the protests which were made by the Archbishop, whose name unbelievably was Piffl, actually resulted in a restraining action, so that the first performance in the Austrian capital did not take place until October 1918. The Berlin Intendant Hülsen was full of doubts as to' whether Kaiser Wilhelm would allow performances of the work to take place. Fortunately Strauss already saw his opportunity of clearing the path for the work in that direction after a performance in November 1904 in which he conducted *Der Freischütz* and at which the Emperor was present. *Der Freischütz* was a particular favourite with the Emperor, as had emerged during Strauss's first encounter with him some four years previously. The composer always enjoyed recounting the conversation. It seems that he was commanded to approach the frowning monarch, who said: 'So you are another of these modern musicians?' Strauss bowed. 'I have heard *Ingwelde* by Schillings;[27] it is detestable; there isn't an ounce of melody.' 'Pardon me, Your Majesty, there is melody, but it is hidden behind the polyphony.' The Emperor looked severely at Strauss and said: 'You are one of the worst.' Another

[27] Schillings was a contemporary of Strauss whose operas have some affinity with those of Pfitzner.

bow. 'All modern music is worthless; there is no melody in it.' Same by-play. 'I prefer *Freischütz*.' 'Your Majesty, I also prefer *Freischütz*.'

So it was a successful performance of Weber's masterpiece which gave Strauss his chance. He was summoned to the Grand Foyer, where the Emperor was extremely cordial, saying that Strauss had made something entirely fresh out of the opera. He then spoke about a play on the subject of *Herod and Marianne* which he actually proposed to Strauss for a libretto. As it was common knowledge that Wilhelm had no great love of biblical subjects on the stage, this was a heaven-sent opening, and Strauss was not the man to waste it. Naturally, having proposed a parallel subject himself, the Kaiser was bound to receive the idea of *Salome* not wholly unfavourably. In the end he raised no objection to the Berlin representations on condition only that the star of Bethlehem be brought into the sky during the last bars, a clever suggestion of Hülsen's. Nevertheless the Kaiser was afterwards reported to have said: 'I am sorry Strauss composed this *Salome*. It will do him a great deal of harm.' Strauss, on hearing this, commented that the harm enabled him to build the villa at Garmisch. This remark is not unlike that of the popular singer whose reply to a critic who condemned his playing to the gallery as inartistic was that he cried all the way to the bank.

The very censorship problems could scarcely have been regretted by Strauss, despite their nuisance value. It has long been recognized that the most certain road to universal fame is to have a work banned by the censor. In America the opera had a chequered career at first. There was a single performance at the Metropolitan Opera House, New York, after which so many influential people were seriously shocked that it had to be withdrawn and was not readmitted into the repertoire until 1933. As for Great Britain, the story of the attempt to stage *Salome* in Covent Garden is told by Sir Thomas Beecham in one of the wittiest chapters of his autobiography, *A Mingled Chime*.

Today the impediments on religious grounds to staging the opera have passed into history and *Salome* is widely accepted as one of Strauss's greatest and most popular works. Yet this is not to say that the moral issues it raises are not still as alive as when *Salome* first appeared. Nor can these be entirely written off as the hypocritical narrow-mindedness of the Victorian era. The movement of which the work forms a part has been described in great detail by Mario Praz in a monograph entitled *The Romantic Agony*. This scholarly treatise traces the origins of such literary excesses back to the early days of the Romantic period, with especial reference to the Comte de Sade and his far-reaching influence on artistic minds of the time. Much of the writing which sprang from this influence is beyond doubt intensely disagreeable, but one cannot deduce its worthlessness on this account alone, and its validity as a truly artistic expression continues to this day to be the object of universal controversy. For Romanticists had, during the second half of the nineteenth century, fought with increasing resolution for the freedom to portray the ugly as well as the worthy or admirable things of this world. Ernest Newman commented wittily on the extravagant opinion which seriously takes into account the corrupting influence of art upon real life when he wrote that we need scarcely 'fear a rise in domestic murder statistics after a few hours of *Othello*'. Yet the notorious lawsuit over the publication of Lawrence's *Lady Chatterley's Lover* revealed, through the widespread fear of the corrupting influence of a book upon contemporary behaviour, that although the trend is still towards greater freedom of expression, Newman's gibe, written over half a century ago, is still as pertinent as the day it appeared.

Nevertheless the case can be presented in other ways. For example, if of two works of art, equally inspired and skilfully executed, one deals with noble sentiments and the other, however sympathetically, with vileness and corruption, is the one by definition incomparably greater than the other? In denying this, Romantic artists and writers insisted upon their right to present and, maybe, to sublimate the weakness, misery, and ugliness of human life and the world around us, equally with the fine and beautiful. In making this claim the artist exalts the impact of his thought upon the subject-matter. Hence, although after a performance of *Salome* one is left with a very nasty taste in the mouth, it may yet be a great work of art on account of the nobility of Wilde's mind. Unfortunately many people have felt that Wilde's very thought suffered as a result of the decadent movement of which he formed a part, and that his choice of subject was itself contaminated. Wilde presented the case for the defence with calculated provocation in the preface to *The Picture of Dorian Gray*:

> The artist is the creator of beautiful things. . . . Those who find ugly meanings in beautiful things are corrupt without being charming. This is a fault. . . . There is no such thing as a moral or an immoral book. Books are well written, or badly written. That is all. . . . The nineteenth-

century dislike of Realism is the rage of Caliban seeing his own face in the glass. . . . No artist is ever morbid. The artist can express everything. Vice and virtue are to the artist materials for an art.

This credo naturally did not allay critical replies, many of which came from would-be admirers, and the same was true in due course when the time came for considered opinions of Strauss's setting of *Salome*. Even Laurence Gilman, who had published an analysis and discussion of *Salome*, wrote of it in another book on contemporary opera:

> The sadness of life, yes; and the evil and tragedy, the terror and violence of life; for the contemplation of these may, through the evoking of pity, nourish and enlarge the spirit of the beholder. But are we very greatly nourished by the contemplation of that which must inevitably arouse disgust rather than compassion? I do not speak of 'morality' or 'immorality', since there is nothing stable in the use or understanding of these terms. But those aspects of life which sicken the sense, which are loathsome rather than terrible—are they fit matter for the artist?

Romain Rolland, too, wrote to Strauss in a letter:

> Oscar Wilde's *Salome* is not worthy of you. It is not that I do this piece the injustice of putting it in the same category as the majority of modern lyric dramas which are solemn trifles or whose symbolism is sleep-inducing. Despite the pretentious archness of its style there is an incontestible dramatic power; but its atmosphere is sickening and stale. . .
> It is not a question of bourgeois morals, it is a question of healthiness. The same passions can be healthy or unhealthy according to the artists who experience them and the characters in whom they are incarnate. The incest of *Die Walküre* is a thousand times healthier than conjugal and lawful love in these rotten Parisian comedies, the names of which I should prefer not to mention. Wilde's *Salome* and all those who surround her, save only that brute of a Jochanaan, are unhealthy, unclean, hysterical or alcoholic, oozing with a perfumed and mundane corruption. It is in vain that you transfigure your subject by multiplying a hundredfold its energy, and enveloping it in a Shakespearean atmosphere; it is in vain that you have lent emotional tones of a moving nature to your *Salome*; you surpass your subject, but you cannot make one forget it.

13

Rolland had first made Strauss's acquaintance already in 1891, when they happened to be together at a lunch-party with the Wagner family at Bayreuth; but it was not until eight years later that the two great men became friends as a result of a visit by Rolland to Germany. This time the contact was firmly established and they remained on intimate terms, corresponding fairly frequently, for the next ten years. Although Rolland wrote very candidly to Strauss with his impressions of *Feuersnot* and *Sinfonia Domestica*, it was in connexion with *Salome* that the letters flowed most regularly. In July 1905 Strauss wrote to Rolland asking his advice over a projected re-translation of *Salome* back into French with a view to performances in Paris and therewith also the French vocal score. A lively interchange of letters followed in which Rolland tried in vain to give Strauss some idea of the subtle inflections of the French language and the flexibility with which a sensitive composer can throw the stresses on the different syllables, with especial reference to Debussy's *Pelléas et Mélisande*. Strauss found this opera infinitely perplexing, and the freedom of Debussy's scansion wayward. He persevered however and virtually completed the translation, Rolland to the end suggesting alterations and improvements.[28]

During all this collaboration, itself the culminating point of a growing acquaintanceship, Rolland was able to form a detailed impression of Strauss, an impression which he outlined with astonishing insight and breadth of vision, together with a number of highly entertaining anecdotes, in a series of entries in his diary. At first he saw Strauss as a personification of the domineering Germany of the post-Bismarck era, to be mentioned in the same breath as Nietzsche and the Emperor of Prussia, Wilhelm II:

> A man more strong than inspired; of vital energy, nervy, morbidly overexcited, unbalanced but controlled by an effort of will-power which rescues music and the musician. It is enough to see him conducting the last bars of the Beethoven A major Symphony . . . to feel the sickness hidden beneath the strength and military tautness.

[28] It is sad, in view of the trouble taken by Strauss and Rolland, that when it came to the point Strauss, never entirely happy about the subtleties of the French accentuation, shelved the entire scheme and the published French version was made by J. de Marliave, an important member of the Ministère des Beaux Arts. The choice was Messager's, at that time the Director of the Opéra, and it is interesting that Messager's wife, Mme Kousnetzova, was the first singer of the title role in Paris.

But a couple of years later, although keeping intact much of his basic impression, Rolland was able to qualify and fill out his picture of the composer:

> His face is unlined, smooth and clear as a child's. A high brilliant forehead, clear eyes, a slender nose, curly hair, the lower part of the face grimacing a little; the mouth often in a horrid pout either ironical or discontented. Very tall with broad shoulders, but his hands attract attention, fine, long, well cared for in a rather decadently aristocratic way which does not correspond with the rest of his person, which is more plebeian and unassuming. He behaves thoroughly badly at the table, sitting with his legs crossed at the side, holds his plate near his chin to eat, stuffs himself with sweets like a baby, etc. . . . Cordial and nicely behaved with us, he is short with others; he scarcely listens to what they say. . . . 'Was?' he mutters. 'Ach! so, so', and that's all.

That Strauss had no illusions as to his own worth is, of course, self-evident. A crowning instance of this occurred at the first performance of *Salome* in Paris:

> He showed himself on the stage at the end. . . to let himself be applauded. The curtain was raised two or three times. But he was used to a different sort of enthusiasm; someone whispered to him; 'I am able to inform you that the President intends to decorate you with the *Legion d' Honneur*.' 'I have well deserved it,' was his reply.

Rolland was soon able still further to qualify his early impressions of the man:

> His conversation shows me how far I was right to see in him the artist-type of this new German empire, the powerful reflection of this heroic pride, near to delirium with this mistaken Nietzscheism, with this egoism and practical ideology, which preaches the cult of force and the disdain of weakness. But attached to this are certain characteristics which I had certainly not seen before, and which are more properly of the people of Munich, of Southern Germany; that is to say, an age-old depth of humorous buffoonery, paradoxical and satirical, of a spoilt child or of Till Eulen-spiegel—It is necessary to remember this if one is not to find some of his opinions odious.
>
> He declares that the war in the Transvaal is a matter of absolute indifference to him; that at first he took sides,

but for the English. 'I like the English very much,' he says; 'they are very agreeable when one is travelling. For example, when I was in Egypt, I was very happy the English were there instead of the Egyptians; you can always be sure of finding clean rooms, all modern conveniences, etc.' Well, it is certainly a point of view to take when assessing the history of mankind. 'The Boers are a barbarian people, backward, who still live in the seventeenth century. The English are very civilized and very strong. It's a thoroughly good thing that the stronger should triumph.'

But Rolland was right when he surmised that this Nietzschean cult of strength was to some extent mere veneer. Indeed, it covered up a basic weakness as a beard so often conceals a weak chin. It was very shortly after he had written the entry just quoted that Strauss confessed to him: 'You're quite right . . . I'm no hero; I haven't got the necessary strength; I'm not made for battle; I much prefer to go into retreat, to be peaceful and to rest. I haven't enough genius.' No doubt this was an over-protestation born of momentary discouragement, but in view of the amiable nature of his later works written at his beautiful retreat in the Bavarian Alps, it is significant that he added; 'I don't want to make the effort. At this moment what I need is to make sweet and happy music. No more heroisms.'

However, even if Strauss had come to feel that heroes and heroics were for him a thing of the past, the time was also not yet come for the sweet music composed in the peaceful retreat. Not only was *Salome* in the process of creation, but the following work was to be the very antithesis of these ideals: *Elektra*, the sister opera to *Salome*. These two stage tone poems represent the twin extremist compositions in which Strauss for the last time came to the foreground as a truly contemporary composer before executing the volte-face as the result of which he was gradually to retreat towards the comfortable estate of respectability.

THE STAGE TONE POEMS (II)

HE author, poet and playwright Hugo von Hofmannsthal was Strauss's junior by ten years, being born in 1874 in Vienna. While still a student he exerted a perceptible influence upon the Romantic literature of his native Austria and was one of a group of young intellectuals who met regularly at a Viennese café in a manner reminiscent of the famous scenes from Murger's *La Vie de Bohème*. Despite his extreme youth he seems to have been one of the strongest figures at these meetings in which literary and other artistic problems were raised and heatedly discussed together with the most abstruse philosophical theories. Nor was this a mere pose of bogus intellectuality. Under the pseudonym of 'Loris' (as a student he was not allowed to use his own name) Hofmannsthal actually wrote a considerable amount of lyric poetry between the ages of fifteen and twenty-five, and it has even been claimed that this laid the foundation of an original post-Romantic literary movement, if stemming to some extent from the example and inspiration of Stefan George. Towards the end of the century, by which time Hofmannsthal had pursued his legal training, completed his military service and taken his Ph.D., the indefatigable young man had turned to the stage and was passing from an early series of shorter dramas towards more ambitious and serious productions.

As he matured it became apparent that Hofmannsthal had an especial gift for re-dressing the works of other periods. He had a strong feeling for the mood and psychology of earlier societies and even civilizations, upon which he stamped the profound perception of his intensely introspective and critical mind. One of the first dramatic works of Hofmannsthal's maturity in which this penchant found fullest expression was an adaptation of Sophocles's *Elektra*, which he completed early in 1903.

Hofmannsthal's first meeting with Richard Strauss took place in Paris as early as the beginning of the year 1900. Hofmannsthal seems to have wasted no time in trying to tempt the already famous and much sought-after composer into a collaboration of some sort, but it was just unfortunate that all the poet had on the stocks at that time were plans for a projected ballet. As we have seen, Strauss had had other schemes for ballets, none of which came to fruition, and it is hardly surprising that he regarded Hofmannsthal's proposals with no particular enthusiasm. Perhaps it was unfairly misleading of Strauss to have appeared so cordial over the scheme when they met. By March Hofmannsthal was eagerly writing to his parents that he had 'begun a ballet which was intended for Richard Strauss', while his letters to Strauss of the following November show that he had progressed far with his book for the ballet, which was to be called *Der Triumph der Zeit*. Two acts, he wrote, were already in fair copy and the third, which would be a kind of apotheosis and relatively short, was at least planned to the extent of a detailed scenario.

At first Strauss made no reply, and when Hofmannsthal pressed him to the extent of sending the draft, he promptly returned it with a note explaining that he had enough projects in hand to occupy him for well over three years. This was no mere procrastination; *Feuersnot* was in the immediate offing, Strauss's own ballet *Kythere* was still under serious consideration and, as he wrote, his symphonic muse was only temporarily dormant, which suggests that the idea of the *Domestica* had begun to germinate in his mind. One might have thought that the poet would lose interest in the scheme after this disappointment, but the work was, in fact, completed and published the following year, though it was never set to music. Many years passed before the two men came together again, and it seems that in all their subsequent association, which even included a ballet production, this first project was never mooted again.

In November 1903 that masterful and ever-enterprising man of the theatre, Max Reinhardt, followed up his successful run of *Salome* with a production of 'a new version of Sophocles' *Elektra*, rewritten for the German stage by Hugo von Hofmannsthal'. The part of the heroine

Richard Strauss with Hofmannsthal

was again taken by Gertrud Eysoldt. Strauss, who had recently visited Reinhardt's *Salome* production, was naturally drawn to this new venture and was immediately struck by its similarity of form and psychological content to Wilde's drama. Accordingly, once his own *Salome* was safely launched, his mind quickly reverted to this twin subject which lay so tantalizingly on the horizon. Ideally he would have preferred to have followed up so grim a tragedy with some gay contrasting piece, but nothing suitable lay at hand to turn his thoughts away from what he already felt to be a work of genius.

Within three months of the première of *Salome*, Hofmannsthal had heard of Strauss's interest and was writing eagerly to the composer to find out for himself how the land lay. This time Strauss's reply came in a matter of days. He was attracted but unsure as to whether it might not be better to postpone *Elektra* until he was a bit more detached from the idiom of the so similar *Salome*. Seizing on some remarks about other schemes on hand which Hofmannsthal had apparently let fall some time previously, he expressed an interest in a proposed opera on a further Greek myth, that of Semiramis. He also plied the author with alternative proposals, such as a two-act drama based on another biblical subject, Saul and David. But Hofmannsthal had set his heart on *Elektra* being their first work of collaboration, and in any case he had nothing else immediately available which he considered suitable for Strauss's style. The similarities with *Salome* were, he wrote in a letter to Strauss, purely superficial; both were in one act, had as title the name of the heroine, were based on subjects of classical antiquity, and had been recently launched in Berlin with Eysoldt in the title role. Nevertheless, when you compared them closely, the one all violet and purple, the other a mixture of the strongest contrasts between night and day, black and white, it became clear that there was not the slightest similarity between them.

That this argument was the grossest wishful thinking is obvious to anyone with any knowledge of the two works. A strong case has even been made[1] for the direct influence upon Hofmannsthal of Wilde's *Salome;* both heroines are continuously on the stage except for a short introductory scene; both heroines react perversely upon the situations in which they find themselves on account of frustrated sex, and so on. The claim is a serious one, though it should be borne in mind how short

---

[1] Jethro Bithell: *Modern German Literature*, 1880–1950.

a time Hofmannsthal would have had to become acquainted with Wilde's
work before completing *Elektra* in 1903. However, he could have
spared himself the trouble of playing down to this extent the link between the two works. The very reasons which Strauss had paraded as
militating against *Elektra* were just those which held him captive to the
work until he had applied his teemingly fertile imagination to its supremely congenial opportunities. In *Salome* he had at last found himself
as a stage composer through the intermediary of the symphonic poem.
But he had by no means written himself out in this medium by the
completion of a single work. Now here, thrown in his very lap, was a
further drama presenting exactly the same solutions to his problem—in
fact, as Hofmannsthal shrewdly pointed out, it was nothing less than a
further stage symphonic poem in potential. Moreover, it centred as
before round a morbidly psychological character study. So far from
waiting until he could detach himself from the idiom of *Salome*, how
much wiser to plunge directly into this even more starkly dramatic
script while the mood was so real upon him. If he worked straight on,
surely nothing could stop him from overreaching even his own most
vivid effects in the portrayal of the grotesque unhinging of the human
mind. He might create yet more fascinating orchestral colours to depict
the hysteria which still ran riot in his spirit. 'To what purpose',
continued Hofmannsthal 'was Strauss enticing him towards some fine
Romantic matter?' (This in answer to Strauss's request :'Something like
a really wild Cesare Borgia or Savanarola would be just what I am
yearning for.')

Even from a formal point of view it would be hard to find a more
suitable vehicle than *Elektra* for Strauss's experimenting in bringing the
symphonic poem to visual representation on the stage, far more even
than *Salome*. The sharply differentiated scenes correspond ideally to
symphonic sections and are interrelated through their very construction
towards the well-planned climaxes, precisely as in a musical work.
Moreover, the author was at hand—eager for collaboration indeed—
and might be persuaded to make any adjustments in the text which
composition might reveal to be desirable or necessary.

So Strauss set to work, though sternly enjoining the delighted
librettist to absolute secrecy lest all did not go as well as he hoped.[2]
He was even so oddly cautious as to suggest keeping the cumbersome

---

[2] Nevertheless the news leaked out and we find Hofmannsthal anxiously
assuring Strauss that he was not to blame.

Semiramis as a second string, while *Elektra* was occupying his mind. By 16th June 1906 Strauss was able to write to Hofmannsthal that he was busy with scene 1, adding that it was not coming easily from his hand. When one examines the wild, savage intensity which drives through this forcible scene, it is difficult to take Strauss seriously in such a comment. Nevertheless alternative proposals were still kept alive and even now Strauss vainly tried to tempt his new colleague with subjects from the French Revolution such as Büchner's *Dantons Tod* or Sardou's *9 Thermidor*. For his part, Hofmannsthal countered with a comedy based on the adventures of Casanova, a scheme which was for a time considered seriously by both as a possible follow-up after *Elektra*. In actual fact the scenario of *Semiramis* did also manage to reach quite an elaborate stage of outline and discussion. Under the title of *Die Tochter der Luft* it was to have been based on a work of the classical Spanish writer, Calderón. It would have incorporated the figures of Memmon, Tiresias, and, of course Semiramis herself; the action would have included a thunderstorm, a hunt, a ballet, and festivities of all sorts, not to mention big scenas for the principal roles. Strauss's outline of the action reads much like a portmanteau version of *Les Troyens*, *Die Aegyptische Helena*, and *Die Liebe der Danae*. Particularly charming would have been the close of Act II, in which, after a great love duet, 'the lover experiences the fatal consequences of Semiramis' favours, and expires forthwith'. But it was not to be. The diffuseness of the complicated plot failed to hold the imagination of its author and gradually faded into the background, although we do not hear the last of it until the autumn of 1910, by which time *Rosenkavalier* was behind him. A suggestion from Strauss that they return to this first idea provoked the wholly conclusive remarks: '*Semiramis* is now miles from my thoughts. No kind of spiritual or materialistic inducement could pump anything out of me on this matter, not even my own strength of mind—indeed will-power is particularly impotent in such matters. Besides, except for the Prologue which I had mentally completed, it was never really a plot, but only the possibility of one.'

Despite his initial qualms, Strauss's progress with the composition of *Elektra* was steady. His procedure in adapting an already completed drama was very similar to that of *Salome*, although with the author still living he was able not only to make cuts as required but change the order of whole paragraphs. In one instance he took a speech out of one scene and transported it into a later scene, where he needed more material in order to build his climax. But on the whole the already printed text gave him all he needed and more.

So passed some eighteen months during which Strauss struggled to fit the ever more urgent flow of inspiration with the demands of his position as conductor. For he still held the post of Royal Kapellmeister to the Imperial Opera House Berlin, which he had inherited from Weingartner in 1898 and which he retained until November 1918. In addition to this he was conducting large numbers of important concerts abroad, including, above all, the series of Vienna Philharmonic Subscription Concerts. In April 1908 the pressure upon him became intense. Weingartner, who had so far retained the conductorship of the Berlin Philharmonic concerts, was called to the Vienna Opera and Strauss was appointed Generalmusikdirektor in Berlin. This position immediately carried with it important prestige tours with the orchestra, such as the extended May journey throughout Europe. By autumn Strauss was at his wits' end and had to press for a sabbatical year from his duties at the Court Opera House. The prospect of more free time to devote to peaceful composition must have been all the more tempting as his splendid new villa at Garmisch was nearing completion. *Elektra* was the first work to be completed at this beautiful home which was to last him until his death forty years later.

In December 1907 Hofmannsthal had occasion to visit Berlin and took the opportunity of spending some time with the composer. This was appropriate, as Strauss was having qualms about the closing section of the work, although he was still far from having reached it in the composition. By the following June Strauss had reached the entry of Orestes and was writing cheerfully that he felt 'in quite good form'. Within a month the great duet between Elektra and Orestes was complete and, according to its composer, 'a great success'. Hofmannsthal had by this time heard Strauss playing and singing a considerable portion of the score and was full of enthusiasm. He now wrote encouragingly that the alterations to the end met with his full approval, as also one or two other cuts which Strauss had proposed.

With the end of the work in sight, Strauss had naturally begun to consider the question of the first performance. Even towards the end of 1907 he had prepared Schuch for the probability of a third Dresden première, promising that despite some tempting offers Schuch could count on his remaining true to him, and on 11th September 1908 Schuch was duly the first to hear that the score was complete: 'the ending is full of juice!'[3] Now the problem of casting arose; 'The title role must before all things be given to the highest and most dramatic soprano who can be found.' This sounds an extravagant demand, but it was no more than the truth. The role of Elektra remains to the present day the most severe and the most cruelly taxing in the history of opera.

Rehearsals began immediately, as Schuch had fixed the first performance for early in the new year. Indeed, matters were put in hand so quickly that the orchestral parts proved to be unusually inaccurate, to the consternation of the different conductors all over the world who were pressing to produce this new extravaganza by the most provocative of modern composers, for such was Strauss widely regarded in 1908. Nevertheless the public's reaction was at first disappointing—even the composer was forced to acknowledge that it had no more than a *succès d'estime*. But he was to live to see the day when it was to be regarded as arguably his finest work and beyond all doubt his most technically advanced and interesting composition. Together with *Salome* and to a greater extent than this sister work, it represents Strauss's *non plus ultra* in the development of the symphonic poem, albeit fulfilled through the extra dimension of visual representation on the operatic stage.

2

The legend of Elektra as we have it today is largely taken from the three widely varying versions by Aeschylus in his *Choephori*, the second part of the Orestian Trilogy, and by Sophocles and Euripides in their *Elektra* dramas. Professor Gilbert Murray well described her as the central figure in the Orestian tragedy of Greek mythology; 'a woman shattered in childhood by the shock of an experience too terrible for a girl to bear; a poisoned and a hunted woman eating her heart out in ceaseless broodings of hate and love, alike unsatisfied— hate against her mother and stepfather, love for her dead father and her brother in exile.'

Briefly the situation is as follows; Agamemnon, king of Argos, has joined the Greek expedition against Troy, but the ships are all becalmed at Aulis, the harbour near Chalcis some forty miles north of Athens. In order to appease the Goddess Artemis into sending a favourable wind,

[3] In actual fact there were still some finishing touches to add, and the score bears the date September 22, 1908.

R.S.–U

Agamemnon sends to his wife Klytemnestra for their daughter Iphigenia and upon her arrival sacrifices her. The necessary wind springs up and Agamemmon sails away, not returning to his palace at Mykene for nearly ten years. During this time Klytemnestra, who can never forgive such a terrible sacrifice nor the insult to her motherhood, takes a lover, a cowardly figure called Aegisthus, and with him plans to murder Agamemnon on his return. This she eventually accomplishes, but is subsequently haunted day and night by fear of revenge, most probably at the hands of her son Orestes, who has spent his life in a far-off land. The versions of the myth diverge as to whether Klytemnestra herself has banished the boy, or whether it was his elder sister Elektra who has safely effected his escape from the clutches of Aegisthus. In due course Orestes returns and at the express command of Apollo murders his mother and her paramour in quick succession. He thereafter suffers persecution at the hands of the Furies, whose function it was to punish the shedding of kindred blood. Actually he would have been equally persecuted by the Furies had he not murdered Klytemnestra, for a second function of these forbidding creatures was to punish anyone who failed to exact blood revenge for the shedding of kindred blood. Orestes, whose mother had murdered his father with an axe, was, as a result, caught hopelessly and doomed to persecution whichever course he decided upon. What seems grossly unfair is that, husband and wife not being blood relations, Klytemnestra was not subject to the same doom as the result of her crime. She is, however, a prey to constant dread and petrifying dreams which gradually demoralize her and undermine her health, both physical and mental.

This appalling story forms the basis of one of the strongest and most dramatic legends of all time. It was a perfect subject for realistic reconstruction by a romantic modernist such as Hofmannsthal, who put into it his most lively inspiration up to that time. He drew largely from Sophocles in the shaping of the drama, but deliberately chose details from the other two Greek tragedians wherever they strengthened his portrayal of the scene or of his characterizations. Moreover, he did away entirely with the Chorus which, although an integral part of all Greek drama, softened the circumstances of Elektra by being at hand to sympathise or offer advice. For Elektra's fate is a life of perpetual isolation and maltreatment, scorned and spurned by even the most menial of servants in her stepfather's palace, which had once been her own when her father was alive. Sophocles adds the figure of a further sister, Chrysothemis, not mentioned by either Aeschylus or Euripides, who provides a valuable element of contrast by her more conventional and placatory nature, and who as a result tries to carry on a relatively tolerable existence. Neither Elektra nor Chrysothemis, however, is allowed to marry or have children lest a son is bred who may perform the deed of retribution dreaded by the wicked parents.[4] This restriction has the consequence of stirring up friction between the two sisters, an idea which is exploited by Hofmannsthal far beyond the more simple bickerings presented in Sophocles' original drama.

The centre-point of all three versions is the recognition scene between Elektra and Orestes, and Hofmannsthal, too, made it the climax of his drama. He intensified, however, the gulf between the brother and sister who after a lapse of over ten years no longer know one another, by choosing Aeschylus' explanation of Orestes' childhood. According to Sophocles, Elektra herself gave her little brother into the very hands of the tutor who now returns with the grown-up Orestes. That she should recognize neither tutor nor brother is unlikely, and moreover the very act of rescue, even so many years before, would provide a link with her distant brother which would to some extent alleviate the poignant loneliness of her position. How much more acute is Aeschylus' account, in which all Elektra knows of the fate of Orestes is that he was sent away by their mother when only a tiny child—even before the murder of Agamemnon, in this version—and whose return, indeed whose very well-being, can only be a matter for hopeful conjecture. After so many years spent in an agony of uncertainty with nothing to support her but blind faith, this too, dashed to the ground by the spurious report of Orestes' death (the ingenious contrivance of most versions to avert suspicion from the presence of Orestes himself in the palace), the flood of emotion which Elektra experiences when she is at last persuaded that it is indeed Orestes who stands before her is convincingly prepared and in consequence profoundly affecting.

Sophocles ends his tragedy with the death of Aegisthus; Hofmannsthal continues a little further and causes Elektra, somewhat like Salome, to dance a wild dance of triumph, after which she suffers a stroke and collapses. There is no precedent for this convenient ending in Greek mythology; Elektra is said to have married Orestes' friend

[4] Even here there is a difference of treatment in Euripides, who shows Elektra married off to a lowly peasant who, however, in deference to her nobility, has touchingly refrained from violating her maidenhood.

Pylades, whom, a silent figure in Sophocles, Hofmannsthal suppresses altogether. The situation, however, created at the end of Hofmannsthal's adaptation is highly imaginative and, as we shall see, breathtakingly dramatic.

3

Hofmannsthal's text divides up into seven unusually clear-cut sections:

(1) Prologue—the five servants.
(2) Elektra.
(3) Elektra and Chrysothemis (I)
(4) Elektra and Klytemnestra.

★ ★ ★

(5) Elektra and Chrysothemis (II) (including a short scene between two serving men).
(6) Elektra and Orestes.
(7) Finale—the murders, Elektra's Dance of Triumph and Death.

So well balanced a scheme must have been a joy to a symphonic composer like Strauss, with the crucial Klytemnestra scene forming the central pivot between the two relatively lyrical Chrysothemis scenes. The whole drama is concerned exclusively with the short period before the appearance of Orestes up to the fulfilment of the murders. Conceived in a single *mise-en-scène*, once more strangely reminiscent of *Salome*, upon which it might have been modelled in many respects, the action takes place in the rear courtyard of Agamemnon's palace. Much of the stern forbidding character of the work emanates from the gaunt, heavy stone façade of the monstrous palace wall with the gigantic door and windows set at intervals along its length.

The opening scene of the servants was an ingenious device of Hofmannsthal's to establish the action in the absence of the Chorus. It reminds one strongly of the opening scene of Maeterlinck's *Pelléas et Mélisande* (a scene not set by Debussy), which may have given Hofmannsthal the idea, as he was well acquainted with Maeterlinck's work. In *Pelléas* the servants discuss by implication Mélisande's impending marriage with Golaud, a curious device of displaced time, since Golaud's first meeting with Mélisande in the forest only takes place in the following scene. The effect is undeniably weird, and sets the atmosphere which pervades the whole play. In a similar way Hofmannsthal uses his introductory scene of the maids to establish atmosphere, though of a very different kind from Maeterlinck's. Here it is an oppressive state of vicious hatred and spite, of bestiality, which is set in the strongest possible contrast with the royal dignity of Elektra's former and rightful position. To emphasise this, Hofmannsthal uses two effects; he first introduces the figure of Elektra herself, very briefly at the outset, so that her appearance 'like an animal darting to its lair' should be as strongly as possible before one; and he also allows one of the maidservants to sympathize with her condition and be ill-treated on account of her loyalty. The remainder all revile her with appalling vulgarity which is only matched by the words Elektra herself has flung at them in retaliation and which they recall with relish. Yet the essence of her existence is her constant preoccupation with her murdered father, and this is established at the outset when the second maidservant says that 'This is the hour in which she howls after her father so that all the walls are set ringing.' It was a feature of Hofmannsthal's text that the name of Agamemnon was never spoken by anyone, as if it were taboo in the house of his slaughter. Not even in Elektra's soliloquy does she address him by name; he is always 'Vater'. It is Orestes who finally breaks the spell in the drama, and then Elektra, with a fine sense of climax, hurls the name in the face of Aegisthus as he is being murdered. Such subtlety Strauss felt to be merely abstruse in the case of a music drama, where it is above all important that the action should be crystal clear at every point. He was particularly obsessed, moreover, by the idea of the spirit of Agamemnon hanging like a cloud over the entire situation. It is from this ominous and towering figure that the tragedy springs in all its horror; from his cruel and tyrannical deeds during his life, and from the brutal manner of his death.[5] Strauss accordingly reverses Hofmannsthal's intention to the

[5] The familiar picture by the distinguished German artist Lovis Corinth on the cover of the vocal score tries to emphasize this conception by the unorthodox method of depicting the scene of Agamemnon's death, an event which took place many years before the action of the opera. This device is rendered additionally obscure by the fact that Corinth gives an oddly false state of affairs. Agamemnon is shown asleep and Klytemnestra is drawing back the hanging of the bedchamber while encouraging Aegisthus on his way in to commit the crime, axe in hand. Throughout Greek mythology it is made plain that Agamemnon was slain on his way out of the bath; Klytemnestra threw a net over his head and while he was thus incapacitated, the cowardly Aegisthus struck the defenceless hero twice with a two-edged sword. Klytemnestra then finished the deed by severing her husband's head with the axe of which we hear so much later. Hofmannsthal adheres to this account in broad outline, as is apparent from Elektra's great soliloquy.

very utmost, introducing the majestic name on every possible occasion and framing the score in its opening and closing pages with a motif based directly upon it.

Ex. 1

A-ga-mem - non

Elektra's abrupt appearance and retreat is described musically by two of her most vehement motifs, the first of which is pure fury ('Poisonous like a wild cat' is the second maidservant's description) and contains a graphic reference in the initial figure ⌐ a ⌐ to the axe-stroke with which Klytemnestra dispatched the bleeding Agamemnon. The sharp juxta-position of two foreign tonalities (B minor and F minor) in ⌐ b ⌐ refers directly to Klytemnestra.

Ex. 2

The second of these motifs represents Elektra's unrelenting hatred, an emotion which has enveloped and transformed her entire being. Although naturally vicious, this theme has a strong suggestion of nobility in its thrusting indignation:

Ex. 3

The chord 'x' of Ex. 3 is used to a considerable extent as an isolated entity and moved chromatically in block progression both in staccato jabs and, later, in sinister smeary legato passages. Ex. 3 is generally taken to represent specifically the consuming hatred which Elektra bears towards her mother and stepfather, and this it fulfils most vividly whether the figure ⌐ a ⌐ is exploited or only the naked chord. The strident polytonality of this chord (D flat and E major) is a pre-eminent feature of the work. If Elektra's madness is portrayed by the super-imposition of two unrelated major tonalities, that of Klytemnestra is later similarly characterized, but by two minor unrelated chords. The whole effect is a further and harsher treatment of the polytonal harmonic technique which Strauss had evolved for the first time in the closing bars of *Salome* (see Ex. 39 above).

As the maidservants describe Elektra's condition and behaviour, two important derivations of Ex. 1 are introduced:

Ex. 4

Ex. 5

Ex. 4 is used to suggest Elektra's ceaseless mourning for her father, while the frenzied Ex. 5 depicts the haggard and unkempt state to which she has been reduced on this account.

In due course the servants refer to her royal descent; Strauss employs three motifs to portray the proud lineage of which Elektra is so vital a representative, and two of them are declaimed now, the third being held in reserve for a more significant first appearance:

Ex. 6   Ex. 7

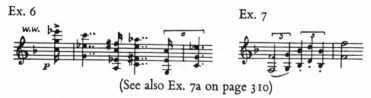

(See also Ex. 7a on page 310)

In this respect Ex. 6 refers more generally to the Race of the Royal House,[6] and Ex. 7 specifically to Elektra herself as a royal princess.

---

[6] I differ strongly from Röse and Prüwer, who in the official Führer to the work attribute Ex. 6 to Orestes, to my mind entirely without evidence or justi-fication. Ex. 21 below is certainly Orestes' motif, as can be proved by countless places in the text. I am disappointed to find Ernest Newman accepting this misleading interpretation without question in his *Opera Nights*.

Memories of whence Elektra sprang and to what she has been reduced evoke the first stirrings of pity in the minds of two of the maid-servants. The fourth maid tentatively suggests that the ill-treatment she received is too severe, but dares go no further. The fifth maid, however, is prepared to fall on the ground before Elektra and kiss her feet, and she says so with considerable fervour, regardless of the treatment she herself will inevitably receive for allying herself with the royal scapegoat. These shows of sympathy are accompanied by a further derivative of Ex. 1, now spun into an extended cantilena.

Ex. 8

Ex. 8 provides the only lyrical relief in a scene which is unique for its angularity and bitter, ejaculatory idiom, to which the hard, pointed style of the orchestration contributes in strong measure.

The fifth maid unwisely retaliates upon her colleagues, saying that it is they who should suffer for the harm inflicted on Elektra. This leads to the climax of the scene in which the overseer throws her into the house for punishment, calling on the other maidservants for support in re-counting the foul slanders of which Elektra has been guilty towards them. The scene ends with the shrieks of the wretched fifth maid, who is duly being beaten. Ex. 8 surges down the orchestra accompanied by violent and repeated birch-strokes in the orchestra, the sounds gradually descending into the very depths and there dying away.

4

There is a rushing chromatic scale in the basses and with vehement statements of Ex. 3 Elektra appears on the stage. Her great solo scene follows immediately,[7] in which we are given a full picture of her terrible preoccupation. In it she calls upon her father and recounts in lurid detail the circumstances of his murder which she has never allowed to

---

[7] This first presentation of the principal character through the immediat appearance of the big aria recalls Radames in Verdi's *Aida*. Though dramatically justified, it imposes a severe test on the performer, who thereby has no opportunity to warm up before embarking on the chief showpiece of the work. Strauss used a similar procedure once before in *Guntram* (see above, p. 99).

fade for an instant from before her eyes. She begs his spirit to return and appear again before her. She then builds elaborate castles in the air, planning her monumental revenge, at the climax of which she intends to perform a sacrificial dance of triumph on a mountain of corpses, built of his slaughtered enemies. Here Strauss adds the name 'Agamemnon' again and again to the libretto, so that the picture of the great king remains permanently before us in his own right and not merely in his role as Elektra's father.

Musically the Scena is a finely constructed symphonic exposition. The first subject is a composite group formed out of Exx. 4, 6, and 7, the motifs of Elektra's mourning and of her royal lineage. As the scene of the murder is described, two motifs which represent Klytemnestra and Aegisthus appear fleetingly. Although they are only fully developed later in the opera, it is important that they should be recognized already now, and I quote them accordingly at this, their first entry.

Ex. 9   Ex. 10

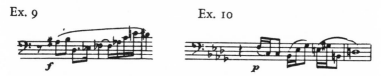

Ex. 9 is the first of a series of sinister motifs which build up the dreadful aura of evil which surrounds the decaying figure of Elektra's tormented mother, while Ex. 10 portrays Aegisthus as a weak-willed, ineffectual personality.

The transition section of the movement introduces a second and most important theme of Agamemnon, a great and soaring octave motif well described by Ernest Newman as 'rising threateningly from the depths to the heights of the orchestra like a great clenched fist'. It was not too fanciful of Newman to press the allusion of this motif forward into seeing the shade of Agamemnon himself towering over the house that was once his.

Ex. 11

In a piece of such concentrated horror and violence a contrasting

element of lyricism comes as a welcome relief. Strauss found his opportunity at the words 'show thyself to thy child'. Although Hofmannsthal
probably intended the use of the words 'dein Kind' as purely factual,
Strauss seized upon them and inserted a long and wistful melody to
suggest the warm and tender emotions stirred in Elektra's breast by the
memory of an affectionate family relationship of which she has been
starved for so long. This third theme of the race of Agamemnon stands
as the central point of the aria, the second subject, so to speak, of the
symphonic scheme. Although treated as an instrumental interlude at
this point, it gradually becomes one of the salient motifs of the entire
opera, representing the emotional ties between herself and her brother
and sister, Orestes and Chrysothemis, as joint inheritors of their noble
father's blood.

Ex. 12[8]

Later in the opera even Klytemnestra refers to this theme when recalling the tender family ties which she, too, has lost.

Elektra now immediately plunges once more into an imaginary
blood-bath as she considers the wild scene of vengeance in which Agamemnon's three children will dance upon the bodies of the enemies
who are at present their oppressors. Beginning with a lurid passage of
chromatic scales in block chords of Ex. 3(x) (which balances formally
with Elektra's description of Agamemnon's murder treated similarly)
the music gradually merges into the material of the actual Dance of
Triumph. This powerful group of themes forms the closing section of
the scena, and it is naturally brought back in a far more fully worked
development at the end of the opera when, the vengeance having been
exacted in full, Elektra actually performs her awful dance.

[8] Cf. the figure ⌐ a ⌐ with the corresponding figure in Ex. 39 of *Sinfonia
Domestica* (Chapter VI, p. 189 above).

Ex. 13

It is of course, immediately apparent that the figures ⎡ b ⎤ and ⎡ d ⎤ are merely variations of Exx. 3 and 1 respectively. Nevertheless so strong is their jubilant character in these new formats that they always preserve a recognizable independence as motifs of Triumph. The elaborate symphonic build-up of Ex. 13 gathers to itself other relevant motifs such as the 'Children of Agamemnon' (Ex. 12); the 'Lineage' theme (Ex. 6) and, last and strongest of all, the fist-like Ex. 11 which occurs at the closing climax of the movement.[9]

There is a tremendous feeling of elation as Elektra calls out twice more the name 'Agamemnon' against the pounding of her dance rhythm. The resolution of the final cadence has been in the key of C, but with a typical Straussian modulation the orchestra, now at full strength for the first time in the opera, rears itself up a third into E. In a more conventional work the moment of arrival in a new key would have been marked by a cymbal clash, a perhaps overfamiliar but neverfailing device for pointing a climax. Here, however, Strauss does something extraordinary. The cymbal stroke is there, but a bar too late, when the justification for it is past. It is, moreover, coupled with the bass drum, and the effect of this double mark of exclamation at an irrelevant moment is jarring and in a crude way wholly in keeping with the savage psychology of the drama.

[9] Strauss takes the voice up to [music] which note, held for nearly a bar and a half, comes not at the end but just before the closing cadence of the aria, a subtle dramatic stroke often lost in performance, since many singers, finding the part cruelly strenuous, omit the note altogether, as also the corresponding and identically situated top C at the end of the Klytemnestra scene.

5

As the climax of Elektra's solo scene dies away, the younger sister Chrysothemis appears framed in the massive doorway of the house and calls
softly to her in a pathetic phrase which returns and is developed much
later in the opera. Abruptly the flow of the music is broken off by the
brass with the violent polytonal Ex. 3 (x) which is immediately stifled to
leave a suspended chord consisting of the simultaneous sounding of the
two chords from the figure Ex. 2 (b).

Ex. 14

This harshly imposed pair of minor triads, which belong to opposite
sides of the tonal spectrum, is further used during scene 4 to describe
Klytemnestra's terrifying dreams. The stage directions at this point
specify that Elektra stares at Chrysothemis as if awakening from a
dream. The link between the two dreams, Elektra's wishful and her
mother's tortured, is most subtly established by the juxtaposition of the
two polytonal clusters, the one built out of two major, the other of two
minor tonalities.

The petulant fragmentary style of the opening scene is now resumed.
Chrysothemis has come to warn Elektra of her mother's intention of
having her removed to a tower of impenetrable darkness. But though
well-meaning, she has no easy time in trying to deliver her message.
Her very appearance is enough to reduce Elektra to an animal-like
creature of hates and fears who only comes out of her daze in order to
hurl unjustly at her the butchering of their father in accusation of her
very condition of relative well-being (for she is only tolerated by
Aegisthus in recognition of her passive acquiescence). Chrysothemis is
portrayed by an agitated, but more lyrical motif which, thrown into
immediate proximity with Elektra's vituperous figures, well illustrates
the difference between the two sisters.

Ex. 15

Elektra hates Chrysothemis, partly because of her weak compliance with the circumstances of their lives, the circumstances against which the elder sister's entire existence is one massive protest, but partly also because she is 'the daughter of my mother', as Elektra says bitterly. Strauss, who introduces at this point new motifs describing Klytemnestra, makes Elektra add the hated name so that the allusion is established firmly.

Ex. 16

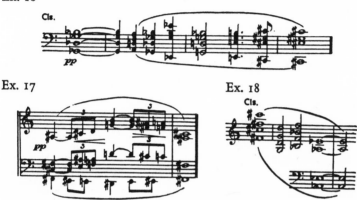

Ex. 17   Ex. 18

Nevertheless, although these themes of shifting chordal sequence catch to perfection Klytemnestra's evil and sinister influence, even perhaps her unspeakable appearance, they do less than justice to a woman whose strength of character and forceful determination was probably unequalled in the whole ancient world. Strauss concentrates on the decaying ruin which we are shortly to see rather than on the tremendous personality she has once been, a figure of such terrifying strength as to have disrupted the lives of all who came into contact with her.

Chrysothemis outlines the dreadful scheme of incarceration which by eavesdropping she has heard Klytemnestra and Aegisthus hatching. Elektra first elaborates her views of Aegisthus' effeminacy:

ELEKTRA: The two women?
CHRYSOTHEMIS: Who?
ELEKTRA: Well now, my mother and that other woman,
the coward Aegisthus. . . . (Exx. 9 and 10)

This description of Aegisthus tallies exactly with Greek tradition. Both Sophocles and Aeschylus emphasize his position as the weak, cowardly and feminine counterpart to Klytemnestra's masculinity.

Elektra next rails at Chrysothemis for stooping to such undignified activities as listening at keyholes. Rather, she says, sit by the gate and pray
for judgement to descend. This evokes Chrysothemis' great outburst
which corresponds with the conventional operatic aria to which the
preceding has been the recitative. It is, moreover, strikingly conventional in idiom compared with the music of the remainder of the work,
and stands as the one weak section of the score. Chrysothemis effuses at
length over how she yearns for a normal existence; love, husband, children are necessary to her, as she sees them all around her, forming part
of the lives of other women. The themes of her music are all extended
melodies of a typically Straussian flow and *Schwung* and are developed
much in the manner of a huge symphonic second subject:[10]

Ex. 19

The latter sections ⌐ b ¬ and ⌐ c ¬ form a kind of refrain to this
cynical outburst.

The main motifs of the race of which Elektra and Chrysothemis are
such prominent members (Exx. 4, 6, 7 and 11) are interspersed into the
development of these melodies, even the theme of pity (Ex. 8) accompanying Elektra's scornful 'Poor creature' in reply to Chrysothemis'
imploring request that she speak to her. The outer sections of the movement are passionately vivacious in accompaniment to Chrysothemis'
despairing outcries, while the central gloomy portion is fully in keeping
with her more hopeless complaint over the stony silence and neglect
amidst which they are condemned to live, 'with no brother returning,
nor a messenger from a brother, nor a messenger from a messenger. . .'

10 Bearing in mind that Elektra's crucial evocation of her father Agamemnon in
her opening solo scene is in C minor, and C becomes the key of her triumph both
in vision and reality, the symphonic analogy can be pursued to show that this
second subject appears regularly enough in the key of the relative major.

The numb grief of her misery is well caught by the cold orchestration which features the lower woodwind group of basset horns, cor anglais, heckelphon and bass clarinet, together with the bassoons and contra-bassoon. This *De Profundis* so to speak, is the best part of the scene, from which the music builds up gradually to the more conventional passionate section in which she screams that she must bear children at all costs, by whomsoever it may be, to a jubilant restatement of Exx. 15 and 19.

At the climax of Chrysothemis' outburst Elektra turns on her with her own savage Ex. 3. She has no sympathy with her characterless sister and one feels that Strauss had little either. Abruptly we are now back at the higher level of adventurous orchestral writing. The final section of the scene is mainly concerned with the growing sounds of pandemonium which presage the approach of Klytemnestra. At this point in the original drama Hofmannsthal had introduced an extended passage in which Elektra describes the nightmare she has been willing upon her mother, a nightmare in which Klytemnestra is hounded by her children to a dreadful death at the end of a terrifying chase. Strauss, however, cleverly transferred this irrelevant speech to the end of the Klytemnestra scene, where it adds most ingeniously to the tremendous build-up near the end. Thus the dialogue which battles against the fast-increasing confusion is reduced to essentials, Chrysothemis explaining that Klytemnestra has ordered endless sacrifices in useless attempts to propitiate the Gods and so put an end to her ghastly dreamings. Elektra insists on remaining to confront her, but Chrysothemis, exclaiming that 'when she trembles she is at her most dreadful', rushes off to avoid the impending conflict. Amidst the ever more frenzied tearing to and fro of strings and wind, unmistakable cracking of whips is heard and a new theme gradually emerges, descriptive of the inexorable driving of the sacrificial animals to the slaughter:

Ex. 20   leading to:

Klytemnestra's many motifs are incorporated as the music builds to a terrifying climax and with them a further vital motif which reveals through the orchestra the nature of her dreams, since Ex. 21 is the motif of Orestes himself:

Ex. 21

The rapid succession of widely varied chords out of which motifs such as those of Klytemnestra (Exx. 16–18) and also these last two (Exx. 20 and 21) are constituted, causes a complete tonal confusion in the mind of the listener especially at the extremely fast tempo of this passage. This effect is naturally enormously intensified when the motifs are superimposed upon one another, and Strauss deliberately plays upon this confusion by using weird and atmospheric orchestral colouring on the one hand and the sharpest possible contrasts of texture or abrupt plunges into dissonant chords on the other.

As the climax approaches, the procession is actually seen passing behind the windows in the great stone wall and culminates in the appearance of Klytemnestra herself.

6

There is nothing in the whole text of Greek literature to prepare one for Hofmannsthal's re-creation of the figure of Klytemnestra. A true product of Praz's *Romantic Agony*, she is easily the most ghastly character in the whole dreadful drama, worse by far in her decadence than Elektra, who is at least strong in her hatred and bitterness. The stage directions[11] tell of Klytemnestra's 'sallow, bloated face . . . she leans on her Confidante while a jaundiced snake-like figure carries the train of her robe. She is entirely covered with precious stones and talismans . . . her fingers bristle with rings, her eyelids are unnaturally large and it seems to cost

[11] In later life Strauss wrote that 'Klytemnestra should be shown not as a weather-beaten elderly witch but as a handsome proud woman of about fifty, whose disintegration is not a physical but a spiritual affair'. Ernest Newman once commented on this change of front, saying: 'If the producer protests that he finds it difficult to reconcile this with the stage directions in the score he can count on my sympathy.'

her an unspeakable effort to keep them from falling.' She herself speaks of how, alive and not even sick, she is rotting away, crumbling, decaying like a tainted corpse, like garments that the moths have eaten. A new motif of chromatic chord sequences depicts this aspect of her existence.

Ex. 22

"bin Ich le -ben - - di-aen Lei - bes " [12]

Even this apparently new theme contains within its structure the opposition of two minor chords a tritone apart which have already made such a striking impression in Exx. 2 and 14. This motivic harmony steadily gains in importance as the scene progresses.

In both Euripides and Sophocles, Klytemnestra finds strength in arguing with Elektra on the grounds of Agamemnon's sacrifice of their daughter Iphigenia. In Aeschylus she only appears briefly in a scene with Orestes in which she pleads for mercy, once again on the grounds of her motherhood. In none of them is she this evil, sinister creature of Hofmannsthal's imagining, whose sole thought is abject paralysing fear of her son's return and how to rid herself of the dreams prompted by that fear. Yet the character study is both logical and credible and on that account the more horribly convincing. Strauss now draws the threads of her relationship with Elektra together by a subtle use of thematic allusion and metamorphosis which is in direct line of descent from Liszt's symphonic technique. By reducing the theme of Elektra's nobility (Ex. 7) to a continuous stream of semiquavers which from now on represents her hold over Klytemnestra through her malicious use of obscure double meanings, Strauss shows its common origin with Ex. 3, viz:

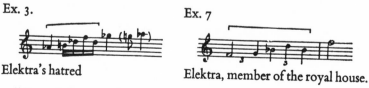

Ex. 3.

Elektra's hatred

Ex. 7

Elektra, member of the royal house.

[12] 'I am a living corpse.'

R.S.—X

Ex 7(a)

Elektra's hypnotic power over Klytemnestra (later also over Aegistus).[13]

Like the preceding duet the Klytemnestra scene falls into three clear sections, but with a difference of climactic structure. In the Chryso-themis scene the ternary design consisted of a kind of recitative, a lyrical aria-like central section, and a return to the freer dramatic recitative from which arises the orchestral interlude of the procession which leads into the Klytemnestra scene. The three subdivisions of this new and central scene correspond more directly with the action of the drama. The first section shows Klytemnestra torn between the restraining influ-ence of her Confidante and Train bearer and her desire to communi-cate with her terrible daughter whom she believes to be possessed of seer-like qualities, much as she fears her implacable hatred. She has come in desperation for advice, and her descent from the house towards Elek-tra, her account of her dreamings, and her solicitations for counsel, form the second section, while the third shows Elektra gaining ascend-ency over her mother through the introduction of Orestes into the discussion.

The first of these three main sections is largely episodic. After the first paroxysms of rage provoked by the very sight of Elektra have sub-sided, Klytemnestra speaks more to herself than to her attendants and scarcely seems to hear Elektra's sardonic comments, each one in any case full of double meanings. But when they are repeated to her she is readier than her companions to find good in them, and even at one mo-ment indulges in nostalgic memories of a time when Elektra was a true daughter to her, understanding her as no one else has ever done. This poignant moment is beautifully caught by Strauss in a passage in which an oboe solo superimposed above Ex. 17 leads into the melody of the family relationship, Ex. 12. The whole of Klytemnestra's tirade of self-pity is accompanied not only by her own motifs (Exx. 9, 16, 17 and 22) but by Elektra's Ex. 7, which flutters around in diminution on flutes and clarinets like an importunate moth.

[13] In the official guide to the opera issued by the publishers this motif is referred to as the 'craft, untruthfulness, and hysterical nature of Elektra', but such an interpretation altogether belittles Hofmannsthal and Strauss's epic heroine.

Elektra moves a little nearer to her mother and, seizing on Klytemnestra's momentary show of sentiment, presses her advantage in order
to alienate her from her two evil attendants who, as Klytemnestra herself acknowledges, turning on them in hatred, exude nothing but the
breath of Aegisthus. Elektra shrewdly brings Klytemnestra to the
realization of how her character has become submerged as a result of
the influences to which she is constantly subjected, and a new melodic
theme appears, the significance of which only gradually becomes apparent later:

Ex. 23

Ex. 23 is used to a considerable extent during the scene, especially at
moments when Klytemnestra believes Elektra to be in an unusually
placatory frame of mind, thus arousing nostalgic memories of a time
when pleasure and happiness pervaded the palace. The reappearance of
this theme towards the end of the opera when happiness suddenly and
poignantly returns is one of the salient features of the work. At present
it alternates constantly with Ex. 22, now adapted to the same swinging
$\frac{6}{4}$ rhythm. A serpentine violin solo which also pervades the texture,
meandering in and out, suggests the insidious Confidante, while a spiky
row of ascending quavers on flute and piccolo characterizes the spiteful
tongue of the Train bearer. Klytemnestra's mounting indignation
against these two evil characters is built upon a symphonic exposition
of this new material which rises to a climax as she abruptly dismisses
them from her presence. The chord sequences of Ex. 22 then sink down,[14]
the two attendants vanish and with them their violin triplets and flute
tonguings. This is a fascinating and highly imaginative page of orchestral composition ending in a remarkable polytonal cadence. Klytemnestra descends from the palace towards Elektra and the orchestration
well depicts the jangling of her endless arm-rings and necklaces as she
moves. The musical effect is that of a new symphonic movement set in

[14] The harmonic progression of this passage, together with the typically Delian
$\frac{6}{4}$ pulse is strongly reminiscent of the Black Fiddler's music from *A Village
Romeo and Juliet*, composed some seven years earlier. Considering that all Delius's
early successes took place in Germany around the turn of the century, it is by no
means unlikely that Strauss would have known something of his work.

two keys simultaneously, F minor and B minor, the keys of the minor
polytonal chord already once heard, Ex. 14, and on that chord the motif of Klytemnestra's dreaming is established, bringing in its train other
polytonal combinations of minor triads through its use of parallel
movements.

Ex. 24

The description of Klytemnestra's night-time experiences stands as
one of the most remarkable passages in a work of genius. In its effect it
has been justly compared by Donald Mitchell with Schönberg's *Erwartung*, to which it is indeed strikingly similar. The horror of what she en-
dures is intensified by the fact that it is so intangible, so negative. As she
says, 'it is no word, it is no pain, it does not oppress me, and yet it is so
fearful that my soul desires to hang itself and every limb cries out for
death'. The creepy-crawly texture of the music which accompanies
this lurid description is pervaded by spaced-out references to Ex. 6,
for ill as she is (despite her protestations to the contrary) she still belongs
to the Race of the Royal House and carries the remnants of its nobility
of bearing. But the figure ⌐ a ⌐ from this motif detaches itself and after
some repetitions on three muted tubas and contra-bassoon, rears up like
some fearful monster:

Ex. 25[15]

The aria ends with Klytemnestra's savage avowal of her determination to shed the blood of every living creature in her desperate attempt
to find the right sacrifice necessary to put an end to her dreams, and

[15] We shall see this figure put to elaborate use in similar contexts in both *Der
Rosenkavalier* and *Die Frau ohne Schatten*.

this gives Elektra her opportunity. She leads on Klytemnestra by indicating that she knows the right victim whose blood must be shed and who must fall beneath the axe. In a series of questions and answers in which Hofmannsthal shows great subtlety and wit, Klytemnestra is drawn steadily into the trap, for it is her own blood, her own neck which must be slaughtered beneath the sacrificial axe. This is made increasingly obvious in the music which refers constantly to the axe theme (Ex. 2(a)), to Ex. 4 (Elektra's mourning theme for her father), and to the music of Elektra's triumphal dance (Ex. 13). Klytemnestra's eager questions are accompanied by Ex. 9, which has from the first emphasized her role of murderess, and the jangling chord sequence with which this section of the scene began and which epitomizes her jewels and the faith she has in the charms which must lie within them. The fluid nature of the symphonic composition is cleverly anchored at one point when Elektra pounces on Klytemnestra's suggestion of a stranger and refers obliquely to Orestes. There is a sudden surge and the music then gently subsides on to a pedal point against which Ex. 23 returns. Klytemnestra begs Elektra not to speak in riddles, and rejoices for a brief moment that they have been able to commune together as mother and daughter. But the leaping octave of Ex. 21 is present throughout the passage and Elektra switches the conversation to a direct attack as to her brother's whereabouts and well-being.[16]

The last section is a steady crescendo to the final climax of the great scene which forms the central peak of the opera. It is in two parts, the first the wrangle over the possible return of Orestes culminating in Klytemnestra's outburst and threats, the second Elektra's exposition of the hunting down and slaughter of her mother, the revealing of her cherished dream of revenge in every horrific detail, at the end of which the positions of the two women are reversed. Klytemnestra is cowering in speechless terror, panting with horrible spasms of fear, while Elektra faces her triumphantly in wild intoxication. It was in the build-up of this tremendous passage that Strauss incorporated into Hofmannsthal's text the long monologue in which Elektra describes in

---

[16] The abruptness with which the twist is effected is due to a cut in the text similar to the moment in *Salome* when Herod suddenly says 'Dance for me, Salome.' Hofmannsthal gradually brings the conversation round by means of some two pages of additional banter between the two women. In so long a scene Strauss tightened the dramatic effect by this use of shock tactics. The atmosphere is very tense as Elektra now suddenly confronts her mother with the forbidden subject of her exiled son.

detail her dream of Orestes' hunt and slaughter of her mother at the feet of Agamemnon's ghost. This tirade had originally belonged to the previous scene and had been declaimed only for Chrysothemis' ears. It is unquestionably apt in this new position and yet it draws out the final climax to the point at which the tension actually flags, and in performance it is now almost invariably cut.

Musically the two climaxes of this closing section of the scene form a synthesis of all the foregoing material. Klytemnestra works herself up in her emphatic refusal to acknowledge the threat from Orestes, but Elektra persists in working upon her mother's ceaseless dread. In the course of this taunting passage a new motif is subtly introduced in conjunction with Orestes' Ex. 21. Although seemingly innocent in this first appearance it gradually assumes a fearful place of importance as the drama reaches its zenith, for it symbolizes the insane, frenzied triumph which the forthcoming murder will bring to Elektra:

Ex. 26

As Klytemnestra forces herself into mock jubilation born of self-delusion, the music assumes an almost dance-like character, the basis of which is the jangling theme now transformed into a horrible waltz.[17] The climax comes after Klytemnestra's words 'I shall find out for my-self whose blood must be shed so that I can once more sleep,' the word 'sleep' being sung to a long-sustained top G sharp, against an ever more frenzied alternation of the bi-tonal jangling chords.

The final section of this duet, Elektra's triumphant tirade, follows impetuously with a violent outburst of the newly introduced Ex. 26, which is now developed as a leading motif together with Elektra's main motirs Exx. 3, 6, and 7. Her description of the ghastly hunt, her fusion of the two dream sequences, the mother's dread and her own desire, is carried on a surge of symphonic polyphony of extraordinary energy and inspiration, in which most of the principal motifs of the opera find their appropriate place. In addition a chordal motif makes a strident appearance on the trumpets as Elektra gloats over her intention to be present at the kill:

[17] At the words 'and if I wish I shall have three armed men sitting day and night with eyes wide open outside my chamber door', there is a curious passage bearing the strongest resemblance to Jochanaan's theme from *Salome*, Ex. 14.

Ex. 27

This is an important example of one of Strauss's most characteristic uses of Wagnerian technique.

The tonality of the music centres round the key of C, which is becoming increasingly associated with Elektra's eventual fulfilment of the will of Agamemnon, and in which key the opera actually ends. The duet ends with a double cadence, Elektra's second top C (see footnote on p. 303 above) soaring over a tremendous statement of the Orestes theme (Ex. 21), but resolving unexpectedly on to a mighty and exultant chord of B flat. The final resolution in C is rightly retained for the end of the opera.

7

The sense of unbearable strain is maintained during the orchestral interlude which ensues. The music follows closely the detailed stage directions which show Klytemnestra receiving from her Confidante the spurious news of Orestes' death, and so gradually changing her position *vis-à-vis* Elektra from the dominated to the dominant character. Her eerie chordal motif, Ex. 16, is strongly in evidence, as is also Orestes' Ex. 21 in diminution amidst the scurrying and hurrying of rapid woodwind and strings figuration suggestive of the rushing hither and thither of countless servants from the house carrying torches. Two odd little motifs appear, which are re-introduced later at a key point in the drama:

Ex. 28   and Ex. 29

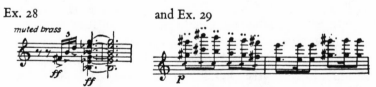

The first of these (Ex. 28) suggests the sudden appearance of light in the house, while Ex. 29 refers to the part played in all this activity by Klytemnestra's hateful but trusted personal servants, the Confidante and Train bearer. This proves to be of particularly sinister significance in due course. Even Ex. 8 is slashed vehemently across the canvas in this mighty central symphonic development, though its appearance is more for musical than psychological reasons as there is no specific mention of the fifth maidservant in the text.

Klytemnestra's exultation now reaches monumental proportions. The chordal motif of Elektra's triumph (Ex. 27) is replaced by a similar triumphal motif, but which is unmistakably drawn from Klytemnestra's Ex. 16. The balance of power has once more returned to the Queen, who stretches out both hands threateningly towards Elektra, then, stick in hand and leaning on her servants, hurries away into the house to the surging of Ex. 17. Elektra is left wholly bewildered as to what news can possibly have so transformed the situation. The fanfare-like Ex. 26 which has hitherto been aggressive in character now sounds a little worried. The violins maintain a high twittering as Elektra gives uneasy voice to her doubts. There is a sudden howling 'as of a wounded animal' and Chrysothemis rushes out of the house.

Strauss regarded this moment as the half-way point of the drama, as of his symphonic poem, for such undoubtedly his score is. He indicated this in two ways, firstly by the orchestra rehearsal figures which, having reached 275, start again at this very bar with 1a to continue to 262a at the very end of the work; secondly by starting the new scene on the second beat of a $\frac{3}{4}$ bar, as in a classical work in which the completion of the bar would come at the end with a single complementary beat, viz:

Ex. 30

Ex. 30 is a motif of extreme anguish with especial reference to Chrysothemis, whose later joy at the end of the opera it also depicts in a major version. Chrysothemis has heard the report of Orestes' death and hastens to share her grief with Elektra, who, however, in desperation refuses at first to believe the news. This section is an elaborate symphonic development of the melody of the Children of Agamemnon (Ex. 12). At the climax it is presented in E flat minor with the chord of D major jammed against it in a stridently dissonant polytonal effect, harsher than any produced previously. For whereas Elektra's dream of revenge is represented by the superimposition of two major chords and Klytemnestra's fear of that same revenge by two minor, this moment of crisis which spells despair to the one and relief to the other is characterized by a combination of major and minor.

A wailing theme is added to the texture which becomes a surging mass of chromatic polyphony in the construction of which Strauss, perhaps unconsciously, incorporated melodic fragments recalling salient motifs from the earlier operas in addition to Exx. 12 and 15, which represent the two protagonists who are actually on the stage.

Gradually the heaving, wailing lament subsides as the two sisters sink to the ground in utter desolation. Abruptly there is a violent change of mood and of colouring as two menservants—one young, the other old—enter the scene, stumbling over the two prostrate figures. These are, in fact, the first male characters who have appeared on the stage since the beginning of the opera. In performance the concentration of women's voices shrieking in almost unrelieved hysteria accentuates to an appalling degree the extreme nervous tension which is such a characteristic of the opera. This interlude for tenor and bass[18] is, however, too brief to supply the deep quality for which the ear is parched, and relief does not come until the great Orestes scene.

Hofmannsthal had extended the scene of the menservants to far greater proportions than Strauss decided to retain. In the original there was also the Head Cook, an impressive but slow-witted character. The whole scene thus presented a kind of foil to the scene of the maidservants with their overseer at the beginning of the drama. An impression of prevailing confusion was created which is to a large extent dissipated by Strauss's whittling down of the passage to a brief and peremptory interchange between the aggressive young man and his bewildered elderly colleague. The former demands a mount that he can ride off to carry the news to Aegisthus as fast as possible. Even a cow would do, he adds with unnecessary facetiousness when the old man gapes at him, but from the galloping rhythm with which the timpani accompanies his exit he was clearly to acquire instantly a steed worthy of his haste if not of his manners.

The music of this scene is typical of Strauss's lighter vein, and is strongly reminiscent of the opening scene of *Feuersnot* with the rowdy Munich children. But the pace is still so hectic that it is easy to miss the basically folky quality of the invention just as one fails to observe the

[18] Sir Thomas Beecham describes a most amusing incident about this scene. See *A Mingled Chime*, pp. 91–92.

fundamentally Viennese flavour which constantly lurked behind the chromatic polyphony of the earlier scene which described the despair of the two sisters at the reported death of Orestes. In fact, this comic interlude is built on the Aegisthus motif which, although presaged near the opening of the opera (Ex. 10), only now begins to emerge in a clear and crystallized form, in which it will later be developed during the appearance of Aegisthus himself on the stage.

Ex. 31

8

The galloping hoofs of the messenger's horse die away and lead into a rapid movement built upon a broken form of Elektra's noble theme, Ex. 7, and also upon the pathetic phrase to which Chrysothemis first called Elektra's name immediately after the solo scene. If Orestes is indeed dead, then the onus of revenge now devolves upon the two last surviving children of Agamemnon: Chrysothemis and Elektra herself. The remainder of this complicated scene shows Elektra's increasingly fervent but ever unsuccessful attempt to secure her sister's collaboration in the horrible enterprise. After the introductory build-up of Ex. 7, the the scene is musically subdivided into clear sections, viz:

(a) The principal seduction passage in which Elektra extols the beauty and strength of Chrysothemis.
(b) An isolated aria in which Elektra promises to be a true sister to Chrysothemis and watch tenderly over her long-desired but so far purely imaginary wedding.
(c) A further clearly defined aria in which Elektra promises to serve Chrysothemis as a slave-girl.
(d) A dramatic coda in which Elektra once more becomes pressing and passionate in her insistence.

Musically these four sections form a group of extremely important developments of themes or passages from earlier portions of the opera, and in one instance the first references are made to a theme (Ex. 38) later to become of primary importance; thus, unlike the excisions commonly made in the Klytemnestra scene, the cuts to which this scene is invariably subjected are much to be deplored.

The first section (a) is a warm, surging E-flat passage in conventional idiom which balances with the earlier similar section in the first Chrysothemis scene (see Ex. 19 above), though now incorporating Ex. 1 as if to impress upon Chrysothemis her responsibility as a daughter of Agamemnon. The second section (b) is based entirely upon the 'family' motif (Ex. 12), while (c), the section generally omitted *in toto*, is an important and unique development of the motif of the sympathetic slave-girls (Ex. 8). This passes by way of a transitional passage, incorporating motifs from the earlier Chrysothemis scene (Ex. 19), into (d), which recalls the closing section from the Klytemnestra scene. Hofmannsthal's text, with its use of repetition, was obviously of great value to Strauss in his planning of the climax. Chrysothemis' reiterated cries of 'Lass mich!' and 'Ich kann nicht!' build naturally and effectively to Elektra's final despairing 'Sei verflucht!'[19]

The viciousness with which the descending figures of Ex. 6 are hurled out at the beginning of this closing section brings the theme close in character to the 'axe' theme, Ex. 2, which is itself similarly hurled during the interlude which follows. Elektra, finding herself alone in her enterprise, and wholly abandoned by Chrysothemis (who has fled in terror), sets to, like a dog digging up a bone, to furrow deep in the earth at the corner of the courtyard for the axe with which her father was murdered and which she has carefully preserved since the fateful day. The music has resumed the frenzied savage character which typified the opening scene, but, as a new wailing theme enters, the fever gradually subsides until it sinks away altogether. The wailing theme is an elaboration of a motif which Strauss has already used several times in earlier works, but here it is developed and extended far beyond any previous treatment.

Ex. 32

---

[19] The whole subject of the musicality of Hofmannsthal's literary style is discussed at considerable length in Dr Karl Joachim Krüger's treatise, published in 1935 as Vol. 35 of *Neue Deutsche Forschungen*.

It heralds the appearance of a man who with quiet dignity stands in
the doorway and gradually steps on to the threshold. Elektra, disturbed
in her secret digging and troubled by his strange manner, tries to bid
him leave, but it is clear from the solemn chords (Ex. 33) which precede
his first words that Orestes, this unknown, unrecognized figure of such
authority, has full control of the situation and has no intention of leaving until such time as he himself considers that he should do so.

Ex. 33

In the same way that Ex. 32 finds precedents in Strauss's earlier works,
Wagnerian chordal themes such as Ex. 33 appear many times in Strauss.
Amongst the most striking instances, the first appearance of Kunrad in
Feuersnot is the most obvious parallel, especially in view of the similar
circumstances of their introduction. A further parallel in *Elektra* itself
needs, however, to be drawn, that of Ex. 27. The relative placing of the
three chords in the two examples is far from identical. Yet the allusion
of the one to the other is unmistakable; Ex. 33 refers to Orestes, but
Orestes has come to provide the fulfilment of Elektra's life and dreams
which was portrayed by Ex. 27. And with the appearance of Ex. 33
the character of the music changes to one of predominant lyricism
which is emphasized by the first extended use of the male voice in the
opera.

Elektra's restless impatience with the new-comer is depicted by a
new figure:

Ex. 34

which alternates with the solemn chords of Ex. 33 until the wailing
theme Ex. 32 returns, forming a background against which Orestes
tells of his own supposed death, the threnody being taken up bitterly
by Elektra. This arouses Orestes' suspicions and he gradually draws

from Elektra her identity. As he does so, a new derivative of Agamemnon's theme (Ex. 1) appears, suggestive of the sad condition in which Elektra appears to her incredulous brother. Moreover, as the stranger gradually and with some circumlocution reveals the truth that Orestes lives, and then hints that he is himself the long-yearned-for brother, a second derivative of the same theme gradually unfolds, full of Orestes' courage and determination. These two themes (Exx. 35 and 36) are brilliant psychological studies and show Strauss at the height of his powers as a tone poet of profound insight and perception.

Ex. 35

Ex. 36

At this point Hofmannsthal introduced an old servant who enters, kisses Orestes' feet and vanishes quickly and silently. Strauss altered these directions so that in the opera the old man is followed by no less than three further servants, who kiss not only his feet but his hands and the hem of his cloak.[20] The intensity and warmth of the music is of a quality unprecedented in the opera as the incredulous Elektra hears her brother say 'The hounds in the courtyard know me well, and my sister not?' At last the truth strikes Elektra and she shrieks out her brother's name.[21] In the tremendous orchestral outburst which follows Strauss actually imitates the bellowing of hounds on six horns, although by the presence of the servants on the stage Orestes seems to imply that the 'hounds' who recognize him are these very menials. The bellowings form the nucleus of an enormously complex polyphonic passage which incorporates not only past themes but motifs to come, such as the major version of Ex. 30 and the great melody of the Recognition Aria,

[20] At one stage Hofmannsthal, possibly with his tongue in his cheek, encouraged Strauss to have as many as twenty old servants all dropping to their knees at the sight of Orestes, but the composer finally settled for a total of four.

[21] The palpable indiscretion of this naturally alarms Orestes, who, in Hofmannsthal's original text, feverishly exclaims, 'If anyone in the house has heard, that person holds my life in his hands.'

Ex. 37. Here is surely one of the supreme emotional outpourings of the
entire Romantic era.[22]

9

This scene is not only the musical climax of the work; it contains the
finest lyrical music Strauss had yet produced in his compositions for
the stage, apart from the closing scene of *Salome*, which is, however,
more an example of erotic excitement than of true lyricism. Here
for the first time Strauss was genuinely moved by a dramatic situation
and by emotions which owe nothing either to sensuality or the grotesque. Certainly the reunion of Orestes and Elektra, one of the most
moving conceptions in all Greek tragedy, is a scene of the calibre to
inspire great music, and Hofmannsthal's interpretation heightens the
pathos in a way which lent itself magnificently to musical setting. Up
to this point Strauss had made many juxtapositions and condensations
of the text, but here he actually asked the poet for some extra lines
which would give, as he wrote in a letter to Hofmannsthal, 'a long
point of repose after Elektra's first cry of "Orest!" I mean to introduce
a softly undulating orchestral interlude while Elektra is gazing on the
returned Orestes; I can make her stammer out the word "Orest, Orest,
Orest!" several times—of the remainder only the words "Es rührt
sich Niemand!"[23] and "O lass deine Augen mich sehn!"[24] fit the mood.
Couldn't you fit in a few beautiful verses here until, at the point where
Orestes tries to embrace her tenderly, I can pass into a more sombre
mood for the passage bearing the words "Nein, Du sollst mich nicht
berühren"? '[25]

Hofmannsthal obliged with eight lines which Strauss used as they
stood, apart from a single word which he altered to suit the vocalization
of a high note. It is apparent, as much by what Strauss retained as by what
he changed or asked for, that the musical fabric stood complete in Strauss's
mind at this point and needed no more than the right number and style
of syllables to put into Elektra's part for the entire section to stand complete in every detail. The result ranks amongst Strauss's highest achievements, and this huge melodic curve is one of the great songs of the world.

[22] Part of this passage is quoted later. See pp. 325 and 352 below.
[23] 'No one stirs.'
[24] 'O let my eyes behold you.'
[25] 'No, you shall not touch me.'

Ex. 37

26 It was this word 'erhabenes' which Strauss altered, the original 'entzückenden' being impracticable for a sustained top B flat. The relative meanings ('sublime' in place of 'rapturous') are very close.

The song ends in tones of the utmost pathos and tenderness, and, as Strauss wrote, the transition is made to the more sombre mood for the interchange which follows between brother and sister. Great use is made of the wailing theme (Ex. 32)[27] and Elektra's new melody Ex. 35, which now seems to have a wistful smile behind its sadness as Elektra in her new-found bliss tells Orestes all that has befallen her, and how her beauty has faded into ashes with ill-treatment. As she describes the desecration of her hair, Ex. 5, one of the earliest derivatives of Ex. 1, which has not been heard since the opening scene, is reintroduced on the basset horn with exceptionally imaginative effect, using as it does virtually the entire range of the instrument. This whole passage stands out as one of the most poetic and colourfully orchestrated of the work. Ex. 30 is also spun into melodies of truly Straussian sweetness as Elektra pours out all the sacrifices she has made for the sake of this very moment which she had forced herself to believe that she would never see.

At last Orestes replies and the scene ends in a conventional duet to a fine new melody expressive of the fulfilment which both brother and sister know lies before them as a result of the deed now so shortly to be accomplished:

Ex. 38

The first incomplete statements of this theme were actually introduced in the scene in which Elektra vainly tried to solicit Chrysothemis' help. They are, however, rarely heard, partly because they only appear hidden in the bass instruments of the orchestra, and in any case they occur during a section of that unfortunate scene which is habitually cut in performance.

Ex. 38 leads through the 'family' theme (Ex. 12) to a final section based on a heroic version of the music of the actual recognition, a C major transformation which sounds in truth somewhat garish and banal

---

[27] The resemblance of the figure to the theme of the soprano song *O Glaube* from the Finale of Mahler's 2nd Symphony is very striking.

after the superb music which has preceded it. This motif, not so far
quoted, finds its true place, oddly enough, in the first love duet of
Strauss's next composition *Der Rosenkavalier* (see Exx. 6 (b) and 6 (c),
Chapter IX p. 352, where both passages are quoted). The whole section
is punctuated by persistent repetitions of the Agamemnon figure
⌐ a ⌐ from Ex. 36 and the wailing Ex. 32 (a).

In the drama the Tutor entered at this moment, an effective point
being made of the way in which he and Elektra become known to each
other for the first time. This was all substantially redrafted, however,
when the music was composed. A duet for Elektra and Orestes was
created by an ingenious redistribution of lines making a motif out of
the words 'selig' (happy) in a way fully in keeping with Hofmannsthal's
strong feeling for musical form. Strauss altered Hofmannsthal's original
intention in so doing, however, sacrificing much of the tutor's appearance which Hofmannsthal had extended precisely in order that his
impact upon Elektra and hers upon him might have their full effect.
The Tutor's motif, nevertheless, is combined with the hammerings of
Ex. 36(a) at the outset of the duet, possibly a survival of a time when
Strauss envisaged an earlier appearance of this stern old man with
flashing eyes and inflexible purpose.

Ex. 39

His entrance marks the beginning of the dénouement and from
this point the action moves swiftly to its climax. With urgent haste and
palpable common sense he upbraids the brother and sister for giving
vent so audibly to their joy and presses Orestes to go directly into the
house and complete the task. The orchestral commentary upon the
complicated stage directions which follow show to their best advantage
Strauss's powers of symphonic organization and his ability to adapt
these to a psychological situation. On a framework of the chordal
Orestes theme (Ex. 33), though with its actual harmonic sequence
subtly altered on each occasion, various motifs flash past: a violent
version of the Agamemnon theme Ex. 1; a hectic memory of the great

song Ex. 37, now used as a restless bass to an inverted form of Klytemnestra's nightmares Ex. 24; the two little motifs Exx. 28 and 29 used as
before to suggest the sudden light and the scurrying of maidservants;
and lastly the sinister motif of Klytemnestra herself, Ex. 22, in its sinking, swaying version and its tortuous resolution into B minor. The last
time this music was heard, Klytemnestra had just contemptuously dismissed her Confidante before descending towards Elektra for their
great scene together. It is with deliberate perception that by bringing
it back here Strauss draws our attention to the gruesome fact that this
very Confidante is now obsequiously ushering into the house the
murderous avenging son whom she knows her mistress has been so
dreading day and night, year after year. Orestes, after shutting his eyes
against the horror of the immediate future, passes through the great
door, closely followed by the tutor. Elektra is left alone once more.

10

The nerve-wracking tension of the passage which follows is built up
by Strauss with a feverish rushing movement of cellos and basses, depicting the maniacal pacing to and fro of Elektra 'with sunken head,
like a captive beast in a cage'. Yet even this frankly onomatopoeic
section is derived motivically from the thematic material in a way
entirely in keeping with the basic symphonic nature of the work.
Elektra's thoughts are fixed naturally enough on the impending murders and each new phrasing of semiquavers begins with the fearful
Ex. 26. There is a ghastly interruption when Elektra suddenly realizes
that she has failed to give Orestes the fateful axe which she has hidden
buried in the ground for so many years for just this moment (the broken
form of Elektra's Ex. 5 returns here, much as it appeared in the second
Chrysothemis scene). With an outburst of diabolical fury she shouts
out against her defiant Ex. 3 that 'there are no gods in heaven'. The
bitonal portion of the 'axe' motif (Ex. 2 (b)) is savagely snarled out and
the music subsides once more to the rushing semiquavers with their
references to Ex. 26. At last Klytemnestra's shrieks from within reveal
that the deed is done and Elektra's elation is portrayed by a conglomeration of five motifs, as demon-like she yells out savagely 'Triff noch
einmal'[28] in her blood-lust. Ex. 26 itself is repeated in utter frenzy; the
rearing octave figure representative of the revenge of Agamemnon

[28] 'Strike yet again.'

(Ex. 11) now builds upon itself in rising minor seconds, the most jarring dissonance possible; the tutor's theme (Ex. 39) is combined with an alteration of two minor chords a tritone apart referring, motivically as always, directly to Klytemnestra; and, capping the whole orchestral tirade, the original principal Agamemnon theme Ex. 1 is proclaimed on trumpet and bass trumpet. Only the themes of Orestes himself are significantly absent. Orestes has performed the appalling act of matricide less of his own volition than as part of the role planned for him by the Fates. His own character is not concerned in the deed, which he has performed much as an objective and mechanical robot.

There is an abrupt change of tempo, and to the theme of sympathy (Ex. 8) the maidservants rush on to the stage, accompanied by Chrysothemis. The sequence of events caused Strauss considerable anxiety at this point. Although the text of Hofmannsthal's play reads substantially as in the opera, there seems to have been a point at which Hofmannsthal proposed the total omission of Aegisthus' entry and murder. Strauss felt this to be wrong:

> . . . he is indispensable to the plot and must be struck down, too, in sight of the audience if possible. If it isn't possible to bring him home earlier, so that he can be slain immediately after Klytemnestra, then we should leave the next scene as it is. Think it over, perhaps. It is not good that all the women come running on after the murder of Klytemnestra, then disappear again, and then come on again with Chrysothemis after the murder of Aegisthus. The thread of the drama is broken too sharply. Perhaps you can think of something else. Couldn't Aegisthus be allowed to come home immediately after Orestes has gone into the house? Then the murders can follow quickly after one another in such a way that at just the moment when Aegisthus has gone into the house and the door has closed behind him, one hears the distant shriek of Klytemnestra; then after a short interval the assassination of Aegisthus would be accomplished, as it stands at present; thereafter comes the whole scene of the women and the finale? I really think this would go well.[29]

To this, Hofmannstal replied with an alternative proposal which,

[29] In the first abridged publication of the correspondence, Strauss's son, Dr Franz Strauss, adds a footnote reading: 'This is the form that was finally adopted.' However much Dr Strauss may have wished to show that Hofmannsthal accepted all his father's suggestions, this, in fact, is simply not so.

denuded of its complicated details, amounts to the replacement of the
scene in which the women rush on, by a dramatic pause; Aegisthus would
then appear abruptly. By thus telescoping the scene of the women into
their later entry Hofmannsthal tried to avoid a 'double curve' in the
action which was worrying Strauss. The result was not, however,
entirely convincing and in the end Strauss went back to Hofmannsthal's
original plan.

Musically the scene is largely constructed from the theme of the
sympathetic maidservants, though the references to Klytemnestra,
men in the house, Elektra and Aegisthus, evoke the appropriate motifs
in the orchestra, the men collectively being symbolized by the dominating figure of the tutor. The turmoil then subsides as the women rush
off and Aegisthus enters to the music of his own Exx. 10 and 31. There
is a brief violent suggestion of an axe-stroke (Ex. 2 (a)) and the music
settles down to an intermezzo-like working out of the Aegisthus motifs
with their *Till Eulenspiegel/Feuersnot*-like geniality. Strauss's treatment
of this sinister scene is most ingenious, and heightens the weirdness of
the charged atmosphere by the introduction of motifs which reveal
thoughts or truths to the audience beyond the suspicions of the un-
couth and slow-witted Aegisthus. Tiny references to Ex. 21 keep flit-
ting across the score, evoking the figure of Orestes, of whose death
Aegisthus is expecting to be told, but who is, in fact, waiting immediately behind the great door to slay him the moment he crosses the
threshold. Elektra makes uncanny play of the role of torch-bearer to
the unsuspecting victim and dances round him with sinister obsequi-
ousness which disturbs and half-hypnotizes the weak-minded
Aegisthus. During this scene Elektra naturally indulges in the same
obscurities of double-talk which so confused Klytemnestra, and
accordingly the various metamorphoses of Elektra's theme Ex. 7 are
brought back in combination—Ex. 3 (in honeyed tones) and the rapid
semiquaver diminution Ex. 7 (a). Above this sinister composium the
violins add the sugary version of the once-anguished Ex. 30 in waltz-
rhythm which anticipates to a remarkable extent the idiom of *Der
Rosenkavalier*.[30] The worlds of the two operas are so far apart, and
Strauss caught the difference so successfully in his settings, that it is
curious to find a *rapprochement* between them occurring at a moment
such as this. To Strauss, however, the dance means the waltz, whether it

---

[30] The origin of this passage has already been seen in *Feuersnot* (see Ex. 28,
Chapter VII, above).

was the Nietzschean Superman, the demented Elektra at her moment of triumph, or the boorish Baron at the Viennese Court at the time of Maria Theresa. Aegisthus finally breaks loose from his uncanny torch-bearer and enters the house.

Immediately violence is let loose once more. His murder does not actually take place in full view of the audience as Strauss proposed, but with his head appearing at a window as he shouts uselessly for help. Again it is the tutor's theme, Ex. 39, which is in strongest evidence, and Orestes is shown only in respect of his descent from Agamemnon, whom he is avenging (Ex. 36). The basic Agamemnon theme Ex. 1 appears at the climax in answer to Aegisthus' 'Does no one hear me?' 'Agamemnon hears you,' shouts out Elektra as she rears herself to this supreme moment. The music sinks down to a growling version of the Recognition music (Ex. 37) as Elektra turns towards the house 'breathing fearfully'. There is a tremendous surge in the orchestra and a change into the bright key of E major as Chrysothemis and the women rush on again for the Final Scene. After the unrelieved tension and agony of all that has gone before, the mood is of intense and heart-rending jubilation.

II

Strauss found the scenario of the closing pages confusing, and indeed so they are in many respects. He wrote to Hofmannsthal in great perplexity.

> One thing more—I do not yet understand your stage directions at the end of the scene. Orestes is in the house—the house door, centre, is shut. On p. 88 Chrysothemis and her women have gone off left, into the house—yet on p. 91 they 'rush wildly out'—from where? left or centre? On p. 93 Chrysothemis comes running out—by what way? Through the yard door on the right? But why? Surely Orestes is in the middle of the house!

The difficulty arises because the action takes place in and around the house, but never in that part of the house which is presented on the stage. Hofmannsthal answered Strauss's questions with a very clear account of the action as he envisaged it, together with a plan of the whole palace, i.e. not merely the rear portion which is visible to the audience. The action in question concerns the fight to the death between the supporters of Orestes and the serving-men who remain true

to Aegisthus, followed by the beginning of the torments of Orestes at
the hands of the Furies. The battle is described in detail by Chrysothemis, but the fate of Orestes is only suggested by implication when
Chrysothemis calls desperately to him, hammering on the great doors,
after the collapse of Elektra in the closing bars of the opera. Strauss
showed a certain *naïveté* over this when he added in his letter to
Hofmannsthal, 'Why at the end does Chrysothemis knock at the house
door? Is it because it is shut?' Nevertheless some pre-knowledge of the
action is indeed necessary here for the climax of the drama to make its
full effect, as the stage is curiously empty, the women having rushed
off yet again, and the throngs of people being only suggested for a
short time by an offstage chorus shouting 'Orest'. Strauss evokes the
general atmosphere of excited confusion by a tremendous build-up in
the orchestra in which many of the motifs which have previously been
associated mainly with gloom and despair now appear in glowing
colours, bringing a surge of emotion through the sudden change from
despair and viciousness to undreamt-of, limitless happiness. Chrysothemis' theme, her call to Elektra, her motif of extreme anguish (Ex.
30) are all transformed; Orestes' Exx. 35 and 36 surge forward as the
unseen chorus bursts in with its paean of praise to the liberator, and at
the climax the theme of happiness from the Klytemnestra scene (Ex.
23) sweeps over the whole polytonal complex.

The remainder of the final scene consists of the last joyful duet
between Elektra and Chrysothemis (for which Strauss again persuaded
Hofmannsthal to produce some additional lines, though they caused
the poet considerable difficulty) and Elektra's Maenad-like death dance.
As the one grows out of the other, they are based on common material
and constitute the Finale of the symphonic poem in which the relevant
motifs are welded together into a culminating synthesis of the whole
work. This supreme moment was anticipated in the closing section of
Elektra's solo scene near the beginning of the opera, a formally satisfying point of structure implicit in Hofmannsthal's poem which is typical
of the way in which the work was so ideal for Strauss's purpose. The
basic of the music, is accordingly Ex. 13, though the figure ⌐ a ¬ is now
replaced by the Recognition theme (Ex. 37), the huge span of the
'fulfilment' melody (Ex. 38), and the great song of the Royal Children
(Ex. 12).

Chrysothemis leaves Elektra performing her grotesque dance, returning later to find her still stumping about like a mad woman. She

calls to her, but fails to interrupt the dreadful exhibition. In the background one catches a brief glimpse of crowds, of faces with torches, but these disappear, and at the moment when Elektra reaches the climax of her dance and falls dead Chrysothemis is alone with her. The climax is brilliantly organized; the chordal motif of Elektra's triumph (Ex. 27) appears in the brass, but fails to reach the last shining chord. Instead, the motif of Elektra's hatred (Ex. 3) and the towering octave figure of Agamemnon himself (Ex. 11) are hammered out simultaneously to the accompaniment of a tam-tam *rubbed* with a metal triangle-beater, 'so as to produce a fearful clamorous howling'.[31] Elektra then remains poised for three bars on a high E flat and collapses to a deep chord of E flat minor on the brass. Four times the great Agamemnon themes (Exx. 1 and 11) peal out fortissimo, but the brass chords remain as still as Elektra's body. In the moment of death she has lost her own identity and the final triumph and vindication remain his alone. In vain Chrysothemis beats desperately on the house doors and calls for Orestes. His drama with the Furies has already begun elsewhere. Here nothing remains but the dominating spirit of the dead king and the lifeless body of the daughter whose uncompromising loyalty to him led her to madness and death. The opera ends with four mighty statements of Ex. 1, a huge chord of C major, and two harsh, rapid chords of E flat minor and C major on full brass and strings.

12

It has already been said earlier that in Greek mythology Elektra does not die demented, but survives to marry Orestes' friend Pylades; similarly the depraved appearance of Klytemnestra is a creation of Hofmannsthal's. Thus despite its origin in Greek mythology *Elektra* is akin to *Salome* as a member of a great line of romantic dramas centering around horrific heroines. The Greeks provided ample scope, of course, in figures like Medea, but the romantic mind piled sordidness on the agony until depraved figures like Wedekind's Lulu (used by Berg for his last opera) were reached. Strauss, however, made no further attempts to follow the movement. For all their viciousness there is strength and nobility in his heroines of the decadent school, and the psychological study of their mental disintegration is accordingly the more fascinating. But now Strauss made a complete volte-face in his

[31] Strauss first discovered this effect in *Macbeth* (see above, p. 61).

choice of subjects, abandoning these pathological studies in human behaviour never to return to them, though he was to write no less than eleven more operas.

Apart from its subject-matter, *Elektra* represents the farthest point for its composer both in his experimentalism with extreme musical techniques and indeed in his development of the symphonic poem. It should be remembered that Stravinsky had not yet written *L'Oiseau de Feu*, Bartók had only just completed his earliest orchestral works, such as the two orchestral Suites and the Portraits op. 5, and Hindemith was still a schoolboy. Only Schönberg was forging new paths for himself and for music in complete isolation, but as yet wholly ignored and largely unperformed. Although Schönberg's chief devotion was to Mahler, whom he revered to the verge of idolatry, his gratitude to Strauss, who on the strength of the Gurrelieder had greatly improved his position in the musical world,[32] was also coupled with admiration. If *Verklärte Nacht*, as we have seen, has much in common with *Guntram* in its treatment of post-Tristanesque harmony and melodic angularity, *Erwartung* is to some extent influenced directly by the more extremist sections of *Elektra*, which preceded it by only two years, although Schönberg had to wait some fourteen years before his work reached the public ear.

From now on, however, Strauss retreated gradually towards greater lyricism in his cultivation of a truly operatic style after what he fondly imagined to be the example of Mozart. *Salome* and *Elektra* both play within the two-hour margin, yet on account of their strenuousness to performers and audience alike they are rarely coupled with any curtain-raiser. Strauss was to write one-act operas again (*Daphne* and *Friedenstag*), but he never again used a symphonic poem technique or concentration comparable with these two earlier monumental works.

In the matter of orchestration, too, *Elektra* represents a climax in Strauss's output. His colouristic imagination was in full swing, and certainly he had given himself every opportunity. *Elektra* was written for an orchestra of well over a hundred musicians,[33] the largest by far that he had yet employed. Not only does the heckelphon appear again, the bass trumpet (for the first time since *Guntram*), eight horns, the

---

[32] See above, p. 114 (footnote).

[33] Sir Thomas Beecham tells an excellent anecdote about an irate gentleman who wrote to him complaining that he could only count ninety-eight musicians in the pit of Covent Garden instead of the prescribed one hundred and eleven.

second quartet doubling Wagner tubas, and the array of clarinets both B flat and A used together and in contrast, but for the first time Strauss resurrects an instrument henceforward to be a favourite member of his wind band—the basset horn. There are two basset horns in *Elektra* and Strauss allocates them a vital and elaborate part in the composition of the orchestral texture.[34] As for the strings, Strauss divides his violins and violas in an unprecedented manner. By instructing six of his violins to double on the viola, he gets a proportion of twenty-four violins to eighteen violas. These groups he divides into firsts, seconds and thirds, each subdivision containing eight and six players respectively. The unusual arrangement enabled him to get a wide range of effects both in the distribution of the complex polyphony and in the layout of the parallel chord progressions. On two occasions, however, during the Orestes and closing scenes, the first group of six violas return to their violins and so restore the conventional balance of sixteen first and fourteen second violins written on two staves, though frequently subdivided into firsts, seconds, thirds and fourths. This reliance upon the versatility of the string department has been known to prove embarrassing to opera orchestras whose violinists do not happen to be experienced viola players.

After these extravagances of orchestral virtuosity, interesting and highly professional as they always were, he gradually turned away from the employment of ever larger forces in the theatre pit. In *Josephslegende* and *Die Frau ohne Schatten*, as we shall see, he still used very large forces, but in the former he had no voices to accompany, while in the second he was far more discreet and sympathetic in his use for the full instrumentation at his disposal, and this new regard for the singers grew increasingly into a philosophy with advancing age. Such discretion was not to be achieved without a corresponding loss of inspiration, but at present he was still at the very height of his powers, and his first attempt in the realm of truly lyrical opera brought him a success before which even those of his tone poems took second place. For to a large majority of music-lovers Strauss will always be primarily the composer of *Der Rosenkavalier*.

[34] Strauss notates his basset horns oddly, using at times the bass clef, which he writes a fourth below, instead of a fifth above, actual pitch as in the old notation of the French horn. Although Strauss probably found the device in Mozart's Masonic Funeral Music, he clearly considered it unsatisfactory, for he never again used it after *Elektra*.

CHAPTER IX

THE CROWNING SUCCESS

U P to this time Strauss had looked to a different author for the libretto of each new stage work. But when he was only half-way through his setting of *Elektra* he wrote to Hofmannsthal complimenting him on being a born librettist. This glowing praise sprang from the additional lines which the poet had supplied for the Recognition Scene, and it is clear that Strauss's enthusiasm arose through Hofmannsthal's outstanding success in rethinking and redrafting his existing text in accordance with the exigencies of the musician. Hofmannsthal was clearly gratified by Strauss's adulation, but was shrewd enough to be able to weigh up the *arrière-pensée* behind his words. The truth is that Strauss already saw in Hofmannsthal an acquiescent collaborator of catholic taste and knowledge who could be counted upon to supply him regularly with the wide variety of subject-matter he needed for the string of theatrical works which he already knew would henceforth form the backbone of his future output. At the same time Hofmannsthal was prone to putting forward ideas and philosophical suggestions, pointing to an independence which often proved inconvenient. In fact, there was here a fundamental conflict which showed itself right at the beginning and persisted between the two men until the day of Hofmannsthal's death in 1929. Many times the collaboration came to the brink of disaster, but was saved by the realization on the part of both men of their essential suitability for each other and the knowledge that out of profound disagreement something entirely new and acceptable to both was sure to arise.

Already from these very early days there seems to have been no doubt in Strauss's mind that he would be looking no further for his librettist for the next opera, even though the actual work was still hidden beneath various disputes. *Semiramis* was always a possibility, but it was too heavy and conventional to be accepted without considering alternatives. Besides it was really a comedy that Strauss was looking for, and there did seem to be something of the kind on Hofmannsthal's stocks if only the poet could be persuaded to be reasonably accommodating. Unfortunately Hofmannsthal proved oddly obstinate in spite of Strauss's flattery. He wanted to work the piece out on his own and even present it in the theatre as a play in the same way as *Elektra*, promising to make the necessary adaptations afterwards for operatic purposes. But this no longer suited Strauss. What he had himself chosen on account of unusual suitability could not necessarily be regarded as precedent. Yet the projected comedy attracted him and he pressed Hofmannsthal repeatedly to make this their next joint endeavour. Entitled *Christinas Heimreise* it was to be based on Casanova's exploits, in an active style not far removed from Beaumarchais. Strauss's arguments were plausible if selfish: it would be against his interests for the comedy to appear in the theatre before the first performance of the opera; if the dialogue were first drafted for a spoken comedy it might be too broken up and at the same time too philosophical for musical treatment; in any case the whole subject was too slender to stand alone (this was splendidly subjective reasoning) and would be pure substance for a libretto which, if worked up the wrong way, might fail on its own ground and so be lost to him, Strauss, as well. For a time Hofmannsthal persevered with the Casanova comedy, making many tempting suggestions as to the adaptation of the work for operatic purposes. He then suddenly wrote saying that he had successfully offered it to Reinhardt after all. Nevertheless all was not lost, for Hofmannsthal had undoubtedly learnt much about Strauss's needs and ways, so that when less than a month later he was able to write again with something positive to propose he knew that he was on fertile ground.

The train of thought which had started when he likened his Casanova to Beaumarchais's *Figaro* had led Hofmannsthal to consider the parallel between himself and Strauss with Da Ponte and Mozart. From the problems which arose when Da Ponte adapted Beaumarchais came the consideration of the psychological aspect of Figaro, Susanna,

Cherubino, and the Countess, and then the existence of these well-known personages as type-characters. From this point it was a short step for Hofmannsthal to look around for a vehicle in which he might cast such figures for Strauss's purpose corresponding broadly to these types. His attention was drawn naturally to other Parisian authors and playwrights, whether contemporaries of Beaumarchais, as, for example, Louvet de Couvray, or earlier, such as the great Molière himself. With these examples before him and the basic characters taking root in his mind, he soon found the action shaping itself, 'almost without one noticing it', and in February 1909, during a brief stay at Weimar as the guest of Count Harry Kessler, he sketched out the following rough scenario:

> I.   The house of Geronte. Geronte is awaiting the arrival of a son-in-law-to-be of good country noble blood. Sophie with the pretty Faublas tells of her forthcoming marriage. She is astonished that he is troubled by it. Arrival of Pourceaugnac and elderly aunts, animals and wonderful luggage (marriage bed.) He summons the Intriguers. Marquise Night-time rendez-vous with Faublas, over which Faublas rejoices but not entirely without reservation. Sophie begs for rescue. The Intriguers.
>
> II.   Bedroom of the Marquise. Night of Love. Morning. Gratitude. Pourceaugnac announced. Faublas remains in disguise. So much like Faublas: yes, all natural children of the noble lady. Hairdresser, servants etc. imposing upon Pourceaugnac. They go away. While the Marquise has her coiffure dressed, P. invites the chambermaid to supper. P. stingy (detailed arrangements where the supper is to be). P. goes away. The Intriguer comes and shows how it should be done.
>
> III.   The room at the inn. Rehearsal of the pantomime. Faublas's boots under his dress. The supper; arrest; Geronte compromised before the Court. The Marquise appears. Geronte wants to go into the bridal chamber. The disguised Faublas reveals himself. Marquise confirms that he is a man.

Allowing for the reversal of the first two acts this presents a fairly close sketch to the more obvious features of the work we know as *Der Rosenkavalier*. The more subtle aspects of the story naturally only developed as the characters themselves came to life. The names Hofmannsthal used for this draft are lifted bodily from his French sources and throw an interesting light on the works he had been reading up for the purpose. Geronte,[1] like the well-known character in Puccini's *Manon Lescaut*, merely signifies an old man, but can nevertheless be found in Molière's *Les Fourberies de Scapin*. Pourceaugnac comes from the play of that name, also by Molière, while both Faublas and Sophie come from Louvet de Couvray.[2] Hofmannsthal himself was greatly taken by his new project, which had the additional stimulus of having been conceived during a lively discussion with his friend and host Count Kessler, to whom he afterwards dedicated the completed text. He at once sent off a brief note to Strauss:

> . . . but what is more important (I hope) for us both; I
> have during three peaceful afternoons worked out a com-
> plete and entirely new scenario for a grand opera (Spieloper)
> with downright comic figures and situations, and action
> as colourful and almost as obvious as a pantomime. There
> are opportunities for lyrical passages, fun, humour and even
> for a short ballet. I find the scenario entrancing and Count
> Kessler, with whom I have been discussing it, is thrilled with
> it. There are two main roles, one for a baritone and one for
> a young and graceful girl dressed up as a man, of the type of
> a Farrar or a Mary Garden.[3] The period: Vienna at the
> time of Maria Theresa. I shall be in Berlin from Sunday
> onwards. Shall we see each other?

Strauss replied with warmth and an historic meeting took place of which Hofmannsthal wrote much later that the effect on Strauss of his telling of the plot was as deeply engraved on his memory as if it had been only yesterday, even though he had taken no notes with him save only the list of characters scribbled on the back of a menu. Strauss immediately exclaimed: 'We'll go ahead with this. We'll perform it and I know down to the last syllable what will be said about it. They'll say that the general expectation had once more been shamefully dis-appointed; that this is by no means the comic opera which for decades

---

[1] From the French word meaning dotard.

[2] Not only some of the principal characters of the future *Rosenkavalier*, but several of the situations, come from Couvray's amusing novel *Les Amours du Che-valier de Faublas*. Even for example, the scene with the Commissary of Police can be found there, while the parallel of Sophie goes deeper than the mere appropria-tion of her name.

[3] These were two outstanding opera singers of the time who were not only justly famed for their artistry but for their appearance. It is interesting to realize that from the first the seventeen-year-old Octavian was planned to have an unbroken voice, an interesting biological point, especially in view of his indisputable masculine potency.

the German people have been longing for. Nevertheless let's keep up a
correspondence while we work on it. You go straight home and send
Act I as soon as you can.'

That Strauss could only see the impending work as the comic opera
awaited with yearning by the entire population of Germany but which
would be totally damned by the critics was a piece of unwarrantable
bitterness combined with the composer's characteristic sense of self-
importance. However, this attitude had no effect upon his artistic
judgement when applied to the task ahead and the collaboration which
followed was amongst the most fruitful which has ever existed in the
field of opera. So attractive was the new scheme that Strauss readily
forgave Hofmannsthal his betrayal over *Christinas Heimreise* and was
even able to write six months later congratulating the poet over his
success with it on the Viennese stage. For his part Hofmannsthal worked
at extraordinary speed and only a month later had the greater part of
Act I ready to read to Strauss. He had already a good idea of the
proposed total duration of the work: 'Two-and-a-half hours, about half
the length of *Die Meistersinger*.' This was a sanguine hope; little did he
dream that by the time it was finished it was to grow to nearly half as
long again. Nor could he foresee that the farce-like pantomime, as he
insisted on describing it, would evolve into a drama in which something infinitely deeper would surround the initial comic situations.
There is a curious parallel with *Die Meistersinger* in the way in which
the broadening of the original scheme was accompanied by the un-
planned emergence of a nobly human central figure, the pathos of
whose personal tragedy comes to enrich the entire dramatic conception; Hans Sachs and the Marschallin have indeed much in common.

2

There seem to have been few problems over the creation of Act I. Its
overall ternary form, the love scenes of the beginning and end enclosing
the appearance of the Baron and the complicated Levée, presented
themselves to Hofmannsthal's mind as soon as he came seriously to
concentrate on the details of the story, as, in fact, did the substitution of
the middle Act of the sketch for the original opening. As soon as this
reversal was established and the general shape clear to the poet, the first
draft followed in a matter of weeks. The first scene was in Strauss's
hands by mid-April and the remainder followed within a fortnight.

Strauss was immensely excited by it and set to work on the opening duet without delay. Hofmannsthal was naturally greatly encouraged by the composer's enthusiasm, but warned him that he might not find it all as congenial as the purely lyrical beginning. Such to some extent proved to be the case, Strauss writing that he was finding some difficulty in putting the middle part into shape, though adding with naïve self-confidence that 'he would manage all right, as he had the whole summer before him'. He also added that he wished he had got to the closing scene of the Act, which he found ravishing. This throws an interesting light on his method of work, which was to take the scenes in strict rotation with a view, as he put it, to preserving the symphonic unity. He was certainly incorporating his symphonic style into the predominantly lyrical quality to a considerable extent, and some sections have the exact style of movements from a symphony. The scene of the Baron's boasting in Act I, for instance, forms almost a detachable Scherzo, and one is not surprised to find that Strauss composed it purely according to his musical instinct and when it was finished had to ask Hofmannsthal for some twenty more lines to go with his preconceived symphonic scheme, ending with a concerted trio for the three voices for which Hofmannsthal had not catered at all, nor, with his lack of experience in working specifically for music, anticipated the need.

But it was not only in respect of lines Strauss needed that he had suggestions to make. His sense of the theatre had developed enormously during his work on *Feuersnot*, *Salome*, and *Elektra*, and his proposals were very well worthy of consideration. This was fortunate, because when it came to putting Act II into shape it was by no means such plain sailing. Hofmannsthal's proposed draft of the action had proceeded little farther than the original scheme of the Weimar scenario and entirely lacked climax. For the first time since work on the opera had begun Strauss wrote a long letter to Hofmannsthal complaining that the poet's sense of structure was at fault. In this he was absolutely right, and it stands much to Hofmannsthal's credit that he realized it immediately and followed Strauss's suggested alterations down to the smallest details. For Strauss had the insight and sense of the theatre to put his criticisms into a most constructive form, and it is no exaggeration to say that the shape of Act II from the entrance of the Baron up to the final waltz scene is entirely according to an alternative scenario outlined by the composer to the librettist in a letter from Mürren on

9th July 1909. This contains the whole crowd scene and the duel between Octavian and Ochs exactly as we have it; moreover, the conception of Ochs's wounding at the hands of Octavian gave rise to the idea of Ochs keeping his assignment with the supposed Mariandel in Act III with his arm in a sling, another comic touch which Strauss foresaw. The letter, drastic as it was, was couched in the most friendly terms and Hofmannsthal was very courteous in his replies. A lively interchange of letters followed, in all of which the concrete proposals came from Strauss. At the end Hofmannsthal openly acknowledged his indebtedness to the composer:

> I see that it is all far more purely theatrical and very much better than the earlier version and I am very grateful to you for the energetic way in which you have tackled it. . . . I hope you are now pleased with Act II, because you have chiefly yourself to thank. This one experience has taught me a fundamental lesson in writing dramatically for music which I shall not forget.

Strauss in his turn, anxious lest he might have offended his new-found colleague, wrote a rather touching letter:

> Please don't allow yourself to be discouraged by my criticism; I can only go on my own reactions, but nothing stimulates my ambition and creative powers so much as adverse criticism from someone whose opinion I respect. My criticism should spur you on, not discourage you. I want to get the best out of you I can!

3

By the middle of September Hofmannsthal had sent Strauss all the lines he needed in order to complete Act II. He then withdrew to a retreat below the Bavarian Alps in order to devote himself to completing *Christinas Heimreise*. With a certain degree of wishful thinking, and believing that Strauss had enough to occupy him virtually indefinitely, he persuaded himself that a gap of a few months in his work on *Ochs von Lerchenau*, as the opera was to be called, 'would only have the effect of maturing and enriching it'. He said significantly that Act III must be the best of all, 'being both gay and full of feeling, while it may soar even further into the upper regions of pathos in the character of the Marschallin'. This is the first suggestion either that the comedy might be something rather more than a burlesque, or that the Marschallin could develop into a personality of primary importance. Act III proved to be a turning-point in the development both of the Marschallin's tragic renunciation and of the deepening conception of the whole work in the minds of its authors.

Hofmannsthal was thus clearly right in the maturing effect of a rest before embarking upon Act III, but he entirely underestimated the speed of Strauss's inspiration when it was at white heat. The composition of the closing scene of Act II was already complete as Hofmannsthal was writing the last textual revisions before disappearing into the mountains. ('The last passages of the second Act are all ready and composed; I really believe this Finale has turned out a hit of the first order. "I am pleased with myself!"[4]') Strauss then proceeded without the slightest pause to the orchestration of what he had completed to date, so that early the following spring Hofmannsthal was shocked to receive a note saying that the composer was waiting with painful anxiety for Act III, as the full score of Act II was already in the press. Well might he answer: 'I am startled to see you write that you are waiting painfully. In the first place I had no idea you were already at home and in peace and quiet, as I keep reading about you being here, there, and everywhere.' There was considerable reason on his side here. Strauss's activities as conductor had not yet abated to any appreciable extent, and he was still at least nominally in charge of the Berlin Opera, a post which he did not relinquish until the following November. He travelled everywhere, moreover, conducting his own works (*Elektra* in London and Prague, festivals of his works in Frankfurt and Munich), and it seems astonishing that he found time to return to the idyllic calm of his beautiful villa at Garmisch to pen the very notes, let alone find inspiration for the hundreds of first-class ideas which abound in *Der Rosenkavalier*. Hofmannsthal was also able, however, to protest that Strauss had by now received the Supper scene and the Police Inquiry and could surely be getting on with these. But the truth was that the latter failed to stir Strauss's imagination, and he acknowledged to the last that this was his weakest passage. He had hoped to have the more lyrical ending in front of him before starting to compose, so as to digest the whole shape of the Act. However, what he had received proved that Hofmannsthal was fully at work once more and he applied himself

[4] This is a quotation twisted slightly from a remark made by Ochs during the scene which Strauss had just finished composing.

to setting the beginning, trusting the poet to produce the remainder before long. Unfortunately, although it did indeed arrive at the beginning of May, it proved to be clumsy, and Strauss, writing more bluntly than ever before, sent it straight back. In Strauss's defence, if he was more curt than courteous, he was naturally very depressed owing to the death of his mother a few days earlier, on 16th May 1910. She had outlived her husband, old Franz Strauss, by only five years and the composer felt her loss very deeply.

Yet even now Strauss was able to put his criticisms into practical form and enclosed a draft alternative script which Hofmannsthal, as the man of letters, was to improve in literary style as far as possible, but should keep to in all main essentials. As with Act II, Hofmannsthal again fully agreed with Strauss's proposals, which were not merely more suitable for musical treatment, but actually more effective and well knit theatrically. Where he went wrong was in mere details, and here with his greater experience and knowledge Hofmannsthal was able to correct and supplement Strauss's sure instinct:

> The way in which Sophie blurts out her longing to be Octavian's bride is too vulgar—the Marschallin would shudder at it; for Sophie and the Marschallin both to sink into chairs on either side of the stage at the end would be in excellent keeping with the conventional burlesque idiom, but ignores the difference in rank between the two women. Sophie must remain standing defiantly while the Marschallin sits sorrowfully on the right. . . .

and so on. But the work had long ceased to be in any such 'conventional burlesque idiom' and the profound implications of the closing scene still occupied the two collaborators for some little time to come.

Hofmannsthal was now realizing more and more the importance of the Marschallin, though he hid what he regarded as a weakness on his part under the pretext that the women in the audience would have an especial sympathy for her. Even so, he was anxious that 'the ending should not make us too sorry for the Marschallin', and he was still extremely apprehensive over the soft ends to Acts I and III, in which her personality blossoms, and repeatedly exhorted Strauss to cut down the length of these Finales. Even after he had delivered the completed libretto to the delighted composer saying that he had enjoyed the work so much that he was almost sorry to have to write the word 'Curtain', he still had misgivings and read the play over to friends many times to see their reactions. Rightly or wrongly, and in any case deprived of the magic of Strauss's music, he felt the end tedious once the hurly-burly of Ochs's exit surrounded by waiters, screaming children, and miscellaneous crowds and minor characters has passed away. 'One can already hear the rushing of the curtain, everything is hurrying to the end. Any tiresomeness at this point (and three minutes could give rise to weariness and impatience) would be death to the success of the whole venture.' So, as much as six weeks after he had completed his part of the collaboration, Hofmannsthal put in the post a shortened version of the first part of the great closing Trio, insisting that Strauss base his composition on this 'definitive version'—otherwise he, Hofmannsthal, would disclaim all responsibility should the last Act fall flat.

With this dismal show of cold feet and lack of understanding of the requirements and possibilities of music, Strauss, with his magnificent setting of the closing pages already on paper, had no patience.

> Your letter [he wrote] I have naturally found somewhat difficult to swallow, but to put your mind at rest I can tell you that (1) I have already made several cuts in the ending on my own account, but that (2) neither you nor Herr S . . . can judge, at this time of day, just what the musical effect of the ending will be. That it is feeble when read aloud is clear. But you can leave it to me with a quiet mind to know how it is just towards the end that a musician, when something special has occurred to him, can get his best and loftiest inspiration. I have all but finished and believe I find the last third the most brilliantly successful. . . . I am pleased to give you a written guarantee over the end of the work after the exit of the Baron, if you will take over the guarantee for the other parts.

Despite this justifiably forceful expression of confidence, Hofmannsthal printed his truncated revision in the published libretto, which shows an interesting divergence from the score of the opera at this passage.

By now it had become plain that Ochs had ceased to be the central figure and the name of the opera was changed by mutual consent from *Ochs von Lerchenau* to *Der Rosenkavalier*. Simultaneously we find Hofmannsthal preaching to Strauss the central significance of the Marschallin as if it has been in his mind all along.

> For true charm of expression as also for the stronger appeal of personality it is to the Marschallin that we should

look. The fact that Quinquin[5] during this tangled double adventure falls for the very first young thing he sees is just the point which gives unity to the whole, and holds the two sides of the action together. Meanwhile the Marschallin remains the dominating womanly figure, with Ochs and Quinquin on either side—against which principal characters Sophie certainly stands a step or so in the rear.

So the 'Pantomime with opportunities even for a short ballet' turned into the gay, cheerful, but profoundly psychological drama, the final vestiges of the earlier conception vanishing as Strauss rejected Hofmannsthal's proposal that the work be subtitled a 'Burlesque opera' on the grounds that this would have the merit of restoring some of the colour which the original and farcical *Ochs von Lerchenau* would have supplied. In spite of the considerable offence which Hofmannsthal took in this question of the heading of the work, Strauss forced the issue and the opera was finally published according to his insistent demands, under the dignified title of '*Der Rosenkavalier*, Comedy for Music in three Acts by Hugo von Hofmannsthal: music by Richard Strauss'.

4

It is not to be imagined that Strauss's mind was concentrated solely on composition during the last few months. As soon as Act III showed signs of flowering, the business man in Strauss asserted himself and he entered into negotiations with Count Seebach, the Intendant of the Dresden Court Theatre, with a view to getting the best terms he could for the work, which he saw clearly was going to be a tremendous success. So sure of himself was he that he nearly overplayed his hand, for he intended, without even giving exclusivity of production rights, to bind the Dresden Theatre to retain his earlier operas in the repertoire. Such extravagant demands naturally outraged Seebach, who, after paying Strauss the courtesy of a personal visit in Garmisch, finally took the step of exposing what he regarded as Strauss's unreasonable demands in an open letter to the Press. Strauss replied in kind and also wrote a lengthy document to the editor of the *Allgemeine Musikzeitung*, the most important and influential paper dealing with the musical

[5] This endearing pet-name of Octavian, the Rose Cavalier himself, is said to have been taken by Hofmannsthal from real life—it belonged to a certain Count Esterhazy von Galantha, born in 1715.

world of the German-speaking countries, in which he presented his legal battle with Seebach as a blow struck for the entire company of German authors and composers. If a composer is unable to stand up for his own works and get the best terms he can without being denounced in this way, what future can there be for the rights of German musicians?

Seebach flatly refused at first to sign a contract containing such a condition and in this he was supported by the Stage Society. As a result Strauss was eventually obliged to accept a mere assurance on this point in a letter apart from the formal contract, which was not at all the same as his demand that for ten years the theatre might not contractually be allowed to perform the best-selling *Rosenkavalier* without including either *Salome* or *Elektra* in the current repertoire.

Nor was this the only incident in the preparations for the presenting of the new opera. During the early stages of the dispute, Seebach had also sent a letter to Strauss with other and more practical objections in the form of censorship of the more licentious passages in the text. These were resolved by a series of compromises in which the offending words appear either in textbook, vocal score or full score, but never in all three, Hofmannsthal producing milder versions which could be shown in the appropriate volume to the Mrs. Grundy of an Intendant if necessary. The deviations survive in the various texts to the present day and make amusing comparison. Some points of production were, however, acceded to by the two authors as merely sensible—for example, they agreed that Octavian and the Marschallin need not be shown actually sleeping together when the curtain rises, but could be out of bed. After all, the truth of the matter would already have been suggested by the music, and what shocked Seebach would also shock a proportion of the audience and set them against the work from the start. On the other hand, a reference to the cowardly Neapolitan General had been changed by Seebach's red pencil to a Russian.[6] This was nonsense, and besides there was no longer a kingdom of Naples to offend. However, such problems of inane censorship were naturally to follow the opera about for some time to come. Count Hülsen, the Intendant of the Berlin Opera, for example, insisted on revising the text himself before passing the work for performance in the capital. Strauss wrote reassuringly to Hofmannsthal that it would not be so bad; when Hülsen spoke of 'softening' and revising the text it was

[6] See below, p. 358.

only words and not to be taken seriously. But, in fact, Hülsen's ameliorations turned out to be substantial and quite laughable, and must have been very distressing to Hofmannsthal. Even so, after the troubles of *Salome* these were mere pinpricks and were soon disposed of, though until recently a large section of Ochs's *exposé* was regularly cut on grounds of indecency, despite the fact that the passage moves too fast for the words to be heard. (It is indeed still excised, together with a few short passages from Acts II and III, from the English translation of the libretto.)

With the settling of the legal problems the questions of performance became suddenly imminent. The choice of a designer gave Strauss and Hofmannsthal no problem; Alfred Roller, chief designer of the Vienna Opera, had been brought into the picture from a very early date and the agreement was concluded already in March 1910. Where trouble arose, however, was in the production. Having already made up his mind that the resident stage manager at Dresden, George Toller, was likely to prove too old-fashioned in his ideas to handle so novel and unconventional a comedy, in which the singers were really required to act, Strauss had even pressed Hofmannsthal to supply a detailed production book. It is scarcely surprising, therefore, that when Strauss went to the first orchestral stage rehearsal he decided on the spot that Toller was proving as inadequate as he had expected, and that immediate drastic action would need to be taken. Remembering that the great producer Max Reinhardt had once expressed a desire to work with him, Strauss approached him without a moment's thought as to possible repercussions, and was delighted when Reinhardt agreed to help put into effect the clear-cut ideas on the staging of the work already held by Strauss and Hofmannsthal. Unfortunately the first intimation which Toller received that Reinhardt had been approached was from reports in the newspapers. Strauss seems to have been oblivious of the tactlessness with which he had behaved and wrote to Schuch, the Dresden conductor who had given the first performances of all the operas since *Feuersnot*, for help in smoothing things over:

> I'm very sorry if the admirable Herr Toller, quite unprepared for anything of the sort, has now been shaken by the Reinhardt bomb and should feel aggrieved. The last thing I want is to hurt the feelings of Herr Toller, whom I value highly and to whom I am greatly indebted for his production of *Elektra*. I am unfortunately one of those men who

when it comes to artistic matters never allow personal
matters to stand in the way, so that I couldn't possibly
have foreseen that so intelligent a man as Toller would
not have been simply delighted to have been helped by a
Reinhardt. Just as even today I would be ready to learn like
a schoolboy from you or Mahler or anybody else without a
thought of being knocked off my pedestal. . . . There will
now be so much incendiary matter piled up in darling
Dresden against me and my poor *Rosenkavalier* that I had
better not be seen at all at the première. . . . It wouldn't be
much fun being stoned.

Seebach himself intervened in this contretemps, insisting that Reinhardt deliver all his dicta from the stalls, never setting foot on the stage.
Strauss was terrified that Reinhardt would withdraw under such an
impossible embargo, but to everyone's relief he agreed to do his best
with the help of the composer.

I myself went on the stage and tried in my own clumsy
way to show the singers as best I could how to play their
parts. After a while Reinhardt could be observed whispering
to Frau von Osten in a corner of the hall and then again
with Frl. Siems, Perron etc. The next day they came to
rehearsal transformed into fully fledged actors. Thereupon
Seebach graciously permitted Reinhardt to direct operations
on the stage instead of watching the rehearsal from the
stalls.

Nevertheless only Toller's name appeared as producer in the billing of
the first performance.

From the start Strauss had said that 'ordinary opera singers' would
not do for the unusually subtle nature of the new work. The part of
Ochs in particular needed the most scrupulous care in choosing a
singer not only with acting ability but with understanding, so that the
role should not degenerate into mere vulgar slapstick. 'Ochs must be a
countrified Don Juan-beau', he wrote in after years, 'of about thirty-
five years old, who is after all a nobleman (even though he has turned
half peasant) and who is capable of behaving properly in the salon of
the Marschallin without having to be thrown out by her servants after
five minutes. He is at heart a coarse and vulgar fellow, but must still
have a sufficiently presentable appearance to prevent Faninal from
recoiling at first sight.' The obvious choice for the creator of this crucial
role was Richard Mayr. Unfortunately Mayr was heavily committed

with the Vienna Opera and could not be released by Weingartner until a fortnight after the proposed date for the first performance. Hofmannsthal was in despair; the alternatives were Carl Perron, a fifty-three-year old singer, and Paul Bender, the resident bass of the Munich Opera House, in neither of whom he had any great confidence. Strauss wrote reassuringly that he fully agreed no merely *adequate* Ochs would do. On the other hand, all he could do was to restate the case and present Hofmannsthal with the power of veto if he and Reinhardt both agreed that Perron could not be brought up to the mark. Bender was fully prepared and could possibly be shared by Dresden and Munich, where Mottl was putting on the opera five days later. The chances of Mayr being released were very slender. Couldn't Hofmannsthal eavesdrop on the Munich rehearsal and get an impression of Bender's suitability? Perron was such a splendid artist, he would understand their reservations and sympathize. Strauss's belief in the readiness of his colleagues to be swept aside, enduring all loss of prestige with cheerful and understanding acquiescence, was sublime.

In the event Bender turned out to be by no means the Ochs Hofmannsthal had dreamed of. 'Well then,' he wrote to Strauss, 'if all Buffo basses must be tall and ascetic, and only Quinquins short and fat, I give up!' So they were obliged *faute de mieux* to fall back on Perron even though, as Hofmannsthal put it, 'what no author or Reinhardt could ever extract from Perron are exactly the all-important clown-like, Falstaffian, comfortable, laughable elements of the character. Act III will be death on wheels with a humourless almost spectral Ochs, instead of a jolly one. Such casting seems to me inconceivable. If only I had heard of it sooner. For eighteen months I have had nothing on my mind other than the paramount importance of getting just the right casting for *this* role above all others. . . .'

Nevertheless when it came to the *Generalprobe*[7] both poet and composer found themselves in an even greater embarrassment on Herr Perron's account, since this worthy gentleman, whether in truth or because he had sensed something of the qualms which the authors had over the quality of his performance, developed a sore throat. A contemporary journalist's account describes in amusing detail the appearance of Strauss on the stage, his face twitching with anxiety as he announces the indisposition of the chief male character. Because of a

---

[7] i.e. the public dress rehearsal which in Germany and Austria is as important an event as the real first performance. See above, p. 63, n.

heavy cold Herr Perron would only be able to mark the part, and the gentlemen of the Press were accordingly requested to be sympathetic. After Act I was successfully past amidst scenes of excited enthusiasm, Count Seebach was overheard telling Strauss and Hofmannsthal that Perron had now developed a temperature and that it was very unlikely that the rehearsal could be continued to the end. In fact, all was well, however, and there seems no doubt that Perron's efforts were appreciated as they may never have been under more favourable circumstances. The report states surprisingly that

> . . . although vocally he only marked his part, he gave as brilliant a performance histrionically as it is possible to imagine [!]. Reinhardt kept calling out 'Splendid! Magnificent!' . . . Even Richard Strauss, whose eyes were nervously shifting from one person to another, was quite unable to conceal a smile of pleasure.' Altogether it seems to have been a very happy occasion, the entire stalls swaying from side to side in time with the waltz from Act II, and Strauss coming on the stage again at the end amidst tumultuous applause, firstly to thank the orchestra and then to tell the public how the following day would bring a well-earned rest to the performers prior to the grand première, for which Herr Perron would, after a visit to the doctor, undoubtedly be able to sing again.

In due course Hofmannsthal and Strauss had their wish and Richard Mayr soon became the most famous Ochs ever to sing the role. But time has shown that the gradual awareness in Hofmannsthal's mind of the shift of importance to the Marschallin was well founded, and of all the great artists who have made their reputations in this most endearing and human of operas it is surely Lotte Lehmann who has reached the greatest heights and won the most hearts with her creation of the great lady who, Sachs-like, sacrifices to a younger rival the love she cannot banish but knows to be hopeless.[8]

[8] Roland Tenschert has shown with fascinating thoroughness that however much Hofmannsthal's conception may have stemmed from Figaro, the finished composition has far greater affinity with Meistersinger. In support of this theory he not only cites numerous instances of detail and turns of phrase, but also tabulates this most interesting side-by-side comparison of the parallel situations:

The resigned older person ....{ Sachs to Evchen
                                       { Marschallin to Octavian

The Proud Father ....{ Pogner to Evchen
                                       { Faninal to Sophie

[Continued on next page]

5

In *Der Rosenkavalier,* for the first time since *Guntram,* Strauss began with
an extended orchestral movement. Strangely enough he did not call it
a Prelude (*Vorspiel*) as he did in the earlier instance, but an *Einleitung*
a term (signifying 'Introduction') which he had used for the far briefer
and more perfunctory opening of *Feuersnot.* The *Einleitung* of *Der
Rosenkavalier* cannot quite stand alone as a concert item, but is nevertheless a very considerable and symphonically worked piece of music
satisfying in construction and, after a series of stormy climaxes
reaching a point of beautiful and lyrical repose. It depicts one of
Strauss's most passionate love scenes, which is so impetuous that it is
just as well that the curtain still hides the action from view. It begins
with the two motifs, one strongly masculine, the other feminine, which
characterize two of the principal persons of the drama, young Octavian
Rofrano and Marie Thérèse, the Marschallin Princess von Werdenberg.

Ex. 1

Ex. 2

These two most striking themes are used in juxtaposition in a way
which derives straight from the love scene of *Feuersnot.* But the ideas
here are stronger and more direct, while an important feature of Ex. 2
is its opening in a totally foreign key, switching abruptly to the tonic by

[Footnote continued from p. 349]

Young Love .... { Walter and Evchen
                                        { Octavian and Sophie

The grotesque wooer .... { Beckmesser to Evchen
                                         { Ochs to Sophie

Art   } in prototype and distort- { Sachs and Beckmesser
Nobility } ing mirror .... { Marschallin (Octavian) and Ochs

means of a chromatic side-slip. This typically Straussian trick is used in this work more than ever before. By now, when he was in his forty-fourth year, Strauss had composed some half-dozen surging orchestral love scenes all essentially similar in character, and it is remarkable that so far from sounding stale and routine this further example of its species is in many ways the freshest of them all.

As in the case of so many of the nobility in eighteenth century Vienna, it is reasonable to suppose that the young Count Rofrano had his fair share of Italian blood, and Strauss may indeed have had this in mind when he gave such lightness and buoyancy to his love music.

Ex. 3

Ex. 4

The orchestral texture is full of trilling flutes and surging horns, all suggesting the youthful exuberance of the boy's first rapturous experiences of love. Twice the music boils over in passionate ecstasy and then at last subsides into a calmer and more lyrical mood. Throughout, Strauss seems to be conscious of an element of absurdity in the extravagance of Octavian's immature emotionalism, for he directs that the working up of the climaxes be played with parodied exaggeration, while the aftermath is punctuated by pathetic little sighs on strings and woodwind.

Ex. 5

[8a] Agitated and very extravagant in execution.

The figure ⌐ a ⌐ is described in the official handbook rather loosely as 'Love's resignation', but it is used during the opera in connexion with the Marschallin's melancholy over her fading youth and the inevitable loss of Octavian which this will bring with it.

As the *Einleitung* draws to a close a further pair of love themes bring a note of deepest tenderness associated with the Marschallin. Her feelings are of a maturity which will endure beyond the more demonstrative gestures of her boyish lover:

Ex. 6 a

Ex. 6 b

Ex. 6 b

[9] Strauss's use of this same formula for the Recognition music of *Elektra* has already been referred to in the chapter on that work (see above, p. 322). For purposes of direct comparison I quote the *Elektra* passage; the gaunter intervals and absence of rich harmonies naturally make for a more strenuous atmosphere. It is thus especially interesting to see to what different use Strauss was able to put such an idea in two consecutive but strongly contrasted works.

Ex. 6 c

Hofmannsthal's original intention was that at the rise of the curtain the Marschallin should still be lying in bed with Octavian kneeling beside her. The prudery of the times has produced the absurdity of both characters merely taking their ease on a sofa in most productions, but fortunately the stage directions have remained as planned. Strauss added some morning sunlight and the songs of birds which create an agreeable diversion to the score.

The opening of Act I consists of a lyrical love scene. There is now no hint of real passion; that has all taken place during the Introduction and is now spent. Octavian is indulging in a good deal of naïve introspection which the Marschallin views with quiet amusement. Although there is only a small difference in rank between them (Octavian being a Count, the Marschallin a Princess), their disparity of age gives rise to a noticeable sense of superiority on the part of the Marschallin. She answers his 'Du' (the familiar second person singular which the English language has long lost) with the slightly derogatory Viennese third person singular which can only be used to an inferior. It is even noticeable that in the printed text the boy is always Octavian while she remains the Marschallin and it is only when he addresses her in adoring tones as 'Marie Thérèse' that we learn her first name at all. Octavian is so young that his voice has not yet broken; we are not told his age at first, but in Act II Sophie, proud of her reading about the personalities of Viennese aristocracy from the equivalent of Debrett, produces it as seventeen years and two months. He is thus a little older than his prototype, Cherubino, and it seems stretching the point to have written the part for a mezzo-soprano. Nevertheless in Vienna such a late maturing seems to have been credible, for some twenty years later Strauss and Hofmannsthal created a similar masquerade in the character of Zdenka who, though in fact a girl, was passed off as a boy without arousing the least suspicion.

As for the age of the Marschallin, here we have a strong bone of contention. Her maternal treatment of Octavian together with her deep consciousness of approaching age cause her to be thought of generally as a woman of some forty-five or fifty. This was far from the author's idea, though Strauss may have overstated the case when he wrote: '. . . the Marschallin must be a beautiful young woman of not more than thirty-two years of age, who in a bad mood thinks of herself as an "old woman" by comparison with the seventeen-year-old Octavian, but in no way a David's Magdelena who, moreover, is also often presented as too old. Octavian is neither the first nor the last lover of the beautiful Marschallin.'

To Lotte Lehmann, Strauss had said that he saw the Marschallin as a woman of thirty-five—between ages. The essential point is that in the Vienna of those days, when a girl might come from a convent at fifteen and marry straight into a position of prestige, authority, and responsibility, thirty-five seemed far older than it does today.

Octavian's meditations on the nature of love take him towards the philosophical sphere of *Tristan* with a comparable preoccupation with such words as 'you' and 'and'. Strauss accordingly obliges with some sly hints at Wagner's chromatically rising love motif mixed in with the surging figures of Octavian's love song.[10]

Ex. 7

The varied 3's and 4's of the bar lengths, which change in their alternation from time to time in a most confusing way, cleverly suggest a reawakening of Octavian's excitement. But soon he calms down once more, overcome at the prospect of losing his very identity in the arms of his love and, much moved, the Marschallin tenderly embraces him to a restatement of Ex. 6 (a and b).

The bird song is heard once more proclaiming the arrival of the hated day (another Tristanesque allusion) which must bring their *entretien* to an end. In a rather childish way he draws the curtains as if

---

[10] Willi Schuh considers that both the text and music are deliberately contrived as a parody of the Love Duet from *Tristan* and refers also to Strauss's uses of the word 'parody' in the orchestral Introduction in support of this theory.

darkness in the room would delay the evil hour and, when the Marschallin gaily laughs at him, protests that he will allow no lackeys to enter nor runners with letters from foreign envoys. The Marschallin's loving mockery, the ringing of the little bells and the general atmosphere of gaiety are all caught with a lightness of touch which Strauss later sought in vain to recapture, in *Arabella*, for example. Even the heroic gesture of Ex. 1, as Octavian says he will let no one enter where he is lord and master, is handled with such delicacy that it is less with surprise than amusement one finds the would-be sentinel of such brave intentions ironically put to rout by the very least of the Marschallin's retinue, her little negro, who comes in to bring the breakfast tray.

<h1 style="text-align:center">6</h1>

The episode of the tiny negro servant is in itself a masterpiece of delicate orchestral inventiveness. It is built on two miniature march-like ideas which are worked together symphonically.

Ex. 8

Ex. 9

There is a short disturbance based on the Marschallin's Ex. 2 when she finds that her foolish lover has left his sword in full view, but otherwise the only additional motivic element is a chordal sequence to which the diminutive Islamic[11] boy bows himself out backwards.

[11] The Marschallin later refers to him as 'der Mahomet'. Thus his place of origin seems limited to a small part of North Africa, unless the term 'negro' is to be understood in the widest sense given it at the time.

Ex. 10

This group of shifting harmonies is palpably in direct line of descent
from the motif of Don Quixote (see Ex. 29, Chapter V), yet is used in a
way which characterizes to perfection the ingenuous bowing of the
little negro.

No sooner has he disappeared than the Marschallin turns on her
young lover, upbraiding him for his thoughtlessness and lack of breeding in leaving his sword in full view. The rapid passage-work which
accompanies her outburst contains references to her 'care' motif (Ex.
5 (a)) and also to a figure which occurs in various forms throughout the
work:

Ex. 11

In a similar way the phrase Ex. 9 (a) is used for its rhythmic value to
denote the scansion of the word 'Feldmarschall' and also as part of the
theme which opens Act II, Ex. 40. In all this apparent thematic connexion there is far less deliberate motivic cross-reference than is to be
found in the symphonic poem operas *Salome* and *Elektra*, in which
practically every apparently insignificant instrumental figuration can
be shown to be derived from one or other of the main motifs describing
the different persons or aspects of the drama. *Der Rosenkavalier*,
though it, too, still makes use of motifs and thematic allusions, uses
them more operatically in the lyric sense; more, that is to say, according
to the purely musical requirements of the moment. At one crucial
point, as will be seen towards the end of Act III, this gives rise to a
quite remarkable and magical use of a theme in unforeseeable and oddly
inappropriate circumstances.[12]

[12] See below, p. 409.

Octavian takes the chiding with bad grace, his Ex. 1 repeating itself with the petulant ill humour of a child. The Marschallin, however, with motherly tact and kindness, woos him out of his offended pride and they sit down together for breakfast. Like the episode of the little negro slave, the breakfast scene is an independent musical vignette. It is described in the score as a Tempo di Valse, but by comparison with the true waltzes which are such a feature of later parts of the opera it has far more the quality of a delicate period piece, a Mozartian Divertimento such as the Court musicians might have provided. It is set for a wind quartet of two clarinets and two bassoons with the lightest of accompaniments by strings and two horns. It is entirely independent thematically and an example both of the fertile originality of Strauss's invention and of his change of technique in operatic composition.

Before long, emotion gets the better of the lovers and there is an interpolation of the love music Ex. 4, though transformed into the prevailing $\frac{3}{4}$ measure. It is at this moment that we learn through Octavian's endearments not only the Marschallin's true name, but that she, too, has a pet name, Bichette.

With breakfast over, a new section begins. It is a more complicated piece of dramatic organization, bringing with it the first moment of real tension. Octavian boasts, in questionable taste, of his enviable situation in the absence of the Feldmarschall. The Marschallin, put out by this, taunts the boy with talk of having dreamt of her husband and, as Octavian rises to the bait, a quarrel ensues. The mock tragedy is followed by real drama; the disturbance in her antechamber which still rings in the Marschallin's ears turns out to be no memory but real, and she becomes quickly convinced that the Feldmarschall has in truth returned. This part of the section is dominated by the figure from

Ex. 9(a) to which reference has already been made: Ex. 12.

Out of this and a collection of rapid little turns and shapes Strauss builds a movement using a Beethoven-like symphonic technique which carries the rapid conversation of the text with skill and ingenuity. The Marschallin, in expressing her fear of her husband's return, recalls an earlier occasion when he came home unexpectedly. In the middle of her recollections she stops suddenly and Octavian is at once tormented by jealous curiosity. It is at moments like this that Hofmannsthal's insight into the character of the Marschallin shows its greatest depth.

R.S.–AA

Lotte Lehmann saw clearly into the poet's mind when she wrote:[13]

> Marie Thérèse is a soldier's wife. Knightliness, imper-
> turbability, eagerness for adventure course through her
> blood. The Field-Marshal has disappointed her as a hus-
> band and a lover, but never as a bold soldier, a strong and
> fearless knight of the sword. For these qualities she ad-
> mires him and is proud of him. This pride rings through
> her words: 'The Field Marshal can move very quickly' and
> the memory comes back to her of a day on which he
> almost surprised her in a similar situation . . . . *almost—*
> for she is still his wife. Had he really surprised her there
> would have been no possibility of any forgiveness. . . .
> She would like to tell Octavian about this, just as she would
> tell a trusted friend. But at the last moment she remains
> silent. Oh no, she couldn't tell this impetuous jealous boy
> about that! To tell him, who believes that he is the only
> one! Laughing, she buries her face in her hands and avoids
> his violent question as to what happened once, by saying
> 'Oh, be good, you don't have to know everything.'

The Marschallin brushes aside Octavian's absurd tantrums in her
genuine anxiety, and before long the two of them are rushing hither
and thither, frenziedly seeking a way out of the predicament in which
they find themselves. Octavian, remembering his sword this time, even
considers standing by the Marschallin, but as she impatiently ignores his
useless show of gallantry he breaks down, asking pathetically what will
become of her if they are surprised together by the Field-Marshal. As
he hides she puts on a bold front, exclaiming that she stands firm, unlike
some Neapolitan General, a rather obscure reference to the Austrian
invasion of Naples in 1744.

This is the corner-stone of the scene, as it now becomes increasingly
obvious that the intruder is not, after all, the Field-Marshal, but a
visitor who by the way in which the lackeys address him and by his
rough stupid voice she recognizes as the Baron Ochs von Lerchenau.
Immediately the thematic content of the music changes, and new
motivic fragments are introduced.

Ex. 13   Ex. 14

---

[13] The quotation is taken from her brilliant chapter on *Rosenkavalier* in *My Many Lives*, Boosey & Hawkes, 1948.

Ex. 13 reflects the Marschallin's gaiety of relief and, together with Ex. 14, the strains of which are the first gallumphing sounds we hear of the ungainly Baron, is organized symphonically, as were the other motifs earlier in the scene. But against them the second part of Octavian's theme (Ex. 1(b)) raises itself more and more menacingly, as if even now the boy is preparing to use force against the threatening intruder. As we shall soon see, Octavian is actually engrossed in an altogether different scheme, and it is probable that, as at other times during the opera, Strauss has used a musical idea more for its constructional value than for its motivic significance.[14]

The new-found joviality of mood on the part of the Marschallin sets in motion a string of waltz measures:

Ex. 15

The presence of the introductory bar of Octavian's Ex. 1 is due to the fact that the Marschallin is reminding him of how she was with him in her coach and never even opened Ochs's letter, announcing his impending visit, when it was handed to her. But a more important transformation of Ex. 1 into an extended waltz tune follows when Octavian suddenly appears in disguise as a chambermaid, having found a skirt, jacket, and kerchief in the alcove.

Ex. 16

Here for the first time is the complete version of Octavian's theme which later becomes so important as to relegate the original motif Ex. 1 to the comparatively slender role of opening phrase.

[14] The official guide by Alfred Schattmann actually cuts the knot by requoting the theme, now labelling it 'Ochs (ii)'!

Octavian addresses the Marschallin in broad Viennese and in the dry ingenuous tones of a country girl not used to city life and manners, an impersonation which is to stand him in unexpectedly good stead as the plot unfolds. Strauss's use of the Viennese Waltz to depict both gaiety on the part of the nobility and plebeian vulgarity has evoked a good deal of criticism over the years. Eric Blom wrote in 1930: 'It is characteristic of Strauss's carelessness in the matter of style that these waltz melodies are flagrant anachronisms. They belong to a time nearly a century later than the period of the play, the time of Lanner and of Strauss's famous namesake, from whom, it must be confessed, he succeeds most happily in claiming artistic descent, if only because he is so clever a musical impersonator.'

There is more than a grain of truth in this accusation, which, as we have seen, applies equally to Zarathustra's Waltz of the Superman. Certainly it is true that although the forerunners of the Waltz, the Deutsche and the Ländler, would certainly have reached Vienna by the middle 1700s, the true Viennese Waltz with its lighter character would not have been part of the folk-music tradition in the way in which Strauss introduces it, especially for a coffee-house band as in Act III. Yet however much it may have been characteristic of Strauss to ride roughshod over the verisimilitude of stylistic detail, the fact is that the idea of using the waltz came in the first place from Hofmannsthal. As far back as April 1909, when Strauss had only just begun the composition of Act I, Hofmannsthal wrote to him: '. . . for the last Act try and think of some old-fashioned Viennese Waltz, half sweet, half cheeky, which should pervade the whole Act.' No doubt Hofmannsthal was speaking loosely and it was 'old-fashioned' which was intended to be the operative word. It is not surprising, nevertheless, that this suggestion put ideas into Strauss's head, and his decision to make the Viennese Waltz an outstanding feature of the whole opera created nothing less than a *succès fou*. It has even been cited as an example of his genius that he makes the very anachronism of time and style into so positive and convincing a characteristic of the work.

7

The Marschallin is charmed by Octavian's presence of mind and wit in carrying out what is beyond question a brilliant idea for extricating himself without attracting attention. She has barely time for a last kiss and request that he should return dressed properly at the earliest opportunity, when the door is flung open and Baron Ochs brushes past the lackeys who try to restrain him. Musically there can rarely have been a more effective entry in all opera. The frenzied but now good-humoured haste of the two lovers builds up to a tremendous diminished seventh chord on the full wind and brass, which is resolved with magnificent aplomb into a comfortable C major by the Baron's first line: 'Naturally Her Highness will receive me'.

Ex. 17

He is no sooner in the room than Ochs notices the seeming chamber-maid who has bumped into him in his/her haste to escape and is now still trying to avoid unwelcome notice. Before even paying his first respects to the great lady into whose boudoir he has so unceremoniously forced his way, he begins making absurd and extravagant apologies to the pretty child whom fate has so unexpectedly and gratifyingly thrown in his way. Octavian for his part is amused beyond telling and finds it impossible to resist playing up to the ludicrous situation. The lackeys are profoundly uncomfortable to see their noble mistress so

ignored, and softly remind Ochs of her presence. He duly makes the
'French reverences' prescribed by Court etiquette and then loses no
time in trying to get his own back on the lackeys by complaining to
the Marschallin of their insolence in barring his way to her room. In
so doing he goes into a long tirade about how he is accustomed to
visiting another Princess (whose identity he disguises by the splendid
nom-de-plume of 'Brioche')[15] while she is in her bath.[16] In all this palaver
Ochs lapses into an easy parlando recitative which is offset by two new
themes, the one describing his vulgar familiarity when addressing
the Marschallin, the other his rapid asides as he comments to himself on
the delicious chambermaid or hazards brief remarks directly to her/him.

Ex. 18

Ex. 19

Ochs's attempt at rebuking the Marschallin's servants in front of her,
over her head even, shows such bad breeding that she interrupts him
sternly and asks him to excuse her on the grounds of a migraine from
which she has still not recovered. (The exact nature of the indisposition
is given in the musical setting by references to two of the love themes,
Exx. 6 and 7 (a).) But the boorish Baron has not forced his way in to
be deterred by such delicate hints and firmly settles down to his composite task of fulfilling his mission *vis-à-vis* the Marschallin and satisfying his interest in the supposed chambermaid. The Marschallin
spends her time in trying to get rid of Octavian, whom she now
addresses as 'Mariandel', and keeping abreast of Ochs's conversation,

15 Translated odiously in the English version by 'The Princess you wot of'.
16 For the Berlin production of the opera, whereas the bed was an embarrassment at the rise of the curtain, the reference to the still more *risqué* 'bath' at this
point proved almost insurmountable, the previously scorned 'bed' having to be
conceded as a disconcerting compromise.

piecing together the picture she would have had of his purpose in visiting her had she read his letter. For his part, Octavian is now thoroughly enjoying the situation and makes only half-hearted attempts to leave the room, the Baron preventing him each time by asking for some of the chocolate and biscuits which still remain from the breakfast brought by the little negro. This comical scene is kept alive musically by an alternation between a rather elaborate form of accompanied recitative and short development-like sections of relevant motifs such as Ochs's (Exx. 14, 17(a), 18 and 19) and the Marschallin's (Exx. 13 and 15 (a)), which latter mostly portray her surreptitious attempts at shooing the rascally Octavian away.

It gradually transpires that Ochs has become involved in an alliance with the young and pretty daughter of a very rich commoner who has just been ennobled and who is anxious to secure a connexion with the true aristocracy to which, for all his uncouthness, Baron Ochs irrevocably belongs. The name of the future bride, Faninal, enters the dialogue and Sophie's motif makes its first appearance:

Ex. 20

Ochs makes it perfectly clear that it is the girl's position as the only daughter and heir to the old and failing Faninal's vast wealth which attracts him, although he views her ravishing prettiness with some relish. He has come to the Marschallin for advice as to the most suitable bearer of the Silver Rose which according to Viennese custom must be presented on behalf of a member of the nobility to the lady of his esteem by a young and equally well-born ambassador.

In the hopes that he will the quicker take his leave, the Marschallin invites Ochs to supper the following evening, promising her proposals then. But Ochs is not yet finished by any means; he has some legal matters prior to the wedding for which he begs the services of the Marchallin's notary. An attempt on the Marschallin's part to send 'Mariandel' away to fetch the notary fails, but brings Ochs's infatuation out into the open. The music has changed back into a waltz rhythm and, to a new and haunting tune, Ochs comments on the sterling quality of the 'maid', who cannot possibly be allowed to mix with the rough and tumble of the other servants:

Ex. 21

The Major-domo now enters and occupies the Marschallin's attention, recounting the list of personnel who, in addition to the notary,
are waiting in the antechamber. The cadence to which he bows before
the Marschallin seems of little moment at first, though it has a curiously
memorable flavour, but it is later transformed into a position of the
very highest importance.

Ex. 22

Meanwhile the music, which has remained in waltz tempo, settles down
to the first of the waltzes which are specifically associated with the
Baron:

Ex. 23

Ochs has taken advantage of the Marschallin's momentary distraction
to invite Mariandel out to a tête-à-tête supper. But as the Major-domo
prepares to retire, the absurd scene is exposed beyond overlooking, and
the Marschallin cannot help laughing as she instructs the Major-domo
that the people in the antechamber be kept waiting a little longer. Even
Ochs is momentarily confused at being shown up so obviously, fearing
that he has gone too far, but soon recovers his good humour when to

[17] It is possible that the fact of this theme being melodically identical with the
opening of Ex. 5 is intentional as signifying the ceremony required in her position
by the ageing Marschallin. The whole opera, is, however, full of motivic similarities between themes and passages which can have no deliberate connexion but a
basic uniformity of style and invention.

his relief the Marschallin smilingly comments that for a bridegroom he shows remarkable alacrity in taking his pleasures where he finds them. His answer takes the form of an extended exposition of his amorous exploits which, as has already been discussed earlier (see p. 362 above), forms a complete and self-contained symphonic scherzo. This extended movement has always been one of the stumbling-blocks of the opera. In it Ochs recounts in some detail the different forms his amours take, according to the month of the year and the character of the various types he sets out to seduce. There would seem a certain perversity on Hofmannsthal's part that in a plot already bristling with *risqué* situations he should write so long an elaboration of the Baron's lewdness, which was bound to give rise to obstacles. Had it been integral to the plot one might understand its *raison d'être*, but in fact it holds up the action as well as presenting Strauss with a problem in setting, which the composer did not altogether solve. With so extensive a monologue to wade through (it runs to no less than eighty lines), instead of pruning it as he might reasonably have done, he makes the Baron gabble the words at such a rate that little of the wit contained in the text comes over the footlights. Thematically it is brilliantly worked out on a collection of small motifs of which Ex. 19 in particular, together with two new figures Exx. 24 and 25, forms the mainstay.

Ex. 24   Ex. 25

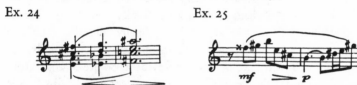

Two further melodic ideas provide lyrical contrast at either end of the episode, Ex. 27 being used for the closing trio which, as we have seen, Strauss caused Hofmannsthal to add.

Ex. 26

Ex. 27

Realizing that the effect of the whole was likely to prove too diffuse, Strauss picked out certain outstanding moments in the monologue for special attention and these remain the most interesting points as well as providing necessary climaxes, but to one of these Hofmannsthal took exception:

> One more thing [he wrote], please let me be quite frank; there is a detail in Ochs's aria which disturbs me terribly; that is the line 'muss halt ein Heu in der Nähe dabei sein'[18] which is only *thinkable*, musically as well as dramatically, in the sweetest of tones. That is to say, whispered as a coarse aside. As a sly, stupid familiarity for the Marschallin's ear, *whispered* with the hand in front of the mouth, but for God's sake not *bawled*! It pierced me right through to see the word 'Heu' shouted *ff*. I must beg and beg of you to change this, not of course just to please me but for the sake of the whole. How wonderfully Wagner uses subtle *nuances* in the declamation of such things.

The appeal, especially invoking the holy name of Wagner, was not in vain, and Strauss was able to mark a *diminuendo* to *piano* on the high sustained F to which Ochs sings the offending word, with infinitely more subtle effect. Yet this was not the end of the trouble, as this reference to tumbling girls in the hay was bound to cause raised eyebrows. Twice it was changed, 'Ein Heu' turning into 'kein Mensch' (i.e. 'there must be no one around') and finally 'Eine Frau' ('There must be a woman in the vicinity'—this presumably was passed by the blue pencil on the grounds of being self-evident) before Strauss finally managed to restore the original 'Heu' in both vocal and full scores.[19] For the even more proper-minded English-speaking countries, however, the passage was rendered with complete disregard of the original sense; 'but if she falls, she will do herself no harm' (which has the virtue of being wholly meaningless in the context) or, as in the translated textbook, entirely omitted together with the whole of Ochs's tirade. In actual fact it became the custom before very long to cut the whole

---

[18] 'There must be some hay in the vicinity.'

[19] Oddly enough the published complete correspondence between Strauss and Hofmannsthal confuses the issue, vacillating between the alternatives in a way which makes nonsense of the argument. From the versions of several letters printed in this collected edition it even appears as if 'eine Frau' was Hofmannsthal's original idea which Strauss changed to 'Heu', perhaps in order to be deliberately more outrageous (cf. the translated abridged correspondence (Knopff, New York, 1927), which differs in quite a number of important respects).

section and it is only in recent years that it has gradually been restored for certain special performances or recordings.

During the closing passage of the Scherzo a return is made to the development of the plot. Ochs actually gets to the point of asking for the services of 'Mariandel' as personal maid for his future bride, a splendid project which the Marschallin quickly sidetracks. Ochs further makes the comment that Mariandel seems to have good blood in her veins, a piece of shrewd perception which, seeing the amused approbation with which it is received, he follows up by telling the Marschallin how such 'natural' children of the aristocracy are to be found everywhere in attendance. He himself always keeps his own illegitimate son ('he has the stamp of a Lerchenau in his features') as his body-servant, and will introduce him later when he comes to bring the Silver Rose.

This has given the Marschallin an idea. With the Baron remaining at Court for some days, as seems likely, he is sure to meet Octavian dressed as himself. If his suspicions are to be allayed they were best anticipated by representing Mariandel as Octavian's bastard sister, whom she, the Marschallin, keeps under her personal protection. To carry out this deception successfully she will need to impress very firmly upon Ochs's mind the similarity between Octavian and Mariandel, and she accordingly calls for her own medallion of Octavian's features with the proposal that this young nobleman, second brother to the Marquis Rofrano, should serve the Baron as Rose-Cavalier. As she speaks to Ochs of Octavian there is a long and nostalgic statement of the waltz, Ex. 21, which accompanied Ochs's description of Mariandel as a 'Goldkind'.[20] This is strangely the last use of a particularly haunting melody which stresses the fact, though Ochs must never know it, of Mariandel and Octavian being the same person, but which seems also to contain a sadness in the Marschallin as if she realizes that there is a danger to herself in suggesting Octavian for the part of ambassador to Ochs's young bride. As Octavian goes to get the medallion he whispers 'Thérèse, take care!'—but she wisely says that she knows exactly what she is about.

The Marschallin presses the medallion on Ochs, who, after much careless inattention, at last falls into the carefully laid trap and comments on the extraordinary resemblance. Her plan complete, she now insists on Mariandel letting in the waiting mob and, despite the Baron's last feverish attempts to detain him, Octavian shouts in rough Viennese

[20] 'Child of gold'—i.e. 'darling'.

dialect through to the antechamber. As the crowd surges in, he then escapes through a little private door which he slams in Ochs's face, leaving him entangled with an old chambermaid who has just entered with a wash-basin.

8

The typically eighteenth-century levée scene is inspired to a great extent by Hogarth's *Marriage-à-la-Mode*. In the fourth picture of the series one can see many of the characters familiar to us in *Der Rosenkavalier*—the noble lady with her hairdresser, the singer with his attendant flautist (though in the opera the singer stands in deference to the Marschallin's rank), the scholar, even the little negro who is serving the chocolate, while in the first picture of Hogarth's series there is a passable suggestion of the Baron trying to bully the notary out of his rigid application of the law by means of the sheer weight of his lineage. There are differences, certainly—Hofmannsthal produced many new characters who would have undoubtedly been at the levée of a Viennese noblewoman, while the little negro, who may very well have been put in Hofmannsthal's mind by the picture, does not actually reappear in this scene. But the essentials are there and clearly prompted the amusing action which follows. The Marschallin at first retires with her old waiting-woman while the hairdressing table is moved into the centre of the stage. The scene has now quickly filled with a hotchpotch collection of assorted characters—a group of noble orphans, a milliner, a vendor of animals, etc., apart from the Marschallin's own cook, notary, Major-domo, and so forth. Strauss gives a suitably pathetic strain for the noble waifs to chant, borrowing from the opening scene of Massenet's *Werther* the device by which the children first shout their piece incorrectly and are then made to repeat it nicely and properly. Their several stanzas are separated by suitably coloured and varied interpolations for, in turn, the milliner and the animal vendor.[21]

Finally the Marschallin makes her entry from behind the screen and everyone bows (Ex. 22). Her first thought is to introduce the notary to the Baron and these two immediately cross over to one side and

---

[21] The animal vendor sings against a passage identical with little Franz Strauss's yells of delight in his bath from the *Sinfonia Domestica*. Since the reference is to monkeys and parrots there may possibly have been the jovial malice of a deliberate allusion.

engage in earnest discussion. An elderly scholar now advances armed with a huge folio, but is brushed aside rudely by an Italian intrigueur by the name of Valzacchi who tries vainly to interest the Marschallin in a scurrilous 'black newspaper' full of court scandals. This roguish character soon becomes of great importance to the action, but although his music, a rapid and rustling tarantella-like movement, is already typical, as yet it only anticipates the less striking of his themes (Exx. 30 (b) and 32 (b) below). Impatiently and with some anger the Marschallin waves him away as she presents the youngest waif with a bag of money and a kiss on the forehead.

At this point the hairdresser springs into action, followed by the singer with his flautist. This is a pure period-tableau and Strauss accordingly falls back on pastiche, writing a florid minuet with an elaborate flute part leading, by way of the formula quoted above as Ex. 11b, into a cruelly clever caricature of an Italian operatic tenor aria.[22]

The Baron's retinue now arrives, three incredibly strange and ungainly figures who seem to have come straight from working on a farm and who seem both ill at ease in formal attire and wholly out of place at court. One of these is a kind of gnome, while another is the bastard son of whom Ochs has been boasting to the Marschallin and who is expecting to be presented in due course. Their music is suitably grotesque as they galumph across the stage, fighting for seniority, tripping each other up and finally forming an awkward group around the Baron, their master, who is engaged in a heated dispute with the notary. The Lerchenaus are an impoverished family and Ochs sees in Faninal, his rich future father-in-law, the instrument by which the family fortunes may be restored. He has fixed on the law of the 'Morgengabe' (morning gift), normally made by the groom to the bride on the very morning after the wedding night, and has decided that the custom shall be reversed in his favour in view of his condescension in marrying a *nouveau riche*. His bride must give him as Morgengabe the old Lerchenau family castle and estates in their pristine privileged condition which his father once enjoyed. While he expounds this

[22] An amusing detail often missed in performance is the arrival of a footman splendidly dressed in rose, black and silver who enters and delivers a note to the Marschallin. She reads it and passes it to the hairdresser to cool his curling tongs which he has shown to be too hot. This is one of many such charming if complicated stage directions with which Hofmannsthal fills the score. Perhaps the note is from Octavian, who would have been concerned lest the Marschallin was worrying about him.

superb scheme to the flabbergasted lawyer, one of the melodic ideas connected with the marriage arrangements winds its way around the orchestra, eventually taking form as Ex. 28:

Ex. 28.

Such a reversal of legal procedure is unknown, however, and the wretched notary tries desperately to think of other ways by which the unscrupulous Baron can achieve his ends without actually using the 'Morgengabe'. The argument is momentarily halted by the Italian singer embarking on a second verse of his aria, this time in unison with the flute, who after his dazzling prelude has been oddly silent in the orchestral accompaniment during the first verse. But the matter of his 'Morgengabe' is still turning over in Ochs's head, as is shown by Ex. 28 which continues during the aria and with which it combines perfectly. The strain of keeping silence is at last too much for the notary and he begins to make his alternative suggestions quietly against the aria. Gradually the Baron loses his temper and shouts 'Als Morgengabe' so loudly that the musicians stop, petrified and confused. The Marschallin, out of humour at this atrocious behaviour, signs to the singer to kiss her hand and take his leave while she turns gloomily to the hairdresser, complaining that he has made an old woman of her today. Once more to quote Lotte Lehmann:

> To sing this phrase with the right expression is of the utmost importance. It would be wrong to say these words too forcefully, wrong to make this reproach too emphatic. Through these words must vibrate her whole helpless resignation disguised as wounded pride. She says them with restraint, quietly, softly, but with decision. With a gesture of suppressed anger she throws the mirror on the toilet table. She *plays* the injured one who is served without sufficient care, the lady who is annoyed by inexcusable neglect. . . .
> But within her heart she has realized that it is through no

[23] These apparent thematic relationships may or may not be conscious references with profound psychological implications (see footnote to p. 364), but see also p. 405 below.

fault of a *friseur* that she who was so radiant has changed into a tired and ageing woman. She knows this—she has the evidence before her, and her irritation is an escape, nothing more. The *friseur* plunges feverishly into trying to improve upon what he has already done well. But the Marschallin with nervous impatience dismisses all those present with a sharp and illhumoured command which is most unusual for her. She only says; 'All are dismissed', whereas usually she has a friendly word for everyone.

Instantly Valzacchi, disappointed at his lack of success with the Marschallin, sets to work upon the Baron, whom he has seen looking anxiously through the little private door in the hope of seeing Mariandel. Valzacchi presents himself as the model of discretion and introduces his niece Annina with whom he habitually works. He offers their services in the capacity of intriguants, private detectives, anything—wherever they can be of use, they are always at hand:

Ex. 29

This shows the Italians up in their true unsavoury colours and Strauss now presents them with all their thematic material fully formed.

Ex. 30

Ex. 31

Ex. 32

The motifs are worked together into a short symphonic set-piece, for which they are supremely suitable, and reappear with striking effect twice more during the opera. Ex. 29 acts as a kind of refrain and Strauss adds, a little inconsequentially, a last 'Wir sind da' to close the movement. Seeing their willingness to unravel any little personal problem, however delicate, Ochs broaches the question of Mariandel to the two Italians. Needless to say, they are nonplussed, having naturally never heard of her, but Valzacchi assures Ochs that Annina will ferret her out if she is anywhere to be found at all.

By now the crowd has largely dispersed and to the strains of the pompous theme of his first entrance (Ex. 17 (a)) Ochs seizes the opportunity of presenting Leopold, his illegitimate son, to the Marschallin,[24] who, with the echoes of Ochs's licentious behaviour ringing in her ears (Ex. 19 pianissimo in the woodwind), cannot help smiling gently. Leopold awkwardly offers her the leather case containing the Silver Rose, which she accepts without allowing Ochs to open it. She is impatient to be rid of him, and his last tiresome attempts at forcing her to call Mariandel irritate her. Fragments of Sophie's theme (Ex. 20) float in the background while against a throbbing bass the broad love theme Ex. 6b softly accompanies the Marschallin's last words to the Baron that Count Octavian will without question accede to her request that he act as Ochs's ambassador to the young bride. The Marschallin is greatly preoccupied now, and very quietly but with inflexible authority she dismisses Ochs so that he has no alternative but make the conventional reverences and withdraw. The feeling of a quiet coda which Strauss writes on Ex. 17 (a) is beautifully timed after so much bustle and confusion. It is at moments like this that his symphonic training was of especial value. The music has been continuous since the beginning of the opera for some three-quarters of an hour and we are about to embark on the most important part of the Act, the Marschallin's Monologue. The sense of repose in the music is just what is needed to put the listener into the more intimate frame of mind in order to follow and understand the melancholy in which the Marschallin, alone at last, finds herself. At first Ochs's Ex. 17 (a) continues as she meditates on the vileness with which such a boorish ruffian can find himself a pretty young wife with a substantial dowry and represent that it is he who

[24] It is here that Strauss in his excitement misread Hofmannsthal's punctuation and committed the splendid mistake of setting to music the stage direction 'diskret vertraulich' (with discreet secrecy). In the vocal score the words appeared in Ochs's part but in the full score the notes have been removed and the passage rewritten. This was not the only such occasion, Strauss making a similar slip when working on Die Aegyptische Helena.

is bestowing the favour. The music rises up to a climax as a sense of the injustice of it all exasperates her, but at last she shrugs her shoulders as she considers that she has no cause to concern herself; such is the way of the world.

The orchestration has been so light in this last passage as to border on chamber music and Strauss now heightens the feeling of intimacy by using, in fact, a chamber ensemble with no more strings than a solo quintet. The simplicity of style and setting is exquisite and must have intrigued Strauss himself, for he wrote his whole next stage work for a chamber orchestra maintaining the delicacy and intimacy of idiom for much of its length.[25]

There is an extended instrumental passage in quiet folk-like vein, not unlike the once-upon-a-time theme from *Till Eulenspiegel* and in the same key:

Ex. 33

A number of after-phrases follow, one of which becomes particularly significant during the Monologue, especially in altered diminution and during the last scene of the Act in augmentation:

Ex. 34

The Marschallin's thoughts have turned towards another young girl who, like Sophie Faninal, fresh from convent school, was thrust into an

[25] *Le Bourgeois Gentilhomme (Ariadne auf Naxos).*

R.S.–BB

unwelcome and cruel marriage with a rough, unloved, middle-aged nobleman. She looks back on life and wonders how she can be the same person as that little Resi who will soon be the venerable old Marschallin. ' . . . ou sont les neiges d'antan,' she says, quoting Villon (though Hofmannsthal might have been better advised to keep to the original French, as the German 'den Schnee vom vergangenen Jahr' is clumsy). There is a brilliant thumbnail sketch of the crowd all shouting and pointing as she, now an old woman, trundles past in her carriage. Then she stops short in her imaginings and asks, bewildered, how the dear God can ordain such things and then endow her with such a clear perception to watch the transformation taking place. The secret meaning of life lies before her—that one must bear these things (the oboe softly gives out her theme of resignation Ex. 5 (a)) and everything depends on *how* one manages to do so. On the word 'how' there is a chord punctuated by a bare octave on the harp, the only use of that instrument in the whole section, as indeed for some thirty pages of score before and fifteen after. The emphasis it gives, isolated in this way, is cf the greatest subtlety and fully in keeping with this profound setting of a deeply moving text.

9

Octavian suddenly bursts in on her musings, now fully dressed in morning clothes and riding boots. He sees she is depressed and tries to brighten her with protestations of love and reminders of the panic they have been through together, which has all ended happily. His love music (Ex. 7 (a)) alternates with her meditations (Ex. 5 (a) and 34 b), together with snatches of the music from the scene immediately after breakfast in which the Field-Marshal was discussed. Octavian now overwhelms the Marschallin with embraces, but she is no longer in the mood for unthinking love raptures, and as she gently turns from him the music changes into the Monologue theme, first in a new broad version and then subsiding on the clarinet in diminution (Ex. 34 b and c). As the 'Feldmarschall' rhythm (Ex. 12) pounds in the bass she considers what it would have meant if the intruder had been her husband—what it might still mean one day; it just so happened that it was not destined to be yet. The thought of her husband, of the iniquitous Ochs, of her ageing little by little, have all brought upon her the imminence of Octavian's own desertion of her. He finds it as hard to follow her thoughts when she begs him not to be as other men, as to understand how she finds his effusiveness too extravagant to be of lasting quality. All his love themes protest his sincerity, Exx. 1, 3, 4, 6 b, and 7 sweeping over each other in the passionate flow of eroticism which, nevertheless, lacks the spontaneity of the love music with which the opera opened. In addition a new idea enters as the Marschallin repulses him, calling him for the first time not Quinquin but Taverl, the diminutive of Octavian.

Ex. 35

The latter section of this pathetic theme soon acquires independence in an urgently repetitive form recalling *Tod und Verklärung* (see above, Chapter 3, Ex. 24) which permeates most of the remainder of the scene. Ex. 35 is combined with the big love melody Ex. 6 b in the first of three important passages which recur at the end of the opera, when the Marschallin's premonitions have been fulfilled and Octavian is deserting her for Sophie. The music then changes to a gentle ⁶₈ as the Marschallin philosophizes, still to the quietly meandering sounds of Ex. 35, which is now developed symphonically at length, together with Ex. 5. Her thoughts have passed through the need for courage to put behind oneself temporal things, on to the relentless march of Time itself, swift and inexorable. Octavian at first takes her strange talk to mean that she wants to be rid of him, but her earnestness gradually grips him as she insists that on the contrary it is he who will before long forsake her. At first he starts up angrily at the very idea, but gradually listens as she sings the wonderful aria 'Die Zeit, die ist ein sonderbar' Ding',[26] in which she describes how Time slips past unnoticed until suddenly one realizes by one's face in the mirror how it is flowing 'silently, like an hour glass'; how sometimes she rises in the middle of the night and stops the ticking of all her clocks. The soft chiming of the celeste and two harps playing harmonics is a magical centrepoint of a most moving aria.

At last the Marschallin seeks comfort in an all-wise Providence of whom Time, too, is a creation. This is too much for Octavian, who is no theologian; he tries instead to offer his own more sensual consolation, but again the Marschallin reiterates her conviction that he will soon leave her for a prettier and younger partner (a passing reference to Ex. 20

[26] 'Time, it is a curious thing.'

tells beyond all doubt who that prettier and younger person is to be).
A heated argument ensues, ending with an outburst of the Marschallin
containing the other two important passages which are brought back at
the supreme moment of renunciation in Act III.

Ex. 36

Heut'___ o-der Mor-gen·　o - - - der den ü - ber-nächsten Tag ²⁷

Ex. 37

['I will make it easy for us both]—one must be light of heart and hand, to hold
and to grasp, to hold and let go also. [Life punishes those who are not so and God
has no pity on them.']

This reference to God again evokes an outburst from Octavian and
this time the Marschallin kindly but firmly tells him that it is time for
him to go. She must attend church and she must visit dear old Uncle
Greifenklau who is lame and with whom she will eat, but later they may
perhaps meet in the Prater, where she will most likely go for a drive.
This enchanting section with its conjuring up of old Viennese life is
sung to a passage of such idyllic yet nostalgic beauty that it ranks
amongst those rare operatic moments which bring the smart of tears to
the eyes. Beginning with repetitions of the Marschallin's original theme
of resignation, (Ex. 5 (a)) it passes through a new idea in consecutive
thirds with characteristic Viennese glissandos. This passes on to a version
of the Marschallin's love theme Ex. 2 which grows a tail, before itself
melting into her tenderest expression of love, Ex. 6 a. I quote both the
new idea in thirds and the extension of Ex. 2, as these return at two
important points later in the score.

²⁷ 'Today or tomorrow or the day after tomorrow.'

Ex. 38

Ex. 39

Octavian is greatly moved and goes away quietly. His back is scarcely turned when the Marschallin is smitten with appalling foresight that she will never again see him and be with him on terms of intimacy as they have just known. He has, moreover, gone without a farewell kiss, and this gives her a pretext which she can offer for immediately re-calling him in this absurd fashion. Frenziedly she summons her lackeys, who dash after Octavian, but in a moment they are back with the news that he has vanished like the wind. Steeling herself to the disappointment, the Marschallin calls for the Mahommedan and when the tiny negro appears (accompanied by his own little motif, Ex. 8) she gives him the case with the Silver Rose. The negro starts running off without knowing where to take the case, but the Marschallin quickly stops him.

The last section, possessed of all the autumnal qualities of a coda to the Act, had been set with classical symmetry in the key of the introduction and opening duet, E major. Briefly the music had moved away from this key for the episode of the lackeys, but now begins to modulate back. In so doing, however, it fails to reach E major and comes to rest in the sadder key of E flat, in which the music remains until the end of the Act, the softer tones of this more subdued tonality adding strangely to the mood of melancholy and nostalgia. To the love music Ex. 6 b the Marschallin sends her negro with his precious burden to the Count Octavian and then, as if realizing that with it she has sent him away from her for ever, sinks down with her head in her hands. Ex. 38 comes sweetly back and leads into the broad version of her Monologue theme (Ex. 34 c), over which Octavian's Ex. 1 soars ruminatively. It has

become the custom for the Marschallin, instead of remaining motionless, buried in thought as required by the stage directions, to look at
herself in the mirror and finger each line on her face. This may well be
more than Hofmannsthal intended, but it seems going too far to in-
struct, as Strauss did some thirty years later, that the Marschallin play
this curtain 'without the slightest trace of sentimentality, nor like a
tragic farewell to life, but instead with Viennese lightness and grace
throughout, one eye wet, the other dry'. If a 'tragic farewell to life' is
one extreme, this direction of the ageing composer is certainly the other.
It is, like the picture Strauss gave at the same date (1942) of his views on
Klytemnestra,[28] hard to reconcile his judgement in old age with his
intentions when writing the operas. The end of Act I of *Der Rosenkavalier* remains one of the most affecting scenes in the operatic repertoire.

10

Act II plunges straight into the hurly-burly of the betrothal preparations
at the Faninal mansion, a palatial establishment filled with lackeys and
servants of all kinds putting the final touches for the great event which
is now imminent. Faninal's Major-domo is pressing his master to leave
immediately lest he meet the Baron's ambassador, the Rose-Cavalier, in
the doorway—an unthinkable breach of etiquette. The opening theme
prepares the scene with the air of dignity in confusion.

Ex. 40

This exciting theme is applied more specifically later in the opera to
the person of Sophie's father, but always in relationship to his plans for
marrying Sophie into the house of Lerchenau. An appendix to it
describes the empty-headed flutterings of the foolish Duenna:

[28] See p. 308 (footnote).
[29] The fact that Ex. 40 begins with the 'Feldmarschall' rhythm (Ex. 12) may
well be coincidental. On the other hand, in view of the resultant prevalence of
this figure in development, there could be a relationship on the grounds that both
Faninal and the Field-Marshal represent the figure of authority; stern, absolute,
and somewhat to be feared.

Ex. 41

Hints can also be heard of a motif which will shortly blossom forth as the motif of Ochs himself in the role of the bridegroom-to-be:

Ex. 42

After a short link provided by the formula discussed earlier (Ex. 11c), Ex. 28 sweeps in gloriously, now in canon with itself at the octave. This leads to a climax at which the same formula inverted (Ex. 11b) is combined with the first complete and imposing statement of Ex. 42 and followed by a magnificent transformation of the ceremonial theme (Ex. 22).

Ex. 43

The curtain has now risen and the sequence is repeated with the voices superimposed of Faninal (who with immense pomp takes formal leave of Sophie) and the Major-domo, who fusses impatiently round his master. Then in a flash they have all gone, leaving Sophie alone to prepare herself for the great honour which is shortly to be paid her. Only the Duenna is in the background, peering through the window and chattering endlessly about the exciting events which she can see taking place in the street outside. Sophie is now portrayed by a new theme characterizing her ingenuous and youthful innocence:

Ex. 44

To this somewhat plaintive theme she sings of how her mother is dead
and she must stand on her own feet. Between interruptions of the
Duenna, who is excited almost to the pitch of hysteria (Ex. 41), Sophie
strives hard to retain her composure, concentrating on the humility
which she has been taught in the convent; but the description of the
Rose-Cavalier is too much for her. Seated in a carriage drawn by six
horses, he is dressed from head to foot in white and shining silver. The
footmen can be heard offstage repeatedly shouting out Octavian's
family name, Rofrano, while the orchestra gives out Ex. 1 majestically
in its fullest form, that is, with the additional phrases which have been
heard first in waltz rhythm (see Ex. 16). Sophie's Ex. 44 becomes
increasingly agitated, the ceremonial cadence Ex. 43 becomes more and
more prevalent, plunging into ever newer and more glittering keys, until
with a mighty effort and a shimmering cymbal clash a resplendent chord
of F sharp major bursts out as the centre doors are flung open. Octavian
is on the threshold, a truly dazzling figure, holding the Silver Rose
out-stretched in his right hand.

11

The presentation of the Silver Rose has rightly become well known as
one of the outstanding episodes in the opera. The translucent orchestral
colouring and beauty of imagination make it one of the most magical
passages in the whole of Strauss's output. It is built almost entirely on
an extended form of Sophie's first, more formal theme Ex. 20, to which
are added two appendages, the first fantastically kaleidoscopic with
Strauss's favourite shifting harmonies, brilliantly set for three flutes,
three solo violins, celeste, and two harps.

[30] As an instance of how Strauss's invention returns to earlier ideas this motif
should be compared with Ex. 35 of *Salome* (Chapter VIII (a)). At that time he made
little use of the theme, which, however, now comes fully into its own.

Ex. 45

Ex. 45 is introduced repeatedly as a refrain after almost every phrase throughout the section. The second appendage, although quoted already, is now only added by way of coda, in which capacity it acquires importance also at the end of the opera.

Ex. 46

Alternately with Sophie's music comes Ochs's Ex. 42, which has still some nobility of expression, partly owing to the manner in which it is handled and partly because we have not yet heard it when Ochs himself was visible on the stage. That dreadful moment of disillusionment still lies before poor Sophie. In the meantime the wonder of the experience overwhelms her, and after a brief formal exchange with Octavian in which, in acute embarrassment, he offers the rose and she accepts it, she pours out an ecstatic song in praise of the scent with which the rose has been artificially imbued.

Ex. 47

Wie himm — — — li-sche, nicht ir - di -sche [31]

Octavian is as dumbfounded at seeing this ravishing young creature as she is at his splendid appearance and their mutual rapture is expressed in a theme which, announced first on the trumpet, is later sung as a duet.

[31] 'How heavenly, not earthly.'

Ex. 48

The formalities at an end, chairs are brought, the Silver Rose (its purpose fulfilled) is taken away by footmen, and Sophie and Octavian relax for a few minutes, waiting for Sophie's father to arrive escorting the principal figure in all this ceremony, her future husband. The Duenna sits down in the background and the music also relaxes into a comfortably flowing ¾ tempo. Sophie opens the conversation, her prattling accompanied by an ingenuous little figure which is fully developed in this miniature intermezzo-like movement. She tells Octavian his age, recites the list (and a formidable one it is) of his baptismal names, to which she adds, a little coyly, 'Quinquin'. He is enchanted and she brightly asks whether he has never thought of marriage. She herself is greatly looking forward to it, she says; it is so very different from remaining single!

Ex. 49

As Octavian has been anything but lonely of late, the orchestra slyly

---

32 There has recently been a great deal of controversy over the note marked with a cross. The study score adds a (♮), as also a few bars earlier where it occurs on the trumpet. No sign of either accidental appears in the full score, in which case the two places would be dissimilar for reasons of key-signature. The study score has a preface stating that its text has been revised by Clemens Krauss and is to be taken as authentic. Nevertheless the passage has always been played by the trumpet in its unsharpened form until recently, when the recording conducted by Karajan was issued with not only the voice but the trumpet part raised according to the study score. So startling and strange was the effect that it aroused excited comment on every side, not all of it by any means favourable. On grounds of euphony the raised trumpet note seems unlikely, to say the least, and although the matter cannot ever be settled conclusively, it is reassuring to find that Strauss himself recorded the flattened version at least in the case of the more striking trumpet note, though he preserved the D♮ in the later bar.

interpolates the breakfast waltz version of Ex. 4. This is a particularly charming self-contained little episode of a kind peculiar to *Rosenkavalier*, although the material is reminiscent of many other passages including, a little oddly perhaps, the Chrysothemis theme Ex. 19 (c) from *Elektra*, in the closing bars.

Suddenly the door opens and, as Faninal and Ochs enter, the music changes character completely. Ochs's Ex. 42, now transformed into a grotesque little march, absurd and self-satisfied, is elaborated and extended, while Ochs examines Sophie, complimenting Faninal on her appearance as if, as she herself puts it, he were at the horse-dealer's making a prospective purchase. An effort on the part of Faninal to introduce the Duenna is brushed aside rudely by the Baron, who asks instead that Faninal greet with him his Rose-Cavalier, Sophie meanwhile being left to stand foolishly on one side. Despite the affront, the Duenna is full of admiration and excuses for Ochs at every turn, but Sophie is outraged, while Octavian, outwardly very correct, is so embarrassed that he can scarcely stand still and watch the boorish exhibition.

The Baron's complete composure is now illustrated by a new theme:

Ex. 50

to the accompaniment of which Ochs tells at length all he knows about Octavian's alleged bastard sister, a recital in extremely doubtful taste. He indulges in a good deal of scandalmongering over Octavian's father, citing the Marschallin and boasting that such is common practice amongst the nobility including, naturally, himself as a person of high social standing. He thus contrives the opportunity of pointing out his son-cum-bodyguard to Octavian. Sophie's indignation now boils over at the thought that this coarse fellow is her future husband, her exasperation and despair heightened at the extra horror of discovering that he is pock-marked:

Ex. 51

(Und das ist mein) Zu - künf-ti-ger   Und blätterstepptg ist er auch   O mein Gott

Faninal's Major-domo and footmen now appear with wine and
refreshments, the Major-domo taking the opportunity of drawing away
the loutish retinue of the Baron, who have been hanging round the
scene after nearly knocking Sophie over at their entrance. Ochs tells
Faninal that he is pleased with him, in a tone of the utmost condescension, remarking to the deeply offended Octavian in an audible aside
that it is as well to put these cheap nobility in their place at once. He
then draws Sophie to him in order to sample her powers of conversation. Strauss here invents a kind of quasi-period dance not unlike the
music of the hairdresser in the levée scene of Act I, but which cleverly
characterizes the self-satisfied Ochs as typical of his time and sure of
himself in the security of his noble descent.

Ex. 52

It is an interesting feature of Strauss's style that this neo-classic form of
invention, introduced at first as deliberate pastiche for period pieces
such as *Der Rosenkavalier* and *Le Bourgeois Gentilhomme,* ended by
becoming an important facet of his normal idiom in works of the
Indian Summer such as the Oboe and Second Horn Concertos.
Sophie's antipathy becomes evident in quick bristling enunciations of
her Ex. 44, while Octavian's irritation can be sensed by his Ex. 1,
treated in the same way. Meanwhile Ochs begins his clumsy wooing to
the sound of a theme the contours of which are by now extremely

familiar from *Elektra*, though it is used here with an utterly different connotation:

Ex. 53

While Faninal preens himself at the thought of a Lerchenau fondling his Sophie with a Rofrano in attendance, Ochs presses home his advantage, pouring scorn over etiquette and good behaviour and, as Ex. 50 becomes more and more insistent, thinks with complacent good humour of his 'typically Lerchenau-ish luck'. Even Sophie's increasing fury delights him the more, so that goaded beyond endurance she finally breaks away from him, hissing through her teeth that no one has ever dared to speak to her in this way—what can he think of her and himself; what is he to her after all? This gives Ochs the cue he has been waiting for, and remarking that it will come to her overnight he placidly hums her his favourite popular song, the gist of which is that 'with me no night will be too long'.

Ex. 54

It is on this undeniably *ben trovato* ditty that Strauss's fame as a writer of waltzes and the world-wide popularity of the opera most securely rests, despite other and more tasteful waltzes later in Act III. As a result of it, his reputation has even rivalled that of his famous name-sake, the waltz-king Johann II, although there is not the slightest question of his having taken the tune seriously in the first place—every indication in the score and even the treatment of it in context reveals it as the purest parody. But its tremendous *élan* and the brilliant way in which it catches the essence of the Viennese waltz caused it to be hailed immediately as a true example—indeed, one of the finest ever written—of the very thing of which it was originally a satire.[33]

In its original form in the opera there are several curious features about this remarkable waltz. In the first place it clearly occurred to Strauss independently of the words, which can only partially be made to fit it. Moreover, it always fails to reach the last conventional cadence, but breaks into a rumbustious section quoted as the figure ⌐ a ⌐ at the end of Ex. 54, an entirely independent waltz in quicker time which is itself fully developed in Act III.

The waltzes gradually become more and more like *Die Fledermaus* as Ochs contentedly repeats his slogan as to his Lerchenau-ish good fortune. This phrase actually gave the two collaborators an astonishing amount of trouble. The fact is that the idea of it was taken from a Ballad by Uhland known to every schoolboy, each stanza of which ended 'Das ist das Glück von Edenhall!' Simply to change Edenhall into Lerchenau seemed too facile—too obvious a quotation. Hofmannsthal accordingly asked Strauss for his ideas suggesting that the accepted version should also be suitable to be sung mockingly at Ochs by the other members of the cast at the moment when he finds himself in the most deplorable circumstances. Although Hofmannsthal had pressed for a quick answer he was surprised to receive no less than four possibilities virtually by return.

Ex. 55

[33] As a comment on the anachronism of its employment out of period it is interesting to find Alban Berg using an almost identical tune as the Ländler played by the beer-house band in his *Wozzeck*, the time of which is only slightly later. Berg's version, however, deliberately has a plebeian Deutsche quality which is far more plausible for the dates in question than the nineteenth-century artificiality of Strauss's waltz.

(d) Nur ein Ler - che - nau ____ hat ein sol-ches Glück

Hofmannsthal found all these utterly unsuitable and out of character, and he accordingly went back to a further idea of his own. But what he could not understand at all was the ease with which Strauss was able to vary with equanimity what to him seemed a crucial refrain. One is reminded of a similar complaint made by Strauss to Romain Rolland a few years earlier as to the unexpected number of possible variants and scansions of the word 'cheveux' in Debussy's *Pelléas et Mélisande* when trying to find a suitable French translation of *Salome*.

Even when Hofmannsthal had fixed on the version which pleased him best Strauss still did not at first arrive at the real solution for the setting. The passage occurs three times during Act II, but although the earlier two are perfectly plausible versions, and, in fact, the first is already based on the relevant melodic turn of phrase, it is only in the last, which occurs during the waltz sequence at the end of the Act, that Strauss really caught, with that essential quality of inevitability, the bumptious self-delight which is implicit in the refrain. For purposes of comparison I quote all three settings which occur during the Act, including the last and most successful, (g), though this only appears somewhat later.

Ex. 55

(e) ich hab' halt ja ____ ein Lerchenau – isch Glück!

(f) Ich hab' halt ein Ler - - - chen-au - isch Glück

(f) also accompanies, with its suggestion of Strauss's great namesake (it is an obvious parody of one of the better-known waltz tunes from *Die Fledermaus*), the Baron's grotesque remark that 'nothing so enflames or rejuvenates him like a real shrew'.

12

Faninal tells Ochs that it is time to attend to the legal formalities of the betrothal, and with a return to his Ex. 42 (there is even a hint of his very first theme of all, Ex. 17(a)) Ochs prepares to retire with the notary, stopping only to invite Octavian to make advances to Sophie and 'break her in' for him if he should feel so inclined, an extraordinary piece of showing off in view of subsequent events. There is a climax with declamatory statements of the 'period' theme Ex. 52 and of the melody connected with the marriage arrangements, before the music fades away. Ochs, Faninal, the notary, and all the lackeys adjourn into an inner room, leaving the stage empty except for Sophie and Octavian and, of course, the eternal Duenna. To a dreary echo of the famous Waltz (Ex. 54) Octavian asks Sophie whether she will really go through with the marriage, which suggestion she vehemently rejects, begging for his help. At first she believes the appeal to be in vain, since Ochs and Octavian refer to each other constantly as cousins, but Octavian quickly assures her that this is mere court parlance.

It is clear that now is the moment for a duet between this new pair of potential lovers. Octavian's sympathy for the poor enchanting creature, and Sophie's admiration for him, coupled with the need for his help in extricating herself from this dreadful fate, make them ideally suited for each other. All thoughts of the Marschallin are far away, and, in fact, neither she nor any of her music appears at all during Act II. All that is needed is to get rid of the Duenna, and this Hofmannsthal does by a trick which is entertaining if somewhat artificial. There is a sudden burst from the orchestra and pandemonium is let loose, screams being heard first off and then on-stage as some of Faninal's maids rush in and out, hotly pursued by the Lerchenau footmen, who have been drinking brandy in vast quantities and have now run wild. The Major-domo comes in for help and the Duenna goes away with him, leaving Octavian and Sophie entirely unattended. A duet does in fact, follow, but is very curious in character. Strauss had at first intended to have a typical outburst of love music, but found the text not nearly passionate enough. The reason for this was partly on account of the changes made when the whole of Act II was redrafted. Hofmannsthal had originally had a much longer conversational dialogue both before and after the exit of the Duenna. This had, however, never reached the level of the love duet, and moreover, although Sophie kissed Octavian's hand, they were to have been interrupted by the Italians before he could return her kiss. When this was changed at Strauss's suggestion Hofmannsthal still found himself unable to alter the essential conversational character of the scene, with the result that, although the kiss is now achieved and followed by a duet, the whole passage remains at an oddly low emotional level. Hofmannsthal wrote to Strauss: 'I am anxious not to bring these two young naïve creatures, who have nothing in common with a Walküre or a Tristan, into any really erotic embracings and shouting to each other in the typical Wagnerian manner.' Strauss agreed that such an emotional explosion would be out of keeping and extremely improbable in the circumstances of the drama, but complained that it was virtually impossible for him to write a love scene in any other vein. At the same time, he also felt at a loss, since, as he put it, he had 'already more than exhausted the lyrical element at the beginning of the second Act'. The calm flow of gentle music with a slightly acid flavour which he finally composed for the scene gives a good element of intermezzo-like calm before the storm that follows, but would scarcely seem to give Octavian the kind of love experience which would tear him away from his adored Bichette. It is largely constructed out of Ex. 53 (possibly to show how the Baron ought to have wooed Sophie, partly perhaps because it is the memory of how he actually did behave

R.S.–CC

which has thrown her into Octavian's arms), Sophie's Ex. 44 and Octavian's Ex. 1 being now drawn out into a number of long and varied melodic strands. There is also a spiky version in diminution of the theme (Ex. 49) in which Sophie had so recently said how much she was looking forward to her marriage, a sadly ironical touch. Out of these elements new melodies appear and alternate but none disturb the prevailing tranquillity of the mood. The effect is to give the two young people the quality of Dresden China lovers, an impression which, as we shall see, returns again at the end of the opera.

During the latter part of the duet the two Italian intrigueurs have suddenly appeared and have been creeping gradually closer. As the final cadence is reached they pounce, Valzacchi holding Octavian with considerable difficulty while Annina struggles with Sophie. In a section similar to their earlier music and consisting largely of Ex. 31 and a new figure Ex. 56,

they scream for the Baron, who quickly arrives and stands with arms folded watching the disconcerted pair, while the Italians bow obsequiously on either side.[34] Ex. 56 describes the screaming not the bowing!

The Baron now has a moment of actual dignity portrayed by a new motif which dominates the following scene:

Ex. 57

[34] It is at this point that the original draft takes an entirely different course from the version suggested by Strauss and finally adopted. Hofmannsthal's plan was that before the Baron actually arrives on the stage Octavian should successfully bribe the two Italians, upon which they immediately change sides and indicate their willingness to serve Octavian in place of the niggardly Ochs. A long scene then followed in which the plans were laid for the pantomime of the following Act. By sacrificing this, Strauss and Hofmannsthal both realized that the Italians' change of front might not be fully explained, but hoped that the audience would guess from some obvious hints at what must have taken place (see below, pp. 393 and 394).

Remembering the instructions which Ochs has just given Octavian before leaving Sophie with him, one might consider that there would be little which he could profitably say by way of reproach. Octavian, however, seizes the initiative and, during an extensive preamble, the Baron continually interrupting in a most offensive manner, makes it plain that Sophie cannot endure Ochs's very presence and has no longer the slightest intention of marrying him. To Sophie's agonized apprehension, Octavian's anger rises to boiling-point, while the Baron merely becomes more and more arrogant and boorish as he tries to manoeuvre Sophie out of the room to the antechamber in which the notary sits awaiting her signature. Seeing that Ochs is on the point of eluding him, Octavian deliberately insults him with the most provocative words and draws his sword. In the meantime the Baron has put two fingers in his mouth, giving vent to a piercing whistle which quickly summons his retinue. Relying on their efficacy in keeping a mere boy at bay, Ochs returns insult for insult and tries still to edge away towards the door, but he is at last obliged to draw and within a matter of seconds has received the point of Octavian's sword in his upper arm.

The cataclysmic ensemble which follows forms the first main climax of the opera. It seems unthinkable that the Act could ever have existed without it, and yet there was no trace in the original draft, most of the very details being supplied with a sure instinct by Strauss himself. The Baron drops his sword and shouts 'Murder' at the top of his voice; thereupon the Italians rush him on to a row of chairs which are quickly arranged in the middle of the room, while his loutish followers indulge in a great many threats, but in fact perform nothing and are easily kept at bay by Octavian's sword. A doctor is sent for and before long the entire Faninal household is assembled and joins in the general débâcle.[35] As this reaches a climax Faninal enters, followed by the notary. His anger and despair find orchestral expression in screaming references to Ex. 56 on the upper woodwind. He turns ferociously on Octavian, who excuses himself as best he may, but is eventually obliged to take his leave, assuring the miserable Sophie that she will have news

[35] Strauss draws to a considerable extent on Sophie's 'looking forward to marriage' theme Ex. 49, amongst the many subjects which are developed together in this passage. Its purpose is more musical than psychological, however, and it gives a fine impetus to the scene. Another odd theme to appear is Ex. 55 g, the first statement in this form of Ochs's 'Luck of the Lerchenaus' motif, a reference which can only be ironical in the circumstances.

of him before long. Faninal then attacks Sophie, a grotesque argument
ensuing to a rapid statement of the wedding themes (Exx. 40 and 28)
as she declares she will lock herself in her room, throw herself out of the
carriage and say 'No' at the altar rather than marry Ochs. Faninal
replies that she will marry him or his corpse if he should bleed to death,
or risk being placed in a convent for life. He repeats the words 'for
life' many times in his rage, hoping too, that they will placate the Baron.
In his distress he even embraces Ochs, who leaps up as Faninal presses
his wounded arm by mistake—an amusing touch. The Major-domo has
gradually been emptying the room, the Duenna takes Sophie away out
of her father's sight and only the Baron remains, attended by the Doctor
and his personal servants, and fussed around to the point of absurdity by
Faninal.

Ochs has by now been made more comfortable and his arm put in a
sling. His ease of mind, fully regained, is beautifully suggested by two
new ideas:

Ex. 58

Ex. 59

Ex. 58 is obviously closely related to Ex. 17 (a), with their common
pompous figure of martial accompaniment. Ex. 59, on the other hand,
is in an entirely fresh vein. It comes three times during Ochs's musings,
suggesting that the disturbance is now wholly resolved and the tension
relaxed. On the first two occasions however, its Viennese sweetness
tails away into chromatic dissonances as memories of recent events come
crowding back into his mind. Faninal, after embarrassing the Baron
with his extravagant attentiveness, at last rushes away, still vowing fearful penalties for the wretched Sophie. Ochs is in the end not displeased
with the turn of events; Faninal is now beholden to him and the sight
of Sophie beside herself with anger is something he would not have
missed for worlds. (He gently carols his refrain about the enflaming

effect shrews have upon him, and the appropriate *Fledermaus*-like Ex. 55 f is softly caressed in the horns and strings.) As for Octavian, now that he is safely out of the way, Ochs shouts threats at his head, the lead being followed by the Lerchenau footmen, who twice sing a vulgar refrain of threatening words at the door through which Octavian departed. The second of these refrains precedes the third statement of Ex. 59 and this time the sweetness of its harmonics remains unalloyed until gently it relapses into the famous waltz, Ex. 54. Ochs, a glass of wine in hand, is now viewing with satisfaction the prospect of a quiet rest in bed (a feather bed, he stipulates to the Doctor) before it is time for one of Faninal's excellent meals.

13

The last scene of the Act is the best known passage of the whole opera. Entirely in waltz rhythm, it gives the fullest version of Ex. 54 alternating with Ex. 16 (the waltz form of Octavian's theme) and Ex. 55 g (the final version of the 'Luck of the Lerchenaus' theme), which now comes fully into its own. There is also a little characteristic figure which is used towards the latter part of the same scene as a cadential linking theme, but which is exploited to some considerable extent as an independent idea in Act III.

Ex. 60

Annina has quietly come into the room armed with an assignment from 'Mariandel' which she reads aloud to him, his glasses being out of reach (an old device for letting the audience hear it, too). He is delighted beyond measure and tells Annina to go and set up a writing table in the inner room, where after dinner he will dictate her the answer. Her importunate gestures for a tip he naturally ignores as being premature, and this incident together with Annina's fist-shaking behind his back are intended to account for Valzacchi's and her betrayal of the skinflint Baron in Act III. This is, however, scarcely convincing, considering that in the first place Annina is already clearly hand-in-glove with Octavian, whose *billet* she bears, and in the second she has no reason to suppose that Ochs will refuse a tip when her part in the assignment has been fully accomplished. Strauss himself was never quite happy about this point. Hofmannsthal had suggested a rather cumbersome explanation: 'Annina demands a tip, the stingy Baron waves her away. Valzacchi backs her up, both Italians become impudent, the Baron calls for help to his men, who drive the Italians out of the room while he looks on, pleased with himself and humming his favourite little song—in this way we get a bustling grotesque ending like a ballet, in which you can introduce your charming waltz motif.' Meantime, however, Strauss had concocted the central débâcle, and was not at all averse to the quiet ending to the Act which Hofmannsthal was so set on avoiding. Accordingly he wrote back: 'We might indeed indicate that the Baron gives the Italians no tip, but the extra scene which you have sent on after is not necessary. The understanding between Octavian and the Italians can be referred to briefly at the beginning of Act III before Valzacchi hands over the chambermaid to the Baron . . . Don't worry about explaining the reason for the Italians' change of front; perhaps you may find an opportunity to introduce the short scene where Octavian outbids the Baron in the middle of the confusion of the big scandal-ensemble with the chorus. But it is not necessary for the sake of the public—they will draw their own conclusions.' But a month later Strauss was less confident. 'How do we account for the turning round of the two Italians? Does that come at the beginning of Act III, so that one gathers that Octavian has won them over because the Baron would not pay them etc.?' To which Hofmannsthal replied: 'It can be better explained briefly at the beginning of Act III than here in Act II, where it would hold things up. Besides, as you yourself quite rightly said, the public are pretty tolerant about such things, especially in matters of professional intrigue.' So the only partial explanation occurs at the opening of Act III, where the Italians are shown receiving a substantial bribe from Octavian, although it is clear that they have already undertaken to organize an intricate plot to discredit Ochs according to his directions. In fact, as we have seen, the initial moves have already been made at the end of Act II—that is, before there had been any question of meanness on the part of Ochs. That these Italian intriguants at the Viennese Court should be so flagrantly double-faced was most probably true to life.

Act III begins with an extended orchestral introduction in the form of an extremely elaborate fugato based on the Tarantella-like material

Exx. 29-32, together with another characteristic figure of mixed origin:

Ex. 61

The first use of Ex. 61 was during Sophie's scene with the Baron and described her snapping anger. More relevant, however, was its featuring when the Italians had caught Octavian and Sophie, presenting them in each others' arms to Ochs with the words 'Ecco!—Ecco!' It is with the memory of that moment in mind that Ex. 61 has so prominent a position in the complex polyphony of this highly original section. Even minor figurations from the first appearance of the Italians in the levée scene are brought back and this Introduction takes on the role of a symphonic reprise. The scurrying figures of the Italians' many themes provide a glittering background. The full version of Octavian's Ex. 1 is presented in this way, phrase by phrase, in a manner not unlike a skittish Chorale Prelude, while at the climax Ochs's Ex. 42 enters in tremendous mock majesty only to be swept away by the Tarantella. It does not require great intuition to perceive that some plot is afoot with sinister designs on the Baron and in which Octavian will play an important role.

The Introduction comes to a well-defined close and immediately begins again from the opening bars as the curtain rises. A new figure now makes its appearance:

Ex. 62

(I quote it in both its rhythmic guises although it is clear that the note formation is identical). This describes Annina—indeed, the second group was probably suggested by the scansion of her name—who is dressed up like a woman in deep mourning. Octavian is also dressed up

—to look once again like Mariandel, and snatches of the waltz-like version of his theme (Ex. 16) are interpolated into the Tarantella. During the long pantomime which follows (no note is sung by any of the characters on the stage) the scene is set and rehearsed with the greatest care. We are in a private room at the inn; in the background there is an alcove containing an enormous bed. Huge beds thus feature in no less than two of the three Acts and it is scarcely surprising that this further bed was forced to remain invisible in many early productions and that the passage referring to it was cut. The room is full of trapdoors, secret openings, and blind windows, and much of the pantomime is devoted to making sure that these work smoothly and to teaching their cues to the sinister characters who are to operate them. Valzacchi and Annina, after receiving a bag of money and kissing Octavian's hand, set about organizing and rehearsing the arrangements, after which the table is laid, the candles lit and the room carefully vacated to give the semblance of complete privacy. Ochs's 'invitation waltz' Ex. 23, is now combined with Ex. 16, and gradually supplants it as Ochs himself arrives, one arm in a sling, the other escorting Mariandel into the room as Valzacchi, bowing low, opens the door and shows him round. The lighting of the candles is illustrated in the orchestra by an amusing series of woodwind trills, after which a backstage band of musicians strikes up with a set of waltzes based, apart from Ex. 23, entirely on new material, some of which is never heard again throughout the opera. Against this, the main orchestra in the pit quietly plays a tune derived from Octavian's Ex. 3, but continuing in a vein strongly reminiscent of earlier works such as Don Quixote and the Sinfonia Domestica. Often missed, this is an intensely characteristic touch of considerable charm and humour.

During this further waltz sequence Ochs closely interrogates the innkeeper, who has rushed forward, eager to satisfy his distinguished guest. The Baron, who is none too affluent despite his rank, sets about reducing the cost; waiters are sent packing, candles are extinguished, he would even send away the musicians if he could—he had ordered none, he says—but on being told merely that they could come nearer if desired, he leaves well alone. Valzacchi is now given to understand that he can expect a tip if he helps to keep the price down; Ochs's own body-servant will wait at table, he himself will pour out the wine. Impatiently he waves away the lackeys who hang around, curious to see what is going to happen, and gradually the supper begins.

14

After a few timorous sips Octavian puts down his glass and, to a
melancholy new waltz, refuses any more wine. Ochs presses him, upon
which he runs away, purposely going the wrong way and revealing the
monster bed. Ochs gently brings him back to the table with soothing
words, even when Octavian reproaches him with being a bridegroom.
His manner is skilful and *coquette* to the last degree and the only suspicions Ochs ever evinces are when he approaches for a kiss and sees a
face so alarmingly similar to the wretched boy who wounded him that
he recoils instinctively with Ex. 1 and the theme of his own lost dignity
(Ex. 57) ringing painfully in his ears. During this scene yet another
group of waltz themes appear for the first time, but these not only
return but are destined for later use at a pre-eminent point in the opera:

Ex. 63

Ex. 64

Ex. 64 consists of two independent waltz tunes which are in fact treated
separately at first, but soon combine admirably as illustrated. At this
point one of the men who are hidden behind trap-doors exposes himself
prematurely and Ochs catches a glimpse of him before he rapidly disappears at a furtive gesture from Octavian. It takes longer for the disconcerted Baron to accept the idea that everything is pure imagination,
but Octavian play-acts to try and reassure the Baron during a new
waltz sequence, based on the linking phrase Ex. 60, but developed as an
independent theme now leading to a violent phrase characterized by
abrupt stops. This describes Ochs impulsively looking over his shoulder,
half expecting to see some other weird apparition:

Ex. 65

Little by little, however, he relaxes, putting these hallucinations down to a slight attack of brain fever, a heaving motif being introduced which hereafter depicts the breathless symptoms of this complaint.

Ex. 66

The relationship of Ex. 66 to that of Klytemnestra's similar if more horrific condition (see Ex. 25, chapter VIII (b)) is clear, even though it is here put to comic effect.

The café band now plays the whole of Ochs's favourite waltz, Ex. 54, which fills him with delight, but reduces Mariandel to a state of acute sentimental melancholia, a condition which, on the stage, most Octavians tend to overdo and which is thus generally somewhat embarrassing. Ex. 54 runs its entire course, complete with Ex. 60 in its original form, and overlapping with itself, by means of an ingenious piece of dovetailing between the stage and pit orchestras. It comes to a full close, the main orchestra taking up the thread with a new *Valse Triste* through which Mariandel sobs dismally:

Ex. 67

A rich climax is built up as Ochs, faced with a situation he certainly never anticipated and has no idea how to handle, takes his wig off to put himself more at his ease, while beginning the principal purpose of the evening by trying to loosen Mariandel's dress. At that moment another trap-door opens and Ochs finds himself looking at a strange man once again. Between the face of the hated Octavian on the now fully passive Mariandel and the Jack-in-the-box effect of the men in the trap-doors Ochs loses his head altogether, seizes the hand-bell and rings it distractedly. This is now the cue for Annina, who appears at the blind window and to her motif Ex. 62 claims Ochs loudly as her long-lost husband. She then vanishes, only to reappear at the door, now accompanied by the innkeeper with a couple of waiters and by four screaming children who cluster round the now nearly demented Ochs shrieking 'Papa, papa'. This was an idea Hofmannsthal found in Molière's *Pourceaugnac* and which was so apt to his own plot that he could not resist incorporating it.

The scene which follows is of the utmost complexity and as we have already seen (p. 341) Strauss had considerable difficulty in summoning up the necessary inspiration to handle it. It remains the least interesting section of the opera musically, and in this respect marks time, relying on the amusing burlesque situations on the stage to keep the audience's attention until the moment when the opportunity arises with the entry of the Marschallin for Strauss's lyrical muse to reassert itself. Meanwhile his technique was quite adequate to bridge the gap with consummate mastery of invention and felicitous touches of orchestral detail. Moreover, Strauss had by this late point in the opera built up a mass of thematic material upon which he could now draw freely; Ochs's waltz tune Ex. 23, for example, is compressed into a violent figure which describes the Baron's agitation perfectly. Strauss also set isolated lines to new and characteristic phrases which he repeated thematically in the orchestra.

To Ochs, who is busily applying a cold compress to his fevered brow, the screaming children are the final straw, and throwing the compress away he opens the window to the street, shouting for the police, a fatal blunder as it turns out. Here is, moreover, a development of the situation which had not been foreseen by the plotters; acting on Octavian's instructions, Valzacchi has arranged for Faninal to be fetched, and the prior appearance of the Commissary of Police accompanied by two burly-looking watchmen is an unwelcome complication in the projected humiliation of the unsavoury Baron. Octavian, however, is not unduly worried and reassures the anxious Valzacchi. The stern Commissary is portrayed by a new motif in stark octaves which, though characteristic, is bleaker than Strauss usually invents, and it is noteworthy that once he had got back into his stride he abandoned it.

Ochs's appearance is nothing short of ludicrous; his arm in a sling, his wig missing—it has vanished unaccountably ever since he took it off prior to beginning his first steps in seduction, and without it he is grotesquely bald. As a result he makes a very unfortunate impression on the police officer, and the latter quickly passes from the miserable innkeeper (who sees the prospect of his inn being shut up and his livelihood taken from him as a result of this evening's escapade) to the astonished Baron. Foolishly Ochs begins by telling the Commissary patronizingly that he is pleased with him, that he can go now and leave him to continue his supper. He can thus scarcely believe his ears when a mere low-born policeman turns on him in all his nobility, refers to him as a great fat fellow and demands his credentials.

At this point Strauss inserted a direction in the full score to the effect that Ochs's body-servant who is greatly concerned at the turn of events, is suddenly seized with an idea as to how the situation can be saved and runs quickly off by the centre door. This complicated manoeuvre, which is, in fact, not in the libretto as published by Hofmannsthal and is in any case rarely noticed in the performance, is explained and justi-fied by a corresponding stage direction later in the Act and it will accordingly be discussed then.

Valzacchi now slyly refuses to vouch for the Baron, and Octavian, choosing his moment with diabolical malevolence, flutters as if by accident to the alcove. The *pianissimo* rushing chord of E major, as the huge bed is revealed, gently illuminated to look inviting, is a most amusing touch on Strauss's part. Ochs is clearly trapped and in an attempt to avoid being arrested for debauchery he pretends that Marian-del is his bride, whom he describes to the Commissary as Sophia Anna Barbara von Faninal (the only time, by the way, that we hear her names in full). No sooner does Ochs pronounce the title of Faninal than Herr von Faninal himself walks in.

Ochs now attempts to extricate himself by disowning Faninal and both men become abusive. When finally Ochs has no option but to recognize his prospective father-in-law, the Commissary confronts Faninal with Mariandel as his daughter. Faninal is naturally scandalized and sends forthwith for Sophie, who is waiting below in the carriage. Ochs's agitation, to which the loss of his wig is a strong contributing factor, is now depicted by a new figure which is added to the texture wherever possible:

Ex. 68

The whole of this section has been played to a kind of hurry-hurry music based on Faninal's Ex. 40 (of which the 'Feldmarschal' figure is accentuated to a considerable extent) and the subsidiary ⌐ b ⌐ from Ochs's motif of gallantry (Ex. 52), now thrown about so that little or nothing remains of its characteristic poise and courtly condescension. With Sophie's entrance, her personal melody (Ex. 44) surges in with fine sweeping *élan* despite the prevailing hectic atmosphere, so that for the first time we are made conscious of the breadth of personality which will one day emerge, Marschallin-like, from her present doll-like immaturity. She is, needless to say, overwhelmed with joyful relief at the turn of events which, she already sees, sets her free from the odious marriage. Neither she nor her father, be it noted, recognizes Mariandel, though possibly under the circumstances and in the general confusion this is not altogether implausible. Even a crowd of onlookers are added to the overcrowded stage in order to allow the chorus to participate, if briefly, in the climax, gleefully shouting; 'Scandal, scandal over the Faninals.'

Herr von Faninal, his world collapsing about him, now feels seriously unwell as realization of the utter humiliation that seems inevitable is borne upon him, and he is carried out, followed by Sophie, who is genuinely fond of him and concerned for his well-being. There is a grand coda section with the respective themes of father and daughter alternating and accompanied by various Ochs motifs (Exx. 52 (b) and 68) treated in rapid descending sequences, as the music sinks gradually to peace once again.

The stage now empties and the Commissary has the remaining stragglers turned out, leaving only Ochs and Octavian, with Annina and the children in the background. Ochs has meantime found his wig and with it his self-confidence. He takes Mariandel by the arm and tries to brazen his way out.[36] He is, however, frustrated both by the Commissary, who is naturally still far from satisfied, and by Octavian, who

[36] Ochs's 'I'll take you home now' is oddly set to Sophie's formal family theme Ex. 20. Strauss's purpose in this is not obvious, but could be intended to suggest that Ochs is still trying to delude the Commissary into accepting Mariandel as his real fiancée.

protests that he does not want to go with Ochs, and breaks free, running to the Commissary as if for protection. The Baron, at his wits' end, is desperately promising marriage as his last trump card when, the music stopping abruptly, he hears Mariandel telling the Commissary that there is 'something formal to announce, but the Baron is not to hear'.[37] Octavian and the Commissary go together towards the alcove, while Ochs still tries pathetically to explain to the attendant watchmen that he has no knowledge whatever of Annina (whom he has at no time recognized as one of the Italians) or the children. To his horror the Commissary seems to be highly amused by something, and is standing by the alcove while Mariandel's clothes are flung out one by one. Mariandel's *Valse Triste* (Ex. 67) is turned into a frenzied $\frac{6}{8}$ and combined with Ochs's no longer pompous Ex. 42 and the motif of his extreme agitation (Ex. 68) as he struggles with the watchmen, who prevent him from going towards the alcove. Feverishly he pleads to be allowed to rescue this young girl who stands under his protection, as he believes, from the evil designs of the wicked Police Commissary.

Suddenly the innkeeper bursts in with news that the Marschallin is on the threshold. There is a short and breathless comma in the orchestra and the great lady sweeps in, her train carried by the little negro. Ochs is overwhelmed with gratification and Ex. 68 rises in all four horns. A huge transformed version of the Marschallin's renunciation theme, Ex. 5 (a), floods over the whole orchestra, while in the cellos and bassoons a rapid form of Ex. 1 surges up through the polyphony to describe Octavian's head pushing through the curtains of the alcove in this last and most unexpected of all the developments in the whole fantastic escapade.

15

The long-delayed reappearance of the Marschallin was, of course, the climax of Hofmannsthal's scheme. Yet he was hard put to it to explain how it could possibly come about that so high a personage should stoop to visiting a sordid tavern in a humble part of the city. The solution, in itself perhaps slightly far-fetched, but at least a reasonable possibility, seems to have been Strauss's idea and can be found in the stage directions

[37] Strauss emphasizes these vital words by having them spoken instead of sung, an operatic device for last Acts much in vogue from Verdi's *La Traviata* to Britten's *Peter Grimes*. Strauss himself used it again at far greater length in *Arabella*.

in the score, one of which has already been mentioned, concerning the curious antics of the Baron's body-servant (see above, p. 400). He, it will be remembered, was struck with an idea and ran out quickly. Now he returns, looking greatly self-satisfied and going to the Baron who indicates that he is much pleased with him. The careful planting of this manoeuvre presupposes that the Marschallin would indeed have come so promptly to Ochs's rescue on being approached in such a manner by his body-servant. However, at least some verisimilitude is attempted on behalf of the Marschallin, who otherwise would appear as a mere conventional *Deus (Dea) ex machina*.

The Police Commissary bows with the utmost deference to the Marschallin, who recognizes in him her husband's former orderly. This rather artificial tying up of loose threads resembles the 'Strawberry mark' which in classical opera plots, including even *Figaro*, removes many awkward complications by introducing some undreamt-of relationship. In the present situation it removes the Commissary, who shortly retires, accompanied by the two watchmen, since with so important a noblewoman in charge he is entirely satisfied. During this recognition scene, Ochs (to the sounds of his Ex. 42) has been trying to impress upon the retreating Commissary his own importance as proved by the Marschallin's appearance, and he is thus greatly infuriated by the sight of Mariandel's head, which is still poking through the bed-curtains. In fact, Octavian is anxiously persuading his Marie Thérèse that he had planned it all quite differently. It is actually, however, a little hard to know just how he *had* planned it, for despite minor mishaps events could not possibly have gone better for the complete exposure and discrediting of the miserable Baron.

Sophie now returns and tries to deliver a last message from her father. Ochs irritably tells her to wait until it is time to be 'presented', but she has not observed the Marschallin at all. The latter, however, has indeed noticed her (it is the first time she has seen her) and Octavian whispers who she is. But the Marschallin is unexpectedly cold—calling Octavian by his family name, Rofrano, for the only time in the work—and to a combination of her own Ex. 5 (a) and Sophie's Ex. 20, says in an aloof tone that she 'finds her *charmant*'. Sophie still notices nothing and, white with rage, delivers her message, which is to the effect that Ochs is never again to come within a hundred steps of the Faninal palace. This violent edict is poured out against explosive ejaculations of Faninal's Ex. 40 which is developed vigorously as Ochs protests and tries to break past Sophie into the room where Faninal is resting.

At this point the Marschallin intercedes. Snatches of Ochs's various themes are heard (Exx. 17 (a), 18 (a) and, ironically, his motif of offended dignity, Ex. 57, the latter is even preceded by the same octave jump which followed the 'Ecco, Ecco' of the Italians at the moment of his greatest self-possession) as she tells him to preserve what dignity remains to him, play the good loser, and make off without delay. When he protests that he is by no means willing, she at last orders Octavian to reveal himself, now once again fully dressed as a man. To his Ex. 1 (with all the extra phrases of Ex. 16 maliciously added one at a time) Octavian presents himself to the shaken Ochs, who comments that everyone is in league against him, and that he thought his eyes had not deceived him (a splendid example of being wise after the event). The Marschallin presses the point home by emphasizing the remark she made when dismissing the officers of the law, to the effect that the whole affair has been a mere farce, a Viennese Masquerade and nothing more, adding with stern haughtiness that she would not have wished that Ochs had in truth seduced her little Mariandel. She then unwisely adds that she has at this moment a grudge against all men (repetitions of her themes of renunciation, Exx. 5 (a) and 38). Ochs is no fool, nevertheless, and has had time to sum up the entire state of affairs, the clue to which is given him by this last remark of the Marschallin. The broad love theme Ex. 6 b rises richly in the orchestra as, after looking backwards and forwards from Octavian-Mariandel to the Marschallin, he pointedly says that he does not know what he ought to think of the whole *qui-pro-quo*. He is, of course, right; he has enough knowledge now to blackmail the pair of them, the price of his silence to be their acquiescence to his marriage despite the débâcle which has just taken place. Indeed, Octavian's grand scheme has been played for Sophie's sake at the expense of the Marschallin, whose secret is now bound to be exposed. With tremendous self-sacrifice the Marschallin acknowledges the inevitable, receiving Sophie's frightened little curtsey with a friendly gesture. But she looks long at the Baron and tells him with slow meaningful words that as a Cavalier she expects him to think nothing whatever.

The Baron naturally takes this as no less than a complete surrender. A recapitulation of one after another of his themes follows, Ex. 42, 52 (a), 50 (a), 18, all with their initial jauntiness restored as they slip in and out of the flat and sharp keys in Strauss's most typical manner.

No Lerchenau has ever been a spoilsport, he says with grand bravado, adding that he will now go and make his peace with Faninal and all will be once again forgiven and forgotten. Ex. 58, the theme of his complacent scene when he was in full control of the situation despite his sword wound, makes a last brief appearance before the axe falls on all his day-dreams and the gay strutting of the measured pulse in the bass, which was from the first the symbol of his self importance (cf. Exx. 58 and 17), is abruptly halted. So sure has he been of the whip-hand he has won that he can scarcely believe his ears when the Marschallin interrupts him, repeating that there is nothing he can do but retire from the scene at once. Still he hesitates dumbfounded, struggling in his own mind against the ultimate defeat which looms ever nearer, until in utter exasperation the Marschallin forces him to realize that his power over her is immaterial to the main issue. To a last sweeping statement of the wedding theme, Ex. 28, she declaims once and for all the fact which Ochs *must* recognize—that from this moment the wedding and everything connected with it is completely over. Yet another Straussian harmonic side-slip gives an astonishing and intensely dramatic hush, Ex. 28 failing to reach the logical cadence in its own highly coloured D flat major, collapsing instead into a bleak D minor in which fragments of Ochs's Ex. 58 linger momentarily. The Baron has at last realized that all his plans have been irrevocably destroyed.

But he is not the only dismayed character on the stage. Poor Sophie has for some time been echoing these awful dicta of the Marschallin ('a farce', 'a Viennese Masquerade and nothing more'), applying these words to the love which had seemed to have sprung up between her and Octavian. Is this, too, connected with the marriage arrangements and hence from this moment completely at an end? Over a ghostlike memory of the melody to which they first looked into each other's eyes during the Presentation of the Silver Rose, Ex. 47, she repeats these words blankly, as does also the Marschallin herself, thinking of her own love affair with Octavian which has been broken by these self-same marriage arrangements. Played so soon after Ex. 28, the Marschallin's resignation theme, Ex. 5 (a) seems here to be intentionally part of the connected psychological idea in the form of Cause and Effect.[38] The Marschallin now shows signs of strain, and Octavian, sensing this, quickly fetches her a chair, but he receives no acknowledgement from her, nor are his movements even covered thematically in the

[38] See footnotes on pp. 364 and 370 above.

R.S.–DD

orchestra pit. At this tense moment he is outside the drama, however briefly.

A token recapitulation of the Prelude to Act III brings back the flow of life and action. Realizing from their various vantage-points around the room that the comedy of which they formed a part is over, the many conspirators swiftly and silently emerge from their trap-doors, etc., and begin to advance upon the defeated Ochs before he can escape. Annina's theme (Ex. 62) and the various Tarantella motifs of the Italians are hinted at in the short shadowy movement which accompanies the approach of Valzacchi, the innkeeper, bill in hand, waiters, musicians, scullery boys, all capped by Annina (who has removed her disguise) and the brood of screaming children. Ochs suddenly sees that the game is up and in one of the most memorable moments of the opera calls peremptorily in broad Viennese dialect to his body-servant: 'Leopold, we're off.' The stage is set for the great finale.

16

Strauss had said from the first that if Hofmannsthal would accept responsibility for the scene with the Commissary, he, Strauss, would look after the Finale. He was certainly true to his word. From the beginning of the next section the music sweeps through to the end of the opera without the slightest flagging of inspiration. It is in the form of a gigantic recapitulation, firstly of the mass of waltz material, which is treated in a number of different ways, and then of the music of the Presentation of the Silver Rose, though this now serves as the background to an entirely new melody. Interspersed between these main sources of material, fragments of the closing duet of Act I appear as occasion warrants. The effect is to give the piece, which has hitherto been more lyrical in the operatic sense than any of Strauss's previous stage works, a coda in fully symphonic style.

The waltzes burst in naturally enough, as Annina and Valzacchi spitefully quote back at the Baron his refrain about 'Lerchenau-ish luck'. Ex. 55 (g) accordingly starts the dance going and leads into a chromatic version of the great waltz (Ex. 54), now relegated to a mere linking function between sentences of other waltzes such as its own last phrase Ex. 54 (a), the supper waltzes from Act III, and, surging through the middle of the orchestra on the horns, the very first of all the waltzes to be heard in the opera, Ex. 15 (a). The innkeeper and all his minions have surrounded the wretched Ochs and are clamouring for payment, recounting at the top of their voices the list of services he has received at their hands.

The climax comes with the appearance of Ex. 65, the characteristic abrupt stopping of which gives a momentary hiatus to the music. Ochs's body-servant has fought a way clear to the door, and he and his master now burst through it, followed closely by the entire seething mob. As the music (which has swung in again with Ex. 64 (a)) gradually subsides, the hurly-burly fades away into the distance, leaving Sophie, the Marschallin, and Octavian quite alone on the stage. The essential practical purpose of the waltzes is over, but Strauss cleverly continues them as background to the love drama which has still to be played out. Ex. 64 pursues its natural course for a time, both its component melodies being played simultaneously as during the supper scene, thus continuing the automatic flow of melodic ideas while Sophie tries to make sense of the fantastic events which have just been enacted before her. With the farcical nature of these events only too clear to her, she is desperately afraid that Octavian has wiped her image clean out of his mind with the passing of the Baron. Octavian's confusion now reaches a point where he no longer knows which way to turn. The Marschallin, her nerves nearly at breaking point, laughs angrily at him and tells him to follow his heart. He, terribly concerned, unable to grasp how she has guessed at what is in his mind, obediently wanders miserably across to Sophie, who seems also to be rejecting him. The poignant harmonies and phrases reached by the waltz accompaniment, which now incorporates the once-upon-a-time crocodile tears of Ex. 67, are most subtly handled. Strauss even invents a new waltz of affecting sweetness and simplicity to support Octavian's plea to Sophie for her friendship:

Ex. 69

This is the section over which Hofmannsthal had so many pangs lest
with the exit of the Baron the audience would begin to collect their
wraps and prepare to leave the theatre. Little did he imagine that, on
the contrary, audiences were from the first to settle the more firmly in
their seats in preparation for one of the supreme experiences opera has
to offer. Strauss was right not to cut a line of the beautiful text, all
of which he needed for his melodic scheme. Ex. 69 gradually incorporates the Marschallin's theme of renunciation Ex. 5 (a) as it merges into
the first of the tear-stained reminiscences from Act I. Octavian's reasonable question as to why Sophie is not jumping for joy at her release
from the odious marriage brings from her the very correct retort that it
might have been wonderful had it come about differently; now she is
ashamed down to the very soles of her feet and wants nothing but to
retire to her father as soon as possible. Octavian's instinctive gesture to
keep Sophie near him causes the Marschallin to rise from her chair in
embarrassment, but quietly she sits once again as she begins sadly to
recall to herself her prophecy of Octavian's forthcoming abandoning of
her, 'today, tomorrow or the day after' (Ex. 36). The melodic line is
built out of the three women's voices[39] in the first of the great Finale
ensembles. The new waltz, Ex. 69, combines with music of the Act I
duet (Exx. 35 and 36) in a sudden burst of emotion, searing in its painful
beauty. It subsides as quickly as it sprang up, though the Marschallin
finds herself obliged to wipe her eyes and the music is left quoting
verbatim the passage from Act I in which she spoke of summoning
the courage to put behind her the weakness of temporal things. She had
prepared herself well, but now that the time has come it is still no
easier to carry out than if she had had no such foresight.

What follows is pitiful: Sophie perceives something which Octavian
is too preoccupied with his own emotions to notice, that the Marschallin
is suffering on his account; quietly she sends him across to her, repeating

[39] The incongruity of Octavian being sung by a mezzo-soprano finds complete artistic justification in the marvellous sonorities of this passage.

that she herself must go to her father. Her little personal theme Ex. 44 flutters bird-like and is answered by Octavian's love theme Ex. 3. He, poor boy, is for once utterly at a loss; he can't even think of anything to say, and the Marschallin is able to forget her own misery for the moment in observing the ridiculous figure he is cutting. Ignoring his thoughtless *cri-de-coeur* to Sophie to remain at all costs, the Marschallin crosses over to Sophie, who gives a series of perplexed little curtseys to the accompaniment first of her innocent little figure Ex. 44 (b) and then of repetitions of the appropriate motif of formal reverence before nobility, Ex. 22. Then, to warm sweeping statements of Ex. 5 (a) she asks the acutely embarrassed Sophie whether she already loves Octavian so much, adding that her pale expression gives her away. This loosens Sophie's tongue and she babbles away about the Baron, the shock, her father, their gratitude—until the Marschallin interrupts her, saying with enormously patronizing expression that she should not talk so much, she is in any case pretty enough. She then outlines her plans for the future; she will go in to Sophie's father and will invite him to come with her in her carriage together with Sophie, herself, and Octavian. This, she rightly reckons, will provide the cure for all his ills, knowing what store Faninal sets on hobnobbing with the nobility. As for Sophie's pallor, she goes on, Octavian will provide the remedy for that.

At this exhibition of self-sacrifice, Octavian and Sophie are not only deeply moved but completely abashed. There is indeed nothing more to be said and Strauss therefore takes the opportunity for a set piece in the manner of the Quintet from *Die Meistersinger*. This is the great Trio which, introduced by the love theme from Act II, scene I (Ex. 48), strangely enough turns out to be based entirely on the waltz 'Nein, nein, I trink kein Wein' from the supper music, Ex. 63, thus continuing the symphonic scheme of recapitulation without regard to the original significance of the material employed. Set for full orchestra in broad shimmering colours, the once trumpery little ditty takes on the panoply of a broad and beautiful cantilena to which the golden tones of the three women's voices crossing and recrossing provide an ecstatic quality. As the melody rises higher and higher other motifs are added to the texture, Exx. 5 (a) and 35 representing the Marschallin, who is singing of her hard-won resolution to love Octavian in the right way, even if this means renouncing him.[40] Octavian's Ex. 1 can also be

---

[40] The parallel with Sachs's part in the Quintet, though not exact, is very close.

heard surging upwards in the cellos and lower woodwind. He has no longer any thought for the Marschallin and is singing only to Sophie. She for her part begins by being profoundly conscious of the Marschallin and in wonder at her goodness; only towards the end of the Trio does she succumb to Octavian's fervent glances. Strauss adds to the splendour of the climax by means of the same device which he has already used so often during the opera, that of side-slipping into a distant key only to veer back again for the final cadence.

The peroration which follows is built largely on Ex. 5 (a), which is combined with itself many times, for this is the moment of actual renunciation on the part of the Marschallin. Yet hidden in the glowing polyphony are the two main themes of the Silver Rose music (Exx. 20 and 47), with Octavian's Ex. 1 still rearing itself on cellos and bassoons. The two young lovers remain with their eyes so riveted on each other that they never notice the withdrawal of the Marschallin, who adds one last phrase: 'In God's name' (still to her Ex. 5 (a)) and quietly leaves the stage.

17

With the final cadence, the orchestral colouring of the Presentation of the Silver Rose is revived. The recapitulation of the waltz themes is over and it is this scene which is now to have its own recapitulation. Against a soft high tremolo Sophie's first theme, Ex. 20, is heard on the oboe just as it was before. Then Octavian's Ex. 1 plunges in and winds its way across the entire range of the orchestra from the deep cellos and bassoons up to the top note of the trumpet. Octavian has gradually moved towards Sophie and as the intense chord of D flat melts into a softly shimmering G major they fall into each other's arms. Ex. 20 is now repeated endlessly against itself to a background of harps and trilling strings and woodwind. The actual modulation formed a motivic sequence of notes which is now used to a great extent as part of the background to the duet which follows.

Ex. 70

The melody of the duet is one so deeply rooted in German folk-song that it is not entirely justifiable to say, as Strauss himself did, that it is stolen from Schubert. If that were so then Schubert could equally be accused of plagiarism, since an almost identical melody appears in *Die Zauberflöte*:

Ex. 71

Strauss thought of this tune quite independently of Hofmannsthal's text and gave the poet exact details of the kind and number of lines he needed. He even wrote four lines of doggerel in the correct metre to give the gist of both rhythm and idiom he had in mind. Hofmannsthal duly obliged, though he found the assignment a little restricting; the highly artificial *naïveté* of the verses Strauss insisted upon did not come naturally to his essentially sophisticated style. This very ingenuousness was, however, integral to Strauss's scheme. After the passionate intensity of the previous section, he wanted to return to Hofmannsthal's own idea of presenting the love between Sophie and Octavian at a deliberately low emotional level. Accordingly, although there is no thematic connexion with their love duet from Act II, this closing section arises out of the earlier scene which it recapitulates dramatically if not motivically. Once again the two young lovers seem to lose their vividness as living human beings and turn into Dresden China.

As the recapitulation of the Presentation of the Silver Rose is an important aspect of the music of this passage, Strauss uses Ex. 48 to a considerable extent in the development of the melodic lines, while Ex. 20 is heard almost continuously in the background. When Sophie plaintively asks Octavian to hold her ('I am only a weak thing'), her rather touching phrase, Ex. 44 (b) is played by the oboe.

The first stanza of the somewhat formal little duet comes to a cadence in the unexpected but significant key of E major. The reason for this is quickly apparent in the change of thematic material as Faninal,with the Marschallin on his arm, crosses the stage on their way from the inner room to the carriage which awaits them. The cadential derivative of the Marschallin's theme Ex. 39 (a) is used as an extension of the duet's own cadence. It thus provides a link to a complete restatement of the music from the closing pages of Act I, during which the Marschallin sent Octavian from her (see above, p. 377, with Exx. 5 (a), 38 and 39). Faninal, seeing the lovers, archly comments that 'young people will always be young people', with which bromide, the Marschallin, the music of her own love sounding with unbearable sweetness in the strings, just manages to agree. They pass out of the scene and Ex. 70 is used again to build a modulation (by way, this time, of B flat and thence back to G, the key of the duet) in readiness for the second verse of the Schubert-Mozart eighteenth-century drawingroom theme Ex. 71. During this last phase of the recapitulation not only does the cadence Ex. 70 continue hauntingly throughout on the third horn, but the tinsel glitter of the Silver Rose music Ex. 45 punctuates every phrase. The coda is reached with Ex. 48 sung in duet much as it was towards the end of the Presentation scene and followed by an extended version of the glittering Ex. 45 as the lovers kiss quickly and run off hand in hand.

The drama is over but Strauss and Hofmannsthal wanted the last taste to be less sentimental than light-hearted. The work had begun life as a burlesque; it must not end as less than a comedy. So Hofmannsthal cleverly added an enchanting little vignette which has a double purpose. Sophie unwittingly drops her handkerchief during the last embrace; it remains on the floor of the empty darkened stage for a moment and then, to a recapitulation of the negro servant's gay music (Ex. 8 and 9) the tiny fellow runs in. He searches for a while, candle in hand, finds the handkerchief, holds it up triumphantly, and runs out as the music rushes to the last brilliant, happy chords in just the bright, light-hearted vein in which the authors wanted the comedy to close. The Marschallin has shown her full acceptance of her abdication in favour of Sophie by sending her own servant to retrieve Sophie's handkerchief. At the same time, it is towards her that our last thoughts are directed as the curtain falls. Like Sachs in *Die Meistersinger*, she both ends the opera and is the most real and memorable character in it.

18

The première of *Der Rosenkavalier* was beyond question the most riotous success that even Strauss had ever had. Yet he himself acknowledged that the evening had been somewhat long drawn out owing to the fact that in his excitement he had set to music the whole of the loquacious text,[41] which even Hofmannsthal had assumed he would to some extent reduce. Nevertheless when, for practical reasons, Schuch made a few cuts Strauss was furious. However much he might view with equanimity the necessity of compromising over the more shockable lines in the libretto, he was at this time unwilling to part with a single note of the music. At first it was, of course, partly the *risqué* character of sections of the plot which caused Schuch to make the first excisions, but he was by nature much given to finding in each opera he conducted a few nicely chosen abbreviations of passages which he considered merely held up the action without contributing anything of great musical quality. However, this was something which one could scarcely expect the composer to appreciate, and he wrote a sharp note to Schuch suggesting that while he was about it he might as well cut the great Trio which was after all quite superfluous. Schuch seems to have been much offended by this sarcasm, though he apparently took the hint.

Many cuts have nevertheless become traditional over the years and it is unusual even today to hear a performance complete to the last bar. Strauss himself in later life not only sanctioned but perpetrated the most extraordinary mutilations in his own score as and when the occasion demanded. These he seems to have done entirely poker-faced, as if he no longer cared, and was quite indifferent to the work which he had once enjoyed filling with exquisite detail and which had undoubtedly called from him as profound a human sympathy and understanding as he ever evinced throughout his long creative career. He allowed a pianola roll to be made of his own decidedly casual strumming of a hotch-potch arrangement of the Waltzes by Otto Singer,[42] thus publicly setting the seal of his approval on the vast number of hackneyed arrangements which turned his brilliant satire into a popular hit. Strauss was not the man to jib if business was good.

[41] Including, as we have seen, one of the stage directions.
[42] He made other equally slipshod pianola rolls of the love scenes from *Heldenleben* (!) and *Feuersnot*, and Salome's Dance of the Seven Veils. Some of these have recently been dubbed on to a long-playing disk, but they scarcely enhance the composer's reputation.

Towards the end of 1924 a film company approached Strauss and Hofmannsthal to allow a film to be made of the opera. Since this was some six years before the advent of the Talking Film, the idea was by no means straightforward. The music would have to be specially arranged and played by an orchestra in the pit. At no time does there seem to have been any question of singers being involved. Strauss was not enthusiastic, but Hofmannsthal saw in the project an opportunity of diffusing a wider understanding of the different characters, for whom he still had the utmost affection, amongst the seemingly unlimited audiences addressed by this new and exciting medium. He urged Strauss to take the matter seriously, he himself having decided to undertake an entirely fresh script so as to throw new light on the characters. He felt that this would rejuvenate the opera, the people who enjoyed the film being sure to rush to see the drama enacted in the flesh. Strauss's task would be not at all to cut down the nearly three hours of music contained in the full version, but to reconstitute it so as to give a corresponding widening of aspect to the musical side of what he, Hofmannsthal, intended for the drama.

But Strauss, whose mind was at this time far more concerned with the plans for *Die Aegyptische Helena* than with the re-heating of stale cabbage, took little interest in the scheme, which proved to be not far short of a new work. For Hofmannsthal wrote a scenario in two parts which contained a large number of entirely new episodes. Ochs's castle, for instance, was shown together with an extended scene in which he was found in bed, woken and dressed by his servants (his famous waltz to be used as background music on a barrel-organ), and prepared for his trip to Vienna in order to visit the Marschallin.

As for this great personality, a flashback was given (as she narrated her own story) of her childhood in the convent and the entry of the Feldmarschall into her life. The Feldmarschall himself then appeared, and later played a considerable role in the rewritten drama.

Ochs's entry into the Marschallin's bedroom followed, and the levée scene, after which the Feldmarschall was shown receiving an important military assignment and departing for war. His prowess in battle was dwelt upon at some length and contrasted with the gaiety of Viennese life, typified by a scene showing its most fashionable park, the Prater.

At this point the film traced Act II of the opera to some extent— the Presentation of the Silver Rose, Ochs's arrival, Sophie and Octavian's love scene, and the duel scene, though this now took place in the grounds of Faninal's palace. Ochs was eventually put to bed and the first part of the film ended with the waltzes from the end of Act II of the opera.

The second part began with yet another battle sequence and then passed to a touching scene between the Marschallin and the little negro servant. Sophie and her father were to be seen next in violent dispute, after which the Italians, Valzacchi and Annina, were shown concocting an entirely new plot to send a messenger warning the Feldmarschall of what was going on in his absence. His hasty return to Vienna, depicted at some length, coincided with the festivities in the garden of his palace in which the gay young Marschallin, despite a wounded heart, was giving a supper-party. Much use was made of a pavilion in which a love scene between Octavian and Sophie took place as well as the Ochs-Mariandel tête-à-tête, the latter surprised by Faninal and his retainers. The Feldmarschall then burst in upon the already confused situation, which involved mistaken identities not unlike the closing scene of *Figaro*. After the party guests had swarmed around the Feldmarschall and Marschallin, a climax ensued in the form of a further duel scene, this time between the Feldmarschall and Octavian. Lastly came reconciliations, recognitions, misunderstandings cleared up, and the inevitable happy ending.

So complete a reconstruction required far more thought than Strauss was prepared to consider and he left the work accordingly for the most part to Otto Singer and the Viennese conductor Karl Alwin.[43] Nevertheless some extra music was naturally needed, especially for the new scenes including the personality of the Feldmarschall. This was supplied by the incorporation intact of various marches which Strauss had written over the years, for this purpose or that: a dreadful *Presentation March* in D, the *Königsmarsch* in E flat, even an entire piece from the music he had written for the Weimar Jubilee in 1892.[44] (This was the same as that which he later renamed *Kampf und Sieg* when, in 1931, he dragged it out of limbo a second time for a ball given by the Vienna Philharmonic Orchestra.) Even so, the film sequences showing the Feldmarschall in his field headquarters proved so extensive that Strauss had to write yet another military march, this time in F. It might seem strange that he did not make use of one of the pair of such marches

[43] He was the husband of the great singer, Elisabeth Schumann.
[44] Not 1894 as he later wrote in the score. See p. 93 above and Vol. II.

which had been published as his op. 57, but there may very well have been problems of copyright.[45]

For the rest, the music consists of a rehash of the music of the opera, juggled and rejuggled out of order, whole sections frequently occurring twice (one occasion usually bearing considerably less relevance to the original context of the music than the other) and often with the most curious transitions. Only in one further instance, however, was a movement introduced from a different work altogether. For the Festivities in Part 2 of the film the Wirbeltanz was borrowed from the *Tanz Suite* of movements by Couperin, which Strauss had completed two years previously, in 1923. This, too, was interpolated complete, as in the case of the Marches and without any attempt at working it into the score so as to soften the quite startling changes of style and texture. Strauss's disinterest in the scheme was positive. He had not even wanted to conduct the first performance which took place in Dresden on 10th January 1926, but changed his mind after an appealing letter from Hofmannsthal. He later came to London, where the film was given at the Tivoli Theatre on 12th April, and the following morning conducted the orchestra in some of the music for a set of gramophone records made in the Queen's Hall by the brand-new system of electrical recording. Today these records are in the nature of an historical document and it may therefore be of interest to outline their contents;

Sides 1-2	Introduction to Act I
3	Presentation of the Silver Rose
4	Waltz Movements
5-6	Trio and Finale Act III
7 (a)	Octavian and Sophie Duet
(b)	Presentation March

The version of the Act I Introduction, in fact, contains part of the opening duet on the first side, while side 2 (still labelled Introduction Act I) contains the wistful music from near the end of the Act to which the Marschallin tells Octavian that it is time for him to go, ending with Octavian's exit. In the film the music ran consecutively as played here, and portrayed the very beginning of the courtship between the Marschallin and Octavian.

---

[45] Unlike the other marches, these were published by Peters.

The Waltz movements on side 4 are neither Otto Singer's popular arrangement, nor a new version composed for the purpose. The four minutes of music are simply made up of two excerpts; the beginning of the Supper Waltzes from Act III, linked by a conventional horn figure to the main exposition of the most famous waltz (Ex. 54) from the end of Act II, as it appeared at the end of Part 1 of the film. Only the order of its phrases is oddly reshuffled from the operatic version, unnecessarily one might have thought, to avoid the entry of the lively figure ⌐ a ⌐.

The whole question of the waltz movements is full of complication. At the request of the publishers various concoctions had been made, for every conceivable combination from full orchestra downwards, by Otto Singer, Doebber and others. Then in 1934 a new and anonymous *Sequence of Waltzes* appeared, this time exclusively from Act III.[46] In many ways this is the best of all the arrangements, being in good and simple taste in its organization of the material and in its brief coda. Finally ten years later still, towards the end of the second World War at a time when Strauss had given up fresh operatic ventures and was merely devising orchestral fantasias from earlier works such as *Die Frau ohne Schatten* and *Josephslegende*, he, too, produced yet a further and entirely new *Waltz Sequence from Der Rosenkavalier*.[47] These original compositions are in many ways quite interesting, containing as they do some new developments of the familiar material, but the later of the two, which is concerned entirely with the music of the first two Acts, begins with an abridged version of the wonderful Introduction and continues with a number of features which are disconcerting to lovers of the original operatic version. Yet Strauss wrote to both Karl Böhm and Clemens Krauss towards the end of 1944 saying that he had made his new arrangement 'with an extended new and brilliant ending' in order to put out of circulation 'the Singer version with its clumsy transitions (badly built and worked out) which had irritated me for the last forty years' (!)

The impression one gets is of the ageing Strauss, sitting in his villa in Garmisch, the world he knew and loved in ruins about him, no longer caring about preserving the artistic value of his earlier works. If the

---

[46] There is some doubt as to the date and origin of this arrangement, which is also reputed to have been the work of Otto Singer.

[47] These last are numbered '1' and '2', not in the order of writing, but in their respective positions in the opera, the later work being specifically entitled *Erste Walzerfolge* (First Waltz Sequence).

world was prepared to pay for arrangements of his music, let them have
what they wanted. How otherwise could he have sanctioned the potpourri published in 1945 as his own work (though it is known that he
took no part in the arranging) under the misleading title of *Rosenkavalier Suite?*[48]

In no way superior to the now discredited fantasias on Italian operas
by the notorious Tavan, this hotchpotch has nevertheless been widely
performed and recorded as a true product of the master. As to who was
responsible for its creation, this remains a mystery, though there are
reports which suggest that the Polish conductor Rodzinsky had a hand
in it.

There is undoubtedly a dearth of satisfactory concert excerpts from
this most popular of operas. Neither of the Introductions to Acts I or III
is playable as a self-contained item. I have myself occasionally performed
an extended symphonic suite in two movements contrived by playing
the appropriate sections in the order in which they occur in the opera
with the aid of a few judicious and more or less ingenious cuts. But in so
doing I have recognized only too well that the result serves more to
give oneself the opportunity of playing and hearing the well-loved
music and marvellous orchestral sounds in the concert hall than to
create a genuine independent work of art, and have come more and
more to doubt the validity of the operation.

19

Der Rosenkavalier stands with *Elektra* at the apex of the second curve of
Strauss's composite output. From this point it will be necessary to
consider the gradual fading of his genius into a combination of talent
and technique until the time comes to discuss the works of his Indian
Summer when, in the last five years of his life, inspiration came to
him once more to enable him to create works of such ineffable, heart-
rending beauty as *Metamorphosen* and the *Four Last Songs*. *Der Rosenkavalier* also marks the turning-point in Strauss's life as a contemporary
composer in the vital sense of the word.

[48] A more valid Suite had been published years before by the, at the time,
well-known arranger, Taubmann (though he reversed his name, by way of an
amusing nom-de-plume, to 'N. Nambuat'). The music was somewhat bowdler-
ized, but the Suite was at least in several short movements. It has, however, long
since ceased to be available.

Yet in *Der Rosenkavalier* his powers of original and vivid intention were still at their peak, and it is only in two or three clear-cut sections that inspiration flagged and Strauss was driven to fall back on padding. Even here, however, he was able to disguise the lack of impetus owing to the exceptional amount of first-class thematic material with which the opera is lavishly endowed. Although it is no longer a tone poem but a truly lyrical opera, the technique of symphonic construction was so much in Strauss's pen when writing *Der Rosenkavalier* that he was often inclined to combine the lyrical element with the symphonic and fill the score with intricate motivic references and relationships. In this he was undoubtedly led on by the quite unusual complexity and psychological detail of Hofmannsthal's drama (for operatic purposes at any rate) of which it has justly been said that it could perfectly well stand on its own feet in the theatre independently of the music.[49]

Strauss's anxiety that it would prove 'too subtle for the public' turned out to be an unjustifiable piece of cynicism, and Hofmannsthal's answer was shrewd, even though it overstated the farcical simplicity of the work:

> Its blending of the grotesque with the lyrical will to a great extent correspond with your artistic individuality to produce something which will be strong enough to keep its place in the repertoire for many years, perhaps decades. . . . Your fear lest the work should prove too subtle gives me no anxiety. The progress of the action is simple and intelligible ⸍ enough for even the most unsophisticated public; a fat, elderly, self-satisfied suitor, favoured by the lady's father, supplanted by the handsome young fellow—surely that is the *non plus ultra* of simplicity. But the working out must be, I fancy, as I have made it—entirely free from anything trivial and conventional; the lasting success of a piece depends upon its working on the coarser *and* finer elements of the public, for it is the latter which creates the prestige without which no piece can live, any more than it can without popular appeal.

Events proved Hofmannsthal entirely right in these last sentiments. *Der Rosenkavalier* became the last work apart from Puccini's *Turandot*

---

[49] This, of course, is equally true of *Salome* and *Elektra*, but the important difference remains that these were both written originally without any intention of serving for opera libretti, while *Der Rosenkavalier* was always what its subtitle says—'a Comedy for Music'.

ever to occupy an enduring place in the international popular operatic repertoire. As has already been said, it established Strauss as a household name the world over, even more than had been the case in the days of the great symphonic poems fifteen years before. Moreover, the widespread popularity of the *Rosenkavalier* waltzes caused Strauss to be confused in many people's minds with the great Viennese waltz kings in a way which could only be considered as gratifying. I have myself heard two elderly ladies asking each other during a concert of his own works given in London by Strauss: 'Now which is this, the father or the son?' Strauss's pride in this confusion with the masters of popular music was perhaps not entirely consistent with his erstwhile role as the greatest and most shockingly modern composer of the contemporary musical scene.

Yet his achievement in establishing his position not merely in respect of the eclectic music-lover but with the broader musical public is not to be underrated, and represents an important facet of a composer's successful mastery of his art. At this point in Strauss's career he stood higher in universal esteem than at any time subsequently, except for a few brief years before his death nearly forty years later. The tracing of the second half of his long life, consideration of the extent to which it represents a gradual and sad decline as well as an overall assessment of his position as one of the world's greatest composers will be the main thesis of the concluding volumes of this survey of Strauss's life and works.

INDEX